ALSO BY ANNE NELSON

SAVAGES *(A Play)*
THE GUYS *(A Play)*
MURDER UNDER TWO FLAGS:
THE U.S., PUERTO RICO, AND
THE CERRO MARAVILLA COVER-UP

Red Orchestra

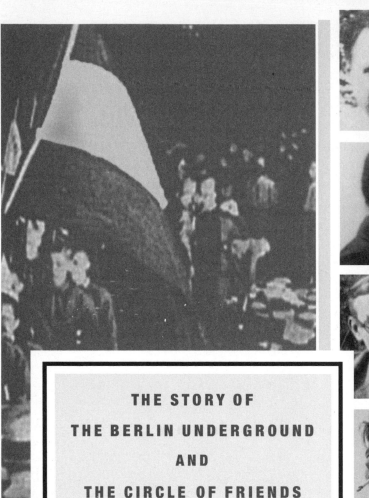

THE STORY OF
THE BERLIN UNDERGROUND
AND
THE CIRCLE OF FRIENDS
WHO RESISTED HITLER

Red
Orchestra

—

ANNE NELSON

RANDOM HOUSE

NEW YORK

Copyright © 2009 by Anne Nelson

All rights reserved.

Published in the United States by Random House,
an imprint of The Random House Publishing Group,
a division of Random House, Inc., New York.

RANDOM HOUSE and colophon are registered
trademarks of Random House, Inc.

Photographs: Gedenkstätte Deutscher Widerstand, Berlin

LIBRARY OF CONGRESS CATALOGING-IN-PUBLICATION DATA

Nelson, Anne.

Red Orchestra : the story of the Berlin underground and the
circle of friends who resisted Hitler / Anne Nelson.

p. cm.

Includes bibliographical references and index.

ISBN 978-1-4000-6000-9 (alk. paper)

1. Anti-Nazi movement—Germany—Berlin—History.   2. World War, 1939–1945—
Underground movements—Germany—Berlin.   3. Rote Kapelle (Resistance group).
4. Espionage—Germany—Berlin—History—20th century.
5. Berlin (Germany)—History—1918–1945.   I. Title.

DD256.4.B47N45 2009

943'.155086—dc22   2008023465

Printed in the United States of America on acid-free paper

www.atrandom.com

246897531

FIRST EDITION

Book design by Barbara M. Bachman

TO THE CHILDREN OF THE ROTE KAPELLE:

Stefan, Hans, Karin, Saskia, Ule, Irene, and so many others

Contents

Cast of Characters

\ \ \

THE COUPLES

THE KUCKHOFFS

Greta Lorke: Sociologist. She met Arvid and Mildred Harnack as a student in Wisconsin in the 1920s. She met Adam Kuckhoff in Germany in 1930 and married him in 1937.

Adam Kuckhoff: Playwright, novelist, journalist, screenwriter. A contemporary of Bertolt Brecht's in Weimar theater.

THE HARNACKS

Arvid Harnack: Economist. He came from a distinguished family of German scholars, and was a Rockefeller Fellow, University of Wisconsin, where he met and married American Mildred Fish in 1926. A number of his cousins—including Dietrich and Klaus Bonhoeffer and Ernst von Harnack—were involved in the July 20, 1944, coup attempt.

Mildred Fish: Scholar and professor of American literature from Wisconsin. She also worked as a professional translator and English tutor in Germany.

Falk Harnack: Arvid Harnack's younger brother and supporter. Also an early member of the White Rose student group in Munich.

THE SIEGS

John Sieg: Journalist, factory worker, and railroad employee. Born in Detroit and grew up in the United States and Germany. Resettled in Germany in 1928 and married Sophie Wloszczynski. Joined German Communist Party in 1929.

Sophie Wloszczynski: Secretary and typist. Her family members were ethnic Poles who suffered under German occupation.

THE SCHULZE-BOYSENS

Harro Schulze-Boysen: The scion of a prominent military family. Student journalist before the Nazi takeover, later joined the Luftwaffe, where he worked in the air force intelligence division. Married Libertas Haas-Heye in 1936.

Libertas Haas-Heye: Film publicist and producer. Granddaughter of a Prussian prince, family friend of Hermann Göring.

THE HUSEMANNS

Walter Husemann: Journalist. Was sent to Sachsenhausen and Buchenwald in the 1930s as a Communist political prisoner; released. Married Marta Wolter in 1938.

Marta Wolter: Actress. Before the Nazi takeover, she appeared in the Brecht/Weisenborn stage premiere of *The Mother* and in the Brecht film *Kuhle Wampe.* Sent to the Moringen concentration camp in 1937 for hiding a political fugitive; released. Friend of Günther Weisenborn; knew John Sieg through Communist Party circles.

THE SCHUMACHERS

Kurt Schumacher: Prize-winning sculptor. Also created decorative work for architectural design. His working-class parents joined the Communist Party in the 1920s. Married Elisabeth Hohenemser in 1934. Drafted into the German army in 1941.

Elisabeth Hohenemser: Graphic artist and photographer. A half-Jew, who was supported as a young student by Jewish relatives in Frankfurt.

THE ENGELSINGS

Herbert Engelsing: Lawyer and UFA movie producer. Introduced the Kuckhoffs and the Schulze-Boysens. A "shadow partner" in the Rote Kapelle resistance activities. His law partner, Carl Langbehn, was involved in the July 20, 1944, coup attempt.

Ingeborg Engelsing: A half-Jew, from a family of prominent lawyers and academics. She and Engelsing used their connections in the movie industry to get Hitler's permission to marry.

HIMPEL / TERWIEL

Helmut Himpel: Dentist. Had many patients in the film industry, thanks to friendship with producer Herbert Engelsing. Long engaged to Marie Terwiel, but was forbidden to marry her under the Nuremberg race laws of 1935, as she was a half-Jew.

Marie Terwiel: Law student and musician. Half-Jew, practicing Catholic.

THE COPPIS

Hans Coppi: Young Communist blue-collar worker. Was repeatedly arrested by the Nazis for protest activity, and sent to Oranienburg concentration camp. Heard Harro Schulze-Boysen speak at a meeting, and later agreed to help with the radio operation. Married Hilde Rake in 1941.

Hilde Coppi: Young activist, involved with Communist youth anti-Nazi underground.

OTHER INDIVIDUALS

Adolf Grimme: Social Democrat official and former Prussian Minister of Culture. Close friend of Adam Kuckhoff since college. After the Nazi takeover, became active in Dietrich Bonhoeffer's branch of the dissenting Lutheran Church.

John Graudenz: Journalist, photographer, and businessman. One-time United Press and *New York Times* reporter in Berlin.

Günther Weisenborn: Playwright and journalist. Brecht collaborator in the 1920s, friend of Harro Schulze-Boysen and Marta Wolter.

Helmut Roloff: Classical pianist. Conservative, friend of Helmut Himpel and Maria Terwiel. Motivated by his anger at the treatment of Jewish friends and neighbors.

Cato Bontjes van Beek: Young ceramicist. Created links between Harro Schulze-Boysen and student circles.

Katja Casella and Lisa Egler-Gervai: Young Jewish art students, and friends of Cato Bontjes van Beek.

THE AMERICANS

Ambassador William Dodd: U.S. ambassador to Germany (1933–1937). Early critic of the Nazis. His work was complicated by his unruly daughter, Martha.

Donald Heath: U.S. embassy official in Berlin (1937–1941). Close friend of Arvid and Mildred Harnack; conveyed Arvid's economic intelligence to the State Department.

THE SOVIET INTELLIGENCE AGENTS

Leopold Trepper: Polish Jewish Communist, recruited as a Soviet intelligence agent in the 1930s. After escaping Stalin's purges, he set up a Soviet intelligence post in Brussels, Belgium. He coordinated some Soviet intelligence operations in Western Europe, but he never met or had any direct contact with the group in Berlin.

Anatoli Gourevitch (code name "Kent"): Soviet agent assigned to Trepper's operation in Brussels. Dispatched to Berlin in late 1941 to restore contact and correct radio problems.

Alexander Korotkov (also called "Alexander Erdberg"): Soviet agent. Sought out Arvid Harnack in 1940, set up communications to Moscow, and left Germany after the 1941 invasion.

Preface

\ \ \

THIS BOOK BEGAN BECAUSE THE REICHSTAG WASN'T FINISHED.
It was April 1999, and a colleague and I, in Germany on business, had
jumped on a train to spend the weekend in Berlin. He was set on seeing
Norman Foster's gorgeous new dome for the Reichstag, the home of the
German Parliament. This symbol of German democracy had been gutted by fire in the days of the Nazi takeover, and pulverized by the Soviet
assault twelve years later. Now it was being reinaugurated as a delayed
consequence of reunification. But we were disappointed. The guard at
the door told us that the building wouldn't open for visitors until the next
day, and we had to depart that evening.

Instead, I took a stroll. As a New Yorker, I appreciated Berlin as a
walker's city. One could still feel the chill of the past in certain places, but
I was struck by the palpable energy for engaging the future.

Turning a corner, I saw what appeared to be a construction site. The
ground was torn up, sheltered in spots by makeshift roofs. People wandered around the area, reading material posted on the walls.

Drawing closer, I learned that we were standing on the ruins of the
Gestapo headquarters on Prinz-Albrecht-Strasse 8. The exhibit consisted of pictures and captions about the people who had been detained
there, many of them tortured and killed. I was surprised to see that a
number of prisoners were identified as *Widerstand* (resistance).

Among these were two women. One who immediately caught my attention was Mildred Fish Harnack, a beautiful literature professor from Wisconsin with a grave, gentle gaze. The caption called her "the only American woman to be executed by Hitler." Another photograph, from a later date, showed a fierce older woman named Greta Kuckhoff. She, too, had studied at the University of Wisconsin, and belonged to the same group, labeled the *Rote Kapelle* (Red Orchestra). Remarkably, she had survived both the Gestapo and the war, and rose to the position of president of East Germany's Central Bank.

The names were new to me. I had heard of Claus von Stauffenberg and the military conspiracy against Hitler, and had seen a movie about Sophie Scholl and the White Rose. But I had no frame of reference for the Rote Kapelle, nor for the idea of Americans who were members of a German resistance movement in the middle of the war. I returned home and began to explore. Initially, it was slow going: a footnote here, an obscure article there. But the more I learned about Greta, Mildred, and their circle, the more compelling their story became.

One reason for this was my own professional history. As a young journalist I had lived under military dictatorships in Central and South America, and had reported on the dynamics of opposition. I had witnessed the strange alliances that take shape in such situations, aligning individuals with differing religious and ideological beliefs through a commitment to a common humanity. I had also noted that under repressive governments, the population tends to divide into three groups: those who approve of the dictatorship; those who dislike it but go along with it; and those who resist. Later I worked in many other countries that were only starting to emerge from a brutal past, among them Cambodia and Romania. The three social groupings held firm; only the proportions shifted.

Why, I wondered, was Nazi Germany different? After all, hadn't we been told that German society underwent a wholesale conversion to Nazism overnight, to become a nation of murderers?

One early revelation came at the Holocaust Museum in Washington, D.C., which wisely directs its visitors to tour the exhibit in sequence, on a route that tracks the evolution of Nazism. The initial floor lays out the story of how Germany's struggling democracy was overcome in the early 1930s, and how its institutions were dismantled and subverted by the regime.

I pursued my questions about Greta and Mildred at the same time that I explored the history of the society that forced them into such unlikely roles. In the minds of many Americans, World War II began in 1941. But there were many crucial historical lessons that unfolded long before Pearl Harbor. The Holocaust could not have occurred if the Nazis had not succeeded in purging the German legal system of its honorable judges and lawyers. The fascists had to intimidate and silence reporters and turn the national media into vehicles for propaganda and mindless entertainment. The Nazis seized upon ongoing international tensions and used propaganda to inflate them into "threats." Then they obliged Germans to prove their patriotism by supporting cruel, ill-considered wars that could not be won. Soldiers were ordered to violate the Geneva Conventions, and officers who protested this breach were marginalized or abruptly retired.

One young member of Greta and Mildred's group expressed her impatience at the Germans' passivity concerning their crisis. "Everybody's talking about it," she said, "but nobody's doing anything." Why did these particular Germans decide to "do something," I wondered. The stakes were unimaginably high—most of the resisters paid for their convictions with their lives. I explored the differences in their motivations and conduct, using my firsthand observations in other countries as a point of departure. Who among the resisters shunned danger, and who found it appealing? How did the actions of young, single members differ from those of older resisters who were married with children? How did individuals weigh the comparative consequences of exile, conformity, and opposition? How did the large percentage of women affect the group's identity?

Underlying each line of inquiry was the question that haunts every book about Nazi Germany: How could they let it happen? This book is not directly about the Holocaust, but the event must cast its shadow over every account of the period. Greta and Mildred's circle had precious few resources to contest the massive evils of their time: the destruction of civil society, the mass slaughter of Soviet prisoners of war, or the Holocaust itself. But they risked their lives to do what they could. Many others, including powerful figures in London and Washington, could not say the same.

Finally, I had to return to the question of why the story of this group was not better known in the West. This query led me into the thicket of cold war politics that arose as soon as the war ended. The Gestapo had invented the idea of the Rote Kapelle as a Soviet conspiracy, and after the war, the Soviets, the Americans, and the surviving Nazis each exploited this misconception to further their own ends. In doing so, they distorted and diminished the historical legacy of the group for over fifty years.

It took German reunification and a new generation of dedicated scholars to begin to set the record straight. I have relied heavily on a remarkable institution in Berlin, the Gedenkstätte Deutscher Widerstand (German Resistance Memorial) and its scrupulously assembled archives and exhibits on the German resistance. I also benefited from the work of Stefan Roloff, a brilliant artist and the son of a member of the group, who assembled a remarkable documentary and book about his father's experiences.

Wherever possible, I have let my characters speak for themselves, through their writings and memoirs. The circle was made up of intellectuals and wordsmiths, and their voices render a unique sense of their time. Early on, I decided to frame the story through Greta Lorke Kuckhoff; first, because she was the connecting link between so many of the other participants, and second, because she was one of the few who lived to tell the story. I had to make a certain leap in citing her memoirs. The book was published in East Germany, and even though she had occupied a prominent public position, she fought a losing battle with the Communist Party over the right to tell her own story as she saw it.

I have included direct quotes from her book, but have tried to mediate between the passages in her voice and the rhetoric that was inserted by the state publishing house to meet the party's requirements.* (Every direct quote in this book is taken from the memoirs and correspondence of, and in a few cases my interviews with, those present.)

---

* I was able to view the correspondence between Greta and her editor, contesting these passages, in the archives at the Gedenkstätte Deutscher Widerstand.

From all available evidence, Greta was an intelligent and decent woman, a devoted wife and mother, and a serious scholar. But she was no secret agent, and it is ironic that her group was painted as "Soviet spies." No collection of individuals has ever been further from the popular image of James Bond. Greta was anything but deft, devious, or glamorous. Instead, she was awkward, ignorant of tradecraft, and a skeptical idealist. But for me, her ordinary quality was part of her appeal. Here was a working mother who tried to defeat fascism when she wasn't doing the dishes. Greta often expressed the belief that if enough ordinary people stand up to an abusive government, decency will prevail.

Later in life, Greta bitterly noted that not enough people stood up to Nazi Germany. But our common history must recognize the courage and the sacrifice of those who did. The story told in these pages chronicles many failures and frustrations, but it should be read in the broader context of the many Germans who argued that true patriotism required them to oppose their own government.

One cannot argue that Greta Kuckhoff, Harro Schulze-Boysen, Arvid Harnack, or any other individual resister changed the course of history. But taken together, the actions of Germany's anti-Nazis are impressive. The head of German military intelligence, Admiral Wilhelm Canaris, helped to deprive the Nazis of the strategic foothold of Gibraltar, clearing the way for the North Africa campaign. His aide, Lieutenant Colonel Hans Oster, offered ongoing military intelligence to the Western European democracies. German antifascists were active outside the country. In Switzerland, Rudolf Roessler passed German military intelligence to the Swiss, the French, and the Soviets, and Fritz Kolbe delivered state secrets to the Americans. The OSS's "Hammer" team of German exiles bravely parachuted into Berlin to guide Allied air strikes in the final days of the war.

Uncounted numbers of other Germans inside the country stood up to the regime out of conviction, with quiet acts of humanity toward its victims, and sabotage of its goals. Many of these individuals were working for the German government at the same time they were helping its enemies, courting accusations of treason as well as death.

A few years after my first visit to Berlin, I was able to visit the Reichstag with my family. The glass dome was worth the wait. As a living symbol of transparency in government, it floods the parliament below with rivers of light. Inside the dome there is a spiraling installation, complementing the exhibit in the Holocaust Museum, both telling the story of how German democracy was lost and regained at a terrible price.

Prologue

1941

IN THAT URGENT SPRING OF 1941, IT WAS EASY TO BELIEVE THAT fascist Germany would rule the world, especially if you were viewing events from the epicenter of Berlin. Austria and Czechoslovakia had fallen to the Nazis in 1938 and early 1939, followed by Poland a few months later. Then went France, Belgium, the Netherlands, Denmark, and Norway, in easy succession, over 1940. Great Britain was supposed to be next, but Hitler had put the invasion on hold. That didn't stop British and German bombers from exchanging violent visits over each other's major cities, leaving behind piles of civilian corpses and smoldering ruins.

In June 1941, the German armed forces launched Operation Barbarossa, their massive invasion of the Soviet Union. The regime informed the German people that this was the beginning of the end of the war. Once their blitzkrieg defeated the Russians, the Reich could gorge itself on the country's vast natural resources and exploit the slave labor of millions. Nothing could stand in the way of global domination. The Americans were steering clear of the war, and soon the British would have no choice but to sue for peace.

Only two decades earlier, Germany had been a spectacle of humiliation and defeat. The Nazi Party promised to transform the country, and so it did, ruthlessly driving the process with the doctrine of *Gleichschaltung*, "make everything conform." Every sector of civil society—the parliament, the military, the schools, the mass media—was rigorously purged of dissent, teaching the survivors the value of silence and submission.

Even so, there were cracks in the monolith. Only four days after the Soviet invasion, a German army monitoring station picked up a coded radio message to Moscow emanating from somewhere in northern Europe—possibly from Germany itself. The intercept raised disturbing possibilities. In the coming weeks, German troops found Red Army units waiting to meet their assaults on obscure hamlets in the Russian countryside. It was difficult to escape the conclusion that the German military machine had a leak.

There were lapses inside the Reich itself as well. Everyone knew that even a passing private criticism of the Führer could bring down a death sentence. The Gestapo had spent years shutting down opposition newspapers, impounding dissidents in concentration camps, and registering every typewriter in the land. Yet on certain mornings, citizens of Berlin awoke to find anti-Nazi stickers attached to the walls of their houses, or anonymous letters in their mailboxes denouncing the regime. Squads of energetic police were dispatched to oversee the scraping of walls, the gathering of flyers, the collection of offending letters.

Yet the leakage continued—even at the borders. Germany's frontiers had been sealed tight for years. But from time to time, one heard whispers. A political prisoner escaped from a concentration camp and made it to Switzerland through an underground railroad of safe houses. A family of German Jews, stripped of civil rights, economic assets, and social contacts, somehow secured the visas and foreign currency to flee the country. These reports were banned from the state-controlled news media, but word traveled nonetheless.

Berliners pretended not to notice such events, as part of their stubborn effort to simulate a normal life. Their urban landscape was sadly altered. Old street signs, which had once honored liberal statesmen, freethinking writers, and Jewish artists, had disappeared or, rather, were magically transformed. The new street names paid homage to Nazi officials who had only recently been shunned as thugs and murderers. Berlin's edgy noise of music, theater, and art from the 1920s had become as safe and leaden as an oompah band in a beer garden.

Greta Kuckhoff blended easily into Berlin's ranks of blond, neatly dressed Aryan housewives, queuing for groceries or picking her way through the rubble to the park with her three-year-old son. In her youth, Greta had dreamed of becoming a professional woman, but now the regime declared that her place was in the home. She spent most of her time coping with rations and shortages, running after little Ule, and keeping things tidy for her husband, Adam.

Like many of his generation, Adam had once fostered high literary ambition. He had achieved some success as a writer before the war, but now the arts were judged according to their service to the Reich. Adam joined many of his former theater friends in the Reich's government-controlled movie industry, some working in Joseph Goebbels's propaganda film units, others helping to produce fluffy musicals to distract the Germans from the war. Adam's work often took him on the road to occupied Prague and Posen (alternately known by its Polish name, Poznań). The German state film company had taken over some first-rate studios in Czechoslovakia, and the public was always interested in footage of the boys in uniform. Adam came back from his trips tired and out of sorts, and it was up to Greta to put a pleasant face on things.

Others in Adam and Greta's circle were even more active in their service to the Fatherland. Arvid and Mildred Harnack, two of Greta's oldest friends, dating from her graduate student days at the University of Wisconsin, were both working for the Reich. Because they were childless, it was easier for them to organize their time. Arvid had always been an academic star, inhibited only by his scruples. Once he joined the Nazi Party in 1937, he had risen briskly through the ranks of the Economics Ministry. Now he was in the middle of the action. He spent his days tending the economic underpinnings of the Reich: tracking the factory output that fed the ravenous military; overseeing resource allocations, labor quotas, and production statistics. As a graduate student, Arvid's passion had been for centralized economic planning. Now, just past his fortieth birthday, he was central to the planning of the most powerful economy in Europe.

Mildred was also doing her part, even if she was an American. It had not been easy to join the Nazi women's auxiliary, and she had to present her Daughters of the American Revolution certificate as proof of her "Aryan purity." But once accepted, she was treated with the same deference as any other Nazi Party wife. Even her Wisconsin degrees in English literature proved useful. She had placed a newspaper ad offering her services as an English tutor, and a young army officer, hoping to distinguish himself in the upcoming invasion of Britain, had signed up for weekly lessons.

Other friends were no less industrious. Perhaps the most glamorous people in Greta's circle were her new friends, Harro and Libertas Schulze-Boysen. Harro was a dashing young intelligence officer in the Luftwaffe, the German air force, whose nerves were frayed by his work on the top-secret plans for the Eastern front. His wife, Libertas, was a social butterfly. The pampered daughter of an aristocrat and an art professor, Libs worked in the movie industry. Her family's aristocratic pedigree made it a magnet for Nazi social climbers, starting with her husband's boss at the Air Ministry, Hermann Göring. Göring thought Libs was absolutely enchanting when they met on a shooting party. Greta and her husband were introduced to Harro and Libs at a dinner party hosted by a mutual friend in the film industry. Now all of them got together on a regular basis.

Not all of Greta and Adam Kuckhoff's friends were aristocrats like the Schulze-Boysens. The Siegs, for example, were definitely blue-collar types, even though John and his little Polish wife, Sophie, were surprisingly conversant in literature and music. Adam Kuckhoff had published John's writing years earlier at his magazine, and thought he showed real promise. But politics intervened. Now John worked for the Reichsbahn, the German state railways. It wasn't a bad life. Through ambition and hard work, he had been promoted to stationmaster at a busy train station in Berlin. The railways were the arteries of the German war effort, transporting soldiers and matériel to the front, and moving booty and captives back to the Reich. It was John's job, quite literally, to make the trains run on time.

Greta's friends all had other friends, of course, and it was common for them to gather in one another's homes on a regular basis. So the four couples would get together in different combinations in living rooms scattered across the city: the domestic Kuckhoffs, the intellectual Harnacks, the socialite Schulze-Boysens, and the proletarian Siegs. They each hosted their own evenings as well, ranging from the spirited singing and dancing at the Schulze-Boysens' to the cerebral tea parties at the Harnacks'. It was the best way to find out what was going on. Public discussions were out of the question, so if people came across juicy news, gossip, or speculation, they shared it in private. Overlapping members carried the best tidbits from circle to circle, fervently hoping there were no informers around to report them to the Gestapo.

But beneath the fun and the gossip of the circles lay an additional tier of activity. Greta and her friends, the four couples at the heart of the enterprise, were living double lives. Beyond their day-to-day service to the Nazi regime, they carried out activities that would have astonished their colleagues at the ministries.

For years, the austere, bespectacled economist Arvid Harnack would say good evening to his secretary and go home with a head stuffed full of intelligence to use against the regime. Luftwaffe lieutenant Harro Schulze-Boysen did the same as he walked out the door of Göring's Air Ministry every night. Their smuggled information made its way clandestinely to Hitler's enemies abroad.

Harro's wife, Libertas, sat at her desk at the Propaganda Ministry, cajoling soldiers into giving her snapshots of atrocities at the front, which she squirreled away into a secret archive. Adam Kuckhoff came back from his trips bearing still more damning evidence. Someday, they told one another, there will be a reckoning, and we must be ready with the proof.

John Sieg, the disappointed journalist-turned-stationmaster, had found a way to employ his writing skills after all. He and his friends ran a secret printing press that published anti-Nazi leaflets, including information gathered from Arvid, Libertas, and other members of the circle. Producing and distributing the leaflets was fiendishly difficult—the mere possession of a copy could mean arrest and torture. Friends of friends of friends, from many interlocking circles, secreted them into mailboxes, dumped them into telephone booths, and even stuffed them into the backpacks of soldiers bound for the front. Greta received each of these individuals in her modest kitchen and helped wherever she could, as translator, courier, and recruiter for the group.

By the summer of 1941 the Nazi state was at its apex, having crushed every preexisting German institution that had stood in its way. And yet the totalitarian system was not quite total. Beneath the frozen surface of the fascist society, as stubborn as a mushroom ring underground, was the small universe of the *Zirkel*. As circles began to overlap, they formed a new geometry. The German word for it was *Querverbindung*, a "network of interlocking relationships." This network's members exerted an immense effort not only to undermine the regime, but to keep Germany's lost culture alive through acts of defiance and the power of the written word.

Sometimes Greta Kuckhoff—Greta the worried mother, the frustrated sociologist, the reluctant spy—wondered how all of this death-defying behavior came about. Why hadn't this small band succumbed to the opportunism, the fatalism, or the paralyzing fear that had afflicted most of Germany's population? And how did this odd collection of individuals, so wildly different in background and temperament, come together in pursuit of such perilous, noble, and possibly doomed activity?

As unlikely as it seemed, Greta herself had been the principal agent of their union, the common thread that ran through the skeins.

But for the moment, the more pressing question was: Which, if any, of them would survive?

Red Orchestra

\ \ \

CHAPTER 1

Greta Goes to Amerika

1927–1929

ONE FINE INDIAN SUMMER MORNING IN 1927, A SLENDER twenty-six-year-old woman stood on the deck of the *President Harding,* watching the New York skyline expand to fill the horizon. The Port of New York was crowded with ships, many of them, like hers, arriving from Germany. After a forced hiatus during the Great War, German immigrants were pouring into the United States once again.

Greta Lorke was not an immigrant; she was a foreign student coming to America for a graduate degree. Although it was the height of the flapper era, Greta was more bluestocking than vamp. She had a slim figure but little sense of style. Her long face, with its high, rounded forehead and searching gray-green eyes, could flicker from stern to wistfully pretty. But Greta, a young feminist, claimed that she wasn't interested in her looks; the important thing was ideas. Looking in the mirror, she commented only that there wasn't "too much to complain about"—then proceeded to complain about her pale freckled complexion and wispy blond hair.

Greta's attention was focused on her education. For the three children in her working-class family, it had been a struggle to attend high school, much less travel abroad for a graduate degree. Her father, Georg, was a metalworker in Frankfurt an der Oder, a grimy industrial town on the banks of a murky river, due east of Berlin. He worked for Ju trichter's firm, the biggest musical instrument factory in Germa little girl, Greta loved to watch her father roll out the sheets of cut into patterns for tubas and flügelhorns, then wander over to adjoining workshops to observe the violin and drum makers.

Greta's mother, Martha, was a seamstress, the daughter of an illiterate tailor. A highly determined woman, she had taught her father how to write his name. The family had inherited a small sum in the 1870s and used it to buy a tenement house on the outskirts of the city. Greta's parents moved in when they married and rented out rooms to help make ends meet.

Greta, who was born on December 14, 1902, inherited her mother's work ethic as well as her Catholic conscience. As a young girl, she was fascinated by the flyers for African mission work in the vestibule of their church. She decided to earn enough pocket money to save an African child's pagan soul. She worked for a year running errands and doing odd jobs, then she tied her coins up in a handkerchief and went to the priest with her order.

"It should be a little black *boy*, Father," she requested. "And please, no older than me—just about eight. And can he be delivered for Christmas? It should be a surprise for my mother."

The kindly priest pulled down an atlas and showed Greta the long and arduous journey that would be required to bring her "black boy" from the tropics to Frankfurt an der Oder. The money she had saved, he explained, was enough to educate an African child for a year, but not enough to bring him to Germany—if, indeed, he should even want to come. Greta wept in disappointment, but donated her pfennigs anyway.

Greta's family made sacrifices for the sake of education. Her parents lived frugally to save for their children's tuition at the *Oberschule*, a necessary prelude to a university education. Quark (a soft white cheese) with linseed oil was a frequent dinner offering. The Lorkes didn't indulge until the holidays, when the family enjoyed meat and fowl, gilded nuts, and lots of singing. Greta's mother sewed blankets and clothing for a Berlin department store to help with tuition, while Greta contributed by polishing shoes and helping her uncle sell religious pictures in his shop.[1]

Greta's childhood struggle for working-class respectability was soon rocked by war and political turmoil. She was about to turn eleven in 1914 when World War I broke out. Many Germans greeted the war with euphoria, but it soon brought unimagined hardship. The winter of 1916 was known as the "Turnip Winter." Germany's food shortage was so severe that young Greta and her family resorted to secret nighttime forages to dig for root vegetables that had been overlooked in the harvest. Toward the end of the war, Greta's father was temporarily laid off from his job at the instrument factory. Resentfully, he walked out of the docile Catholic Workers' Association and joined the militant Metalworkers Union, hoping it would be more forceful in defending his interests.

Greta Lorke was just turning fifteen when the war drew to a close, and talk of socialism filled the air. However, Greta, like many of her countrymen, was uncertain exactly what "socialism" meant. She preferred to experience politics through literature and the arts. "We looked for every piece of theater that gave us a taste of the new developments."[2]

One leader who embodied the "breath of the new" was the revolutionary Rosa Luxemburg, the daughter of a small-town Jewish businessman in a Russian-controlled region of Poland. Luxemburg was active in the German Social Democratic Party (SPD), but left in protest of its early support for the kaiser's war. In 1916 she cofounded a splinter group called the Spartacist League, which later evolved into the German Communist Party (KPD). In November 1918, as the revolt gathered steam, Luxemburg helped to found and edit a newspaper, the *Rote Fahne* (*Red Flag*), to coordinate strikers' councils.

Luxemburg was a reluctant participant in the 1918 revolt, and she paid a heavy price for her involvement. On January 15, 1919, paramilitary Freikorps forces captured, tortured, and killed Luxemburg and her colleague Karl Liebknecht in Berlin. Luxemburg's allies continued to fight for a revolutionary government, but they were finally defeated by the Social Democrats in concert with the Freikorps.

Rosa Luxemburg's legacy would loom large in Greta's life. Like Luxemburg, Greta would be caught up in the tensions between Socialists and Communists and forced to choose between the roles of scholar and activist. Luxemburg's letters displayed her brilliance but also revealed that she loved deeply. (Greta called them "deeply moving.")[3] Her passionate feminism did nothing to abate her longing for a home and children—the same tensions that Greta experienced throughout her life.

Germany settled into an uneasy, poverty-stricken peace. Some 2.4

million German soldiers had died in the Great War, and many left destitute widows and children.[4] In the winter of 1919, Spanish flu settled on the country like a curse fulfilled, preying upon the weak and the hungry. Hundreds of thousands died. On urban streets, the ranks of the have-nots festered and grew. The marketplace near Greta's home in Frankfurt an der Oder filled with mass demonstrations, rallying three thousand workers at a time.

Munich's malcontents included an embittered young Austrian veteran named Adolf Hitler. He had struggled as a painter of sentimental landscapes in Vienna before the war, then served as a courier on the horrific front lines, earning a medal for valor. He was shattered by Germany's surrender and the dissolution of his native country, and after the Armistice he joined other angry veterans in the street-fighting Freikorps. In September 1919, Hitler was assigned to report on a political meeting organized by a small, muddled group calling itself the German Workers Party. Sensing an opportunity, Adolf Hitler signed up for membership—and the future Nazi Party was on its way.

By 1923, Germany had entered its infamous phase of hyperinflation. The government's presses ran overtime printing worthless bills, and the value of German currency sank to over four trillion marks to the dollar (valuing a U.S. penny at 4 billion marks). Millions of citizens lost their life savings. Pensions, accumulated by workers through decades of struggle, vanished overnight, along with their trust in the middle-class values of diligence and thrift.

All in all, it was a depressing outlook for an ambitious Catholic schoolgirl. Nonetheless, Greta persevered. In 1924 she began her studies at the university in Berlin. Greta enrolled as an economics student and got a work-study job in an orphanage among the grim tenements of Neukölln, an industrial neighborhood in the southern part of the city. There she looked after twenty-three boys, helping with everything from nitpicking their head lice to tutoring them for school.

On the nightmarish streets of Berlin in the mid-1920s, one could see crippled officers reduced to begging, decent girls driven to prostitution, and aged pensioners forced to sell off their few possessions. But the cruelest sight was the children suffering from hunger and cold. Most of Greta's "orphans" had parents who could no longer support them. An international relief worker described children like Greta's in Neukölln: "Tiny faces, with large dull eyes, overshadowed by huge puffed, rickety foreheads, their small arms just skin and bones, and above the crooked legs with their dislocated joints the swollen pointed stomachs of the hunger edema."[5] Neukölln was one of the most ravaged areas of Berlin. Greta suffered along with her young charges, angrily wondering who should be held to blame.

Still, her experience did not convert her to the orthodox left. In fact, she found the Communist students at the university to be obnoxious and rude. "They struck me as loud, with the way they said hello by ostentatiously slapping each other on the shoulder, trying to show off how 'proletarian' they were," she wrote later. She tried to engage them in conversation, "but the first thing they did was demand, 'Are you with us or not?' I was also put off by the way they expressed their disapproval in the lecture hall by noisily shuffling their feet." Greta decided to keep her distance. Nor did she get very far with their literature. She managed to read Marx and Engels's brief tract, "The Communist Manifesto," but she had less luck with Marx's exhausting tome *Das Kapital*. "I just couldn't get through it," she confessed.

Still, Greta was serious about economics. It was a volatile period in the field, as massive social experiments were launched in Russia and the American economy roared. The young people of Europe believed that the old European institutions—monarchy, aristocracy, church—had made a mess of things, and it was time to start over. The world was no longer subject to the old models of autocratic command and control; instead, human society was to be documented, analyzed, and rationally organized. Greta, fresh from the front lines of Germany's slums, was ready to join this intellectual army to set the world right. "My idea about life in general," she recalled, "was to make the world a better place through scholarly research."

In 1925 one of Greta's American friends at the university made a startling proposal for Greta to come back to America with her and apply to Columbia University in New York. Greta saved up five hundred marks in newly adjusted currency and began to plan her adventure.[6] She was more than ready to leave the university in Berlin, whose rector was so hostile to women students that he refused to shake hands with them.

Still, it wasn't easy to say good-bye. On the night before her departure, her father sorrowfully asked her where he had gone wrong, raising a daughter who would rather wander the world by herself than settle down to a nice teaching job, a good husband, and some apple-cheeked children.

Greta was susceptible to such guilt, especially since her father had lost his job in the instrument factory. He now got by with marginal work, commuting twice a day to Berlin to pick up bundles of Catholic newspapers, returning to sell them in Frankfurt.

The ocean voyage was a novelty, but nothing compared to the sensation of New York. Greta roamed the city with her friend, inhaling the experience, from the streets of Harlem to the glitter of Broadway. New York was compelling, but it was also expensive, and Greta realized that her modest savings would not go far at Columbia. Her friend had just received an assistantship at the University of Wisconsin in Madison, which was becoming a magnet for progressives, reformers, and freethinkers. It would be easier for Greta to earn money there, too. Greta was dizzied by the precipitous change in plans; as a German she was used to endless layers of bureaucracy. These Americans, she marveled, didn't even require residence permits. She took a deep breath and boarded the train for Madison.

Wisconsin was a pleasant surprise. In Germany, professors were proud and remote; a mere student didn't dream of a personal conversation unless he had excellent family connections. American academia was more democratic. "In Madison not a week went by without a number of professors coming by and sitting on the carpet in our small dwelling," Greta wrote.[7] "They nibbled cheap peanuts and drank equally cheap coffee, wanting to hear every possible new detail about post-war developments in Germany."

Greta was dazzled by the sheer diversity of the people around her— "Japanese, Chinese, South American; Mormons, Baptist, Methodist and Presbyterians," she noted breathlessly in her memoirs. They were all interesting, and they were all full of questions about Germany. But Greta was disturbed by the white students' reluctance to socialize with her black friends. In Greta's tally of America's virtues and flaws, race relations went down in the debit column.

Greta's sociological field trips included a visit to a Ford auto plant, where she got to see an assembly line for the first time. She thought the workers looked miserable, driven for hours on end at breakneck speed. She contrasted their situation with the memory of an early morning in the sleeper car on the way to Wisconsin, when the train woke her up with a sudden stop. She stuck her head out of the window just in time to see young Edsel Ford step out to meet his father, Henry, on the platform— "at a small private train station reserved for the Ford family and their guests," she noted pointedly. Such privilege seemed to mock democratic principles. America, too, she thought, was ripe for reform.

The University of Wisconsin was full of people who agreed. Greta was pleased to be invited to "The Friday Niters," a weekly discussion circle hosted by John Commons, a distinguished professor known for his explorations of the relationship between economics and law. Her friends among The Friday Niters included Elizabeth Brandeis, the daughter of the first Jewish justice on the U.S. Supreme Court, who later joined Roosevelt's Brain Trust herself. Greta's roommate, Elsie Gluck, later became a prominent American trade unionist and labor historian.

There were relatively few German students in America at the time, and Greta enjoyed her air of exclusivity. Thus she was less than pleased one day when another student addressed her in flawless German. This, she learned, was the other German on campus, Arvid Harnack.

Arvid did not wear his learning lightly. His lean, bespectacled face radiated intensity, and some thought him cold. He was only a year and a half older than Greta, yet in 1924, when she was just beginning her undergraduate work in Berlin, he had already completed his law degree and was about to move on to a stint at the London School of Economics. Whereas Greta was a striver from a blue-collar family, Arvid was born into one of Germany's most prestigious clans of lawyers, scholars, and clergymen. Aspiring intellectuals competed for a place at the family table, just to hear them talk. Arvid's uncle, Adolf von Harnack, was one of Germany's leading liberal theologians.

Arvid's younger cousin and childhood neighbor, Dietrich Bonhoeffer, followed in their uncle's footsteps as a theologian, and came to study in the United States a few years after Arvid. The Harnacks and their close relations the Bonhoeffers, the Delbrücks, and the Dohnanyis belonged to a society that attached prestige to intellectual accomplishment. They even looked alike: a tribe of sturdy, bookish people with fine features and keen eyes, most of them framed by wire-rimmed spectacles.

Greta found Arvid's credentials more impressive than endearing. She had had to labor for every pfennig to finance her trip to America, while Arvid had arrived in Madison on the wings of a much-coveted fellowship from the Rockefeller Foundation, one of only four in the whole country. Greta acknowledged Arvid's brilliance, and noticed how even Professor Commons deferred to his views. But at the same time, she bristled at his air of superiority, especially in regard to their fellow Germans. Greta quoted him mockingly: "They're deeper thinkers. They do this and that better. They even have more cultivated tastes in food and drink." In short, Greta found Arvid to be a classic German intellectual snob. Greta tried to avoid him after that, but a second meeting changed her mind.

The meeting took place at an ice-sailing and skating party she attended with a group of students. Greta cozied up to the bonfire beside the lake, inhaling the aroma of pork chops crackling over the flames. Suddenly she looked up and saw two figures skating toward her, their bodies swaying in unison over the ice. As they approached, she could see it was Arvid, accompanied by a pale, willowy young woman with a gentle smile. Arvid was much improved, Greta thought, by his wife's company: "more relaxed, more serene, altogether more pleasant."

Arvid Harnack had met Mildred Fish shortly after his arrival in Wisconsin in 1926. One day (or so the story went) he wandered into the wrong hall looking for John Commons's class. Instead, he found a young teaching assistant beginning her lecture on literature. She was slim and fair, radiating a serene and intelligent beauty. Entranced, he stayed to listen and introduced himself after class. The two agreed to swap English and German lessons, and within a few months they were married by a Methodist minister, on her brother's farm.

Mildred Fish Harnack was only three months older than Greta. She was born in Milwaukee, a German-American enclave, but her forebears were New England Yankees. (They included such gloriously named Puritans as Preserved Fish and Grizzle Strange.) Like Greta, Mildred had been obliged to earn her education, and counted on the moral support of a devoted mother. She developed an ardent interest in literature and languages. She memorized long passages of poetry in German and ancient Greek, and planned to make her mark as a writer and critic. Together, she and Arvid made a golden couple, tall, blond, and austere.

For all of his family's prestigious connections, Arvid also survived a troubled youth. His father, a melancholy scholar, had drowned himself when Arvid was twelve, and his mother lost her modest pension in the economic crisis. Toward the end of World War I, Arvid ran away from home to join the army. He was sent back home for being underage, but joined the right-wing Freikorps immediately after the war, intent on battling the Communist insurrection.[8] Once he settled down to his studies, he excelled at them. But Arvid had little use for academic theory unless he could find a way to apply it to the social realities around him.

Greta and Mildred quickly became friends. Greta found Mildred a little dreamy, especially in her notion of Germany, which, dappled with castles and enchanted forests, seemed straight out of a Grimms' fairy tale. But she was good-hearted and earnest, and Greta admired her passion for American literature, a subject that was just beginning to be taken seriously in Germany. Mildred was the kind of woman men admire and other women envy, as she floated lightly above the fray. Still, her penniless New England pedigree led some students to whisper that Arvid was out of her league.

Greta made friends with Arvid, but she never completely warmed to him. He was fierce in a debate and enjoyed scoring points with his relentless logic. Still, he was a good person to know, especially since he received a steady supply of German newspapers from home. Arriving by ship, the papers were a few weeks out of date, and the news they brought only went from bad to worse. Unemployment back home was climbing steadily, and the coalition government in Weimar never established firm control.

In his irritatingly pedantic fashion, Arvid would tell Greta that the real problem lay in the economy, and that the solution lay in giving more power to the workers. The big factory owners had made huge sums of money manufacturing armaments during the war, and multiplied their profits through speculation during the troubled peace. As long as profiteers could turn disasters like hyperinflation and unemployment to their own ends, Germany could never achieve peace and stability. Germany's only lifeline, Arvid told her, was the United States and its offer of loans to see the country through.

Life in Madison was not all grim political debates. Arvid and Mildred liked to host Shakespeare readings in the evenings, and Greta was a frequent participant. She was amused by the way Arvid always claimed the most difficult leading roles—Lear, Coriolanus, Henry IV—soldiering through them with a sophisticated grasp of the content but hobbled by his thick German accent.

Greta was also fascinated by movies of every description. Over its first decade, the Soviet Union produced a bounty of widely acclaimed avant-garde work. Greta was gripped by Sergei Eisenstein's film *The General Line,* an arresting look at the new phenomenon of collectivized farms. But she was also enthralled by *Hallelujah,* an early American film with a black cast, and delighted by Walt Disney's first Mickey Mouse talkie in July 1928.

Greta and her friends were passionate about fiction, and avidly read the newest works by Theodore Dreiser, Sinclair Lewis, Upton Sinclair, William Faulkner, and other writers who were forging a golden age of American literature. As Germany grew more pinched and chaotic, America felt increasingly like the land of infinite possibility.

By 1929, Greta's student visa was running out and she was in the final stage of her doctoral examinations. She was not eager to return and go job hunting in Germany's conservative university environment. She had found it cramped and misogynistic when she left Germany, and she doubted it had changed. But she did miss home. She wrote her parents:

> I'm coming back. I'll find a real job, and I'm tired from studying for so long. I'm afraid that I'll lose my foothold in reality if I remain immersed in my books, and I don't think I'll ever make it to professor anyway. . . . I still have my old desire to wake up someday with the sure sense that I can write a convincing book. I would give up everything else for this.[9]

Greta packed her bags reluctantly. Her last stop in America was Brooklyn, where a student friend from Madison named Saul invited her to stay with his family on her way back. The two roamed the Hudson waterfront to find the best view of the bridge, and finished the night with a bagful of fresh hot doughnuts. Saul took her to his favorite little Jewish restaurant. Greta thought about how safe and familiar it seemed, all the while mournfully aware that her time in America was running out. When she boarded the ship, a tender telegram from Saul was waiting for her. "I will build a bridge over the ocean," he promised. But the romance had no future.[10]

Greta's two years in America had been provocative, irritating, and exhilarating all at once, giving her a superb command of the English language and sealing a relationship with the country that would last her whole life. In October 1929, Greta said good-bye not only to a student adventure, but to an entire era. Around the time she returned to Germany, she posed for a photograph on a bridge. America had made a new woman of her. She is now sleek and severe, even stylish in her dark coat and fitted hat. But her expression is troubled. The figure in the photograph is a woman on the edge.[11]

\ \ \

CHAPTER 2

Greta and Adam

1929–1930

GRETA RETURNED FROM AMERICA WITH A NEW PERSPECTIVE. At the University of Wisconsin she had been treated with respect, and it was far easier to pay her own way in Madison than it had been in the slums of Berlin.

"I was a little smarter when I landed back in Hamburg," she wrote. She was able to pursue her studies without worrying about her room and board, and reflected, "These two years in America not only freed me from the pressures of these old problems, they also put international issues in a new perspective."[1] Part of that perspective was her appreciation for a more egalitarian society, where tenured professors listened to her ideas, and where even the daughter of a metalworker could aspire to high office.

On her voyage home she had renewed her assault on leftist literature, taking the analyses of class conflict personally. "I never forgot that I was the daughter of a blue-collar worker," she wrote.[2] Gazing out at the Atlantic, she reflected on how her father's unemployment had blighted his life and hampered her ambitions.

Germany had changed in Greta's absence—in many ways, for the better. The country's grueling efforts at recovery were paying off, and Berliners enjoyed a brief period of prosperity known as "the Golden Twenties." To optimists, it looked like the road to progress. Unfortunately, 1928 was to be its peak.

Much of the credit went to an influx of American loans, which allowed the German government to pay its reparations to the French without crippling the country's productive capacity.[3] The new prosperity brought a flowering of artistic expression and political freedom. It seemed that finally Germany could tolerate, and even celebrate, a free marketplace of ideas. Germans were not used to such liberties, and would not know them again for a generation to come. By 1928 the government felt secure enough to lift its ban on extremist parties and allow them to present candidates for the Reichstag.

Basking in the national prosperity, the moderate Social Democratic coalition triumphed in the September elections; the Social Democrats won almost twice as many seats as their nearest rivals. The newly legalized Nazi Party, on the other hand, made a dismal showing, winning only 12 out of 491 seats (just over two percent). Adolf Hitler and his colleagues had disgraced themselves with a failed coup attempt in Bavaria five years earlier, and most Germans found it hard to take them seriously. But there were signs of a rebound. Right-wing student groups multiplied in regional universities. In rural villages, traditional sports clubs and music societies were hijacked by tough-talking nationalists. This was of little concern to Berlin's intellectual and cultural elite, who disregarded developments in the provinces.

Like many of her friends, Greta preferred political theory to messy party politics. Many Germans saw their democracy as a caricature, with a Reichstag filled with fat middle-aged men shouting ineffectually at one another before they staged yet another petulant walkout or revolving-door election. Industrial workers and provincial farmers often cast their votes under instructions from their trade unions or religious leaders, while many artists and intellectuals took a whimsical approach, changing parties as casually as their clothes. Their serious allegiances were reserved for artistic movements.

Intellectual advances were the good news in Germany. Berlin was the cradle of major developments in every conceivable field, from Albert Einstein's mathematical breakthroughs at the university, to Arnold Schönberg's adventures in atonality at the Prussian Academy of Arts. Newspapers and periodicals were thriving, with pages stoked by debate and coffers swollen by advertising. Anyone who aspired to be a player, including Greta, wanted to be in Berlin.

Berlin had more than doubled in size in the new century, from a population of 1.8 million in 1900 to more than 4 million in the 1920s.[4] New theaters, music halls, and galleries sprang up across the city. Old-fashioned operettas and classical paintings existed side by side with raw new works, many of them generated by angry young artists, scarred by the Great War in body and soul. The fruit of Berlin's artistic labors could be spotty, but it was abundant.

Then came Black Friday. Wall Street crashed on October 25, 1929, only days after Greta arrived back home. Initially, the Europeans heard it only as a distant echo from New York, but within months the American crisis became a worldwide phenomenon. No country was hit harder than Germany. American loans (called the "German life insurance") evaporated as Americans tended their own disaster. The foreign investments that had flowed into Germany now flowed out, and the few Germans with money to invest sent their own capital out with it. Factories closed and construction ground to a halt, casting hundreds of thousands of workers into the street, angry, confused, and desperate. Unemployment rose from 1.5 million to 2.5 million in the month of January 1930 alone.

That year a Berlin newspaper reported that the number of customers selling their belongings in the city's pawnshops had doubled. A quarter of them were unemployed women.[5] Greta might have been one of them. Her financial outlook was bleak, and she had to revise her American dreams of academic glory downward to a life of editorial piecework and tutoring to pay the bills. She spent the winter and spring of 1930 at a series of odd jobs, seeking a new sense of direction.

"My thoughts began to turn back to my old love of theater," she wrote, recalling her high school theater days when she consumed German, French, and English dramas at the rate of four or five a day.[6] "I swam ecstatically in that flood of plays."

So Greta was excited to learn of the Fourth International Theater Congress, scheduled to take place in Hamburg for nine days in June 1930. The event promised many glamorous highlights, including presentations by the Comédie Française and an experimental theater company from Moscow. Impulsively, Greta scraped together the money to go.[7]

Once in Hamburg, Greta was drawn to the French delegation. Greta spoke enough French to fit in comfortably, and she reveled in the Gallic spirit. The Congress was all she could have hoped. The honorary president of the assembly was legendary producer Leopold Jessner, one of the three most powerful figures in Berlin theater. Jessner headed the Prussian Staatstheater, which occupied a neoclassical building on Unter den Linden just down the block from Greta's university.[8]

Greta's eyes were fixed, however, on a less-renowned colleague of Jessner's who accompanied him to the Congress. Dr. Adam Kuckhoff was Jessner's head dramaturge, a position that offered playwrights a stipend in return for editing scripts and mediating discussions between writers, directors, and management.[9]

Adam Kuckhoff was a square fireplug of a man, just short of forty-three, with a moody gaze, blunt features, and a full mouth. Given his august position, Greta was half-expecting him to present a formal lecture on the mechanics of theater administration. Instead, Kuckhoff gave a passionate speech on nothing less than "the nature of theater and film in the new Era."[10]

The previous year, Kuckhoff had already laid out many of his ideas in an essay entitled "*Arbeiter und film*" ("Worker and Film"). He was contemptuous of the "sentimental lies of the typical society film," and just as critical of the "patriotic hurrah" of nationalist cinema:

> This outmoded spirit, which unfortunately still persists today, slowly poisons the breathing forces that first brought the new cinema to light as a popular art form. . . . But film, like all other expressions of the spirit, is determined by socio-cultural conditions.[11]

Greta listened, so visibly rapt that Kuckhoff approached her after his lecture. He addressed her in French, based on her location in the French section. Did his talk correspond to her experience, he demanded? She answered him in French, continuing the little game. Kuckhoff decided they needed to discuss "the problems of dramaturgy" further, on a romantic boat tour of the Hamburg harbor. From the boat they went on to dinner, and from dinner to other diversions. It was the story of a thousand conferences, in which countless charismatic older men have ensnared countless dreamy-eyed young women sitting starstruck in the stalls.

On her last day in Hamburg, Greta confessed to Kuckhoff that she loved him. It was only after she returned to Berlin that she learned he was a married man.

Adam Kuckhoff was rife with complications. To begin with, he was born in 1887, making him fifteen years Greta's senior. The son of a needle manufacturer, he grew up in Aachen, the ancient city on the Belgian border where Charlemagne once ruled and was buried. The region had passed back and forth between German- and French-speaking rulers for centuries, and its inhabitants tended to be intermarried and bilingual. There were rumors that the Kuckhoff family had Jewish ancestors, but Adam was raised in the tradition of the Rhineland's easygoing Catholicism.

Like many students of his time, Kuckhoff tried out half a dozen different disciplines, ranging from literature to law, in at least four universities. He finally found a subject that united his enthusiasms: the eighteenth-century German writer Friedrich Schiller. Kuckhoff identified with the playwright's mission to create poetry out of his passion for liberty and equality. One of his most famous quotations was *"Eine Grenze hat Tyrannenmacht"* ("There is a limit to the power of a tyrant").[12] Kuckhoff completed his degree with a thesis on Schiller's theory of tragedy, and Schiller's influence colored the rest of his career.

At the same time Kuckhoff explored literature, he was also experimenting with more practical matters. In 1912, at the age of twenty-five, he fathered a son, Armin-Gerd, neglecting to marry the child's mother, actress Marie Viehmeyer, until the following year.* In 1914, Kuckhoff, swept up in Germany's war fever, enlisted in the army. Shortly afterward he was assigned as an actor to the army's "front theater" in the French town of Laon. Less than two hundred miles from Kuckhoff's hometown, this beautiful but treacherous region of French countryside was called the Aisne after the river that meandered through it.

Kuckhoff and his company had been posted to one of the most fiercely contested theaters of the Great War—not as hellish as the

---

* Marie and her sister Gertrud worked under the stage names "Paulun."

nearby battlefields of Ypres and the Somme, but brutal by any other measure. The first Battle of the Aisne, in September 1914, was an early experiment in trench warfare and machine-gun slaughter. The second, a bitter three-week engagement in the spring of 1917, was an unabated bloodbath. French casualties were listed at 96,000 but believed to be higher. The German casualties numbered over 160,000.[13]

The front theater included both civilians and professional actors who had joined the armed forces. Many, including director and producer Erwin Piscator, would go on to become major figures in the theater after the war. Female roles were played by both imported actresses and soldiers in drag. The companies staged their productions under the most primitive conditions. One memoir described how actors drove to the front and converted a delousing station into a theater on the spot, improvising their lighting from truck headlights and still managing to "raise the curtain" within an hour of their arrival.[14]

Adam Kuckhoff emerged from the army full of theatrical energy. He wrote a play, *Der Deutsche von Bayencourt* (*The German from Bayencourt*) describing a border dweller who is torn between his German patriotism and his cultural identification with the French. Kuckhoff's work in theater administration led to a succession of higher positions with larger theater companies. By 1923 he was the director of the touring company for a theater in Frankfurt.

Kuckhoff, drawn to both theater and a literary career, pursued both at the same time. In 1927 he was offered a tempting new opportunity. Eugen Diederichs, a prominent publisher, invited him to edit his political and cultural monthly, *Die Tat* (*The Deed*). Diederichs hoped that Kuckhoff could revitalize *Die Tat*, which had fallen behind the times. Known for promoting German nationalism and economic self-sufficiency from a conservative standpoint, *Die Tat* had spawned its own political circle, the Tatkreis, made up of influential figures from politics, business, and the military.

But with Kuckhoff, Diederichs got more than he'd bargained for. His new editor gave the magazine a sweeping new subtitle, "the monthly magazine for the formation of new realities," and a new leftist profile to go with it. He brought in an eye-catching list of new contributors, including Armin Wegner, a Prussian aristocrat who had valiantly exposed the Turkish massacres of Armenians that he had witnessed as a medic during the war.[15] Wegner's was one of the twentieth century's first voices to be raised against the crime of genocide.

Another of Kuckhoff's discoveries never achieved Wegner's fame, but he was destined to play a far larger role in Kuckhoff's future. This was a young German-American journalist named John Sieg.[16] Kuckhoff took a liking to the young man and his atmospheric essays, and the two became good friends.

Kuckhoff's editorship of *Die Tat* came to a sudden end in 1929 after he had a falling-out with Diederichs, who feared that he was taking the journal too far to the left. Kuckhoff, like many other intellectuals in Berlin, had lost patience with the hapless Social Democrats and began to regard the Communists with greater interest. There is no evidence that he ever joined the German Communist Party, but he was well-versed in the concepts of Marx and Lenin. Growing ranks of middle-class intellectuals were gravitating to the left. The question that resounded endlessly, in rehearsals, editorials, and coffeehouses, was whether theater and other art forms could be harnessed to the interests of the workingman. Kuckhoff was eager to leap into the fray, but Diederichs was not.[17] Kuckhoff was fired.

Despite the bleak economy, Kuckhoff's period of unemployment was brief. Rescue came at the hands of Adolf Grimme, the new Prussian minister of culture. Grimme, a respected educator and committed Social Democrat, had been one of Kuckhoff's closest friends since they were twenty-year-old students together in Halle. Now Grimme pulled some ministerial strings to get Kuckhoff appointed first dramaturge at Leopold Jessner's Staatstheater in Berlin. It was this post that took him to the Theater Congress in Hamburg a few months later.[18]

So this was Adam Kuckhoff, the man who swept the wistful Greta Lorke off her feet. And for all his complications, Greta was loath to let him go. After the thrill of her adventure in America, Greta feared that at the age of twenty-eight, she would settle into the dreary existence of an underemployed old maid. Adam Kuckhoff may have been unprepossessing with his high-flown theories and gnomish appearance, but his thoughts on the great questions of the day were wonderfully similar to her own. Furthermore, an association with him could propel her from her secretarial backwaters into the whirlpool where Berlin's experimental theater and leftist politics converged.

Berliners were eager to drag their high culture off its pedestal and mix it up with the life of the street. Classical theater was reworked to the rhythms of cabaret satire and barroom ballads. But there were dark reasons behind Berlin's frenetic cultural energy. Many important artists were driven by anger, nihilism, and despair. An entire generation of young Germans had watched the kaiser's hubris drag the country through an insane and devastating conflict. Now they doubted the ability of the Social Democrats to put it back together again. Furthermore, many young artists had served at the front and personally experienced the unprecedented carnage. That trauma was played out ferociously and obsessively in their work.

One of Adam Kuckhoff's rivals in the Berlin theater world was a scruffy young playwright named Bertolt Brecht. Over much of the 1920s the two writers' careers ran on parallel tracks. They worked with many of the same actors and faced similar tribulations. Both men experimented with form, reworking the same source material into drama, fiction, and screenplays. Brecht, eleven years younger than Kuckhoff, came from a comparable background, and served as a teenage medic in the final stage of the war. Afterward, both Brecht and Kuckhoff were surrounded by the maimed and shell-shocked "walking dead" on the streets of Berlin. Their generation's wartime experiences were translated into a new dramatic form called the *Heimkehrerdrama,* depicting the soldier's homecoming to "face the difficulty, or impossibility, of reintegrating into a society which rejects them as symbols of a recent past that it wishes to forget."[19]

Both Brecht and Kuckhoff wrote poetry and drama. But poetry was self-expression; theater was supposed to change the world. Their work came to life through the efforts of extraordinary producers. Leopold Jessner, Adam Kuckhoff's patron, combined innovative stagecraft with strong political engagement. Producer and director Erwin Piscator was more radical and even more influential. Piscator held that the purpose of theater was to serve as an engine of social change.

Much of Piscator's theatrical work was driven by his rage against the war. In 1928 he produced an unexpected hit in the form of a new antiwar play. *U-Boot S-4* was the work of an unknown twenty-six-year-old graduate student named Günther Weisenborn, who would work closely with both Kuckhoff and Brecht in the future. The play, drawn from newspaper stories, depicted six American sailors trapped in a submarine off the coast of New Jersey. The production featured Heinrich George, a major star of both commercial theater and the Communist avant-garde, fresh from his appearance in the film sensation *Metropolis.*

Weisenborn's *U-Boot S-4* was denounced as pacifist propaganda by the nationalist press, but this was to be expected (and may have contributed to its great success). The author, a slight, engaging young man with beetle brows and a toothy grin, promptly moved to Berlin. Piscator introduced him to Brecht, and the two writers soon became friends and collaborators.[20]

In early 1930, Erwin Piscator asked Weisenborn to work on a stage adaptation of Maxim Gorky's 1906 novel *The Mother* for his Volksbühne company. Brecht took an interest in the project and asked Weisenborn to collaborate on a further adaptation based on the Volksbühne script. The Brecht-Weisenborn version of the play opened in Berlin in 1932, directed by Brecht and starring his wife, Helene Weigel. She was joined in the cast by a blond, nineteen-year-old actress named Marta Wolter, who had just finished filming a new movie with Brecht.

Die Mutter (The Mother) began to tour workers' halls and clubs, but the Nazis considered the play an outright provocation. They disrupted performances and the police closed it down in February. (It would be Brecht's last stage production in Germany before the Nazi takeover the following year.)[21] Weisenborn maintained his friendship with Brecht for decades, and also remained close to the young actress Marta Wolter, who would play a critical role in his resistance activities in the future.

Before the war, German theater was rooted in nineteenth-century conventions, decked out in literary flourishes and elaborate costumes, sets, and lights. But the front theater taught a generation of dramatists like Adam Kuckhoff and Erwin Piscator that theater could thrive under the most extreme conditions and speak to contemporary experience. Avant-garde theater moved into the basements of Berlin, with additional pockets in regional centers such as Hamburg and Munich. Over the 1920s it gathered momentum. Many artists saw a natural convergence occurring between Marxism, political reform, and creative experimentation. Bertolt Brecht decided to abandon his middle-class background and adopt the proletarian affect of a convict haircut and black leather jacket. By 1928 he had begun to make a conscious effort to write plays with Marxist themes.[22] When he opened his new musical *Threepenny Opera* that year, the production included his favorite actors from Communist theater groups, including a sloe-eyed beauty named Carola Neher, who was cast as the ingenue Polly Peachum.[23]* Brecht converted to Marxism the same year he became a commercial success.

Brecht's and Kuckhoff's lives intersected again in the person of an exceedingly handsome young actor from Dresden named Hans Otto. Adam Kuckhoff had met Otto in 1920 in Frankfurt am Main.

Otto made his professional acting debut at Kuckhoff's theater, playing the lead in *Kabale und Liebe* (*Intrigue and Love*), an early Schiller classic.[24] Otto, who had just turned twenty, was gorgeous in his nineteenth-century powdered wig and lace cravat, playing an aristocrat who falls tragically in love with the daughter of a humble musician.[25]

Kuckhoff and the company soon realized they had a star on their hands. Soon Otto was writing grandly to Kuckhoff about his contract, suggesting programming and making demands: "Regarding the clause 'Possible accommodation in unheated quarters'—I object."[26] Otto also caught the attention of Adam's wife of ten years, Marie, who saw him as "a high-strung, strikingly pale young man, a man who, without being a wet blanket, was standoffish—a real loner."[27] (Marie, in contrast, was called "slight, stylish and clever" by Otto's sister Elspeth.)

The stylish, clever Marie and the high-strung Otto fell in love. She divorced Adam Kuckhoff and married Hans Otto in 1923, and Adam married Marie's sister Gertrud. In short order, Hans Otto simultaneously became Adam Kuckhoff's ex-wife's husband and his new brother-in-law. By all accounts, the union of Marie and Hans Otto was a happy one. Even under these most complicated of circumstances, Kuckhoff, Otto, and the Viehmeyer sisters all remained good friends.

"Dear Gertrud and Adam," Otto wrote cheerfully in 1928. "This abundance of work makes it hard for me to write—forgive me! Maybe

---

* Her father was played by another Brecht discovery, the young Hungarian actor Peter Lorre.

I'll come to Berlin next year after all. It's so hard to decide. Should one pursue success, or one's interests?"[28]

Otto pursued both. He and Marie fell in with a group of Communist artists in Hamburg, and Otto joined the German Communist Party, or KPD, in 1924. Soon he was recruited to staffs of their arts publications and collectives. In 1926, Otto starred in a production of Bertolt Brecht's play *The Life of Edward II* and Otto and Brecht became fast friends.

Everyone seemed to like Hans Otto. He grew more outgoing as he matured, and people were attracted to his frank, warm gaze and dark curly hair. He approached both communism and theater with a passion for the workingman. Otto exerted a strong influence on Brecht, who mentioned him frequently in his correspondence.

By 1930, Otto, Kuckhoff, and Brecht were all working at Jessner's Staatstheater in Berlin. Otto was an extraordinary example of that Weimar phenomenon: matinee idol combined with leftist firebrand. In 1930 he drafted a flyer promoting the agitprop theater program of the KPD's German Workers' Theater Association. He called "the masses to the gigantic task" of creating a workers' cultural movement. Music clubs would sing "new revolutionary songs that the masses should learn," gathering in workplaces and recreational facilities.[29] The following year he starred in Jean Giraudoux's delightful comedy *Amphitryon 38* with leading actresses Elisabeth Bergner and Lil Dagover.

But by 1932, Otto raised the stakes with a pamphlet confronting the Social Democrats' minister of culture, Adam Kuckhoff's old friend Adolf Grimme. He accused the Social Democrats of betraying German artists by closing theaters for budgetary reasons. Their police, he complained, had closed down a theater collective's production of Bertolt Brecht's (and Günther Weisenborn's) play *The Mother*. The ministry dared to say it supported the "Theater of the People." Otto pointed instead to the Soviets, who, he claimed, had increased the numbers of theaters and audiences over the previous two years.

Adam Kuckhoff steered a middle course between his friends, the bureaucratic Adolf Grimme and the incendiary Hans Otto. He was still trying to meld his political convictions to his dramatic art, but it was not easy. Even Piscator and Brecht, with their open allegiance to Marxism, frequently ran afoul of the Communist Party. The Russian Bolsheviks, now under the rule of Joseph Stalin, made a fetish of their proletarian and peasant roots. They were particularly suspicious of the worldly German Marxists, who combined an air of superiority with an annoying degree of independence.[30]

In his usual fashion, Adam Kuckhoff was ensnared in conflicts that had nothing to do with ideology. Unable to commit himself wholeheartedly to either of his disciplines, he split his time between them. Kuckhoff continued as dramaturge at the Staatstheater, but he was also working on a novel, *Scherry,* based on the character of the celebrated Swiss clown named Grock. The book explored the overweening ego of the performer, which overpowered weaker beings in its path.[31] (The theme may have been inspired by Adam's recent experience of losing his first wife to an actor.)

Greta Lorke, who had found Adam Kuckhoff so irresistible in Hamburg, had removed herself from his travails. She called the discovery of his marital status "a major blow." Adam tried to explain away the complexities of his married life with the Viehmeyer sisters, but Greta was having none of it. Crushed, she pulled away. "I buried myself in my work," she wrote later, "although given the conditions, I couldn't expect any satisfaction from it, beyond making enough money to support myself, with a little extra to send home to my parents."[32]

CHAPTER 3

Berlín

1928–1930

GRETA'S FRIENDS FROM WISCONSIN, ARVID AND MILDRED HAR-nack, spent 1928 and 1929 in the small university towns of Jena and Giessen. There they became aware of a disturbing new phenomenon. A radical right-wing party called the National Socialists was enjoying extraordinary success in recruiting student supporters.

Mildred understood the Germans' frustration, but she feared the direction they were taking. She wrote to her mother: "There is a large group of people here which, feeling the wrongness of the situation and their own poverty or danger of poverty, leaps to the conclusion, since things were better before the war, it would be a good idea to have a more absolute government again."[1]

Arvid reacted by joining competing student groups that favored pacifism and the Social Democrats, struggling to apply his academic training to the crisis at hand. As the German economy sank deeper into chaos, he took a growing interest in the idea of a centrally planned economy. He was not alone. As the Western capitalist nations floundered in the Great Depression, Americans lost their life savings in uninsured bank accounts, British workers marched in the streets, and Germans panicked at the threat of renewed starvation. Could economic planning protect society from such hardship and disruption? In London and Washington, officials were starting to explore the radical ideas of economist John Maynard Keynes. Arvid Harnack asked similar questions, and wondered whether the new Soviet economists could create a more rational system by starting from scratch.[2]

In 1930, Arvid and Mildred moved to Berlin, where she received a fellowship to study at the university. They were pleased to return to the comfort of his family, and Mildred was thrilled with the prospect of life in the big city. "Yesterday I went to Jena and bought myself material for an evening dress to wear in Berlin," she wrote her mother. "White crepe de chine (waist close-fitted, somewhat short, skirt to feet, two yellow satin appliquéd flowers). Wore to theater."[3] Six weeks later she wrote, "My days [in Berlin] are full until midnight. . . . Full of study, lectures, seminars, concerts, meetings with various members of the family and others."[4]

But Berlin was not to everyone's liking. Adolf Hitler, for one, despised the city as a decadent sinkhole, full of Communists, audacious artists, and Jews—three groups that he tended to conflate. Hitler called Berlin a *Trümmerfeld,* a "field of rubble," and condemned it as "cosmopolitan": a place where German culture was corrupted by decadent foreign and avant-garde influences.[5] (In the Nazi lexicon, "cosmopolitan," "foreign," and "avant-garde" were often slightly veiled terms for "Jewish.")

Berlin was proudly and undeniably cosmopolitan. Some observers were fond of comparing Berlin to Chicago, but most Berliners felt a stronger affinity to New York. By the end of the nineteenth century, both cities had helped transform their nations from agricultural economies to industrial and financial powerhouses. These dynamic conditions couldn't fail to excite intense interest in Greta as a sociologist, Mildred as a literary critic, and Arvid as an inquiring economist.

Berlin's Central Park was the Tiergarten, the old royal hunting park graced with decorative fishponds and romantic walks. Arvid and Mildred often joined their fellow Berliners in weekend strolls along its paths. The Tiergarten intersected with Berlin's spacious promenade, Unter den Linden, which featured elegant hotels and embassies, as well as the University of Berlin, where Greta, Arvid, and Mildred studied and taught.

Friedrichstrasse was Broadway and Madison Avenue combined, with bustling shops and restaurants to complement the theaters where Adam

Kuckhoff and his colleagues produced their work. There were echoes of the Lower East Side in the southeastern working-class neighborhood of Neukölln, where Eastern European immigrant families crowded into tenements and Greta had picked lice from the orphan boys' hair.

Berlin was founded in the twelfth century on a marshy patch of land (its name was said to have come from the word *birl,* or swamp). For centuries it remained a political and cultural backwater. But in the seventeenth century a canny reformist ruler, Kaiser Friedrich Wilhelm, modernized the city. He promoted it as a haven for persecuted French Protestants and Viennese Jews, and both populations took root and prospered. As of 1871, when it was named capital of the new unified Germany, Berlin's population was just over 800,000, half the size of New York's. By 1880 the city had some 45,000 Jewish residents, almost ten percent of Germany's total.[6] Germany's Jewish population peaked in 1910 at 615,000, roughly one percent of the country's population.

Berlin's Jews attained levels of status and influence that were undreamed of in most of Europe. Nonetheless, anti-Semitism still plagued German society. Some of it arose from a tendency to scapegoat Jewish bankers and businessmen for financial panics. Other forms of intolerance resulted from the pogroms in czarist Russia, beginning in the 1880s. These attacks drove floods of Polish- and Russian-speaking refugees into Berlin—thanks in part to international Jewish relief agencies that promoted Berlin as a welcoming destination for resettlement.[7] Berlin's worldly, assimilated Jews, who had struggled for years to win full enfranchisement in German society, now expressed ambivalence about the arrival of the *Ostjuden,* whose dress, speech, and religious practices were redolent of a different century. They feared, with some justification, that the influx of aliens could prompt a backlash among the malicious and the ignorant of their fellow citizens. At the same time, many non-Jewish Berliners denounced anti-Semitism as barbaric. In 1880 a group of Berlin's leading professors, politicians, and businessmen signed the "Declaration of the Notables," deploring anti-Semitism as a "national disgrace" and cautioning against the "ancient folly."[8]

The cataclysm of World War I affected Berliners even more drastically than other Germans. Following the Bolshevik revolution, Russian refugees poured into the city. Another result of the war was the reconstitution of Poland. The new government launched a new series of attacks against Polish Jews, and many fled west to Berlin.

By 1930, Berlin's collection of four million souls was more eclectic than ever, a heady collision of cultures, languages, generations, and ideologies. This made for rough politics but great literature. Ever since the Rhinelander Johannes Gutenberg refitted his fifteenth-century wine press with movable wooden type, Germans had been passionate consumers of the printed word. It was no coincidence that Adam Kuckhoff and the Harnacks managed to publish their work; there were plenty of opportunities. Germany had more newspapers than the United States (with less than half the population), and more than France, England, and Italy combined.[9]

Intellectuals like the Harnacks could follow political developments from dozens of different editorial perspectives. Every major political party was represented among the publications owned by the parties or their supporters. The oldest ones belonged to the Social Democrats and the Catholic Center Party, followed by the Communist Party papers, and finally that of the Nazis.[10] Berlin's independent quality press was dominated by two large publishing houses, Ullstein and Mosse, both of them Jewish-owned. The thriving business in small-town newspapers offered regional diversity, and as of 1928 over eighty percent of the country's papers were family-owned.[11] It was a good time and place to be a journalist.

This was clear to Adam Kuckhoff's young protégé, John Sieg, who approached journalism with single-minded zeal. Many members of Kuckhoff's circle had leftist sympathies, but John was among the few who could lay any claim to actual "proletarian" experience. He also had another exotic quality that fascinated the worldly Berliners: John Sieg was, at least arguably, American.

Ignatius John Sieg was born on February 3, 1903, in Detroit, Michigan, the son of a working-class German Catholic couple who had migrated to America in their youth. His father died when John was seven years old, and the boy was taken to Germany by his grandfather for a visit a few years later. Their return to America was prevented by the outbreak of the Great War, and John found himself attending high school in the West Prussian towns of Schlochau and Krone.[12] In 1920, at the age of seventeen, John, identified as "Johann," became a naturalized German citizen. In 1923 his education was disrupted once again, when John's grandfather died and his mother summoned him back to Detroit.

He must have gone with some reluctance. He was midway through his studies at a teacher's college in Prussia, and he had a Polish sweetheart named Sophie Wloszczynski. They made an attractive couple. Sieg was a handsome man; compact and energetic, with an easy boyish grin and a thick shock of dark blond hair. Sophie was a few years older than John, with the tiny frame, dark ringlets, and winsome gaze of a young Lillian Gish. Sophie followed John to Detroit six months later. On her arrival, she was hired as secretary to the flamboyant Russian conductor of the Detroit Symphony Orchestra, Ossip Gabrilowitsch. As one of the perks of her job, Sophie and John Sieg enjoyed symphony concerts twice a week.

John's career was less genteel. In 1924 and 1925 he worked in the big Ford and Packard auto factories—perhaps on the same assembly lines that Greta Lorke would observe as a visiting sociology student a few years later. John worked the night shift so he could attend daytime classes at the College of the City of Detroit.* Ford had introduced the assembly-line method in 1913. Model T's had swept the country, and within five years they accounted for half the cars in the United States. John joined the long line of job applicants at Ford's Rouge auto plant outside Detroit, which would soon become the largest industrial complex in the world. These experiences would provide the seeds of his writing career.

Henry Ford was not an easy master. Assembly-line work was grueling, with a high worker turnover. Ford reacted by shortening hours and raising wages. But many employees bridled at Ford's paternalism and intolerance—he was virulently antiunion, and even more stridently anti-Semitic. Beginning in 1920, Ford took it upon himself to publish the U.S. edition of *The Protocols of the Elders of Zion,* the notorious anti-Semitic tract that was used to develop Nazi race ideology over the same period.

John Sieg was one of many young workers who leaped into union activism. Sieg was not yet a Communist, but he was fired from his job at

---

* Now Wayne State University.

the Ford plant as a suspected Communist agitator nonetheless.[13] He managed to stay in college until January 1926, but hard times forced his hand. He moved from city to city looking for work, from the construction sites of Pittsburgh to the slaughterhouses of Chicago, taking in the people and places with a writer's eye.

Finally John and Sophie decided to go back to Germany. They arrived in Berlin in February 1928 to an atmosphere of high excitement. Everything was building up to the month of May, when national elections were held. Of the eight major parties, the Social Democrats were clearly dominant, with 153 out of 491 seats. The Social Democrats and the Communist KPD made modest gains; the conservatives lost a significant number of votes; while the unruly Nazis almost disappeared off the parliamentary map.

But the elections were not the only political action in town. May also brought May Day, when the traditional workers' marches expanded into mass political rallies. These often degenerated into slugfests between Communists, Nazis, and police. John's sympathies clearly lay with the leftist trade unionists. He soon joined Rote Hilfe, a solidarity group that had started off as a relief fund for striking workers, and evolved into a welfare effort for imprisoned and injured leftist organizers.

On May 30, 1928, John and Sophie married in a quiet ceremony in their modest apartment to the north of the city. Money was still tight, but Sophie was able to return to a previous job working as a stenographer and clerk for a Jewish lawyer named Harry Wolff in his office on Potsdamer Strasse.

John had his heart set on writing. He set to work, and within a few months he could boast that he had published an article in Dr. Adam Kuckhoff's prestigious political and literary monthly, *Die Tat*. Kuckhoff decided to try out his new author on a book review. His publisher's firm had just released a book by a contentious writer named Adolf Halfeld. *Amerika und Amerikanismus* portrayed American society as primitive, uncultured, and materialistic. "The American lives and traffics in the present," Halfeld wrote, "idealist in word, realist in deed."[14]

Kuckhoff asked John Sieg, recently arrived from the "Amerika" in question, if he could respond to Halfeld's critique. He showed Kuckhoff a series of autobiographical letters and sketches he had written about his experiences in the United States, and Kuckhoff edited them to address Halfeld's points.

John's letters begin in 1925, describing John's homecoming to Detroit and the flood of childhood memories it provoked. America's vitality makes Germany look like a leaky, sinking ship, he writes. "She's acquainted with the compass, but she doesn't even know she needs a rudder." But America has its problems, too. John appreciates the vitality of Chicago's Frank Lloyd Wright and Carl Sandburg, but when he goes looking for work in the city's slaughterhouses, all he can think of is Upton Sinclair: "There I saw and understood what 'the Jungle' really is."[15]

Back in Michigan in 1927, he notes that some factories have closed. It's a shame for the workers, he says, even though he thinks it's crazy to stand on an assembly line "repeating the same hand motion 8,500 times a day."

In his final letter, John stares out on the immense New York night, meditating on its essence: the sound of saxophones on the streets of Harlem, the sea of humanity pouring out of movie theaters and concert halls—the gorgeous other face of *Amerikanismus* that must be experienced firsthand.

There is something to the criticisms of America, John concludes. Yes, the factory work can be brutal and alienating, and yes, Americans can be small-minded and infatuated with technology and money. And yet. When John turns his gaze on New York and other great American cities, he perceives an energy and an unexplored potential that the distant German theorists fail to grasp. He doesn't even bother to read German newspapers pontificating on the subject of America anymore, he says; they're ignorant and shortsighted. John has his own beefs about America, but they're based on his personal experience and tempered with considerable affection. "Amerika, my home," he concludes, "here I leave you."

John's farewell to America turned out to be a fine entrée to German journalism. Adam Kuckhoff was pleased, and offered him more assignments. In April 1929 he published more of John's American sketches, and the June issue offered John's travel piece, "Southern Wanderings."

John was in excellent company. *Die Tat*'s list of contributors displayed Kuckhoff's ever-expanding reach. It included Leo Schestov, the

Russian Jewish existentialist philosopher; Thomas Ring, a renowned astronomer; and Kurt Grossman, the Jewish general secretary for the German League for Human Rights in Berlin. John Sieg, with his history of assembly-line jobs and community college classes, might have felt a little awed by such august associates.[16]

On the other hand, John's rough edges and real-life experiences were part of his appeal. Kuckhoff was fired from *Die Tat* shortly after, but he and John remained lifelong friends. Kuckhoff introduced his protégé to members of his circle, including Hans Otto, the handsome young actor who had married Kuckhoff's first wife, Marie. As a five-year veteran of the German Communist Party, Otto was active in both party affairs and the workers' theater movement. John Sieg and Hans Otto found they had much in common, including an interest in the Communist Party.

John's articles for *Die Tat* opened other doors. In August 1929 the prestigious *Berliner Tageblatt* published a piece about his experiences working on an American skyscraper construction crew. Hermann Grosse, the city editor of the Communist paper *Rote Fahne* (*Red Flag*), noticed the piece and approved of Sieg's sympathetic portrayal of the working class. He tracked down the twenty-seven-year-old writer and recruited him to write for his paper. Soon John was a member of the KPD as well.[17]

John was entranced with the German Communists, and they with him. Grosse published a series of his articles, sketches, and stories under the pseudonym "Siegfried Nebel."[18] John's proletarian authenticity helped him stand out. "In Grosse's eyes [John] had something of the Jack London about him," recalled a friend. "A worker who had mastered Marxism, self-taught. . . . A thoughtful man, physically agile but not showy. . . ."[19]

Within a few months Grosse offered John a job on the editorial staff. In the harsh winter of 1929, a job in journalism with a steady paycheck was doubly welcome.

The *Rote Fahne* was now the largest of the fifty Communist papers in Germany. By 1932 its circulation reached 130,000, about the same as the mainstream liberal daily *Berliner Tageblatt*. *Rote Fahne* was an unapologetic party organ, and played a role in undermining the government and promoting political violence. But it also published an impressive roster of artistic contributors, including both obedient party members and free spirits from the avant-garde, including literary critic Walter Benjamin and composer Hans Eisler, with illustrations by George Grosz and John Heartfield.

John Sieg joined the German Communist Party at a time when its very identity was under assault, although the offensive, unfolding in far-off Moscow, was invisible to most party members in Berlin. The discord between the Germans and the Soviets went back to the very origins of socialism. The German Communists and the Stalinists shared Marxist rhetoric, but the Germans held a proprietary attitude toward Marxism; beginning with Karl Marx himself (who was, after all, born in Germany, the descendant of a long line of German rabbis). Stalinism, on the other hand, began life in the brutal incubator of Bolshevik terrorism; Stalin was so vicious and intolerant that even Lenin—no stranger to violence himself—condemned him as a scoundrel. But Lenin had died in 1924, unable to derail Stalin's path to power. This failure was to have fatal implications for the Germans.

The early KPD was rich in its diversity, including idealistic artists and intellectuals, as well as trade unionists, unemployed workers, and street-fighting thugs who saw communism as an organizing principle for gang warfare. Unlike the Russian Bolsheviks, the KPD functioned as a legitimate party in Germany.

But the German KPD had been a leading member of the Communist International since its founding in 1919. This forum was where the world's Communist parties gathered to discuss policy and strategy. Stalin had little use for their ideas, but he saw a way to use the organization to his own ends.[20] Over the years he brought Communist International under his control and, with it, the various national Communist parties. As historian Alan Bullock points out, "No other Communist party suffered or resented this subordination more than the German."[21]

By the time the Sixth Communist International Congress convened in 1928, Stalin's scheme was complete. At his urging, the Congress resolved that all local Communist parties must be subordinate to the Communist International. Stalin then rammed through an additional resolution stating that Communist parties everywhere should view socialist parties as their most dangerous enemies, "more dangerous than the avowed adherents of predatory imperialism."[22] In German terms, this meant that the KPD and the SPD, which had sometimes cosponsored social legislation, would now be incapable of collaboration.

The stakes were desperately high. In the 1928 German parliamentary elections, the two leftist parties accounted for more than forty percent of the vote in a field of eight parties. (The Nazis, by comparison, had dropped off to less than three percent.) If a working coalition between them had been promoted—instead of sabotaged by Stalin—it could have blocked the juggernaut of the right.

As the 1920s drew to a close, Germany was poised on the brink of a new economic crisis. It would pit desperate urban workers, with their smashed hopes of industrial prosperity, against country people who feared abandonment to poverty and isolation. Many longed for the authoritarian days of the kaiser; others listened to the fairy tale of the Soviet workers' paradise. Democratic Socialism increasingly looked like a failed ten-year experiment.

Most Berliners forgot to worry about the Nazis, who were still regarded as a joke. But they were also unaware of the menace of Stalin, who played his hand behind the scenes. Stalin was secretly antagonistic toward non-Russian Communist parties, and had murderous designs on ethnic Germans and other minorities under his rule. German Communists were doubly vulnerable.

But such critical insights were unavailable to political dilettantes like Adam Kuckhoff and party foot soldiers like John Sieg.

\ \ \

CHAPTER 4

The Masses and the Media

1929–1932

GRETA SAW NO REASON TO LINGER IN GERMANY. THANKS TO THE crash, jobs were scarce, and her new love interest, Adam Kuckhoff, was a married man. Germany was changing, and clearly not for the better. Public discourse had become impossibly shrill, the press was sharply polarized, and passersby had to dodge brawls in the street.

Greta was rescued by an invitation from a lawyer friend who wanted her to accompany his family to Switzerland. He asked only that she put his large private library in order and teach his children some English. Zurich was an island of luxury and calm. Greta was paid generously on top of her free room and board, and the family included her in their activities as an equal.

It was a taste of the good life, she recalled. "I can't deny that I liked it too. . . . There were Perigord truffles, and shellfish flown in from Berlin."[1] In the springtime, the view from her room was transformed into a carpet of violets. Greta was able to send money home to her parents, assuaging her guilt for abandoning them to their working-class poverty. "Occasionally I would dream about my father. I would see him lifting his newspapers into the luggage compartment of the train twice a day, without a word of complaint."[2]

Greta enjoyed a romance on the rebound with a Swiss artist named Leo Leuppi. One of his untitled portraits from this period shows a young woman with a long face like Greta's, posed against a field of blue and graced by a single rose.[3]

It took her mind off her problems. "Adam Kuckhoff's face slowly blurred," Greta wrote later. "His letters came seldom, and I wrote to him even less."[4]

Once she finished the job in Switzerland, Greta reluctantly accepted a position in Frankfurt, this time as a girl Friday for a sociology professor. Karl Mannheim was a brilliant theorist, but the job was less lucrative and less satisfying than the one in Zurich. She worked long hours putting yet another massive library in order, yearning for time to finish her doctorate. After hours she would retreat to a neighborhood coffee shop, where students passionately debated the dismal state of the nation, agreeing only that the ruling Social Democratic government was a disaster. Here, too, Greta ran into Communist students, who pressed her to join the party. But she wasn't comfortable with the idea.[5] She didn't understand their debates and she didn't share their vocabulary. She maintained her own different perspective and kept her distance.

But Greta's friends Arvid and Mildred Harnack found it increasingly difficult to skirt ideological debates. Arvid's initial shock at the Nazis' momentum spurred him to join a Social Democratic campus organization in Giessen. But as the German economy went into a tailspin, the Social Democrats became more vulnerable to criticism from the left as well as the right.[6] Arvid Harnack joined the leftward drift. He gradually came to think of himself philosophically as a Communist (though no evidence has been found that he ever joined the Communist Party). The KPD had many unattractive attributes for a man like Arvid. Its public street brawls were matched by internal divisions, and the party underwent frequent splintering and purging.

Arvid Harnack, deeply immersed in his research, had no taste for infighting. He was set on advancing his career. He had already produced a thesis on the U.S. labor movement, and planned to publish an analysis of Soviet economic planning. Mildred was far more interested in American Transcendentalists than Soviet Bolsheviks. But once she settled in Germany, she found that politics were unavoidable.

Mildred, a newlywed abroad for the first time, was eager, observant, and more than a little homesick. Her frequent letters home offered a detailed and intimate account of her new country's rapid decline.

In October 1929, Mildred described their modest life in the university town of Giessen, where Arvid was completing his studies. Dinner, she noted, consisted of cabbage, potato, and sausage soup, costing fifteen cents. One could eat for thirty-five cents a day "if you eat simply as we do . . . I think it is the best policy not to call attention to oneself in any blatant way, for among the poor Germans it is not kind to look rich."[7] Three days after Christmas she asks for her mother's help in cashing a coupon on a bond. Like others all over the country, she says, "We're in money difficulties."[8]

A few months later Mildred wrote that economic conditions had worsened:

> The situation is hardest on many children of the middle and lower classes, who don't get enough to eat and are in economic fear. . . . The trouble was that the war wasn't only against the Kaiser. The people of Germany were half bled to death, and their hard times are not over. There is no pity or love between nations, yet nations are composed of people and the people must suffer. . . . You can see why we are careful with our money.[9]

Arvid proudly introduced his bride to his family, including his uncle Adolf von Harnack, an eminent theologian who had led campaigns against anti-Semitism in the Lutheran Church. The meeting took place in Berlin in early 1930, only a few months before his death, and the elderly sage made a deep impression. A few months later the young couple visited Adolf's son Ernst von Harnack, a prominent Social Democratic official. Mildred wrote home about his impressive residence. The same letter, with an eerie foreshadowing, described her experience with a decapitated specter.

> Dearest Heart: Enclosed is a picture of the beautiful castle in which I was the guest of Arvid's cousin Ernst von Harnack and his wife Aenne on my way to Berlin this week. Ernst is the *Regierungspräsident* [regional governor] of a portion of Germany and lives in a magnificent, if simple manner in the great stately rooms of the castle of Merseburg, a suburb of Halle. I slept in a room at the left behind the trees. . . .

When we came home Ernst told me a story of the headless ghost of a page who haunted the castle and especially, he said, my room. The result of his story was that I dreamt all night about the unfortunate fellow.

Germany was growing more unstable by the day, and even a political novice like Mildred could see a new crisis in the works. She assigned some of the blame to a vicious new faction:

> The leaders of the group are paid by the big industrialists who wish to use the movement as their weapon against organized workers, against the insurance of the working-man, etc., and finally against Communism, which wants by working in a temporarily violent way, to pull the rich man down and to pull the poor man up until both are on the same level, until all have enough, and no one has too much or too little.
>
> The group names itself the National-Socialists, although it has nothing to do with socialism and the name itself is a lie. It thinks itself highly moral and like the Ku Klux Klan, makes a campaign of hatred against the Jews.

Mildred shared her husband's view of the conflict, and hoped that Germany could maintain peace through the cooperation of the Social Democrats and the Communists. She retained the Harnack family's Social Democratic perspective, and feared the KPD's threat to public order:

> The existence of [the Nazis], as well as the smaller one of the Communists, whose aims are finer, endangers the government in Germany. Neither group wishes to work through the Reichstag (the German Parliament) although both sit in it. If the "Nationalist Socialists" succeed in erecting a dictatorship, there may be much agitation, because the party of [Democratic] Socialists together with that of the Communists makes a strong left wing in the Reichstag and will oppose the efforts of the right-wing (conservatives to lower wages, reduce the amount of unemployment insurance etc.).

Just now a big strike of the Metal-Workers has begun, because there is an attempt to reduce their wages (none too high to live on now) 8%. . . . [10]

Sophisticated Berliners were used to regarding the Nazis' boorish brownshirts as a bad joke.[11] Now, suddenly, they had good reason to worry. In September 1930, from one election to the next, the Nazis went from last place (in a field of nine), to second place after the Social Democrats. They multiplied their parliamentary seats nine times over, benefiting from Stalin's secret decision to fracture the left.

Berlin's intellectuals were shocked. The city's most prestigious liberal daily, *Berliner Tageblatt,* railed against the "monstrous fact . . . [that] six million and four hundred thousand voters in this highly civilized country had given their vote to the commonest, hollowest, and crudest charlatanism."[12] The Nazi victory seemed to come out of nowhere, but only because the *Tageblatt* editorialists and other urban intellectuals had been inattentive, more absorbed in avant-garde and ideological hairsplitting than in the slums and farms of their own backyard.

The Nazis' strategy was simple: to exploit the fissures of Weimar political culture. Germany was rife with opportunity. The countryside, the mass media, and the streets were the three main targets.

Traditional parties were vulnerable on all three fronts. The Social Democratic government had an unfortunate history of cronyism, favoring its own affiliated trade unions and civic organizations. The leftist parties cultivated urban areas at the expense of rural constituencies. The Nazis exploited the vacuum by attacking civil society from the grass roots. Mildred Harnack had watched them move in on her college town. Between 1924 and 1928 the Nazis infiltrated local singing societies, sports clubs, and even church groups. Some towns resisted the onslaught. Others rancorously divided into two biking clubs, two drama societies, and, in one Hessian community, two competing volunteer fire companies.[13] In one small town, the forty-six local members of the Nazi Party belonged to no fewer than seventy-three religious and civic organizations.[14]

The party grew rapidly, with a unique organizational structure. As of 1928 there were 100,000 Nazi Party members organized into tightly knit cadres throughout the country. Over the next two years, the party quadrupled its membership, with over 3,400 branches, and 2,000 trained speakers for its national recruitment efforts. It continued to expand quickly over 1931 and 1932.[15]

The Nazis' success was fueled by sheer panic. Between 1928 and 1932 suicide rates rose fourteen percent among German men, and nineteen percent among women.[16] The Nazis offered a reassuring message: if Germany was failing, it was because the country had been weakened by internal divisions and victimized by foreign enemies. That condition could be reversed if Germans could unite under a banner of strength and self-discipline.

The Nazis were ready to take the lead, participating in the electoral process only in order to destroy it. This philosophy was spelled out in April 1928, in an essay by Joseph Goebbels, a candidate for the Reichstag.

> We are an anti-parliamentarian party that rejects for good reasons the Weimar constitution and its republication institutions. We oppose a fake democracy that treats the intelligent and the foolish, the industrious and the lazy in the same way. . . . We enter the Reichstag to arm ourselves with democracy's weapons. . . .
>
> If we succeed in getting sixty or seventy of our party's agitators and organizers elected to the various parliaments, the state itself will pay for our fighting organization. That is amusing and entertaining enough to be worth trying. . . .

The Nazis needed someone who could market their message to the underdogs of German society, and Joseph Goebbels was their man. Under slightly different circumstances, he might have been another of Adam Kuckhoff's protégés. The two men had much in common.

Like Kuckhoff, Goebbels was born a Catholic Rhinelander, a small, frail man left crippled by a childhood infection. He studied at a succession of German universities in search of a vocation, and finally earned his doctorate in German literature and drama in 1922 from Heidelberg. Goebbels, too, aspired to be a writer, and had high hopes for his autobiographical novel, written just after he received his degree. His melodramatic work was called *Michael: ein Deutsches Schicksal in Tagebuchblät-tern* ("Michael: A German Destiny in Journal Pages"). It told the story of a young student who is inspired by German folk ideals but driven to suicide by his despair over Germany's decline.[17]

Young Goebbels submitted *Michael* to leading publishers, only to have it rejected by all. He wrote two plays—one of them, *Der Wanderer* (*The Wanderer*), was based on the life of Jesus Christ—but they went unproduced. Goebbels offered dozens of articles to *Berliner Tageblatt*. But the paper turned down Goebbels's articles as well as his application for a job as reporter.

Goebbels finally found acceptance in the embrace of the Nazi Party. He attended a Munich rally in 1922, and he joined the Rhineland branch of the party soon after. He became one of Hitler's strongest supporters, driven by passionate personal loyalty.[18] The party, in turn, acknowledged his literary talents (as the German publishing industry had not) and assigned him to edit party publications.

In 1926, Hitler sent Goebbels to "Red Berlin." This was a challenge; the city's well-entrenched Socialist and Communist culture was more resistant to Nazi ideology than the countryside. Shortly after he arrived, Goebbels founded a weekly called *Der Angriff* (*The Attack*), which conveniently let him publish as much of his own writing as he pleased. He won his seat in the Reichstag in 1928, and became the party's chief strategist for propaganda, which allowed him to pursue his passions for the dramatic arts, the cult of celebrity, and the mass media.

Goebbels was a born propagandist, and is often credited with the creation of the myth of Hitler as all-powerful Führer. He also had a talent for stagecraft, imbuing the Nazi movement and Hitler's personality cult with perverse mutations of Catholic pageantry and iconography.[19]

Over the 1920s, the German news media underwent a massive consolidation process. The resulting concentration of ownership benefited the Nazis. Many media properties ended up in the hands of conservative media baron Alfred Hugenberg. By the end of the decade, his holdings included a major book and magazine publisher, a newspaper chain, an international wire service, and Germany's leading film company, Universum-Film (UFA). Hugenberg began to court the Nazis. They quickly took over his empire and used it to transform the German mass media environment, with Goebbels in charge.

In November 1930, Goebbels won party financing to take his newspaper from a weekly to a daily publication, which also allowed him to lower the newsstand price and expand the content. (One of his first new features was serial fiction, launched with his own novel, *Michael.*)[20] Goebbels used *Der Angriff* to fashion a parallel Nazi universe of ideology, behavior, and myth. Like other newspapers, it covered political and economic issues, but Goebbels added women's pages, book and music reviews, even sports coverage, all of it delivered from a Nazi perspective. As scholar Russel Lemmons writes,

> *Der Angriff* was part of an attempt by the [Nazi Party] to lay the foundation of a future totalitarian society; one in which the Führer and his minions would have the last say on all matters, public and private, and no one would have the information to oppose them. *Der Angriff,* and papers like it, would provide a valuable training ground for the future leaders of the Third Reich's propaganda apparatus, and this trend toward the creation of an all-encompassing world view would continue, indeed accelerate, during Hitler's years in power.[21]

Perhaps not even Goebbels realized it at the time, but his vision of *Der Angriff* would serve as a blueprint for the Nazis' future policy of *Gleichschaltung:* "shaping everything into conformity" by reaching into every sector of society to root out dissent and envelop the public in Nazi values.[22]

Goebbels's focus transcended the argumentative realm of print. He worked closely with Hitler in staging mass rallies for outlying cities, offering a thrilling spectacle to the beaten-down audiences, and showcasing Hitler's oratory.

Goebbels saw infinite promise in the movies. A failed playwright, he paid close attention to plays and films and systematically reviewed them in his journal, taking special note of the 1930 film production of Brecht's *Threepenny Opera.* Goebbels was engrossed in the question of how film could be adapted as a political tool, and he considered *Threepenny Opera* to be a negative model. Although it projected the Communists' message of solidarity with the poor and the powerless, he believed that the polemic was diluted by humor and cynicism.

Still, Goebbels recognized that the Communists were several steps ahead of the Nazis in politicizing the arts and the media. One reason for this lay in the extraordinary figure of Willi Münzenberg, the media czar of the left. Münzenberg, who cultivated the scruffy image of his working-class past, was also a public relations genius. He soon parlayed the relief initiative into his own mass media consortium known as the Münzenberg Trust. Over the next nineteen years it grew into an international media empire that included two daily newspapers, a mass-circulation weekly, and a collection of trade magazines. He also financed Erwin Piscator's agitprop theater for the masses, and founded Prometheus Productions to underwrite left-wing films.

But Münzenberg lacked the Nazis' rapacity and financial expertise. His occasional cinematic successes were interspersed with turgid propaganda-laden flops.[23] In 1931, as the political situation approached a boiling point, Münzenberg decided to produce a script coauthored by Bertolt Brecht. The proletarian epic was called *Kuhle Wampe* (literally translated as "Cold Stove," but also Berlin slang for "empty belly"), and told the story of a family of unemployed workers and their refuge in a tent city outside Berlin.

The film's young heroine was played by Marta Wolter, the delicate nineteen-year-old actress who had recently joined the KPD. It was to be the first and last feature role of her career. The Nazi cataclysm was only months away, and with it, leftist filmmaking would come to an abrupt end. Münzenberg and Brecht would be flung to opposite ends of the earth. Marta Wolter would stay in Berlin and learn a new role as part of the resistance.

Kuhle Wampe was released in 1932. The Nazis banned the film within the year, but they examined it closely nonetheless. Some authors have speculated that *Kuhle Wampe*'s scenes of workers' rallies and athletic contests inspired similar tableaus in the Nazis' *Olympiad* and *Triumph of the Will*. Earlier, Joseph Goebbels had borrowed from Brecht's *Threepenny Opera*. The propaganda minister, who played a little piano himself, told his diary that he abhorred the film, especially the jazz-influenced score by Jewish composer Kurt Weill. All the same, he gave orders to make similar popular music available to the German public on the Reich radio system.[24] It was easy enough to censor cultural expressions, but sometimes it was more useful to co-opt them.

\ \ \

CHAPTER 5

Things Fall Apart

January 1932–January 1933

I T GREW HARDER, EVEN FOR MODERATES, TO IMAGINE HOW DEMOC-racy in Germany could survive. Mildred Harnack, a captive audience to Berlin's ugly dramas, was stirred to indignation by events on the streets. In January 1932 she witnessed a fracas between the Nazis and the Communists in front of the Karl Liebknecht Haus, which served as KPD headquarters as well as the *Rote Fahne* newspaper offices. Mildred wrote home expressing her outrage at the government response. "The police openly assisted and protected the Fascists, struck at the protesting workers with their rubber batons, and put a great cordon about the whole square, allowing only Nazis to get through."[1]

It wasn't enough for the Nazis to gather strength; in order to take over they required a breakdown of the status quo. On this count, the fates obliged them at every turn. Violent police actions were only one symptom of the social collapse. The same October that witnessed the Crash on Wall Street brought the death of Foreign Minister Gustav Stresemann, Germany's most gifted statesman. Stresemann had brokered economic and political treaties that led to recovery in the mid-1920s, and shared the Nobel Peace Prize with French foreign minister Aristide Briand in 1926. Now, in the midst of crucial negotiations with the French, he died suddenly at the age of fifty-one. Stresemann had urged his quarrelsome colleagues to unite against extremists, warning, "We are dancing on a volcano and we are facing a revolution, if we are unable to achieve conciliation by a wise and decisive policy."[2]

There was a critical vacuum in leadership. Part of the problem was structural. The 1919 constitution endowed the office of president with many powers, including the ability to call parliamentary elections, to appoint a chancellor, and, in cases of emergency, to rule by decree. Since 1925 these powers had been held by Prussian field marshal Paul von Hindenburg. The old general had been a war hero, but he had no idea how to respond to the growing political chaos. After 1928, Hindenburg went through four chancellors in four years.

The parliament was equally unstable. There had been five parliamentary elections in the nine years following the founding of the Republic in 1919. But now the political upheavals produced four elections in the two and a half years between September 1930 and March 1933. Each election saw a decline in the Social Democratic Party's standing, and growth for the radical parties trying to displace it.

The German Communist Party (KPD) was one of the parties that gained parliamentary seats. The party recruited angry unemployed workers to carry out Stalin's orders to sabotage the Social Democrats. They were met by gangs from Nazi paramilitary organizations: the SS (Schutzstaffel, or Protection Squad), founded as a retinue of Hitler bodyguards, and the SA (*Sturmabteilung*, or Storm Division), known as the "brownshirts." Communists and Nazis knocked heads frequently and sometimes fatally. The brawls were called *Zusammenstösse* (collisions). Police often, but not always, favored the Nazis.

It was still barely possible for middle-class Berliners to mind their own business and hope it would all blow over. Adam Kuckhoff, for one, was busy with another professional reincarnation. In 1931 he quarreled with the management of the Staatstheater and left his position as dramaturge to become a freelance writer. He coauthored a comedy aptly called *Wetter für morgen veränderlich* (*Changeable Weather Tomorrow*) that was produced in Berlin in 1932. Then he started on a new novel and picked up extra work as a reader for Ullstein's book division.[3]

The Harnacks also clung to normalcy. Mildred resumed her studies at the university in Berlin, and was delighted to get an offer to lecture there on American literature. She happily set about getting to know her husband's family, while Arvid joined his wife exploring Berlin's lively American community.

It must have been a welcome island of sanity. Berlin was teeming with American and British expatriates, attracted by the highly favorable exchange rate and the exotic atmosphere. Christopher Isherwood, W. H. Auden, and Stephen Spender came in search of the "divine decadence" that Isherwood subsequently portrayed in his Berlin stories. Mildred and Arvid's activities were more wholesome: luncheon lectures at the American Women's Club, supper forums at the American Church, and U.S. embassy teas. The American community was a mixed bag of students, tourists, and businessmen, but many members held a liberal perspective, reflecting the dawn of the Roosevelt administration back home.

The Harnacks shared a keen interest in the Soviet Union, like many of their German and American counterparts. Mildred was thrilled by Russian fiction and cinema and inspired by news of Soviet social reforms, especially those affecting women. She eagerly shared her views with her students. Arvid was more convinced than ever that the Soviets' experiments in centralized planning offered hope for the West. After all, he pointed out, the Soviets were impoverished, but they had escaped the worst of the Great Depression. Arvid decided to set up a new study group called ARPLAN, a German acronym for the Working Group for the Study of Soviet Economic Planning. It was launched in January 1932, with Arvid as secretary and a number of prominent German scholars as members. They were assisted by two Soviet officials posted to Berlin, Sergei Bessonov, a leading economist, and Alexander Hirschfeld, an embassy official.[4] The Soviets had instructed Bessonov to recruit German technocrats for visits to the USSR, and to extract useful information for the Soviet trade legation.[5]

It was clear that 1932 was going to be a decisive year. The Social Democrats were in disarray, and the Nazis and the Communists were both on the rise. Germany held presidential elections on March 13, with a runoff on April 10. The three leading candidates for president were Hindenburg, Hitler, and Communist Party candidate Ernst Thälmann, a rough-hewn dockworker and Stalin loyalist.

President Hindenburg was still Germany's power broker, but he was ill-served by aides who convinced him that Hitler could be easily manipulated. Equally grave, at eighty-four, he was tired and increasingly senile. Still, in the public mind, the field marshal represented order and discipline in the face of growing turmoil. Despite an ugly campaign, Hindenburg won the runoff elections easily, with the support of every major party other than the Nazis and the Communists. Hitler came in a distant second, with Thälmann trailing an even more distant third. Altercations between Nazis and Communists sharpened, with a mounting death toll. A political chill set in, and the influence of the Nazis began to reach beyond the streets.

In May 1932, Mildred Harnack's job became an early casualty. She was a gifted and popular teacher, but the American studies division of the university had been taken over by a prominent Nazi.[6] He received reports of Mildred's liberal leanings and passion for Russian literature, and terminated her contract.

The next blow came the following month, when the Harnacks were obliged to move. Mildred wrote her mother that, unfortunately, "the people with whom we live are National Socialists." She and Arvid found a new place on the border between the neighborhoods of Kreuzberg and Neukölln, both working-class neighborhoods and political tinderboxes. Mildred was pleased with their new quarters; they were sunny and comfortable, near the open spaces of parks and the Tempelhof airfield.[7]

The Harnacks were ready to take a break from Germany's turbulence. In August, Soviet economist Sergei Bessonov invited the twenty-three members of Arvid's group to take a three-week study tour of the Soviet Union. Mildred had her heart set on going, but she had found a new teaching position at a night school and the ARPLAN trip conflicted with her schedule. She decided to go separately, booking her own trip to Leningrad and Moscow a few weeks ahead of the group.[8]

Mildred and Arvid each received a "Potemkin Village" tour, rooted in the long-standing Russian tradition of showing outsiders a whitewashed version of their actual conditions.[9] The Soviets devoted great effort to such tours in an attempt to build support for their country in the West. The Harnacks were shown that food was plentiful, and were shielded from the vast numbers of the population who were suffering from a devastating famine. As Arvid was shepherded around model factories and public works, he was impressed by their scale and efficiency, while Mildred eagerly learned of Soviet reforms for women such as birth control and maternity leave.

It has been alleged that Arvid was contacted by Soviet intelligence while he was on the study tour, but this is not confirmed by his own records.[10] Whatever the case, Arvid met with a range of Soviet officials, but paid his own way and continued to function as an academic. He took systematic notes on large-scale economic projects and wrote them up as a book upon his return in September. The manuscript was accepted by Rowohlt, a major publisher in Berlin.

On their return, Mildred and Arvid were quickly swept back into Berlin's political drama. It was still possible to hope that the November elections could lead the country back to normalcy. The Nazi Party's electoral support had peaked the previous July. In November they lost two million votes and thirty-four seats in the Reichstag, while the Social Democrats held steady and the Communists made gains.[11]

But these numbers left out the wild card of coalition politics. Hindenburg had been reelected president, but Adolf Hitler, whose eroding minority party still had the largest number of seats in the Reichstag, demanded that Hindenburg appoint him chancellor. Hindenburg's conservative advisers urged him to agree, in hopes that the Nazis would help them consolidate their power.

It was a hard sell. Hindenburg didn't see Hitler as chancellor material, and continued to dismiss him as "the little Bohemian corporal." He tried to stall, but his advisers prevailed. On January 30, 1933, Hindenburg, beaten down by the conflict and fearing a disintegration into civil war, appointed Adolf Hitler to be Germany's chancellor. General Erich Ludendorff, a conservative politician and Hindenburg's former chief of staff, took his old commanding officer to task:

By appointing Hitler chancellor you have handed over our sacred German fatherland to one of the biggest demagogues of all time. I solemnly prophesy that this wretched man will plunge our country into the depths and will bring unimaginable suffering to our nation. Future generations will curse you in your grave for this action.[12]

Joseph Goebbels immediately organized a torchlit parade through the heart of Berlin, long considered enemy territory. There were similar marches all over the country, met by Communist demonstrations against the new government. Fighting broke out. Within a few days, the Communist newspaper *Rote Fahne* was banned and copies confiscated. Storm troopers attacked Communists and trade unionists in their offices and homes, and the attacks were soon extended to Social Democrats.[13] The previous year Hindenburg's administration had purged Social Democrats from the Berlin police force. Now the police stood by while Social Democrats and Communists were beaten and killed.

Yet another round of national elections was scheduled for early March. By mid-February the Nazi brownshirts had begun to attack members of the Catholic Center Party in addition to Communists and Social Democrats. Center Party newspapers were banned for criticizing the government.

On February 20, several dozen of Germany's wealthiest individuals gathered at the home of Nazi minister Hermann Göring. These were the men who controlled iron mines, steelworks, and munitions factories—all of which had labored at a disadvantage under Versailles restrictions and trade union demands.

Adolf Hitler, the featured speaker, assured the businessmen that he had their interests at heart. "Private enterprise cannot be maintained in the age of democracy," he told them. He promised to eliminate the Marxists and rebuild the army, whether or not his party won in March. "Now we stand before the last election. . . . Regardless of the outcome, there will be no retreat, even if the next election does not bring about a decision."[14] Göring told his guests that it was a good time for them to make a contribution to the cause.

Göring purged the police force of unsympathetic officers and replaced them with Nazi recruits. On February 24 his police raided the abandoned Communist headquarters at the Karl Liebknecht Haus. (Much of the Communist leadership had already fled the country or gone underground.) Göring's forces confiscated piles of political leaflets, but they were still unable to produce evidence that a leftist uprising had been planned.

Then another opportunity arose. On the evening of February 27, a massive fire was set at the Reichstag, and within hours the symbol of German democracy was a charred ruin. The police quickly arrested an unemployed Dutch laborer named Marinus van der Lubbe and accused him of committing arson under Communist orders. Rumors instantly spread that the Nazis had set the fire themselves.[15]

Hitler had been enjoying a quiet evening with the Goebbels family. When they heard the news of the fire, the two men rushed to the scene. They joined Göring and Rudolf Diels, head of the Prussian political police, on a balcony to survey the damage. Years later, Diels recalled the event:

> Hitler turned to the assembled company. I now saw that his face was flaming red with excitement and from the heat that was gathering in the cupola. He shouted as if he wanted to burst, in an unrestrained way such as I had not previously experienced with him: "There will be no more mercy now; anyone who stands in our way will be butchered. The German people won't have any understanding for leniency. Every Communist functionary will be shot where he is found. The Communist deputies must be hanged this very night. Everybody in league with the Communists is to be arrested. Against Social Democrats and *Reichsbanner*[16] too there will be no more mercy!"[17]

The police interrogation indicated that van der Lubbe had acted alone, but the evidence was irrelevant. Within hours the police pulled lists of Communists from their files. Four thousand Communists and Social Democrats were arrested, including Reichstag deputies whose office gave them legal immunity.[18] The next day Hitler and the Nazi ministers convinced Hindenburg to sign a decree that suspended all constitutional guarantees of civil liberties, placing restrictions "on the right of free expression of opinion, including freedom of the press; on the rights of assembly and association."

A final round of elections was scheduled for March 5. Now the Nazis enjoyed full control of the state radio, and extensive government resources and private financing for their campaign. Opposition rallies and newspapers were banned, and politicians faced arrest, beatings, or death if they dared to appear in public.

Remarkably, the majority of Germans still voted against the Nazis.

The party's share of the vote rose to forty-four percent, but even combined with the National Party, this was not enough to guarantee control. The Nazis now turned to a new piece of legislation called the Enabling Act, which would allow the chancellor to create laws without the approval of the Reichstag or the president. This constitutional amendment required a two-thirds quorum and two-thirds of the votes of those present. The Nazis guaranteed this outcome by eliminating the eighty-one seats of the Communist deputies, brutalizing the Social Democrats, and leaning hard on the Catholic Center Party.

A week later, an eviscerated Reichstag overwhelmingly voted to render itself obsolete. Hitler and the Nazi Party were now in full control of the executive and the legislative branches of government. The judiciary was not expected to present any obstacles. On March 3, Göring had promised a crowd in Frankfurt that "my measures will not be crippled by any judicial thinking . . . I don't have to worry about justice; my mission is only to destroy and exterminate, nothing more!"[19]

In short, there were no remaining democratic institutions capable of reversing the new national condition. Through a long, tragic series of conspiracies, blunders, and lies, the Germans had bartered away their freedoms and allowed their feeble democracy to collapse into dictatorship.

Now, at the very moment Mildred Harnack had the most to tell, her letters to her mother became more circumspect. It was a frightening time—all around her, friends, neighbors, and colleagues were being fired, beaten, or arrested. Any communication that was sent by mail fell under Nazi scrutiny. Mildred wrote to her mother, taking stock of their situation. Neither spouse was a Communist Party member. She hoped that their interest in the Soviet Union would escape notice. "Our curious ideas are not known here," she wrote nervously.

"We are not active politically. We are safe, very well, and happy. Who would bother himself about two students sitting off in a corner and thinking thoughts about the future of the world? So don't feel any worry about us at all. And best keep still. If any one asks you about us, we are not interested in the world from a political but from a scientific standpoint. That's all you need to say."[20]

In reality, of course, they were highly vulnerable. A number of

Arvid's cousins had been openly critical of the Nazis' rise to power, including Social Democrat official Ernst von Harnack and the Bonhoeffer brothers, Dietrich and Klaus. Professor Friedrich Lenz, the president of Arvid's Soviet study group, was purged from the university in Giessen for "political unreliability."

Mildred trusted her mother to read between the lines. On May 2, 1933, she wrote urging her mother to visit while it was still possible.

The day before, the Nazis had staged an enormous May Day parade right across the street from Mildred's apartment. For generations, May Day had been a celebration of solidarity for the German trade unions. But this year was different. Over a million people were jammed into the Tempelhof airfield, and the marchers were regimented into a configuration of twelve giant squares, with Nazi banners flying overhead.[21] Mildred described the event for her mother in detail, trying to signal the dangers ahead.

Mildred's diction had changed. She was still the literature professor who loved honesty and clarity of expression, still the Wisconsin liberal who loathed militarism and the Ku Klux Klan. But from now on she would contort her language into code for the benefit of Nazi censors, trusting her mother to know when she meant the opposite of what she said. "How beautiful it was!" she wrote archly.

> Thousands and thousands of people marched in order, singing and playing through the majestic streets which radiate from our home. . . . The new and the old national banners marched with the people. I thought of the preparedness parades in our country at the beginning of the war. . . . There is a great impulse in masses of people which can be roused—a very great and beautiful impulse. You know that I thought this impulse was directed rightly in the war and I think it is being directed rightly in the same way now. That is, it is being given the right motives: vs. the Jews & radicals etc. . . .
>
> If it were being used wrongly, it would mean that it would become empty and that the people would become resentful and disappointed after a period of time. Or it would mean still further deception in a great war for the purpose of profit. But now it is

being used rightly here as it was at home in the World War. Well, it is a very beautiful serious thing—serious as death,—and I hope it will never be perverted again![22]

The same day Mildred wrote those lines, the Nazis made a coordinated assault on the offices of every Social Democratic trade union in Germany. Their publications were closed down and their funds were seized. Union leaders were taken into the "protective custody" of concentration camps—or killed.[23]

Now the Nazis had full control of the chancellorship and the cabinet, the Reichstag, and the state radio. The two most effective opposition parties were smashed, and those that remained were bullied into submission. The Nazis controlled the police forces, and began their assault on the courts.

Some Germans still hoped that these brazen moves were the answer to their country's slide into chaos. Others, like the Harnacks, had the opposite impression. They saw fewer and fewer institutions that could impede Germany's march toward war. It was, as Mildred noted, a "serious thing—serious as death."

CHAPTER 6

The Takeover

1933

MOST GERMAN ARTISTS WERE NOT NAZIS, AND THE TAKEOVER obliged them to choose quickly among three unattractive options: run for cover, flee the country, or try to conform. A sudden chill set over the theaters, galleries, and cafes where Adam Kuckhoff and his colleagues had gathered to talk politics and art.

The golden age of Berlin theater was officially over, its presiding geniuses dispersed. Max Reinhardt, the Jewish impresario, fled to his native Austria. Adam Kuckhoff's mentor Leopold Jessner, even more at risk as a Jewish Socialist, escaped to New York. Erwin Piscator was not Jewish, but he was a member of the KPD, and elected to stay on in Moscow where he was working at the time.[1]

Some writers could make themselves less conspicuous. Adam Kuckhoff remained in Berlin, deciding to wait and see. Brecht's friend and Piscator's protégé Günther Weisenborn took a riskier approach. His new play, *Warum Lacht Frau Balsam?* (*Why Is Mrs. Balsam Laughing?*), provoked a right-wing riot in the theater when it premiered on March 16, 1933, and was immediately closed.[2] Weisenborn would not be able to produce a play under his own name for the next twelve years.

Bertolt Brecht had no intention of testing the waters. He was reportedly in the hospital on February 27, 1933, when the Reichstag fire broke out. He went straight to the train station the following day, accompanied by his wife and their eight-year-old son. (Their two-year-old daughter, Barbara, was left behind, to be brought out later.)

Once the Nazis laid the blame for the Reichstag fire on the Communists, they launched an all-out attack to annihilate them as political rivals. On the night of the fire an estimated 1,500 people were arrested in Berlin alone.[3] By April 1933 over 45,000 antifascists had been arrested, the majority of them Communists and Social Democrats.[4] Historian Eric Johnson writes: "One can well argue that the destruction of the left, particularly the Communist left, was nearly the sole focus of the Nazi terror in the first year and a half of Hitler's regime."[5]

All across Germany, but particularly in the epicenter of Berlin, leftist intellectuals were forced to evaluate their options and their odds. Anyone who had taken the trouble to listen to Hitler or to read *Mein Kampf* knew that anti-Communism and anti-Semitism were fundamental to his outlook. Nonetheless, while Jews were frequent victims of street violence, they were not yet the primary targets of official attacks—unless, of course, they had been Communists, Social Democrats, or public critics of the Nazis before they came to power.

One such figure was Jewish novelist Lion Feuchtwanger, an early patron of Brecht's and a popular member of Berlin's leftist literary circle. Feuchtwanger was on a speaking tour of the United States at the time of the Nazi takeover, and guest of honor at the German embassy in Washington. The following day the German ambassador resigned from the diplomatic corps and warned Feuchtwanger not to return to Germany. The writer moved to Los Angeles and launched a successful second career. But he remained loyal to his vision of Germany, and wrote from exile, "The [Nazis] could not kill or imprison all their adversaries, for their adversaries comprised two-thirds of the population."[6]

Mildred and Arvid Harnack had seen the crisis coming, and now hastened to lower their profile. The couple was safe on religious grounds, since both of them came from "Aryan" families and were active members of the American Protestant church in Berlin. Their political status, however, was questionable. The couple shared an interest in Marxist theory, but neither was a member of the Communist Party. Still, they feared the consequences of their trips to the Soviet Union the previous year and Arvid's writings on labor and the Soviet economy. His Soviet study group, ARPLAN, was disbanded in March just after the Reichstag fire; the affiliation cost its president, Professor Friedrich Lenz, his job. Arvid's publisher canceled the contract for his book on the Soviet economy and destroyed the printing plates. Another of his manuscripts had to be smuggled out of the country.

The Harnacks left Berlin in March to lie low in a little hotel in the countryside. Once they returned to Berlin, Arvid's cousin Klaus Bonhoeffer came to his rescue with a job as a lawyer at his employer, Lufthansa. This allowed Arvid to earn a living while he studied for another round of examinations, required for government work.[7] Years earlier, as a prospective bridegroom, he had written a letter to Mildred's mother about his desire to work for the German Labor Ministry on international labor issues.[8] Now he was about to realize his dream, though in a very different fashion than he had anticipated.

The Harnacks were settling into their new apartment near the Tempelhof airfield. In the beginning, Mildred was pleased with it, and wrote to her mother that the only problem was "a bit too much music from the restaurant downstairs."[9]

Following the Nazis' takeover, the noise took on a different character. Mildred wrote: "The traffic seems to us to have increased tenfold here in the last two years. Heavy trucks are continually going through to the barracks and places of detention not far from here."[10] The trucks were conveying political prisoners to an airfield facility called Columbia-Haus, an obsolete military prison. At the beginning of the takeover, Communist, Social Democrat, and trade unionist victims had been hauled into *Wilde Lager* ("wild camps"), improvised in warehouses, pubs, and cellars. But these were soon filled, and Columbia-Haus was reopened to provide additional facilities for torture and interrogation. Although the Harnacks were probably not aware of it, some of the trucks that sped past their apartment carried people they knew, such as Paul Massing, an agricultural economist and member of Arvid's Soviet study group. Massing was beaten and interrogated at Columbia-Haus, then sent to the Oranienburg concentration camp for five months' solitary confinement.[11] The Harnacks, distressed by the daily "traffic," began to look for new rooms once again.

Mildred, fired from her position at the university, was now teaching literature at a night school for working-class adults. Once again, she quickly won the respect and affection of her students, although they were sometimes taken aback by her American spontaneity. (Sometimes she livened things up by leading the class in American folk songs.) She filled the rest of her time with occasional lecturing, writing, and hosting literary teas, and began to publish reviews and essays in the Berlin daily press. There was no problem writing about most topics in American literature, as long as they didn't stray into the areas of German controversy. Arvid, for his part, did his best to disappear into the role of a colorless legal bureaucrat.

Mildred and Arvid's friend Greta followed the crisis from a distance. In March, just after the Reichstag fire, she had traveled to London. There she received a letter from her old flame, Adam Kuckhoff. She read it, her "heart pounding," on the steps of the British Museum. Most of her friends had discouraged her from returning to Germany, she recalled, telling her that "it would be wiser to wait for at least a few months. I would be naïve to think that I could continue my study of sociology (as if I believed it!)."

But Adam's letter carried a different message. Adam had written: "Come—I'm waiting for you."[12] Her friends' warnings were quickly dismissed, and she decided to return.

But Greta received another letter in April, this one from her father: "Yesterday we read in the newspaper about the professors' leaves of absence. Frankfurt-am-Main alone had six listed. Unfortunately Professor Mannheim was among them."[13]

This was bad news. Sociologist Karl Mannheim had retained Greta as his secretary and librarian the year before, eager to mine her knowledge of academic developments in the United States. The professor was in the process of laying the intellectual foundation for the sociology of knowledge, but he was also a Hungarian Jew, and was summarily dismissed once the Nazis took power.[14]

Greta's return to Frankfurt was tense. Her academic program was closed down and her typewriter had been confiscated. Her landlady trembled when Greta told her that she was going to see the Nazis to get her typewriter back.

The new officials were expecting her. They had some questions.

"Where is your airplane?" they demanded, waving a flyer bearing Greta's signature that they had found posted in the sociology department. The paper gave the details for a "flying group" meeting on nearby "Zeppelin Street." Greta could only laugh, explaining that their study group met "on the fly" in different locations. Fortunately, the Nazis laughed, too. But the incident reminded Greta that in the new Germany, casual misunderstandings could have dangerous consequences.[15]

There was nothing to hold her in Frankfurt, and Adam was in Berlin. Greta returned to the capital, where she would spend the rest of her life. Soon after she arrived she encountered Arvid Harnack. She was certain it was not a coincidence. Arvid was putting together a discussion circle, or *Kreis*, made up of opponents of the regime. Would she join? Greta wasn't sure she had much to offer. She had been away from Berlin a long time, and her contacts among workers and slum dwellers were out of date. But Adam Kuckhoff was also pressing her toward activism. And so, in the spring of 1933, Greta Lorke, a thirty-year-old sociology student just short of her doctorate, left Frankfurt for Berlin and abandoned academia to join her lover. Perhaps it was not clear to her at the time, but in the process, she joined the anti-Nazi movement.

Adam Kuckhoff's career was once more in flux. He worked as a freelance reader at Ullstein, wrote fiction and drama, and published the occasional review.[16] It was not a brilliant career, but for the moment, his obscurity worked in his favor, allowing him to stay in the country.

By now, many of Kuckhoff's colleagues from journalism and theater had fled, meeting hardship along the way. Most were not wealthy, and there was little demand for German writers in non-German-speaking lands. Prague was an easy destination, but the Czechs made a practice of deporting German Communists back to the Gestapo's enthusiastic welcome. Paris had its own aggressive immigration police. Other Germans headed east to Moscow, where Stalinists viewed them with distrust. Every destination had its problems, whether they were political, economic, or cultural.

But the choices were also fiendishly difficult for antifascists who stayed. Their plight was illustrated by the case of Armin Wegner, Adam Kuckhoff's author who had denounced the Armenian genocide. A few days after the Nazis' April 1933 boycott against the Jews, Wegner wrote an impassioned open letter to Hitler denouncing anti-Semitism. He knew that no newspaper would dare to print it, so he sent it directly to the Nazi headquarters in Munich with the request that it be forwarded to Hitler. Wegner made his appeal, he wrote, "as a descendant of a Prussian family which can trace its roots back to the days of the crusaders":

A tormented heart speaks to you. The words are not only my words, they are the voice of fate admonishing you: "Protect Germany by protecting the Jews" . . . Restore to their position those cast out, the doctors to their hospitals, the judges to their courts. Don't exclude any longer the children from their schools. Heal the afflicted hearts of the mothers, and the whole nation will be thankful to you.

Wegner predicted that his generation would be remembered as one that "thoughtlessly gambled away our country's fortune [and] disgraced its name forever."

A few days later Wegner was arrested by the Gestapo and thrown into a cell in Columbia-Haus, where he was gagged and beaten until he lost consciousness. He survived seven other prisons and concentration camps before he finally escaped to Italy.[17]

Other authors from Adam Kuckhoff's stable fared just as badly. John Sieg, the dashing young autoworker from Detroit, was rounded up in the Nazis' initial March foray. This was not surprising, since he was a member of the KPD and on staff for the party newspaper *Rote Fahne,* and therefore high on the list of targets. Sieg was hauled into the storm trooper barracks on Hedemannstrasse.[18]

His detention facilities were described that month in the British daily *The Guardian* via a letter from "a private correspondent in Berlin":

These Storm troopers are arresting Communists in their homes or on the streets. . . . In the Nazi barracks they whip the Communists and break their fingers in order to get from them confessions and addresses. In the Nazi barracks in Hedemannstrasse there lay in one room about 135 Communists who had been tortured until they were half dead. . . .

They were all undressed, and when they were naked had to run the gauntlet until they broke down. [One] comrade is lying half dead in the hospital. . . . We have no means of bringing these outrages and horrors to the notice of the public, as our press is forbidden. We beg you to see to it that these facts become known in foreign countries, because they are real facts. We have no possible way of getting help. According to the new police decree no police official is allowed to help us.

The horrors . . . are part of a systematic Terror organized and directed by the authorities with the object of exterminating the Communists. . . . All the news received here from Germany suggests that nothing like the Terror now existing in Germany has been known in Europe within living memory. . . . Refugees are pouring into France, Switzerland, and Poland. All the German Socialist leaders, unless in prison, are fugitives and have either escaped from Germany or are in hiding.[19]

Following his ordeal in the barracks, John Sieg was transferred to the Plötzensee prison in the northern part of the city. This was an improvement, since Plötzensee had long served as a traditional prison for common criminals, and retained its old staff and procedures. Sieg was finally released in June, after the legal proceedings against him stalled.

According to Sieg's city editor from the *Rote Fahne*, Hermann Grosse, Sieg owed his freedom to the quiet heroism of Theodor Haubach, a prominent Social Democratic journalist. Haubach had been the police press spokesman under a previous government, and he took it upon himself to make the police dossiers on the *Rote Fahne* editors "disappear."[20] The Nazis knew who was on the staff, but still had to go through established legal channels for sentencing. When the Nazis prepared to prosecute the editors, no files were to be found. "John Sieg was unknown at the police stations, and other arrests and measures of persecution were initially avoided."[21] Within a year Haubach himself was locked up in Columbia-Haus as a result of his opposition activities, and he continued to struggle against the Nazis for the rest of his life. His gesture showed that, whatever the rivalry between Communists and Social Democrats, there were also instances of generosity and mutual support.

Many Communists saw that the advantage lay with the Nazis and changed sides, but John Sieg was not among them. While he was in detention at the Hedemannstrasse barracks, he was approached by Karl Ernst, the SA Group Leader for Berlin. The storm trooper offered Sieg his immediate freedom if he would work for the Nazi press. Sieg refused.[22]

Following his release, John Sieg returned to Neukölln, the heart of the Communist Party underground. Several of Sieg's *Rote Fahne* colleagues lived in the area, trying to rebuild a network from whomever was left after the killings, the exiles, and the arrests. Hundreds of thousands of Communist Party members and sympathizers had been released from detention or escaped arrest, but it was difficult to organize and take action. Many of them had earned their living from trade union or professional party positions. With these organizations closed down, economic survival was the priority.

John Sieg's newspaper was one of these defunct operations. He was now unemployed and virtually unemployable. His wife, Sophie, still had her office job, but the lawyer who employed her was Jewish, making her situation precarious.

The Nazis realized that powerful forces in German society opposed them, and moved to consolidate their regime. They had already dismantled rival political organizations. Now they set out to impose their ethos of conformity on the rest of German society, with special attention to institutions that affected public opinion through media, culture, and education. The Nazis installed their own candidates in leadership positions, while leftists and Jews were purged.

At the helm of this process was Joseph Goebbels. His first objective was German broadcasting. When the Nazis took over the government, the newspaper and movie industries were still privately owned, and they realized that it could take a few years to bring them into full compliance. But German radio had been state-regulated since 1925, and this simplified the control of its content.

Less than two weeks after he took office as minister of propaganda, Goebbels addressed the managerial staff of the state broadcasting house in Berlin:

> I hold radio to be the most modern and the most important instrument of mass influence that exists anywhere. . . . I am also of the

opinion—and one shouldn't say this out loud—that in the long term radio will replace newspapers. . . . You have in your hands the most modern instrument in existence for influencing the masses. By means of this instrument you are the creators of public opinion. If you perform this well, we shall win over the people. . . .

As the piano is to the pianist, so the transmitter is to you, the instrument that you play on as sovereign masters of public opinion.[23]

Within a year the German broadcasting system had been purged and unified into the Reich Radio Company. The nine regional broadcasters were downgraded to "stations," run by general managers under Goebbels's control.

Goebbels maintained his interest in drama of every variety. His most celebrated piece of street theater took place on May 10, 1933, on Unter den Linden, just across the street from the University of Berlin, where Greta Kuckhoff and Arvid and Mildred Harnack had studied and taught. It involved the burning of books.

Over 40,000 Berliners gathered for Goebbels's spectacle, watching and chanting as students and storm troopers heaped some 25,000 books on the sidewalk and set them aflame. The burning ceremony, or *Verbrennungsakt*, was conducted as a pagan perversion of a Christian rite. Huge bonfires erupted into the darkness; their flickering light transforming stolid German faces into ominous masks. The crowd of thousands chanted a litany of "fire oaths": first, an offense, then a remedy, and finally the name of the writer to be cast out.

Against class warfare and materialism;
For the community of the *Volk* and an idealistic way of life.
Marx, Kautsky

Against decadence and moral decay;
For discipline and decency in family and state.
[Heinrich] Mann, Ernst Glaeser, [Erich] Kästner

Against democratic-Jewish journalism, alien to the *Volk;*
For responsible cooperation with rebuilding the nation.
Theodor Wolff, Georg Bernhard

Against the literary treason committed against the soldiers of World
    War One;
For educating the nation in the spirit of military might.
[Erich Maria] Remarque.

Among those blacklisted were many of Germany's most popular writers. Kästner was an antifascist, but he was best known for his enchanting children's books. Theodor Wolff, one of Germany's leading journalists and civil rights activists, was the Jewish editor of the prestigious *Berliner Tageblatt.* Erich Remarque's autobiographical novel *All Quiet on the Western Front* spoke for the "generation that was destroyed by war, even though it might have escaped its shells." The book touched such a profound chord in German society that it sold a million copies in 1929, the year it was published.

Joseph Goebbels took his place before a podium draped in a Nazi banner. His resonant tenor voice, always marked by precise enunciation, was raspy that evening, perhaps from the smoke. But his message rang clear. The German *Volk* and their wholesome cultural values were going to be restored. Germany would be purged of urban, avant-garde, cosmopolitan culture.

The era of extreme Jewish intellectualism has come to an end, and the German revolution has again opened the way for the true essence of being German. This revolution was not started at the top, it burst forth from the bottom, upwards. It is, therefore, in the very best sense of the word, the expression of the will of the *Volk.* There stands the worker next to the bourgeois, student next to soldier and young worker, here stand the intellectuals next to the proletariat. . . .

Over the past fourteen years you, students, have had to suffer in silent shame the humiliations of the [Weimar] Republic; your libraries were inundated with the trash and filth of Jewish "asphalt" literati. . . . The old past lies in flames; the new times will arise from the flame that burns in our hearts.[24]

The flames consumed thousands of the books that had given Berlin's "golden twenties" their luster, by Jews as well as by Catholics, Communists, feminists, social scientists, and Americans. Bertolt Brecht's plays burned next to Freud's treatises. The prints of Marc Chagall (a Jew) and Georg Grosz (a leftist) smoldered next to books by Americans Ernest Hemingway, Helen Keller, and Jack London, condemned for their pacifist or socialist tendencies.

The pyre also included works by Brecht's young friend Günther Weisenborn. His most recent play had been closed down on the same day it opened two months earlier. As far as the Nazis were concerned, the thirty-year-old playwright's career was over.

There were consequences for every writer in Germany, even those whose works escaped the flames. The bonfire consumed political texts that Greta Lorke and Arvid Harnack had studied in graduate school, and the works of Adam Kuckhoff's authors from *Die Tat*. The American authors included the subjects of Mildred Harnack's lectures and critical essays.

But the Nazis were acting to silence the intellectuals, not eliminate them. They needed time to strengthen their base, and knew they would require the ongoing productivity of Germany's skilled laborers, technocrats, and intelligentsia. The most effective means of harnessing them to their system was through systematic terror, rendering noncompliance too fearful to bear. Central to this effort was the new institution of the concentration camp, which combined elements of a prison, labor camp, and execution facility.

On March 14, 1933, the newly appointed Nazi head of the Munich police, Heinrich Himmler, described the innovation as a humane measure:

Certain individuals . . . have to be taken into protective custody under the direct protection of the police. The individuals involved, who are often of the Jewish faith, have through behavior towards the nation of Germany, such as through offending national feelings, and so on, have made themselves so unloved among the people, that they would be exposed to the anger of the people unless the police stepped in.[25]

The following week Himmler gave orders to convert an abandoned munitions factory into a "concentration camp for political prisoners," to handle the huge number of people being taken into "protective custody." The grounds, a few miles northwest of Munich, lay just outside a market town called Dachau, known for its lovely views and picturesque fountains.

Over the following year the camp acquired almost 5,000 prisoners, the great majority of them Communists, as well as many Social Democrats and trade unionists who had been swept up in the raids. The early concentration camps tended to be relatively nonlethal, temporary operations. Over the second half of 1933, Dachau usually held about 3,800 prisoners at any given time. Anywhere from 600 to 2,000 chastened prisoners were released per month, replaced by newly arrested individuals.[26] Officials gave press tours to journalists from major newspapers, to assure the public that conditions were civilized.

Shortly after the opening of the camp at Dachau, another concentration camp was created outside Oranienburg, just north of Berlin, adjoining an area called Sachsenhausen. Rumors of its brutality spread, and the regime quickly released a propaganda film showing the Communist and Socialist prisoners, clad in their own suits and sweaters, learning how to line up in an orderly fashion, and engaging in wholesome activities such as gardening and calisthenics.[27] Within a year, Berlin's grim Columbia-Haus was redesignated as a concentration camp as well. It is reckoned that over the course of 1933, about 100,000 people were sent to concentration camps, although this figure does not include those who were taken to the "wild camps," tortured, and released. Between 500 and 600 prisoners were killed.[28]

Germany's artistic community faced a choice between detention, exile, and compliance. The Nazi leadership tended to patronize artists, viewing them as useful pets and moral imbeciles. In 1938, for example, a Nazi official produced a 1933 Communist manifesto that had been signed by one of Hitler's favored sculptors, Josef Thorak. Hitler brushed it aside, saying, "We should never judge artists by their political views. . . . Artists are simple-hearted souls. Today they sign this, tomorrow that; they don't even look to see what it is, so long as it seems to them well-meaning."[29] Thorak, with five years of faithful service to his credit, kept his position.

Hitler also made special allowances for the theater. His courtiers noted his "amazing knowledge of stagecraft, his interest in the diameter of revolving stages, lift mechanisms, and especially different lighting techniques." As chancellor he moonlighted as a stage designer, sitting up at night for weeks on end drawing fully executed set designs for his favorite operas.[30] Theater was central to his political philosophy. "We must bring the masses illusions," he said in 1930. "Just because life is grimly real, people have to be exalted above the routines of every day." [31]

Much of Berlin's creative community, including Adam Kuckhoff's friends and collaborators, conformed to the new order. But not everyone fell into line. One prominent exception was Hans Otto, Brecht's friend and Kuckhoff's brother-in law. Otto, who had joined the German Communist Party in the early 1920s, was an enthusiastic participant in workers' theater, mixing his classical roles with parts in revolutionary works. Otto made the leap to Berlin in 1930, around the same time as Adam Kuckhoff. Otto's star continued to rise. In the 1930–31 season he appeared in almost two dozen stage productions, and had his first starring movie role in a UFA comedy called *Das Gestohlene Gesicht* (*The Stolen Face*).

But as the political tensions mounted, Otto stepped up his activism. He served as a leader in the Communist Party's theater and film unions, contributed to party publications, and directed Marxist study groups in his theater.[32]

The endgame was near. January 21, 1933, marked the premiere of a stunning new production of Goethe's *Faust, Part II*. It was to be the iconic play of the Nazi era, the story of a man who sells his soul to the devil in exchange for worldly gain. The production starred the theater's new regional acquisitions, Gustaf Gründgens as Mephisto and Hans Otto as the Kaiser. Herbert Jhering, Berlin's leading theater critic, gave the actors a rhapsodic review:

The courtyard scenes, the interplay between the Kaiser and Mephisto, and the striking realism of the money scene were superbly realized. There was no cheap modernization. The form and the poetry of the piece were protected in every regard.

But Hans Otto as the Kaiser (especially good), Paul Bildt as a chancellor, and Wolfgang Heinz as the treasurer gave such witty and nimble performances that it seemed as though a new comedy ensemble had just been formed.[33]

The following week the Nazis came to power. Within a month, the Reichstag was burning and the purge was under way.

On February 27, 1933—five weeks after his triumph in *Faust*—Otto received an official communication from Franz Ulbricht, the new director of the Staatstheater:

Esteemed Mr. Otto!

I truly regret to be obliged to inform you that the collective artistic group of our theater finds it impossible to extend your contract after its expiration.

With the greatest respect, FU[34]

On May 23, 1933, Hans Otto played the Kaiser in *Faust, Part II* one last time. It was to be his last performance. Otto's friends urged him to leave the country. Many of his leading collaborators had already been forced into exile. His popular costar Elisabeth Bergner, a Jew, was driven out of the country. Max Reinhardt, the Jewish producer who had launched him in Berlin, contacted Otto from exile and invited him to join his theater in Vienna.[35] Other offers came in from Zurich and Prague.

But Otto was reluctant. As a gentile with a successful stage career, he had the option of staying in the country and fighting fascism from within. His decision was sealed one evening after his dismissal, as he took a stroll with his wife and a friend near the park in central Berlin. The three spotted a freight car crossing the railway bridge, guarded by storm troopers. It was crammed with political prisoners en route to a concentration camp. After this experience, Otto refused to consider emigration.

Instead, he plunged into clandestine activity. It is difficult to know exactly what actions were involved, but one set of clues exists in a roman à clef called *Mephisto,* by Thomas Mann's son Klaus, who had worked with Otto and Gründgens in the 1920s. It is believed that Klaus Mann's 1936 novel depicts Hans Otto as a character named Otto Ulrich. At one time, Otto "had been an amiable, even tender-hearted man," but after the Nazi takeover "he was no longer amiable, no longer tender-hearted. His gaze had developed a threatening gravity. Otto Ulrich was a man poised between caution and boldness, between attack and flight; he was playing a perilous game."

Mann describes how Otto Ulrich contrived to remain at the Staatstheater for as long as possible, ingratiating himself with theater patron Hermann Göring and his circle. He glided between roles, making "Heil Hitler" salutes to Nazis one moment and holding clandestine meetings with antifascist stagehands the next. Mann writes that the actor had been briefly shocked into paralysis by Nazi terror, but then "he overcame his despairing apathy." "'When you have witnessed those horrors, you have only one choice,' he said. 'You can either kill yourself or go back to work with greater dedication than before.' He went back to work."

> The objective was to gather together the dispersed forces of Resistance, to weld into a single movement an opposition composed of mutually antagonistic ideas and backgrounds. . . . And so he spread the net of the conspiracy wider than his close party comrades. He was much more anxious to contact opposition Catholics, former Social Democrats or independent republicans. At first the Communist encountered distrust in middle-class liberal circles. . . .
>
> "But you are just as much against freedom as the Nazis," protested the democrats. "He answered, 'Look—we are all for the overthrow of tyranny. We can all come to an agreement about the kind of order that should be set up afterwards.' "[36]

The actual Hans Otto threw himself into the same sort of underground activity with similar zeal.[37] The Communist Party was in disarray, its membership gutted by arrests, desertion, and flights into exile.

Greta Lorke as a Catholic schoolgirl from Frankfurt an der Oder.

At the University of Wisconsin, Greta befriended German economist Arvid Harnack, a Rockefeller fellow, and his American wife, Mildred Fish, a graduate student in literature.

In 1929 Greta (and the Harnacks) returned to Germany and an impending crisis.

In 1930 Greta fell in love with Adam Kuckhoff—novelist, playwright, editor, and roué.

John Sieg married Sophie Wloszczynski in 1928.

Nazi minister Joseph Goebbels (below) pioneered the use of mass media for propaganda.

In March 1933, Nazi storm troopers acting as auxiliary police rounded up Social Democrats, Communists, and trade unionists for torture and imprisonment in "wild camps."

On May 10, 1933, the Nazis burned books in a giant ceremonial bonfire in Berlin, an act that was repeated across the country, destroying works by Jews, leftists, pacifists, and humanists, among them Ernest Hemingway and Helen Keller.

Field Marshall Hermann Göring, commander of the Luftwaffe, married actress Emmy Sonnemann in 1935.

Hans Otto and Elisabeth Bergner were two stars of German stage and screen. Bergner was forced to flee the country because she was Jewish. Otto, a committed Communist, was Adam Kuckhoff's friend, theatrical collaborator, and relation. He refused to compromise with the Nazis and was murdered in storm trooper barracks in November 1933.

U.S. embassy official Donald Heath was a friend and intelligence contact to Arvid and Mildred Harnack. The State Department transferred Heath from Germany to Chile at a critical juncture in 1941.

Ambassador William Dodd with his family; Martha and William Jr. are on the left.

Greta and Adam Kuckhoff's son Ule was born in 1938. After Ule's birth, Greta's husband and friends were more cautious about involving her in resistance activities.

Harro Schulze-Boysen and his wife met the Kuckhoffs at a dinner party hosted by film producer Herbert Engelsing. Harro was the scion of one of Germany's leading military families. He was also a passionate anti-Nazi.

An der Schreibmaschine. Ajh. 44

Schulze-Boysen's aristocratic wife, Libertas, began her career as a publicist in MGM's Berlin office. The Kuckhoffs soon introduced the Schulze-Boysens to their friends the Harnacks.

Listening to Hitler's speeches was part of the job for Libertas (fourth from the right) and her fellow MGM employees.

Metro hört die Führer-Rede

The Gestapo headquarters on Prinz-Albrecht-Strasse was once the School for Industrial Arts and Crafts, where Libertas Schulze-Boysen's father taught. The Gestapo took it over in 1933. The basement held a warren of cells to hold political prisoners for torture and interrogation.

In 1937, John Sieg got a job with the Reich railways, which offered unique opportunities to work against the Nazis. His Berlin neighborhood of Neukölln served as a base for Communist underground activities and the production of anti-Nazi flyers.

John Sieg and his circle hid one of their hectograph machines in this paint and carpet supply shop on the outskirts of Berlin.

Film producer Herbert Engelsing often socialized with Libertas (left) and Harro Schulze-Boysen. He also used his position to assist Libertas's resistance work.

Ingeborg Engelsing became a close friend of Harro and Libertas Schulze-Boysen. Her husband and friends left her in the dark about political activities, since her status as the half-Jewish mother of young children made her particularly vulnerable.

Germany's UFA film conglomerate was the secret home of the Antiwelle, a movie industry anti-Nazi network. This feature film, made as anti-British propaganda entertainment, was produced by Herbert Engelsing with dialogue by Adam Kuckhoff. The star, Olga Tschechowa, was a Nazi favorite, but spent the war secretly assisting Soviet intelligence.

Marta Wolter Husemann was another member of the Schulze-Boysen salon. Before the Nazi takeover she was a promising young actress, shown here in Brecht's 1932 film *Kuhle Wampe*. In 1937, she was sent to the Moringen concentration camp.

Günther and Joy Weisenborn's wedding on January 25, 1941, provided a rare opportunity for the Schulze-Boysen group to gather in public. The wedding couple is in the foreground, while Libertas Schulze-Boysen stares anxiously into the camera on the lower right. Harro, in uniform, is seated at left. Walter Husemann celebrates in a desert helmet.

Harro and Libertas's salon included a number of left-wing artists and intellectuals, including prize-winning sculptor Kurt Schumacher. One of his works was selected for Hermann Göring's country estate.

In June 1941, Kurt Schumacher was drafted and sent to guard French workers in Poznań. He continued his resistance activities in Poland.

Soviet agent Alexander Korotkov sought Arvid Harnack's help as an intelligence source.

In late 1940 Harro Schulze-Boysen (second from left) pictured here in the German Ministry, learned of the Nazis' secret plans to invade the Soviet Union. He and Arvid Harnack supplied the Soviets with a vast store of intelligence to use against Hitler. But Stalin chose to ignore the warnings.

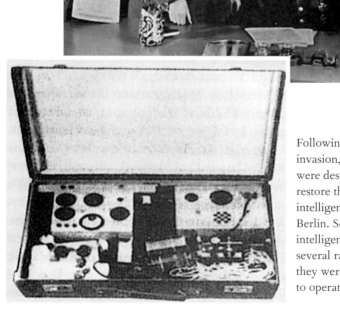

Following the German invasion, the Soviets were desperate to restore the flow of intelligence from Berlin. Soviet intelligence sent several radios, but they were a nightmare to operate.

Herbert Engelsing's dentist friend Helmut Himpel and his fiancée, Marie Terwiel, brought many new members into the group. The couple was forbidden to marry because she was half-Jewish. They supported Harro Schulze-Boysen's work by producing and distributing anti-Nazi flyers, and helped persecuted Jews.

Helmut Roloff, a classical pianist with conservative politics, was brought into the group by Helmut Himpel. Roloff was angered by Nazi anti-Semitism and helped the Schulze-Boysens with anti-Nazi leafleting campaigns. He offered his Jewish neighbors, including the Kuttner family, critical moral and logistical support.

John Graudenz, pictured here with his daughters, had been a United Press and *New York Times* correspondent in Berlin in the 1920s. He worked with Harro Schulze-Boysen on anti-Nazi flyers and helped Jewish friends, including young Sophie Kuh and her stepfather.

Cato Bontjes van Beek, a skilled ceramicist, recruited students and artists to help with leafleting and other resistance activities. Cato came to doubt Harro's judgment in the period before their arrests.

Katja Casella and Lisa Egler-Gervai were two of Cato's art student friends who joined the resistance group. The two beautiful young women hid in plain sight of the Nazis, who were unaware that they were Jewish. Katja hid fugitives in her studio.

In May 1942, propaganda minister Joseph Goebbels organized an exhibit in the heart of Berlin called "The Soviet Paradise," designed to justify Nazi atrocities. The exhibit attacked the "Jewish-Bolshevik conspiracy" and portrayed horrific executions on the Russian front as security measures.

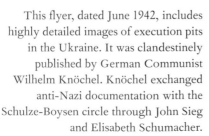

Ständige Ausstellung
Das NAZI-PARADIES
Krieg Hunger Lüge Gestapo
Wie lange noch?

These stickers were Harro Schulze-Boysen's response to Goebbel's "Soviert Paradise" exhibit. His group used a child's stamp set to print stickers reading "Permanent Installation: The Nazi Paradise: War, Hunger, Lies, Gestapo. How much longer?" Schulze-Boysen's young band roamed Berlin on their midnight "sticker-posting operation."

This photo (presumably taken by a German soldier) surfaced after the war with the inscription, "Last Jew in Vinnitsa." In 1942 the Schulze-Boysen group began to collect similar atrocity photos from soldiers returning from the front. Libertas Schulze-Boysen secretly copied and archived them at the UFA film studio for use in future war crimes prosecutions.

Das
Friedenskämpfer
Sonderausgabe Juni 1942

This flyer, dated June 1942, includes highly detailed images of execution pits in the Ukraine. It was clandestinely published by German Communist Wilhelm Knöchel. Knöchel exchanged anti-Nazi documentation with the Schulze-Boysen circle through John Sieg and Elisabeth Schumacher.

Leopold Trepper was a professional Soviet intelligence agent based in Brussels. In late 1941 Moscow ordered him to make contact with the group in Berlin. Trepper, who was unacquainted with the Berliners, was horrified when Moscow sent their names and home addresses over the radio. The German military intercepted the message and soon decoded it.

Anatoli Gourevitch, a Soviet agent in Trepper's Brussels operation, was sent to Berlin to contact the Schulze-Boysens and establish radio communications.

The Gestapo arrested Harro Schulze-Boysen on August 30, 1942. Other arrests quickly followed. These police photos shows Harro Schulze-Boysen (above), Helmut Himpel, who already shows signs of abuse (right), and Arvid Harnack (below).

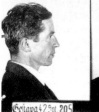

Also arrested were
nineteen-year-old
Liana Berkowitz
(right),
Greta Kuckhoff,
and Adam Kuckhoff.

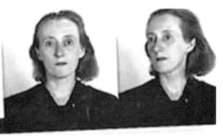

Hermann Göring
summoned Luftwaffe
judge advocate
Manfred Roeder from
Vinnitsa, Ukraine,
and ordered him to
prosecute Schulze-
Boysen and his group.

Most of the Rote Kapelle executions took place in this room at Berlin's Plötzensee prison. The women and some of the men were guillotined. A special beam was equipped with meat hooks to slowly strangle the men who were considered central to the case.

Greta Kuckhoff was one of a few survivors of the Berlin circle. She worked with the Nuremberg investigators to bring Manfred Roeder to trial for war crimes, but he was protected by U.S. Army intelligence. Greta settled in East Germany, where she was later purged from her government position. The East Germans heavily censored her memoirs.

Katja Casella is the last known survivor of the *Rote Kapelle*. She and her friend Lisa were the two Jewish art students who hid fugitives for the group. Katja became an accomplished painter, she now lives outside Berlin.

For the next six months Otto traveled the city, seeking out the survivors. One gathering might take place in an old suburban mansion; another clandestine encounter might occur on the subway. Some meetings included Otto's wife, Marie, and her sister, Gertrud, who was still married to Adam Kuckhoff. It was a desperate situation in which little progress was possible. Otto and his friends continued to produce and distribute anti-Nazi flyers, but the work was tremendously dangerous. Given that the meetings involved leading celebrities from stage and screen, it was hard to be inconspicuous.

On the evening of Wednesday, November 13, 1933, Otto arranged to meet Gerhard Hinze, an actor from his underground group, at a little cafe on Victoria-Luise-Platz south of the Tiergarten. A signal was given and five storm troopers entered and arrested the men—someone had betrayed them.[38] Otto and Hinze were taken to the Comet Cafe, a storm troopers' restaurant at a lakeside resort just outside Berlin. There the two actors were flogged, punched in the face, and kicked in the gut, as the music of a dance band played inside. The storm troopers demanded the names of other members of the underground, but Otto refused to talk, even after they pounded his head into the wall.

After four days of torture, Otto and Hinze were dragged off to another neighborhood. They were thrown into a stinking basement with a number of other battered men and women who appeared to have been there a long time. They were moved again, interrogated and beaten along the way, then delivered to Gestapo headquarters on Prinz-Albrecht-Strasse for more interrogation. Their last stop was the SA barracks on Volkstrasse, just down the street.

Hinze and Otto were separated. Hinze recalled their final encounter:

During this ghastly night I saw Hans Otto once more. It must have been approximately around midnight. He no longer was able to speak but could make only indistinct sounds. His mouth and his eyes were thick and swollen. And then, seeing me, he tried to smile. . . . A few hours later I saw him for the last time. He was half naked and I could no longer recognize his face. His body was one bloody lump. He was unconscious. They kicked him and poured water on him to try to restore consciousness. In vain. A few hours later they threw his battered body down on the pavement.[39]

Hans Otto died in the Berlin public hospital on November 24, 1933. Word traveled quickly that his murderers were three SA men named Witzke, Möder, and Kubik.

This was not the official story. Otto's wife was informed that her husband had committed suicide by leaping out of the top floor of the storm trooper barracks. It was said that Goebbels himself signed off on this account. There was a news blackout on Otto's death, and the regime warned that the act of attending Otto's burial would be considered an offense. Only a few friends and relatives showed up, closely monitored by the Gestapo. But it was impossible to keep Hans Otto's death a secret.

The German diarist who wrote as Sebastian Haffner described the shock of the German public:

> Brilliant young Hans Otto, who had been the rising star of the previous season, lay crumpled in the yard of an SA barracks—yes, Hans Otto, whose name had been on everyone's lips, who had been talked about at every soiree, had been hailed as the "new Matkowsky"[40] that the German stage had so long been waiting for. He had "thrown himself out of a fourth-floor window in a moment when the guards had been distracted," they said.[41]

The impact of Otto's death rippled through the city. Adam Kuckhoff was one of the brave souls who dared to attend Otto's funeral. It was days before he could bring himself to talk about the experience: the lurking Gestapo agents, the sorrowing family, the inspiring eulogies. Kuckhoff had lost a friend, colleague, and relation, and this galvanized him into action. For Otto's friend and fellow party member John Sieg, his death was a reminder of the deadly perils of underground party activity.

German theater had changed forever in the course of a single year. An entire generation of playwrights, directors, and actors had vanished. Many of those who stayed behind (at least those who were not Jewish) found they could reach an accommodation with the new regime. Gustaf Gründgens, Hans Otto's friend, costar, and comrade-in-arms in leftist theater, made a public show of his new allegiance. So did Heinrich George, another Staatstheater star who had worked closely with Piscator, Weisenborn, and Brecht, and had joined Otto as a Communist theater union organizer.

Hans Otto's death also resonated abroad. It gave stern notice to the artists in exile that things would get worse before they got better. Letters, articles, and protests concerning Otto's fate flew across the continent.

Bertolt Brecht was finishing up a project in Paris, en route to Denmark. But he took the time to write an open letter about Otto to Heinrich George, who had, at least until recently, been a friend and collaborator to them both. For once, Brecht's voice was neither ironic nor direct; it wavered between an accusation and a plea:

> We must address a question to you. Can you tell us where your colleague from the State Theater, Hans Otto, is? He was supposedly arrested by the SA, held in secret, and delivered to the hospital with terrible injuries. Some of us would like to know whether he died there. Can you not go and see about him? You know that this is not about a negligible man. . . . Where is he?[42]

Hans Otto was one of the first prominent artists to be murdered by the Nazi regime. He was thirty-three years old.

CHAPTER 7

Denial and Compliance

1933–1934

THE NAZIS' MOST DARING OPPONENTS TOOK DRASTIC MEASURES. On March 3, 1933, German police arrested a group of Communists led by a shipwright in the Baltic port city of Königsberg. The conspirators had met secretly twice over the month of February to plan a bomb attack on Hitler at a Nazi rally on the eve of elections. They were released at the end of the year for lack of evidence, but the plot was the first of many attempts on Hitler's life over the course of the Third Reich.[1]

But over the Nazis' first year in power, most antifascist Germans were not yet disposed to assassinate. Their first concern was to buy time. It was difficult enough for them to comprehend what had happened; it was impossible to predict where things were going. The liberal and left-leaning intellectuals who remained in the country had lost their usual means of engaging in politics, and they stood to lose their livelihoods as well.

Mildred Harnack's situation illustrated their dilemma. Resolutely anti-Nazi, she was also a dedicated teacher who encouraged antifascist sentiments among her students. But if she wanted to continue teaching at the night school, she was obliged to become a member of the National Socialist teachers' organization. She joined in June 1933.[2]

Compliance had its rewards. In the throes of the Depression, good jobs were scarce, and the country's civil servants were hard pressed to save their paychecks. As thousands of Communists, Socialists, and Jews were eliminated from public life, their positions became available. Nazi

Party members quickly moved up the ladder. It was little wonder that in the three months between February and May 1933, 1.6 million people joined the Nazi Party (compared to a total membership of only 108,000 in 1929).[3]

Every aspect of German life had been hijacked by politics, even romance. Greta Lorke had been lured back to Berlin by Adam Kuckhoff, but he seemed to make his courtship conditional on her political engagement. "It is because I love you that I cannot give up having you at my side in the political struggle," he told her.[4] Adam was strongly influenced by the Communist commitment of his "other family"—his former wife, Marie, and her husband, Hans Otto, who had been raising Kuckhoff's son Armin-Gerd. Kuckhoff's convictions were only deepened by Otto's murder.

Because the German Communist Party (KPD) and the Soviet Union had loudly opposed Hitler from the start, Germany's remaining antifascist intellectuals and artists decided to initiate new points of contact. Many of them naturally assumed that the KPD and the Soviets acted in unison. But they required very different avenues of approach. Most of the surviving KPD militants were blue-collar workers, often bearing a class-based grudge against intellectuals and aristocrats. The Soviets, on the other hand, tended to operate out of the embassy, moving in different social circles entirely.

There is no record that Adam Kuckhoff ever joined the Communist Party, but he was among those who turned to the Communists hoping for a coherent response to the crisis. His theater work and journalism had brought him into contact with many Marxists, both militants and dilettantes, and now they offered resources that were lacking among the rest of the political opposition.

Adam challenged Greta to abandon the detachment she had learned as a social scientist. She shouldn't just stand back and offer analysis and advice, he told her; she should get involved. Greta had returned to Germany intent on joining opposition activities, but she was still taken aback to find that her love affair was contingent on political action.[5]

Greta found a room to sublet, in a boathouse on a lake in the far western suburb of Pichelswerder. She remained in close touch with Arvid Harnack, who also pressed her to join anti-Nazi activity. Greta visited the Harnacks at their Tempelhof apartment once, but usually they met in out-of-the-way spots near her rented room.[6] Arvid told Greta about his recent visit to the Soviet Union, and worried aloud that the Nazis would go to war against the Soviets in order to acquire lebensraum in the East. It was up to Germans like them, he argued, to thwart those plans. Resistance would require new lines of social communication, cutting across class divisions and prejudices.

Arvid pressed Greta for her working-class contacts even though she was uncertain of what she could offer. The key to their future work, Arvid replied, lay in expanding their circles of acquaintances, their *Bekanntenkreise*. He urged her to find a job that would reach into new communities. Arvid had connections to opposition circles that produced antifascist literature, and he shared their goal of warning German workers not to be seduced by the Nazi propaganda. Both Arvid Harnack and Adam Kuckhoff had early connections to the Soviets, but their origins are not entirely clear. Arvid's government work brought him into contact with officials in both the Soviet and the U.S. embassies, and as his antifascist convictions grew, he strengthened his foreign ties. Adam Kuckhoff had a broad range of political contacts through his former authors for *Die Tat*, among them KPD member John Sieg, but German Communists and Soviet intelligence agents did not necessarily overlap.

Whether or not Harnack and Kuckhoff attempted to contact Moscow directly at this point, Moscow was clearly trying to reach people like them. One indication came to light recently with the release of Soviet intelligence files.

On May 20, 1933, a Moscow official named Karl Radek sent a message to Boris Vinogradov, a Soviet intelligence agent and embassy official in Berlin. Radek, one of the founders of the German Communist Party, had settled in Moscow to work with the Communist International, and was recruited for intelligence functions.[7] Radek instructed Vinogradov to hold "discreet talks" with several individuals, including Oskar von Niedermayer, "Grabovski," and "the people from '*Tat Kreuz*.'" He urged Vinogradov to proceed "whether Faigt and Ku are in Berlin or not."[8]

With their KPD contacts scattered, the Soviets were struggling to assemble alternate sources of information. The Oskar von Niedermayer mentioned by Radek was a German army intelligence officer who had overseen joint German-Soviet training exercises in the 1920s.[9] Far from being a Communist ideologue, he served the Nazi regime throughout the war. "Grabovski" was probably Adolf Grabowski, a prominent political science professor from Berlin and a member of Arvid's study tour of the Soviet Union. The "*Tat Kreuz*" was a mistranscription of *Tatkreis* (Tat Circle). This was the group of conservative intellectuals that formed around Adam Kuckhoff's former magazine *Die Tat*. (At least one author, Stephen Koch, believes that "Ku" signified Adam Kuckhoff.[10])

There is no record of Vinogradov's response to Radek's instructions, but they would have been simple to implement. The Russian diplomat could have encountered many of the individuals listed on his usual rounds. Diplomats also encountered the Harnacks and Greta Lorke on the circuit, as well-connected members of Berlin's intellectual elite.

John Sieg's connections were of a different sort, and they demonstrated the risks and benefits of Communist Party membership. His KPD affiliation had led to his arrest and imprisonment, but it also offered him an avenue for activism on his release. Germany's Communists had a long history of secrecy and front organizations, and they had laid the foundations for underground activity long before their public organizations were erased.

A few weeks after John Sieg walked out of Plötzensee prison in June 1933, he and his wife, Sophie, moved into their new apartment in Neukölln, where Greta Lorke once tended her orphans. The neighborhood lay to the south of the city, in a district of sprawling cemeteries, forbidding tenements, and grimy corner shops. Behind the gray walls lay honeycombs of Communist cells. Living in Neukölln put Sieg at the center of the action.

For many anxious Germans like Harnack, Kuckhoff, and Sieg, the Communists represented the only functional opposition to fascism. But despite the KPD's emphasis on hierarchy and party discipline, the party was anything but orderly and united, thanks in large part to Stalin's obsessive machinations.

Stalin had reason to fear political compromise in Germa⟨...⟩ country's Social Democrats had enjoyed good relations with t⟨...⟩ ern democracies, calling on them in times of crisis for assi⟨...⟩

united front between Germany's Communists and the Social Democrats evoked Stalin's worst nightmare: a united West confronting the Soviet Union. The dictator found the idea of a divided Europe to be far more congenial. Stalin was aware that his approach would provoke the Nazis to crush the KPD, but he was unperturbed by the notion of thousands of German Communists undergoing torture, exile, and concentration camps. Stalin's cynical maneuvers were invisible on the ground. Many German Communists assumed that any criticism of Stalin was simply right-wing propaganda, and could not imagine Stalin delivering them into the hands of their fascist enemies.

The KPD's first concern was the Nazis. Immediately after the takeover, thousands of KPD members fell victim to Nazi violence. One of the first was presidential candidate Ernst Thälmann, who had come in third in the national elections only months earlier. Thälmann had belatedly called for a Social Democrat–KPD joint effort (after years of thwarting such a possibility), and was swept up in the first wave of March arrests. His trial was repeatedly postponed, then canceled, and he was eventually executed.[11]

The KPD had been a major force in German society, recording 300,000 members in 1932, and reaping nearly 6 million votes in the November elections. But the Weimar police's detailed files on the Communists made it absurdly easy for the Nazis to arrest them en masse. It was estimated that over 1933, 2,000 Communists were killed and 60,000 were made prisoner. Thousands left the party, and thousands more fled to Paris, Moscow, and Prague. By the end of the year, only 60,000 to 150,000 KPD stalwarts remained in Germany, uncertain of their course and bereft of leadership.[12]

When John Sieg was released from his three months of torture and imprisonment, all that remained of the KPD in Germany was a ragged network of cells. These small groupings functioned in factories, trade unions, or other discreet communities over a matter of years. John Sieg's new neighborhood of Neukölln was a KPD enclave, but like most working-class neighborhoods, it also hosted notorious storm trooper clubs that doubled as commissaries and torture centers. One of them, Sturm 21 at 35 Richardstrasse, operated just a few blocks east of the Siegs' Jonasstrasse apartment.[13]

As soon as he arrived, Sieg contacted Kurt Heims, the former labor correspondent for the *Rote Fahne*. Heims belonged to the southern Neukölln district organization of the KPD, and his home on 91 Berliner Strasse became a meeting place for regrouping party members. Sieg was instantly welcomed back into the circle, which included Otto Dietrich; Werner Mendelsohn, a Jewish Communist; and Herbert Grasse, a twenty-three-year-old printer.

Sieg, the displaced journalist, took a special interest in the group's principal project, an illegal newspaper called the *Neuköllner Sturmfahne* (Neukölln Storm Flag). Grasse printed the paper secretly in Otto Dietrich's home in an unassuming building a short walk from Sieg's apartment.[14] "Newspaper" was something of an exaggeration; the *Sturmfahne* involved a few crude mimeographed pages featuring clumsy illustrations and hand-lettered text. The "news" consisted of denunciations of Nazi officials and urgent KPD concerns, such as the ongoing imprisonment of Ernst Thälmann, information that was censored from the state-controlled press. It was a challenge for the group to distribute the copies to moribund Communist cells; anyone caught producing, disseminating, or even in possession of such literature was severely punished.

Sieg was glad to find people who were taking action, in contrast to the millions of Germans who succumbed to Nazi propaganda or sank into passivity. As the Nazis intimidated and took over the country's mainstream news organizations, the underground press served notice that Nazi control was not absolute.

Sieg needed more than an outlet for activism—he was also broke. Through the Neukölln crowd, John Sieg met Karl Hellborn, a trade unionist who worked for the Reichsbahn, the state railway. The railway workers' union had been subjected to *Gleichschaltung* by the Nazis, but the old union networks survived in secret. Hellborn promised to try to get Sieg a job through his connections.[15] In the meantime, Sieg had to settle for odd jobs and construction work, as he once did in Chicago and Detroit.

Sieg and his friends found that even mundane political transactions were painfully difficult. It was no longer possible to exchange information in accustomed ways. Meeting halls, party newspapers, and even cabarets were closed down or converted to fascist use. The neighborhoods Neukölln, "Red Wedding," and Wilmersdorf continued to brew opposition activity, but they were also rife with informers. The Gestapo lacked vast numbers of agents, but it received ample assistance from ordinary Germans who were all too eager to spy on their neighbors.

The antifascist opposition had few resources to counter the regime's propaganda machine, which now turned to the mass production of hatred. The Nazis used every means at their disposal to blame the country's problems, past and present, on "Bolsheviks" and "Jews," suggesting the two were synonymous. Ubiquitous caricatures showed Jews as hooknosed businessmen clutching their moneybags or as glowering, lurking *Ostjuden* in long black robes. Leftists were bespectacled, effete intellectuals who trafficked in the politics of "complexity," instead of subscribing to Hitler's simplistic gospel of national unity.[16] The Bolshevik was portrayed as a swarthy proletarian (often with vaguely Asian features) in a cloth cap with a menacing scowl, sowing chaos in an orderly land.[17] Thanks to the machinery of *Gleichschaltung*, these vicious images were multiplied in street posters, textbooks, Nazi newspapers, feature films, and cartoons.

Only a few years earlier, the Communists had answered Nazi propaganda with its own mass media, employing some of the best minds in the business, notably Willi Münzenberg. The epic film *Kuhle Wampe* raised the bar. The Communist melodrama depicted the suicide of a handsome young worker, driven to desperation by unemployment. But his family and friends (including the teenaged Marta Wolter) triumph over adversity by uniting in proletarian solidarity. Just as the plot threatens to completely disintegrate, the joyous Communist youth of Berlin assemble for wholesome athletic contests and elaborate bicycle formations. Many of the movie's elements were to reappear, with polish, in future Nazi films.

One early imitation came quickly on the heels of the takeover in 1933. The plot for *Hitlerjunge Quex* was based on the story of a Hitler Youth who had been killed by Communists in a street brawl the previous year. The film expropriated familiar Communist mythology and turned it upside down. A wholesome towheaded youth, Heini (nicknamed "Quex," or "Quicksilver") lives in a slum surrounded by seedy Communists, the most brutal of whom is his drunken Communist father, complete with cloth cap and menacing scowl. One day Quex stumbles across Hitler Youth camping in the countryside. He is entranced by their clean-cut appearance and mystic rituals. He secretly joins the Hitler Youth, performs heroic acts of rescue, and is beaten to death by Communist thugs. In the misty finale, phalanxes of Hitler Youth march triumphantly into the foreground to the strains of a Nazi anthem.

The Nazis scored a major propaganda coup by casting Heinrich George in the role of the drunken Communist father. George was one of the country's leading actors. His leftist credentials were also extensive, including a number of Erwin Piscator's agitprop productions, among them young Günther Weisenborn's antiwar play *U-Boat S-4*. He had been directed by Brecht, and collaborated with Willi Münzenberg's Prometheus Productions. He had spoken at KPD rallies and served as Hans Otto's comrade-in-arms, organizing Communist theater workers' strikes. In March 1933, the Nazis banned Heinrich George from working in the National Theater. After an anxious interlude, he came to an "arrangement" that allowed him to work again. Part of the price was his role in *Hitlerjunge Quex* as the boorish Communist father who batters his noble Nazi son and lives to regret it. German movie audiences witnessed one of their foremost actors publicly convert from communism to Nazism on the silver screen.

Quex was not a Goebbels favorite. The propaganda minister privately disparaged overt propaganda films, believing that the masses could be lulled into submission more effectively through a diet of mindless entertainment.[18] But he publicly praised *Hitlerjunge Quex*, as did many others. Before the film opened at Loew's Yorkville Cinema in New York in the summer of 1934, the distributors removed Hitler's name from the title, replacing it with the anodyne *Our Banner Flies Before Us*. The *New York Times* gave *Hitlerjunge Quex* a positive review, recommending it to "persons desirous of getting a pictorial idea of how the Nazi doctrine was spread among the rising generation in Germany." It went on to note, "Technically, the picture is well done . . . the action moves fairly fast and many of the scenes, particularly in the humble home of the young hero and in the streets during the political campaign, are genuinely entertaining."[19] The *Times* gave special mention to "such excellent players . . . as the massive Heinrich Georg [sic], as a rank-and-file Berlin Communist," and "the likable young Claus Clausen" as his Hitler Youth son.[20]

In 1937, Goebbels named George an official "State Actor," and soon after, he was appointed head of the prestigious Schiller Theater.[21] Heinrich George was living proof of the assertion made by theater-lover Hermann Göring: "It is easier to turn a great artist into a decent National Socialist than to make a great artist out of a humble party member."[22]

\ \ \

CHAPTER 8

Going to Ground

1934-1935

THE CATACLYSM OF 1933 WAS FOLLOWED BY WAVES OF KILLINGS, exiles, and arrests, transforming German public life. But it was impossible to regulate the private transactions that take place on a daily basis among a population of sixty-six million people. Much of life seemed to go on as before. One could criticize the regime as long as it was done within a closed circle that guaranteed confidentiality. Such conversations persisted at family dinner tables, in pubs and cafes, and in workers' huddles on factory floors.

Still, as the Gestapo made its presence known, thousands of zealous new Nazis competed to inform on their neighbors. It became increasingly dangerous to trust anyone. A jealous relative or disgruntled coworker found it all too easy to settle old scores or eliminate a competitor; a simple denunciation would do. Trust could no longer to be taken for granted.

Arvid and Mildred Harnack were lucky to belong to the close-knit Harnack family, which prided itself on its liberal values. Now the extended family's long, philosophical dinner conversations took on a new urgency. Arvid and his cousins Dietrich and Klaus Bonhoeffer were cut from the same cloth: cerebral, but unwilling to limit their work to theoretical realms. The entire clan—extended by marriage to the Delbrücks, the Dohnanyis, and the Schleichers—represented an impressive range of liberal German social scientists and civil servants.

A remarkable proportion of the family had taken an active stand against Nazism, extending their professional ties to fashion a dozen strands of resistance. The Harnack clan was offended by the pseudo-sacred rhetoric of the Nazis, and repelled by the resurgence of anti-Semitism. They stood by their many Jewish friends, and went to great lengths to defend them. The Bonhoeffers' ninety-one-year-old grand-mother took the lead when she defied the first anti-Jewish boycott by marching past a cordon of brownshirts to enter the Jewish-owned KaDeWe department store. Soon Mildred Harnack began to work her connections at the U.S. embassy to help her Jewish friends emigrate. Ernst von Harnack arranged for a number of his Jewish friends to leave for England. (Some of them were annoyed at his insistence, convinced that "it would all blow over.")[1]

Arvid's younger cousin Dietrich Bonhoeffer never wavered in his opposition to fascism, but it wasn't always clear what path he would take. He had originally intended to become a psychiatrist like his father, but to everyone's surprise he gravitated toward theology and found a vocation as a Lutheran pastor. In 1930 he followed in Arvid's footsteps to the United States, arriving in New York only a few months after Arvid and Mildred returned to Germany. Bonhoeffer did postgraduate work at Union Theological Seminary near Columbia University.

Bonhoeffer was fascinated by his Harlem neighborhood, and soon attached himself to the African-American Abyssinian Baptist Church on 138th Street, just north of the seminary. He was deeply influenced by the nonviolent civil rights movement taking root in the black Christian community, and collected recordings of gospel music to take back to Germany. Once he returned, Bonhoeffer accepted a teaching position at the University of Berlin around the same time that Mildred joined the faculty.

Like the rest of the family, Bonhoeffer watched the political developments in his country with growing alarm. On February 1, 1933, he gave a radio talk deploring the way young Germans were imbuing the "Führer" with the qualities of a sacrilegious icon, but the microphone was cut off as he spoke.[2] A few days later, he drafted an essay called "*Die Kirche vor der Jugenfrage*" ("The Church and the Jewish Question"), declaring that Christians had an ethical responsibility to defend the Jews. That same week Dietrich and his brother Klaus reached out to American

Jewish theologians, including the prominent Rabbi Stephen Wise.[3] That spring Bonhoeffer witnessed the spectacle of Goebbels's book-burning on the pavement just outside his classrooms. In August the university informed him that his services were no longer required.

Like many Germans, Bonhoeffer was torn between leaving a country that trampled his most deeply held values, and staying on to fight for its soul. He believed that the international community, especially ecumenical organizations, had a duty to thwart the Nazis' plans for conquest and bloodshed. He spent the next year in England as a pastor to Lutheran congregations, making many friends. Just as Greta Kuckhoff had used her trip to England to alert British trade unionists to the dangers of Nazism, Dietrich Bonhoeffer sounded the alarm among British academics and church people.

It was not an easy task. Many Britons regarded Hitler and the Nazi movement with sympathy, just the thing to subdue the Bolsheviks and get the German economy back on its feet. Anti-Semitism was commonplace in British society, and Britain incubated its own version of fascism. In 1931, British aristocrat Oswald Mosely undertook a political study tour of Italy and Germany, and returned to found the British Union of Fascists the following year.

Bonhoeffer finally decided that his place was in Germany, where both Catholic and Lutheran churches showed worrying signs of accommodation. The Vatican reached an agreement with the Nazis in July 1933, signing a Concordat that allowed the dissolution of Catholic trade unions and the Catholics' Center Party. In return, the Catholic Church was allowed to go on functioning in Germany as a religious institution, and the Church retained its property. Some courageous Catholic clergy and laypeople objected, but they were a minority.

The Lutheran Church was more influential than the Catholic, and even more complicit. The 1925 census identified 40 million of Germany's 65 million people as Lutheran, compared to 21 million Catholics and 620,000 members of smaller denominations.[4] The Nazi regime moved quickly to subvert the Church into a state institution that synthesized Nazi ideology and conservative Protestant tradition.

This campaign was offensive to many Lutherans, including Pastor Martin Niemöller, a World War I submarine commander and a onetime

Hitler supporter. Niemöller reacted by founding the Pastors' Emergency League, which evolved into a dissenting branch of the Church known as the (*Bekennende*) Confessing Church. When Dietrich Bonhoeffer returned to Germany from England in 1934 (only twenty-eight years old) he joined the effort and became its leading theologian. The Confessing Lutheran Church attracted thousands of German Protestants with its argument that true Christianity was incompatible with Nazism. Bonhoeffer interpreted his calling as a mission to create a sanctuary for principled opposition, grounded in faith. This was the community that sustained the anti-Nazi activities of Adam Kuckhoff's friend, Social Democratic minister Adolf Grimme.

Over 1933 and 1934, Arvid and Mildred Harnack remained in close touch with their Bonhoeffer relatives. Mildred, seeking alternate sources of income, launched a lecture series sponsored by the U.S. embassy, presented in Klaus and Emmi Bonhoeffer's home.[5]

Arvid was immersed in preparations for his examinations, but the young couple's social circle continued to grow. Their simple but welcoming salon attracted liberal writers and publishers, and served as a meeting place for Berlin intellectuals and American expatriates. Arvid and Mildred Harnack saw America as a symbol of hope. Franklin Delano Roosevelt had just come into office, and they were cheered to learn that his administration was hiring their friends from the University of Wisconsin for crucial positions in government. Suddenly their shared causes, such as labor reform and economic planning, were official policy objectives in a program called the New Deal, implemented by people they knew and admired.

The couple received an additional boost in July 1933 with the arrival of the new U.S. ambassador. William Dodd arrived in Berlin with Mrs. Dodd and their two grown children, Martha and Bill. Mildred was especially interested in Martha, a twenty-four-year-old University of Chicago dropout and occasional journalist. The two young women were opposites in many ways. Mildred was tall, gentle, and grave, while Martha was a tiny, dark-haired spitfire who liked to live dangerously. But they shared literary interests and became fast friends. Soon they were coauthoring a book column for the local English-language paper.[6]

Martha had cultivated a number of celebrated American writers. She wrote to her friend Thornton Wilder about the Harnacks' literary circle, and described her new friend Mildred as "very poor and real and fine and not much in favor though the family is old and respected." Martha, prone to self-importance, announced that "the Harnacks and I (since we have concluded we are the only people in Berlin genuinely interested in writers) conscientiously encourage all such free intellectual endeavor as there is left."[7]

Mildred and Arvid's literary teas were more than mere social occasions. The guests were survivors of a beleaguered and depleted culture, seeking shelter in one another's company. Mildred wove a path among her guests, offering liverwurst sandwiches and fruit. All the while she and her husband were testing the waters. Which of the assembled acquaintances shared their political views? Could they be trusted with secrets? Who might cross the line from private skepticism to active opposition?

The Harnacks understood the degrees of opposition. Many intellectuals opted for "inner emigration," trying to sit out the Nazi period in rural retreats, by neither complying nor opposing. The next level was called *Resistenz*, "resistance" in the sense of a substance that fails to conduct an electrical current. These Germans expressed their positions passively through everyday acts of noncompliance, such as refusing to contribute to fund-raising drives or failing to return a Nazi salute. Under the wrong circumstances, even such passive rebellion could result in criminal charges. The third and most serious level was called *Widerstand*, literally "taking a stand against" the regime through acts of opposition. The Harnacks believed that this was the only effective course to take.

Ambassador Dodd arrived in the early days of the Nazi regime, before either the American press or diplomatic corps had a clear sense of its nature. (Roosevelt was inaugurated March 4, 1933, the day before the German elections that brought Hitler to power.) But the Nazis presented extraordinary challenges in diplomacy, and the new ambassador soon had a growing caseload of Americans who ran afoul of the regime. His consular headaches were reflected in an October 15, 1933, *New York Times* article. It reported that the Germans, responding to diplomatic pressure, had arrested storm troopers for beating up a U.S. citizen who failed to return a Nazi salute.

Ambassador Dodd was hampered by Hitler's successful public relations campaign, which won him a sympathetic audience among influential Americans. Many of them were open to the Nazis' early policies, and condemned the New Deal reforms of social security and public works as creeping Marxism. Father Charles Coughlin, a Catholic priest with a vast following in the United States, peppered his radio talks with effusive praise for Hitler and Mussolini and crude anti-Semitic remarks. In 1934, Boston businessman and politician Joseph Kennedy, who was awaiting a political appointment in the Roosevelt administration, sent his nineteen-year-old son Joe Jr. to Germany for an eyewitness report on conditions. Joe Jr. returned full of enthusiasm:

> The German people were scattered, despondent, and were divorced from hope. Hitler came in. He saw the need of a common enemy, someone of whom to make the goat. . . . It was excellent psychology, and it was too bad that it had to be done to the Jews. This dislike of the Jews, however, was well-founded. They were at the heads of all big business, in law etc. It is all to their credit for them to get so far, but their methods had been quite unscrupulous . . . the lawyers and prominent judges were Jews, and if you had a case against a Jew, you were nearly always sure to lose it. . . . As far as the brutality is concerned, it must have been necessary to use some. . . .[8]

Within four years, Joseph Kennedy Sr. would be the U.S. ambassador to Great Britain, and would turn often to Joe Jr. for advice.

The ambassador's daughter, Martha, approached Germany differently. A vivacious woman who considered herself a femme fatale, she initially found German fascists intriguing, and even charming in a sinister way. Her father's position made her a desirable social commodity, and she spent her early weeks in Berlin dating a succession of Nazis, ranging from young storm troopers to high officials. Her mother diplomatically had tea with Mrs. Göring and Mrs. Goebbels (who made a good impression). Hitler himself kissed Martha's hand.

But the niceties of Berlin society provided scant cover for the brutality going on around them. On a motor tour of the countryside, Martha was startled by the sight of Nazis brazenly assaulting Jews. Her family soon realized that the phones in their residence were tapped, and that many of the guests at their social functions lived in a permanent state of fear.

Martha had a quick mind and an observant eye, but little bent for analysis. She trusted Mildred to interpret the situation and to connect her to Germans who were disaffected with the regime. "I knew intimately no other woman in Germany who possessed such sincerity and singleness of purpose," she recalled later. "She was never glib, never sarcastic at someone else's expense, never hasty nor bigoted. . . . Her words were cautious, persuasive, charged with unobtrusive but incontrovertible logic."[9] Mildred, for her part, found Martha to be an eager partner in exploring the German scene, writing to her mother that she was "clear and capable and has a real desire to understand the world. Therefore our interests touch . . ."[10]

It was still just possible for the stubbornly optimistic to believe that the fascists could be swept away as abruptly as they had come to power. But other former opponents were coming around. Many among the traditional elite, including the Prussian aristocracy and the army officer corps, were repelled by the Nazis' crass style and brutish methods. At the same time, they acknowledged change on the horizon. For the first time since Versailles, Germans saw the potential for their national prestige to be restored, their economy reenergized, and their lost territories reclaimed. Many found the social cost acceptable. Most of the elite had never been overly fond of Jews and Social Democrats in the first place, and many had openly battled Communists.

Still, as the dictatorship entered its second year, the situation was far from stable. As the institutions of democracy were irreversibly dismantled and the concentration camps filled to bursting, even conservatives had second thoughts.

In June 1934, the situation came to a head through an internal Nazi Party crisis. The SA, or brownshirts, had grown rapidly under the leadership of Ernst Röhm. Now they were threatening to spin out of control. With over two million members, the paramilitary group far outnumbered the German army.

On June 17, Röhm convened the SA leadership for a retreat at a small resort outside Munich. Hitler issued orders that were executed with shocking speed. The SS (the elite military force founded as Hitler's bodyguards) moved across the country as coordinated death squads, mowing down strategic pockets of Hitler's rivals and opponents, including Röhm and the SA leaders.

On July 13, Hitler gave a speech about the seventy-two-hour blood-letting, calling it "The Night of the Long Knives." He acknowledged seventy-seven deaths. (Sixty-one were described as executions, and the rest as "suicides" and "killed resisting arrest.") Other estimates ran into the hundreds. Hitler justified his actions under an impromptu law that stated: "The measures taken on June 30 and July 1 and 2 to strike down the treasonous attacks are justifiable acts of self-defense by the state."[11]

The Night of the Long Knives turned Ambassador Dodd's low opinion of the Nazis into full-blown disgust. The ambassador, no born diplomat, decided he would refuse to take part in any voluntary meetings with the Nazi hierarchy. His wife's health began to suffer from the nervous strain. The couple had their hands full with their daughter Martha, who had transferred her favor from Nazi officials to a handsome Soviet diplomat, First Secretary Boris Vinogradov. Now she began to play another dangerous game, sharing her father's confidences with her new beau. Stalin's state security intelligence service, the NKVD, noted the development with interest and made plans to draw Martha into their network of informants.[12]

It was becoming more difficult to make social contact with Soviet officials; the Nazis had stepped up surveillance of the Soviet embassy. Nonetheless, Arvid Harnack remained in touch with his Soviet embassy contact, and relied on his wife to do the same with the Americans. In April 1935, Arvid passed another round of rigorous professional examinations. This qualified him for a position at the Ministry of Economics, which gave him access to extensive economic intelligence.

On May 8, 1935, the U.S. embassy in Berlin hosted a major literary event. The ambassador's daughter, Martha, held an embassy tea in honor of Thomas Wolfe, the towering young American novelist, and Random House publisher Donald Klopfer, both in Germany on a visit.[13] Wolfe, thirty-five, was at the peak of his powers. A Germanophile, Wolfe had already made several trips to the country, and a leading German firm had just translated and published his best-selling novel *Look Homeward, Angel.*

Martha Dodd asked her friend Mildred Harnack to assemble the German guest list. But from the viewpoint of the ambassador's spoiled daughter, the party was a flop: "a dull, and at the same time, tense afternoon." Mildred Harnack had invited "about forty people, writers, poets, publishers and magazine editors," many of whom were already involved in secret anti-Nazi activity. But Martha, for all her intrigues, still responded as a petulant child, unable to observe anything in the room beyond its failure to entertain her:

> This was the party at which I had hoped to hear amusing conversation, some exchange of stimulating views, at least conversation on a higher plane than one is accustomed to in diplomatic society. But this party was so full of frustration and misery; of the strain laid upon the last scraps of minds and opinions of any freedom, by the ferreting-out conducted by the Secret Police; of tension, broken spirits, doomed courage or tragic and hated cowardice, that I vowed never to have such a group again in my house.[14]

Greta Lorke approached the party with an entirely different agenda. Mildred Harnack had personally visited Greta Lorke and Adam Kuckhoff to deliver the invitation and give Greta her assignment, described in her memoirs:

> A range of writers and journalists would be there. . . . Martha, who was still very young, was hoping to engage us in a lively debate. . . . The meeting at Martha's looked like a conventional get-together of friendly harmless people, who came from different circles. Arvid Harnack, who didn't go himself, had given us the task of establishing contact with as many guests as possible and carefully evaluating their positions. Harnack was concerned that in order to explore the extent of the anti-Nazi front and its possibilities for expansion, it was necessary to make acquaintances and

establish contacts between different circles and groups, and increase the sources of information.[15]

The reception provided a welcome opportunity for anti-Nazis to gather in a group. It included leading American journalists Sigrid Schultz of the *Chicago Tribune* and Louis Lochner of the Associated Press, both outspoken critics of the Nazi regime. Mildred's German guest list gathered novelists, poets, and journalists from beleaguered Berlin dailies. Adam Kuckhoff brought John Sieg, who no longer fit the definition of a working journalist, but produced and distributed clandestine anti-Nazi leaflets to factories and trade unions.

Most of the evening's tense political discussions went over the heads of the American guests of honor. Thomas Wolfe and Mildred Harnack took an instant liking to each other, and he granted her an interview. She proudly published the results in both English-language and German periodicals. Wolfe had less respect for Martha Dodd, calling her "a little middle western flirt—with little stick out teeth, and a little 'sure that will be swell' sort of voice."[16] Nonetheless, Wolfe soon joined Martha's long list of conquests, and their turbulent affair lasted until he sailed for New York at the end of June.

Arvid Harnack continued to cultivate his contacts in the U.S. embassy, but made little progress. The Americans still had no defined policy toward the Nazi regime, and U.S. intelligence capabilities were almost nonexistent.

An alternative soon appeared. That August, Arvid was contacted by Alexander Hirschfeld, an acquaintance from the Soviet embassy, who asked for a meeting. Hirschfeld told Harnack that his new job in the Economics Ministry could provide useful information, and offered to set up a mechanism to convey it to the Nazis' enemies in Moscow. Hirschfeld laid out the first rule of collaboration: maintain a low profile and keep well away from any kind of political activity. In particular, Harnack was instructed to keep his distance from anyone involved with the illegal German Communist Party, and to avoid working with the resistance.[17] Arvid heard him out, but he declined to comply.

Each man was holding out on the other. Hirschfeld, as political counselor for the Soviet embassy, was aware that Stalin was pursuing multiple agendas in Germany. Harnack, for his part, was never interested in becoming a Soviet agent.[18] He identified himself as a Communist, but he focused his concern on his own country's future. He would provide information to any power that promised to shorten Hitler's reign, whether American or Soviet. Harnack showed no regard for NKVD's instructions on tradecraft, and explored every opportunity to turn his fellow Germans against the regime, even if it placed his intelligence work—and his life—in jeopardy.

Between 1935 and June 1938, Arvid Harnack provided the Soviets with extensive information about the German economy, foreign investments, and trade agreements. Against the wishes of his Soviet contacts, he circulated related information to both Communist and non-Communist resistance circles in factories and government offices.[19]

Harnack remained true to his mission to "establish contacts between different circles and groups, and increase the sources of information." A memo in his KGB files, drafted a few years later, described his approach to proselytizing among the intelligentsia.

> Within the larger circle, centers have been formed, each of which is dedicated to the education and training of a small group. . . . Although [Harnack] cannot personally vouch for every person, every one of these sixty people, the whole network of people who have the same background, think alike and come from the same social strata. . . . The aim of them all is to prepare personnel to occupy administrative posts [in the German government] after the [anti-Nazi] *coup d'etat.*[20]

By 1935 the Harnacks' contacts had grown to an impressive array. They included Arvid's Social Democrat and dissenting Lutheran relations, Mildred's night-school students, their U.S. embassy contacts, and their literary and academic friends. The circles often shifted and sometimes overlapped.

But even Harnack had his limits. That same year, another Rockefeller Fellow from his Wisconsin days, sociologist Rudolf Heberle, offered to introduce him to his wife's cousin, who was also a fervent anti-Nazi. Harro Schulze-Boysen was an urbane young aristocrat who had joined the Air Ministry the previous year. Like Arvid, Harro had penetrated a fascist stronghold with the express intent of undermining it. Heberle thought the two men should meet, and the Harnacks invited Schulze-Boysen to their home.

Afterward, Arvid asked Heberle to tell Schulze-Boysen that he "appreciated meeting with him" but didn't care to see him again. The two men were utterly different in temperament: Schulze-Boysen was bold and impulsive, while Harnack was cautious and deliberate. In Arvid's opinion, another meeting would be "too dangerous."[21]

CHAPTER 9

The Prague Express

1936–1937

JOHN SIEG AND HIS NEUKÖLLN CROWD WERE ROUGH AROUND THE edges, but they knew how to get things done. Before the Nazi takeover, their district's cheap housing and high unemployment had made it a prime recruiting ground for radicals of every stripe, including the KPD, the *Rote Fahne*, trade unions, and the Rote Hilfe (as well as their Nazi archrivals). But the waves of arrests deprived them of their established leaders and organizational structure.

Thanks to this leadership vacuum, John Sieg quickly evolved from a journalist gadfly to a dynamic political operative. Although the group's objective was nothing less than overthrowing the Nazi regime, its members' immediate goals were necessarily short term: to break the Nazi monopoly on news and propaganda; to help victims of political persecution; and to create whatever obstructionist mischief they could.

Shortly after the war, the survivors from the Neukölln group recorded a series of testimonies about their Nazi-era activities. Buried for decades in East German state archives, the files conveyed a vivid portrait of clandestine life.[1] Similar groups operated all over Germany, both before and during the war, but two factors made the Neuköllners unique. First, they operated in the heart of the German capital, only blocks away from the Nazi high command. Second, thanks to John Sieg and a few other well-placed individuals, they had more access to other strata of German society than the industrial workers' cells. This placed them among the few actual Communist Party members within the artists and intellectuals' network that would come to be known as the Rote Kapelle (Red Orchestra).

The German Communists inside the country were increasingly isolated from both the exile communities in Western Europe and the bureaucrats in Moscow. Sometimes it was hard for members of the German underground to restrain their resentment of party officials living in safety outside the country, who churned out piles of unrealistic speeches and manifestos for them to distribute in Germany at the risk of their lives. They also wanted more autonomy in running their operations. Taking orders from abroad had yielded poor results; they had suffered badly for following Stalin's instructions to oppose the Social Democrats in 1933.

After the Comintern's Seventh (and last) Congress in Moscow in 1935, the German Communists held a follow-up meeting to assess the damage. The proceedings opened with a grim report. Of 422 leading figures in the KPD, 219—over half—were in German prisons and concentration camps. Another 125 were in exile, 41 had left the party, and 24 had been murdered.

Only 13 of the 422 were still active inside the country. Local committees had been repeatedly wiped out by arrests and killings. Leaders were soon replaced, but the life span of these individuals and groups was often measured in weeks.

The German delegates in Moscow, fed up with Stalin's minions, called for a new election. They discarded Stalin's favorites and voted in a surprise raft of new leadership, all veterans of underground work in Germany who had witnessed the destruction of their groups and lost faith in Moscow's directives.

The German Communists set to work reshaping their operations. Earlier, the KPD had established border stations outside the German frontiers. Now these were upgraded into border secretariats called *Abschnittsleitungen,* with specialized functions. The Prague secretariat was responsible for central and western Germany, including Berlin, while the Zürich office oversaw the south. Other regions were assigned to bureaus in Brussels, Amsterdam, and Copenhagen. The Paris bureau had the added responsibility of organizing a cultural popular front. Party workers called "instructors" traveled in and out of Germany from the border secretariats, carrying messages and writing reports on party operations.

The KPD no longer imported large quantities of printed materials into the country; it was simply not worth the risk. The report on the 1935 meeting itself was smuggled into Germany with great care, bound in a cover labeled "Proper Care of Cactus Plants."[2] (The KPD often chose its titles with a measure of wit. Willi Münzenberg's famous "Brown Book of the Hitler Terror and Burning of the Reichstag" appeared as "Electric Home Heating," while the 1934 Communist Party program was published as a "Cook Book with Seventy Approved Recipes.")[3]

Over his career, John Sieg had written moody poetry and impressionistic essays from America, and colorful newspaper stories in Berlin. Now he transferred his talents to the shadowy world of underground flyers, or *flugblätter*.

The centerpiece of his Neukölln publishing operation was a mimeograph-like machine called the hectograph. (The group sometimes referred to it as "the apparatus.") The device used chemicals and wax plates to reproduce written materials in moderate quantities, and merely to own one was to invite a Gestapo interrogation. It appears that the Neukölln group had access to several machines, one of them hidden in a cellar after 1933 and later installed in Otto Dietrich's apartment on Biebricher Street.[4]

Another hectograph hiding place was Max Grabowski's hut in Rudow, on the southern outskirts of Neukölln. Max and his brother Otto had been active in Sieg's group since the beginning. Max's hut was little more than a shed that was set up for a construction business. Its exterior bore commercial signs for paints, varnishes, and wallpapers, providing a convenient excuse for deliveries of supplies and equipment.

The hectograph was a finicky machine and required extensive cleaning. "Dirty work," one member wrote. "You can't even smoke there because of the Benzine. The apparatus already has an illegal past. It escaped capture, but its lord and master sits behind bars." Its "lord and master" was young printer Herbert Grasse, who had been arrested in 1936 and sentenced to two and a half years in the penitentiary. His loss had been a blow to the group's technical operations as well as its morale. But its members took comfort in the fact that no further arrests followed, indicating that Grasse had remained silent under Gestapo interrogation.

The hectograph's wax plates and paper were difficult to procure. The Gestapo kept close tabs on the bulk purchase of everything from office supplies to stamps, in hopes of detecting just such operations. Some of the flyers were handwritten, but John Sieg preferred to use a typewriter—another dangerous possession. Sieg's prior imprisonment in 1933 made him a strong candidate for house searches. The typewriter became another piece of bulky machinery that had to be hidden and moved, along with the supplies.

It had been different back in the early days of 1933, when boxes of flyers could be smuggled in from Switzerland. Members of the group carried the boxes into the subways, five thousand flyers at a time, right under the noses of the police and the informers. But it turned out that their luck was indeed too good to be true. The police were actually tracking the members and biding their time until they could make a mass arrest. When they pounced, they hauled in twenty-five members at once. Now the group was more cautious. Flyers were produced in runs of a hundred, two or three hundred at most, and distributed surreptitiously in mailboxes.

The flyer contents evolved along with the political situation. Over the summer of 1936, the Nazis convened the Olympics in a splendid new stadium in a northern district of Berlin. The city glistened, as unkempt Gypsies and anti-Semitic signs were temporarily removed from public view. While the rest of the world gawked at the Games, the push for a united front gained momentum. That summer, the international edition of the *Rote Fahne* published a joint statement by leading Social Democrats, Communists, and members of the exiled intellectual community in Paris. Its banner headline read:

BE UNITED, UNITED AGAINST HITLER!
A PEOPLE'S FRONT TO RESCUE GERMANY FROM
THE CATASTROPHE OF WAR

The Neukölln group echoed this policy from their grassroots perspective. Members compared notes about which of their acquaintances was a "reliable" Social Democrat committed to fighting fascism, and which was an ideologically "obsessed" Social Democrat who would rather cozy up to the Nazis than cooperate with Communists.

Many of the Social Democrats had decamped to Prague, with additional publishing operations in the Czech town of Carlsbad, on the German border. In 1934 they began to publish reports on conditions in Germany, but they made for depressing reading:

> People say "Things can't go on like this," and they also say, "Things can't be worse after Hitler," but behind these phrases there is neither the will to overturn the system nor any conception of what should take its place. . . . These extraordinary swings of mood . . . place great strain on the mental strength and resilience of everyone involved in illegal opposition.[5]

The Neukölln group met as often as it could, shifting locations. The members gave reports on various activities, including the challenges of recruiting new collaborators while remaining on guard against *Flitzer* (informers). Industrial workers were crucial to their effort, and at first glance Germany's factories looked like fertile grounds for recruitment. The KPD's pre-1933 membership had been heavily blue collar, concentrated in urban areas such as Berlin and Hamburg. But the Nazis were adept at thwarting worker initiatives. In 1934 and 1935, after elections for factory worker delegates went badly for Nazi candidates, Hitler simply canceled further elections.[6] Over the course of 1936 and 1937, tensions mounted between industrial workers and the Nazi regime. German workers were initially enthusiastic about the new jobs generated by the Nazis' public works programs, as well as new benefits such as subsidized holidays, cafeterias, and recreational facilities. But gradually they realized that once their unions were destroyed or absorbed into Nazi fronts, the possibility of collective bargaining vanished with them. The workers mounted a series of strikes and protests over 1936 and 1937, but Nazi shop stewards and the Gestapo guaranteed that their actions remained small, scattered, and temporary.[7]

The Neukölln resisters not only had to endure the perils of their work, they also had to overcome a sense of futility. Most members of the group were blue-collar factory workers and small tradesmen. Under Germany's rigid educational system, they had been placed on an apprenticeship or trade-school track at an early age, with limited exposure to the liberal arts or the professions. For such Germans, higher education held a mystique, and this worked to John Sieg's benefit. By Harnack standards, Sieg's academic credentials were slight; limited to some teacher training in West Prussia and a few night-school classes at the City College of Detroit. But this was more than most of his Neukölln counterparts had, and Sieg was a published author as well. The Neuköllners appreciated the way he organized meetings as study groups and led the participants through Marxist catechism as well as operational plans.

One of the Neukölln group's riskiest undertakings was foreign travel. The Nazis had been steadily tightening travel restrictions, but with so many Communist exile operations based in Prague, couriers were necessary. Under normal circumstances, the train ride from Berlin to Prague (some 230 miles, a little farther than New York to Washington) was a day's scenic journey. Over the years of 1936 and 1937, however, the trip was anything but normal.

The archival files on John Sieg include one account of a journey by a Neukölln courier called "Franz." The identity of Franz has not been established; if it was not Sieg himself, it was possibly one of his circle.

The young man boards the train at a Reichsbahn station in central Berlin in February 1937. His mood is both anxious and somber. The past year has been hard on his circle. One member died of tuberculosis and another committed suicide. Still others were caught in the brutal revolving door of prisons and concentration camps, though a surprising number of them resumed their illegal work as soon as they were released.

The first leg of Franz's journey is a few hours' ride through the neatly cultivated hayfields of Brandenburg, graced by weeping willows. The stop in Dresden offers a glimpse of the splendid city of the Saxon kings, under the suspicious gaze of local Nazi officials. After Dresden, Franz's route veers west. It would have been more direct to proceed due south, along the Elbe and its fabled sandstone cliffs, but the dogleg in Franz's route allows him to skirt the heavy surveillance at the main border crossing. The towns are even smaller now, with quaint local details such as the pointed Saxon domes that crown old buildings like inverted radishes. This is a rougher landscape, steeply graded through dense pine forests. As the train approaches the Czech border, tensions rise. Immigration and customs inspections lie ahead.

It is not a congenial spot for a member of the underground. The Nazis have long been aware that the Socialists and Communists were running opposition activities out of the Czech borderlands, as well as out of Prague. But recently the Nazis had taken an additional interest in the area. The westerly rim of Czechoslovakia, known as the Sudetenland, was a predominantly German-speaking territory, assigned to the new nation of Czechoslovakia with the breakup of the Austro-Hungarian Empire after the Great War. In recent years a local ethnic German party had been complaining of mistreatment at the hands of the Prague government, and the German Nazis leaped to advance their claims. Czech president Edvard Beneš, a staunch anti-Nazi, was trying to steer an uneasy course between his dislike of the fascists and his country's neutrality, with only sporadic support from the Western democracies.

Franz avoids the German border officials altogether. Fourteen hours after boarding the train in Berlin, he gets off in Plauen, a small industrial city on the German side of the border known for its lace. There he is met by an older man. They establish their bona fides, and the guide talks him through the positions and habits of the border patrols.

"The illegal crossings have been a lot tougher since the Nazis got so interested in the Sudetenland," the guide tells him. "In the old days you only needed to say that you wanted to go and get soused on good beer and they were fine. They don't go along with that anymore. So look sharp, stay back fifty paces, and stick with me."

Snow lies in patches. Franz's feet are soon soaked, but there is no time to attend to them. He startles at every noise; freezes at the sight of a tree stump or a half-rotten fence. His guide simply watches and waits. No other human is to be seen, and the guide continues without interruption. Two hours later the guide turns to him. "So, we're over the border. The big job lies ahead." Franz is handed off to a succession of German immigrants, unpacking news from Germany at each stop along the way. A Berliner he doesn't recognize calls his name, asking for news of the city streets, businesses, bars—"Have all the girls in Berlin become Nazis yet?" Franz dodges him. That night Franz makes it to Prague, where a

German family hosts him in their rented rooms. He should enjoy a few days in a city without Nazis, they tell him, to say nothing of the strangeness and beauty of Prague itself.

The next day he proceeds to a pub to meet with two exiled party representatives. They warn him that the familiar precautionary measures still apply. Gestapo informers are all over the city, and they take full advantage of its democratic freedoms like everyone else: one photograph sent off to Berlin, and unfortunate consequences are sure to follow. The party leaders then devote themselves to discussing how to support the underground work in Germany. Franz thinks they overestimate the possibility that the Nazis could infiltrate the organization, but it seems that some bad experiences inform their conversations.

Franz has a few days to produce his written report. The weather is turning unpleasantly cold, and Franz, a little homesick, has no wish to postpone his departure. The evening he is to go, Franz strolls through Wenceslas Square in the center of Prague looking for a pub. If he drinks enough, he thinks, maybe he could string enough Czech together to express himself to the locals. He feels a sudden need "to talk to people who are not contaminated by fascism—to tell them about the other Germany, the better Germany."

Instead, he is suddenly greeted in German by someone he knew slightly before 1933. "What are you doing here?" the man exclaims. Another cat-and-mouse game ensues. "Vacation," Franz says nervously. "To drink good Czech beer and eat cheap."

"And not have to listen to that Nazi propaganda, right?" answers his acquaintance.

"I'm not interested in politics," Franz replies quickly. He disentangles himself from the encounter and takes a different route back to the house in case he's being followed. Then he makes his way back to Berlin. This time his guide across the border is a woman with a red market satchel, which Franz worries could be clearly visible in the fair, springlike weather. The Sudetenland seems more ominous on the return trip. Suddenly Franz hears a voice in German addressing the woman: "Halt! Where are you going? What do you have in there?" Franz hangs back, unseen. The border is hot today—one wrong step could mean a charge of treason. But the woman is allowed to pass, Franz is undetected, and he reaches his train to Dresden and Berlin with an hour to spare.[8]

John Sieg was involved in many such border crossings. In March 1937 he was offered an exciting new opportunity by Karl Hellborn, a member of the Neukölln group and stationmaster for the Berlin suburb of Charlottenburg. Hellborn used his union connections to get Sieg a job at the freight yards of the Stettiner train station, in a northern zone of the city.[9] The idea appealed to Sieg, who had lacked regular employment for four years since the *Rote Fahne* had been closed down. Barely thirty-three, he had already done stints as a Ford factory worker, a freelance writer, a staff reporter, and a semiemployed construction worker. Now the Reichsbahn—the German state railway—would provide him with his final and most dramatic career.

Once Sieg proved himself loading freight, he was offered a permanent position. This required him to submit an official autobiography to the Nazi officials. It had to be a sanitized version, of course. (This was a necessary formality. Officials could easily find evidence of his Communist past, but they could not afford to disqualify the millions of former Communists and Socialists from employment.) Sieg's carefully written statement explained that he had interrupted his studies at the City College of Detroit because "my loyalty to Germany was so strong that I returned to Berlin." His literary career consisted of "translations and travel writing." Unfortunately, he added, "I was unemployed for certain periods."[10] He declined to mention that his loss of employment at the *Rote Fahne* was accompanied by a brutal SS beating and three months' imprisonment. Likewise, Sieg omitted his wife's former secretarial position with a Jewish lawyer who had fled the country. The autobiography was a good illustration of *Gleichschaltung:* simply erase the inconvenient aspects of the past, and everyone emerges as a satisfied beneficiary of the regime.

In 1936, Hermann Grosse, the *Rote Fahne* city editor who had brought John Sieg to the paper, emigrated to Czechoslovakia. The following year he sent word to introduce some new members to the group.

Walter Husemann, another reporter from his stable, was a dark-haired young man with fierce eyes. His beat of labor and court proceedings had placed him on the front lines. In the final days of the Weimar Republic, Nazi paramilitary squads would execute workers accused of disorder, even if they had been tried and acquitted in court. After Husemann covered one such incident, he was placed on a hit list himself. Following a failed assassination attempt, he fled from Berlin to the western cities of Essen, Cologne, and Mannheim, where he wrote for local Communist newspapers.[11]

Husemann was well known in Communist circles, but the greater celebrity was his partner and future wife, the actress Marta Wolter. Many of the Neukölln Communists recognized the slender blonde from her performances in Brecht and Weisenborn's stage production of *Die Mutter* (*The Mother*), and in Brecht's film *Kuhle Wampe*. Marta was only twenty-four, but she had already led an eventful life. Trained as a seamstress, she enjoyed a brief but glowing career in Communist theater. She met Husemann in 1930 and joined him in Mannheim in 1932, where he was swept up in the first wave of Nazi arrests in January 1933. After his release the couple returned to Berlin, where Husemann lived illegally.

Marta Wolter sold novellas and short stories to Berlin dailies to make ends meet, sometimes submitting the blacklisted Husemann's work under her own name. Her old theater friend Günther Weisenborn helped place her writing in Ullstein publications. When the Gestapo searched Husemann's rooms, Weisenborn gave Marta a place to stay. Walter Husemann concentrated on producing underground flyers and activating contacts to other Communist networks, such as the Jewish group that gathered around the young electrician Herbert Baum in central Berlin.[12]

On November 26, 1936, Husemann, his father, and Marta Wolter were arrested for sheltering a fugitive Communist official. Husemann's brother Wilhelm managed to escape to Moscow, but Walter and his father were sent to the concentration camp at Sachsenhausen without trial. Marta Wolter was consigned to the Moringen concentration camp, also without trial, from March until June 1937. She was said to owe her release to a camp visit from Heinrich Himmler, the head of the SS; Himmler ordered her to be freed because she looked too "Aryan" to be there.[13] Dark-haired Walter Husemann was not as lucky. In 1937 he was transferred to Buchenwald, where he worked as the camp librarian.

Marta Wolter rejoined John Sieg's Neukölln circle soon after her release, and served as a link between the workers and her theater friends. Günther Weisenborn, ever supportive, introduced her to his friend Harro Schulze-Boysen, whom he had met at a left-wing student gathering in 1932.[14] Marta soon joined Schulze-Boysen's floating left-wing salon of theater people, artists, and aristocrats, most of whom detested the fascists and sought outlets for their rebellion. After Walter Husemann was released from Buchenwald a few months later, he, too, was welcomed into the group. He and Marta married soon after.

Harro Schulze-Boysen and his wife both came from money, and took special pleasure in inviting their less privileged friends to spend the day on Harro's sailboat. A set of photos survive from the spring of 1938, when Weisenborn invited Marta along for a lakeside holiday. Barely a year out of the concentration camp, the young woman appears in a strapless bathing suit, laughing at Weisenborn and Schulze-Boysen as they try to hack off a slice of corned beef.

CHAPTER 10

The Gentlemen's Club

1937

ARVID HARNACK WAS STILL SEEKING A COURSE OF ACTION, AND he agonized over his next step. Germans were increasingly surrounded by the high walls of Nazi propaganda, and mounting censorship and travel restrictions left them more isolated all the time.

Arvid Harnack and Adam Kuckhoff turned to the radio in search of uncensored news, but the Nazis had made it both illegal and impractical to monitor foreign broadcasts. It was hard enough to lay one's hands on a working shortwave set, and by the time the device was placed in a secure location and tuned to a foreign station, the broadcast was often over.[1]

But the Harnacks and the Kuckhoffs firmly believed that the German people should know what was being said about them in the outside world, and the broadcasts offered crucial evidence. Mildred and Greta translated the banned speeches of Roosevelt and Churchill from English to German, and their husbands helped distribute them to various discussion circles.

Mildred was unhappy; homesick for America and worried about her mother, who was terminally ill. She wrote plaintive letters to friends back in the States, asking if there were any available teaching jobs. But it was the depths of the Depression, and responses were not encouraging.[2]

In early 1937, Mildred Harnack traveled back to America to visit her ailing mother. She lectured at New York University, Haverford College, and other universities, seeking recommendations and job openings along the way. Her inquiries were once again fruitless. Mildred's family and friends found her greatly changed: reticent, austere, and tense.

That January, the Nazis tightened their grip on the German civil service. They proclaimed a new law that allowed them to dismiss any tenured employee who was judged untrustworthy. Soon ninety percent of the Prussian civil service were members of the Nazi Party. One of them was Arvid Harnack, who joined in May 1937 and became party member number 4,153,569.[3] This number hardly qualified him as one of Hitler's favored "old fighters," nor did it include him as one of the "March Violets" that suddenly blossomed in the spring of 1933. Arvid's Nazi Party card indicated that he was a practical man who worked for the government and wished to keep his job. Party membership notwithstanding, Harnack continued to offer information to the Soviets and the Americans, as well as to antifascist circles in other government ministries and circles of German society.[4]

Arvid and Mildred Harnack had deep and strong ties to the United States, and continued to look to America for personal and political support. Ambassador Dodd's embassy offered them a sympathetic hearing and a safe haven, but his concern did not take them far. Few U.S. officials shared Dodd's sense of urgency, and many of them considered him amateurish for putting his commitment to human rights on a par with traditional matters of state.

Dodd had arrived in Berlin in 1933 full of nostalgia for the Germany of his student days, but he was alarmed by the country's transformation at the hands of the Nazis. His initial mandate was to represent the interests of American firms, such as claims from National City Bank and Chase Manhattan on massive German loans that had gone into default. But as conditions worsened, Dodd transferred his attentions to American and German Jews who came under attack.

One of Dodd's biggest frustrations was the inability of Americans at home to grasp the nature of the Nazi threat. In November 1934 he met with Frank Gannett, a prominent New York newspaper owner and friend of President Roosevelt's, who was seeking an interview with Hitler. Gannet informed Dodd that many "well-to-do people at home . . . are arguing for a Fascist system there, with a sort of Hitler to head it. They use the facts of perfect order and absence of crime in Germany as arguments for such a move." Dodd's diary records that he "told [Gannett] there were other phases of the regime which would shock Americans to the limit."

But Dodd was swimming against the current. In 1936 the Nazis staged a major public relations campaign in the form of the Berlin Olympics. There were widespread calls to boycott the Games, but the plans went forward in triumph.[5] The Nazis took the trouble of removing visible signs of anti-Semitism from Berlin for the duration of the Games, and welcomed the throngs of visitors with a carefully managed veneer of normalcy.

In early 1937, *National Geographic* took the bait, and published an article called "Changing Berlin," written by Douglas Chandler, an American Nazi sympathizer. In his eyes, the Hitler Youth was "a substitute for Scout training," while the Nazis' Winter Aid, a barely veiled extortion racket, was "aiding the needy," supported by "voluntary workers contributing their services." Chandler closed with a vignette of small boys singing "that moving modern national song," the Horst Wessel storm trooper anthem. Chandler neglected to remind his American audience of the recent Nuremberg Laws that stripped Jews of their civil and political rights, and omitted the Nazis' four-year record of purges, prisons, and concentration camps.[6] Instead, the *National Geographic*'s vast American readership was shown an enviable picture of German peace and prosperity.

Over 1936 and 1937, Ambassador Dodd's attitude toward Hitler, Göring, and Goebbels shifted from indignation to outright repulsion. He began to renege on his duties as ambassador, boycotting official functions and avoiding face-to-face meetings with top Nazi officials. He watched in disgust as American businessmen cut deals with the Nazis and European democracies acquiesced to Hitler's brash forays abroad. He devoted an increasing amount of time to persecuted individuals and asylum-seekers who would have been assigned to a lower-level consul in less dire times.

By early 1937, Dodd, plagued by nervous headaches and what he called "unbearable tension," was ready to leave. Washington asked him to hold on until March 1938.[7] For the rest of the year his diary served as an outlet to denounce the latest Nazi outrages. On April 17 he described a list of ninety-one Germans who had been deprived of their nationality, including a child of two.[8] The following week he received a telegram from Washington regarding the case of Helmut Hirsch, a twenty-one-year-old Jew who had been accused of trying to bomb a Nazi rally in Nuremberg. The cable described Hirsch as a U.S. citizen (his father had lived in America) and instructed Dodd to visit the Foreign Office to press for a legitimate trial. Dodd returned from his visit in a state of disbelief, having been told that Hirsch "must be executed though he did not actually try to commit the crime."[9] Dodd, whose son was Hirsch's age, threw himself into the effort to save the young man, and sent a personal appeal to Hitler himself, to no avail. On June 4, the ambassador recorded that "poor Hirsch had his head chopped off this morning at sunrise."[10]

Dodd had agreed to stay in Germany until March 1938, but suddenly Roosevelt informed him that he would be recalled at the end of 1937. The president was reacting to "pressure" (though Dodd was uncertain whether it originated with the Nazis or his enemies in Washington). The ambassador and his family sailed for the United States on the last day of 1937. Germany had been a heartbreaking assignment, and the last of his long career. (Within a few months Dodd's wife was struck down by a heart attack, and the ambassador himself died two years later.)[11]

American policy was in a muddle, and the nation's amateur diplomats were sending mixed messages to the world. Roosevelt understood that Europe was heading toward war, and knew that in a contest between Germany and Britain, he would favor the United Kingdom. But he muted his sentiments, knowing that he faced both clear-cut opposition and public apathy that could quickly turn into disapproval. For most Americans, Europe's problems still seemed very far away.

But Washington was not much better informed than the public. As of 1937, as the Nazis stepped up their persecution of the Jews and Hitler completed his plan to dismember Europe, the U.S. government's understanding of Germany was partial, contradictory, and badly out-of-date.

One senior American diplomat later wrote, "It must be confessed that our Intelligence organization in 1940 was primitive and inadequate. It was timid, parochial, and operating strictly in the tradition of the Spanish-American War."[12]

This dismal state of affairs had a simple explanation: there was, to put it bluntly, no functioning U.S. intelligence service. The Office of Strategic Services (the OSS, which would eventually evolve into the CIA) was still five years away from creation. The army and the navy had intelligence services, but the two branches did not collaborate. Their officers were cynically described as military attachés who would go out and count tanks when parades passed by.[13]

Embassy officials gathered data that pertained to their individual departments, especially in the all-important spheres of trade and economics. But no one collated or analyzed information that arrived from the various departments and countries before it was sent to the White House, which was itself chronically short-staffed and consumed with breaking domestic crises. In desperation, Roosevelt turned to a socialite friend, Vincent Astor. Astor had set up an amateur spy club with his friends at a town house on New York City's Upper East Side, and liked to send Roosevelt intelligence reports from his yacht as he circled the globe.[14] Such antics drove the British intelligence professionals to distraction.

The Americans' disarray had important consequences for the antifascist circles in Berlin. Arvid Harnack now had a secure position at the heart of the Reich's Economics Ministry. As a trusted member of the Nazi Party he enjoyed access to important officials and documents. He had intentionally positioned himself to do whatever he could to undermine the Nazi regime. He considered himself a Marxist, but thanks to his experiences in Wisconsin, his wife's patriotism, and the couple's many friendships at the embassy, he also closely identified with the Americans and sought ways to share his intelligence with them. The problem was that the Americans had no one in place to make use of it.

Part of the Americans' complacence resulted from an acute lack of information. The German opposition saw Adolf Hitler's book *Mein Kampf*, published in two volumes over 1925 and 1926, as a chilling blueprint for Nazi policies to come. But non-German readers were left in the dark, and there was no initial interest in an English translation. When one was finally commissioned for the British and U.S. markets in 1933, the German government demanded the right to approve the text, and excised the most extreme anti-Semitic and militaristic passages. (One example was the deletion of Hitler's opinion that Germany should have gassed "twelve to fifteen thousand Jews" during World War I.) Furthermore, the English-language edition gave no indication where the deletions occurred.[15]

Greta Lorke shared the desire to alert the West to Hitler's intentions, and the book offered her an unusual opportunity. In 1936 she moved to a new apartment, where a neighbor introduced her to another tenant, a picaresque Irishman named James Murphy. Greta learned that Murphy, said to be a defrocked priest, was a professional translator. (He had recently translated works by the eminent physicist Max Planck.) Murphy had been taken ill and needed an assistant on an upcoming project. Greta's landlord vouched for her competence and industriousness.

When Greta met with Murphy, she learned that his illness was closely linked to the consumption of alcohol. Soon Murphy asked her to assist him on his next assignment: a complete translation of *Mein Kampf*, including the racist, militarist, and anti-Semitic passages. Greta found the work repellent but significant—she wanted the Western democracies to understand Hitler's menace. The "Murphy edition" of *Mein Kampf*, published in 1939, was one of the first complete translations to appear in English.[16]

Berlin had become an anxious and foreboding city, but personal lives continued to unfold. In 1937, Adam Kuckhoff and Greta Lorke decided to get married. There was a pressing reason: at the age of thirty-four, Greta was four months pregnant. Adam was still legally married to Gertrud, his first wife's sister, and he was not eager to ask for a divorce. He balked at the idea of getting an *Ariernachweis*, the proof of "Aryan purity" that was now required for marriage in Nazi Germany. Relatives, churches, and registries across the country had to be contacted for evidence of ancestry.

Furthermore, Adam worried over the prospect of a child. They lived in dangerous times, when friends were disappearing into prisons and concentration camps. "The child will need you for years," he told Greta. "What if something happens to you?" But she insisted on having the baby. The couple agreed that marriage was important for the child's sake, and they assembled the required documents.[17]

Adam and Greta's August wedding party gathered their oldest and closest friends, many of whom occupied sensitive positions. The best man was Greta's old friend Hans Hartenstein, whom she had known since her student days. Hartenstein had been wrestling with his own political problems. A longtime Social Democrat, he avoided joining the Nazi Party after the takeover, and retained his position in the Economics Ministry because of his indispensable specialization in currency policy.

Hartenstein's career at the Economics Ministry ended around the time of Greta's wedding, when he was recommended for a promotion that required Nazi Party membership. Hartenstein refused, and left the civil service for private industry. He quietly supported the Kuckhoffs' resistance activities, and remained Greta's loyal and trusted friend.[18]

The other witness at the wedding was another prominent Social Democrat, Adolf Grimme, the former Prussian minister of culture. Grimme, who had once moved in circles with Thomas Mann and Albert Einstein, lost his position in the political shuffle that immediately preceded the Nazi takeover. He now filled his time by freelancing for publishers, studying languages, and writing a scholarly commentary on John the Baptist.[19] He also worked with Adam Kuckhoff's antifascist circle, drafting anti-Nazi flyers and serving as a link to the dissenting Confessing Lutherans. Sometimes Grimme brought Lutheran flyers for Arvid Harnack to analyze. Grimme's stolid Lutherans responded to different rhetoric than the leftist intellectuals. They objected to Hitler as "plebeian," and chastised Göring for his greed and Goebbels for his "big mouth."[20]

Hartenstein and Grimme maintained their august bearing. At the wedding ceremony, Greta wryly noted that the registrar was visibly impressed by the two men, who outranked him by countless rungs in the German civil service universe. The local official was still obliged to order them to attention and give the "Heil Hitler" salute, an instruction they pointedly declined to follow. This threw the petty bureaucrat into a lather of officiousness, discomfort, and awe. The gathered company found him so comical that they decided not to be irritated.

The city around them was suffused with suffering and fear, but Greta managed to enjoy her wedding anyway. It was a day, she recalled, "when the very air tasted like wine."[21]

CHAPTER 11

\ \ \

A Faraway Country

1937–1938

HITLER WANTED A WAR, AND HIS OPPONENTS FOUND IT INCREASingly difficult to see any way to avert it. They believed that no matter where the conflict began, it would necessarily lead to a confrontation with the Western democracies. But Arvid Harnack and his genteel relations found it astonishingly hard to engage the very nations that had the most to lose.

Harnack and his circle made a point of maintaining contact with the U.S. embassy, but its relevance was diminishing by the day. When Dodd was recalled in November 1937, he was replaced by Hugh Wilson, a career diplomat who immediately made it known that he would take a softer line toward Hitler. One of his first actions was to accept an invitation to the annual Nazi Party rally at Nuremberg, which Dodd had been boycotting. Dodd tersely commented that "Mr. Wilson . . . was very welcome to the Nazis."[1]

More cordial gestures followed. In January 1938, Nazi SS officials Heinrich Himmler and Reinhard Heydrich invited police from around the world to tour their new criminal police headquarters in Berlin. Edmund Patrick Coffey, head of the FBI's new crime laboratory, was one of the honored guests. The Nazi newspaper *Völkischer Beobachter* heralded the FBI official's visit with the headline "German Security Police as Model," describing Coffey's "great pleasure" at the work of the German police forces.[2] German antifascists were appalled.

Many American businesses profited from a close relationship to the regime. One of these was John Sieg's old employer, the Ford Motor Company, run by the notorious anti-Semite Henry Ford. The company had opened its German branch in 1925, in time to profit from Hitler's massive roadworks. The Nazis' military mobilization represented a Ford windfall, and between 1934 and 1938, company revenues increased 400 percent. The Nazis were pleased to officially designate Ford a German company, making it eligible for government contracts. The German plants could not meet the increased demand. Prebuilt components were secretly imported from the United States to complete the 3,150 trucks needed for the incursion into Czechoslovakia planned for 1938. In July 1938 the Nazis awarded Henry Ford the Grand Cross of the German Eagle, the highest decoration a foreigner could receive. Ford's U.S. operations were still providing trucks to the German army as late as 1941.[3]

November 7, 1938, brought a major political development. A seventeen-year-old Polish Jewish student named Herschel Grynszpan, distraught over his parents' deportation from Germany to Poland, entered the Germany embassy in Paris and shot an official (who was unrelated to the deportation). The diplomat died two days later, and the Nazis used the incident as an excuse to unleash a wave of violence against Germany's Jews. The event came to be known as Kristallnacht.

The following week, U.S. secretary of state Cordell Hull recalled his ambassador in protest, leaving a chargé d'affairs to handle outstanding matters in Berlin. The Nazis retaliated by withdrawing the German ambassador to the United States. The two countries would not restore diplomatic relations until the end of the war. For the Harnacks and the Kuckhoffs, this meant the loss of an important American haven and potential advocate.

They had few other places to turn. The French government was enmeshed in complicated negotiations with both the Nazi regime and its own vexing Communist Party. The British seemed to offer a better option—at least they had the benefit of their professional Secret Intelligence Service, begun in 1909. Arvid's cousin Dietrich Bonhoeffer, who had served as the pastor for the German Lutheran church in London, worked tirelessly to cultivate allies in the United Kingdom. But the British also responded to the Nazi regime with ambivalence. Winston Churchill's 1935 book *Great Contemporaries* was published after two years of Nazi rule. Germans had been wantonly beaten to death by thugs acting in the name of the regime. Leading figures from opposition parties had been held hostage, first in "wild camps," then in permanent concentration camps. Jews had been progressively stripped of their rights, and the German legal system had been attacked and corrupted at every level. Yet Churchill still found the evidence inconclusive:

> We cannot tell whether Hitler will be the man who will once again let loose upon the world another war in which civilization will irretrievably succumb, or whether he will go down in history as the man who restored honour and peace of mind to the great Germanic nation and brought it back serene, helpful and strong, to the forefront of the European family circle.[4]

That left the Russians. In intelligence terms, the Soviets held many practical advantages. Secret police and espionage agencies were long-established institutions in Russian society, and had an impressive international reach. The Soviets had liberally seeded their embassies with intelligence scouts (such as Sergei Bessonov, one of the officials who cultivated Arvid Harnack in 1932), and drew on networks of Communist sympathizers around the world.

In late 1936, an obscure encounter transpired that would determine the fate of the Harnacks and the Kuckhoffs.

That December, two stocky middle-aged men met in Moscow. Both were survivors of the savage early decades of international communism. Their encounter took place in the "chocolate house," a small brown building on a side street near the Kremlin that housed the Intelligence Service of the Soviet army.

Jan Berzin, the Soviet officer behind the desk, was a forty-six-year-old Latvian with cropped, graying hair and a falcon's gaze. Director of the Red Army Intelligence Service, he had weathered some of the most violent struggles of the Old Bolsheviks at the dawn of the revolution.

Berzin's guest was a stolid forty-two-year-old Pole named Leopold Trepper. Trepper was the embodiment of Adolf Hitler's worst nightmares. "I became a Communist," he declared, "because I am a Jew." Like Hitler, Trepper had been born in an outpost of the vast Austro-

Hungarian Empire, his birthplace ceded to Poland after World War I. Trepper led a peripatetic youth, abandoning Poland in the 1920s in reaction to a rash of anti-Semitism. In Palestine he joined the local Communist Party and organized Arab citrus workers to strike against Jewish landowners, to the ire of British authorities. In 1928 his community in Palestine was broken up, and most of his fellow Communists left for the Soviet Union.[5] The British deported Trepper, who went first to France and then, in the summer of 1932, to the USSR. On his way he passed through Berlin, where he observed the Nazis' momentum and worried that the German Communists weren't taking them seriously enough.

Once in Moscow, Trepper enrolled in the University for National Minorities, which included some seven hundred students in twenty different sections.[6] But he also joined a larger closed community of several thousand international Communist agents-in-waiting.

Trepper received intensive instruction in the Soviet intelligence system, which was divided into three branches. Trepper was attached to Soviet military intelligence under the command of Jan Berzin, who cultivated international Communist militants and sent them out under cover to report back to Moscow. The Comintern had a parallel network of agents, also mostly non-Soviets. The third branch of intelligence was the NKVD, the internal state security. The much-feared secret police was responsible for the control of foreign agents on Soviet soil, but was always ready to extend its mandate.

Trepper and Berzin agreed that the Soviets needed to do more to monitor the Nazi threat, and they contrived a plan for a vast network of agents across Europe, with an outpost in Germany itself.

Trepper and Berzin were not alone in their concern, but already, political alignments were not as simple as they seemed. After 1933, Moscow's exile community swelled with hundreds of Germans fleeing the Nazis. Their arrival coincided with Stalin's growing anxiety that he was losing his grip on the Soviet Union and the Communist International apparatus. Stalin made noises of solidarity to welcome the exiled German comrades, but he regarded them as more of a threat than an asset. The German Communists had a long history of factionalism and insubordination, and many of the artists and intellectuals who washed up in Moscow had never bothered to join the party at all. More disturbingly,

Stalin knew that many German leftists supported his blood enemy, Leon Trotsky, who had once nearly derailed Stalin's path to power. Trotsky would not get a second chance.

Stalin reacted with brutal resolve. In 1934 he orchestrated the assassination of his perceived rival Sergey Kirov. This event served as an excuse for a massive campaign of arrests and executions, whose scope and savagery has had few parallels in history.

Stalin's agents began by rounding up leading Soviet Communist Party members and subjecting them to highly contrived show trials in connection with Kirov's murder. The public watched in confusion as Old Bolsheviks, who only recently had been held up as heroes of the revolution, were publicly humiliated, tortured into unlikely confessions, and executed. Trotsky had been driven into exile years earlier, but now anyone with any remote connection to him was in peril. The arrests spiraled into the thousands, then hundreds of thousands. Over 1937 and 1938, millions of Soviets were dragged off to labor camps, most of them never to return.

Informed guesses place the casualties of Stalin's Great Purge, including those who died in the camps, at nine to ten million.[7] The numbers are painfully uncertain. The Soviets kept less meticulous records of their victims than the Nazis did. There was no postwar liberation of Stalin's prisoners, or an international tribunal for his crimes. The scope of Stalin's atrocities were obscured for almost two decades, and their full details will never be known.

Foreign Communists were directly in the line of fire, and Stalin reserved special vitriol for the Germans. His victims included Hugo Eberlin, one of the founders of the KPD; four members of the German Politburo; and ten members of the Central Committee.[8] John Sieg's colleagues from the *Rote Fahne* suffered heavy casualties. Former editor in chief and Central Committee member Heinz Neumann, once a Stalin confidant, was shot in 1937, accused of hiring a traitorous reporter for the paper in 1930.[9] Other *Rote Fahne* victims included editors in chief Heinrich Susskind and Werner Hirsch, and four of their assistant editors.[10] In April 1938 the German representative on the Comintern's Executive Committee reported that 842 German antifascists had been arrested by the Soviets.[11]

Bertolt Brecht, with his unfailing instinct for self-preservation, managed to steer clear of Moscow over this period. He puzzled over events from his outpost in Denmark, manically listing friends and colleagues in Moscow who had disappeared:

> koltsov too arrested in moscow, my last connection there. nobody knows anything about tretiakov, who is supposed to have been a "japanese spy". nobody knows anything about [carola] neher who is supposed to have done some business for the trotskyists in prague on her husband's instructions . . . literature and art are up the creek, political theory has gone to the dogs . . .[12]

Brecht's collaborator on the *Kuhle Wampe* screenplay, experimental novelist Ernst Ottwald, was denounced for artistic "diversionism" in the Soviet press. He disappeared into a Soviet concentration camp, where he was shot in 1943. When *Kuhle Wampe*'s blond starlet, Marta Wolter, was arrested in Germany with her fiancé, Walter Husemann, in 1936, Husemann's brother Wilhelm had counted himself lucky to escape to Moscow. But now he was arrested and shot by the Soviets.[13]

Brecht's amber-eyed muse, Carola Neher, was another early victim. The actress who created the role of Polly in *Threepenny Opera* had fled to Moscow with her second husband in 1934, and the couple was arrested two years later on suspicion of links to Trotsky. Her husband was shot and Neher was sentenced to ten years' hard labor. She failed to complete her term. One report stated that Neher was loaded onto a transport to a labor camp in Central Asia in 1942 and died shortly afterward of typhoid fever. A later account holds that she was shot in a Soviet prison camp in 1941.[14]

Even the Soviets fighting in Spain could be vulnerable. One was Leopold Trepper's contact Jan Berzin, the Old Bolshevik who headed Soviet military intelligence. Berzin was sent to Spain in 1936 to help organize the Loyalists' defense. A practical man, he complained that Stalin's purge of the internationalists was damaging his field operations.[15] Berzin was recalled to Moscow in June 1937, arrested the following May, and executed six weeks later.

With Berzin's execution, Stalin forfeited one of the most successful intelligence officers in the world. Berzin had recruited a spectacular network of spies that was now positioned across Europe, crucial to the war ahead. But Stalin seemed to be determined to destroy his country's military capacity. Over the course of the two-year purge, 30,000 Soviet officers were eliminated through imprisonment, torture, or execution. These included 3 of the 5 marshals, 14 of 16 army commanders, 60 of 67 corps commanders, 136 of 199 divisional commanders, and 221 of 397 brigade commanders.[16] Their posts were assigned to inexperienced and incompetent personnel without a unified vision of strategy or command.

The impact of Stalin's purges traveled far beyond the Soviet Union. The Soviet diplomatic corps was decimated, including the embassy staff in Berlin. Boris Gordon, one of Arvid Harnack's first acquaintances at the Soviet embassy, was summoned back to Moscow in 1937 and executed. Sergei Bessonov, the economist who had arranged Harnack's trip to Russia in 1932, was recalled to Moscow and arrested that same year. Bessonov withstood months of questioning, but finally succumbed to torture and a notorious treatment called "the Conveyor," consisting of sleep deprivation and endless interrogations. The diplomat "confessed" that he had acted as an emissary for Trotsky and was sentenced to fifteen years in prison. He was shot on September 8, 1941.[17]

Five of the eight intelligence officers from the Soviet embassy in Berlin were recalled and executed.[18] Boris Vinogradov, the Soviet intelligence agent who had won Martha Dodd's heart and recruited her as a source, was shot in 1938.

Stalin's purges left the antifascists in Germany even more isolated than before. Arvid Harnack was now perfectly positioned to supply vital economic intelligence from the Reich ministry, but the Soviet embassy was gutted of diplomats and intelligence officers, leaving him without a working contact. Harnack had only the vaguest information about what was happening in Moscow, but he was distressed by the little he could learn.

In later years Martha Dodd wrote that Arvid Harnack "did not like what Stalin was doing." He "spoke vehemently" to her about it, and had "agonizing doubts about the turn of the propaganda" coming from the USSR.[19]

Fortunately, the Americans now offered him a practical alternative. At the end of 1937, the State Department appointed Donald Heath to the post of first secretary in Berlin. Heath, forty-three, was a tall Kansan with a broad mustache and an understated manner. After serving in World War I, he worked as White House correspondent for the United Press before joining the State Department. Assigned to serve under Ambassador Hugh Wilson, he stayed on in Berlin after Wilson's recall.

Heath's State Department assignment was only half of his position. He was also assigned to a secret intelligence role as monetary attaché, reporting directly to Roosevelt's treasury secretary Henry Morgenthau. This reflected the bias in Washington at the time: there was far more emphasis on monitoring German economic policies than on documenting concentration camp conditions or disenfranchisement of the Jews.

The Harnack-Heath connection began when Heath's wife met Mildred Harnack at a social occasion. Heath was excited to hear that Mrs. Harnack's husband had studied in the United States, and set out to meet him. He tracked him down at his desk in the Economics Ministry and suggested they have lunch. Arvid Harnack happily agreed.[20]

Donald Heath's needs and Arvid Harnack's intelligence were complementary, and the two men quickly forged a partnership. Harnack's work at the Economics Ministry concerned Germany's balance of payment and foreign exchange. According to one coworker, he was:

> in direct contact with all the various country desks; and his position as chief of a basic desk [trade policy] allowed him to participate in all decisions that were made. . . . He systematically acquired a reliable overview of our current economic capacity, our production and our reserves, and he evaluated our foreign trade situation at any given time. In this way, Harnack became one of the persons most knowledgeable about the state of the economy.[21]

Harnack was among the first and most important of Heath's sources. It was a struggle for Heath to explain the political profile of German antifascists like Harnack to his superiors, whose suspicions were aroused by their Nazi Party membership. Their positions within the regime, he argued, were precisely what made them useful.

Heath's informants tended to be from the second tier of government officials, approached in weekend settings in which they could speak freely. Most of them had begun their careers under the previous regime as serious and well-trained public servants. If the majority were now Nazi Party members, Heath reported to Washington, "It is indeed a practical necessity for them to be members if they are to advance or even retain their positions in the government."[22] This was a perfect description of Arvid Harnack and his friends and relations.

Heath tried to describe the attitudes of Berlin's cultivated parlor leftists to his American superiors:

> The majority of this group are inclined to be moderately Socialist in their views. They do not disapprove of the increase of state intervention and the control of industry and commerce under the National Socialist regime. What they object to is the restriction on personal liberty, freedom of thought and the present policy of military aggression, instead of international cooperation, which they feel will eventually lead to a European war.[23]

At the same time Heath was drawing on Arvid Harnack's storehouse of secret information, he and his wife, Louise, enjoyed a public friendship with Arvid and Mildred Harnack as members of Berlin's American expatriate community. Heath took his young son Donald Jr. on walks with the Harnacks to promote the appearance of an innocuous family friendship. When the men's conversation turned to intelligence matters, the boy learned to fall in step with Mildred, whom he greatly admired.[24]

Arvid Harnack was only one of Heath's many sources. Heath continued to troll Germany's economic waters, netting bigger and bigger fish, including Reichsbank director Emil Puhl and Arvid's former boss Hjalmar Schacht, a prominent banker who had helped Hitler come to power.[25] (Schacht resigned as minister of economics in 1937, in protest over the regime's military buildup and anti-Semitism.)[26]

Both Heath and his German sources understood that they were skirting the boundaries of treason. In 1937 the German government warned its citizens that providing economic information to foreigners could carry the penalty of death.[27]

On March 13, 1938, the Germans marched into Austria with the collusion of Austrian Nazis. The Nazis deliberately avoided calling it an invasion, substituting the word *Anschluss,* a term with almost tender connotations of an attachment or an embrace. A plebiscite was held a month later, under strict Nazi vigilance, which confirmed public approval by a massive majority. In September 1938, Hitler turned his sights on the Sudetenland, attacking Czech president Beneš in a Nuremberg speech.

The German public greeted these events with jubilation. Some Germans disapproved of Hitler's provocations, but there was no longer any possibility of public opposition. Tens of thousands of Germans languished in concentration camps at any given time. Political parties, trade unions, the media, and academia had all been suppressed and purged.

Propaganda Minister Joseph Goebbels was not satisfied with passivity. The regime sought universal enthusiasm, and he argued that the key lay in his new model of totalitarian communications. Under his initiative, the regime had promoted the mass production of small, inexpensive "people's radio" sets, whose dials were restricted to local stations, all of which were controlled by the Nazis. An improved design was introduced in 1938. A square brown Bakelite box with a large round speaker, the set was soon dubbed the *Goebbels-Schnauze* (Goebbels snout). The cheap radios flooded the marketplace. In the decade after the Nazis came to power, the number of German households with access to a radio almost quadrupled, reaching seventy percent of the population—ranking among the densest radio penetration in the world.[28]

Germans now had more "news" but access to far fewer sources of information. The Reich stepped up the penalties for listening to foreign broadcasts. Nazi radio wardens were instructed to convince their neighbors to listen to party programs, to report foreign-broadcast listeners, and to forward local feedback on programming back to a central agency. When they reported that audiences were tiring of endless propaganda and speeches, the ministry sweetened the mix with light musical offerings.[29]

German antifascists condemned the maddening docility of the "ninety percent" who had acquiesced to the regime, but their own "ten percent" was eroding from exile, execution, and defeatism.

Nonetheless, the seeds of an anti-Hitler conspiracy continued to take root, some to wither, some to grow. One plot enlisted ten former Prussian police officers who had been ransomed from German concentration camps. In 1938 they planned an attack on Hitler, but the conspiracy ran into difficulties and dissolved.[30] Another 1938 conspiracy looked more promising. It was spearheaded by a member of Arvid Harnack's clan, Ministry of Justice official Hans von Dohnanyi. As Hitler's machinations against Czechoslovakia came to a head, Dohnanyi enlisted an impressive circle of German military officers and intellectuals, among them psychiatrist Karl Bonhoeffer (Dietrich and Klaus's father).

The plot was straightforward enough. Hitler's plans for aggression constituted such an egregious breach of international relations, Dohnanyi argued, that it would surely trigger a swift retaliation from the Western powers. This would embolden his critics in the German military, and disgrace him in the eyes of the German people. The Dohnanyi group would step neatly forward and take Hitler into custody, then set about getting German democracy back on track.

The assignments were handed out with care. Dohnanyi assembled a criminal dossier on Hitler. The eminent Dr. Bonhoeffer prepared to certify that Hitler was mentally ill. Army relations would be handled by General Ludwig Beck, a conservative opponent of Hitler's who had recently been forced to resign as chief of staff. Hitler's arrest was assigned to military intelligence officer Hans Oster, aide to Admiral Wilhelm Canaris. There was no doubt about the goal, but the group disagreed on tactics. Oster believed that Hitler must be assassinated for the plot to succeed, while others hoped he could be institutionalized. Oster and his supporters therefore planned a conspiracy within the conspiracy, the staging of an unfortunate "incident" during the arrest that would lead to Hitler's death.[31]

The conspiracy hinged on one critical event to trigger the plan: an open confrontation between Hitler and the governments of Britain and France. Hitler had summoned the British and French prime ministers to Munich. As the meeting progressed, a call came in from London to say that the British now expected to go to war against Germany on Czechoslovakia's behalf. Back in Germany, the conspirators' phones were ringing with calls from new supporters volunteering to assist in the coup.

Then came the stunning news: on September 29, 1938, the parties reached an agreement. The British prime minister expressed his relief to his countrymen in a radio address: "How horrible, fantastic, incredible it is that we should be digging trenches and trying on gas masks here, because of a quarrel in a faraway country between people of whom we know nothing."[32] Germany gained the Sudeten region, and Hitler's popularity surged.

Back in Berlin, the conspirators gathered in Hans Oster's apartment for a gloomy postmortem. "You see, gentlemen," one of them mused bitterly,

> for this poor foolish nation he is once again our big dearly beloved Führer, sent from God, and we—we are a little pile of reactionary and disgruntled officers or politicians who dared to put pebbles in the way of the greatest statesman of all times at the moment of his greatest triumph.[33]

In May 1939, Donald Heath told his Washington superiors that his German antifascist sources were sorely disillusioned with the European democracies. They believed that "a firm stand would be made against Hitler," in which case he "would have been afraid to go to war and the check to his prestige would have been sufficient to bring down his regime." France and Britain's approach was a bitter disappointment. Heath concluded that "their one hope is in President Roosevelt, in whose democratic ideals and ability they have a very considerable belief."[34]

Many German antifascists, including the Harnacks, labored to win the Americans over to their cause, but the Nazis appeared to be winning the public relations campaign. The antifascists found their united support chiefly among German exiles and Jewish communities in New York and California. The Roosevelt administration trod cautiously, under mounting pressure to steer clear of Europe altogether. Memories of World War I were still raw, and "America First" isolationists argued against any involvement in the mounting conflict. American Nazi groups flourished. They littered New York subways with anti-Semitic literature and held a mass rally in Madison Square Garden in February 1939 that drew a crowd of 22,000. Jewish protesters were met by American storm troopers who beat them on the street in front of Macy's.

U.S. embassy officials in Berlin were obliged to keep a low profile. The United States had never replaced its ambassador, but in May 1939 a new chargé was appointed. Alexander Kirk was a laconic American diplomat of the old school, but in the eyes of his aide George Kennan, he was a decent and intelligent man who "despised the Nazis and held them at arm's length with a barbed irony." Kirk, the heir to a cleaning-product fortune, liked to deflate pompous Nazis by extending his hand and declaring, "My line is soap. What's yours?"[35]

Kirk was supportive of the German opposition, and held a number of secret meetings with Count Helmuth von Moltke, a member of Dietrich Bonhoeffer's resistance circles. Moltke, a political visionary, could already perceive the seeds of the Nazis' destruction, and was studying the American Federalist Papers for ideas on reconstituting post-Nazi Europe. But few of Kirk's superiors in Washington shared his sympathies.

In the summer of 1939, Arvid and Mildred Harnack traveled to Washington, hoping to recruit American support for their cause. Arvid Harnack's official assignment was to guarantee international copper and aluminum supplies to Germany before war broke out. He fulfilled his public duty with U.S. trade officials who were happy to supply Germany's arsenal.

But Harnack also wrote a secret memorandum to the State Department, offering his assistance against the Nazis.[36] He succeeded in meeting privately with officials from the U.S. Treasury Department, probably with the help of Donald Heath. Tragically, the U.S. officials dismissed him out of hand.[37] Even with the Nazi takeovers of Austria and Czechoslovakia and the impending crisis in Poland, Americans believed they could still keep Europe's troubles at arm's length. They did not want their prejudices to be disrupted by information. More traditional American diplomats took a dim view of German dissident officials, regarding them as "suspicious," and were not even interested in their intelligence value.

The Harnacks stayed with Mildred's family in Maryland, but her relatives found her increasingly remote. They thought Arvid was even worse—cold and uncommunicative, a "typical German." The couple were undoubtedly aware that there were Nazi spies in Washington and that they were monitoring the Harnacks closely. A frank conversation, with even a close relative, could always be repeated to the wrong person. But the effect of their caution was unfortunate; at least one of Mildred's family members took Arvid's demeanor as proof that he was a zealous Nazi.

The Harnacks returned to Germany in mid-August 1939. The Nazis had been busy in their absence.

\ \ \

CHAPTER 12

The Dinner Party

1938–1940

ONE EVENING IN 1940—SHE COULDN'T RECALL EXACTLY WHEN—
Greta Kuckhoff put on a freshly ironed dress, a precious pair of Italian
silk stockings, and a cape, and set off with her husband to a dinner party.[1]
It was a big occasion. Their host, Herbert Engelsing, was an executive
producer at the Tobis Film Company, making him a major player in the
German movie industry. Greta was less than enthusiastic. Their son,
Ule, was still a toddler, and she felt uncomfortable leaving him at home,
but there were compelling reasons to go. Herbert Engelsing could help
Adam get work. Since Adam had left his regular employment, he was
concentrating more on his own writing, and they needed the additional
income from contract work for the Reich's film studios.[2]

Adam was still striving for literary success, but he had to balance it
against other considerations. He was well aware that by now, any form of
writing—or not writing—was a political act in Germany. Lion Feuchtwanger and Thomas Mann published screeds of anti-Nazi essays and fiction from their safe havens in America, but this was not possible for those
who had stayed behind. Adam Kuckhoff belonged to a growing school of
writers who used coded situations to critique German political realities.
Many chose to describe the calamity of World War I as a warning against
the next one. Others created character studies of men who sold out to vicious interests in the name of ambition, or who withdrew into ineffectual
silence in the face of injustice.

In 1937, Rowohlt, a leading German publisher, released Adam's novel *Der Deutsche von Bayencourt* (*The German from Bayencourt*), adapted from a play he had written during World War I. Like many writers, Adam spent his career returning to a central overarching theme: the tension between patriotism and social ethics. Adam intended his novel to be the first volume of a trilogy, but he was cheated of the opportunity to write the subsequent two volumes.

Der Deutsche von Bayencourt told the story of a German farmer named Bernard Sommer, who had settled in a small French village long before the Great War. His loyalties are tested when a stranded German patrol asks him for refuge. He is found out by the French, court-martialed, and executed. His pacifist son argues that the real enemies are the warmongers and profiteers on all sides who unleash "the boundless horror of this war."

Adam composed his book with care, but even he must have been surprised when it was favorably reviewed by both the leading Nazi newspaper, *Völkischer Beobachter,* and the leading Nazi cultural journal, *Nationalsozialistichen Monatshefte.*[3] Fascist reviewers heralded Sommer's tragic gesture as an act of patriotic self-sacrifice, and ignored the other characters' calls to pacifism and social justice. German critics called the book Kuckhoff's "masterwork," and an American professor put it on his short list of important works in his "Survey of German Literature During 1937."[4]

Film producers immediately began inquiring after movie rights, but after the Nazis' enthusiastic reception, Kuckhoff was wary. He had witnessed Goebbels's strange gift for fabricating Nazi propaganda out of anti-Nazi material. (The most notorious example was currently in production: the film version of the 1925 novel *Jud Süss,* an attack on anti-Semitism by the Jewish writer Lion Feuchtwanger, which had been transformed into an attack on Germany's Jews.) Adam found it all too easy to imagine his novel turned on its head and rendered into a Nazi propaganda film to justify war against the French.

But Engelsing and Kuckhoff had other interests in common. Both men were natives of the city of Aachen on the Belgian border, and Engelsing responded warmly to the themes and conflicts expressed in Kuckhoff's work. Engelsing had entered the film business a few years earlier as a lawyer for Tobis Film.[5] After the Nazis purged Tobis, Engelsing was offered a newly available position with the title of *Herstellungsgruppenleiter* (director of production groups). Engelsing retained his right to practice law by joining the firm of Carl Langbehn, a prominent attorney.[6]

Herbert Engelsing lived on the very knife-edge that ran between accommodating the regime and undermining it. Engelsing's law partner and close friend, Carl Langbehn, socialized in the highest Nazi circles, but he was secretly involved in conservative anti-Hitler conspiracies.[7] Engelsing himself maintained a high profile in the film business and a low profile in the resistance, but he played the role of consummate producer in both fields: making introductions, brokering deals, securing locations; then disappearing once the action was under way.

Tobis Film was a small company compared to the giant UFA, but it still released over a hundred films between 1937 and 1945.[8] Its stars included some of the greatest names in Germany, including the legendary Emil Jannings, Gustaf Gründgens, Heinrich George, and the German-Russian actress Olga Tschechowa, niece of Anton Chekhov himself.

Although Tobis Film functioned under Nazi control, it tended to produce the light comedies and romances that Goebbels used to sedate the public, instead of dealing overtly with politics. Even entertainment could have political overtones. The films of Austrian writer, actor, and director Willi Forst sounded Austrian nationalist themes all the more emphatically after his country was digested by the Reich. Other films were set in Ireland or India with story lines that disparaged the British. But most political references required reading between the lines; cultural expressions of protest that could be disavowed if necessary, just as Adam Kuckhoff and his fellow novelists critiqued the regime through deniable allegory.

Herbert Engelsing also expressed his antagonism to the Nazis obliquely. His position offered him unusual access to the highest reaches of power. The Nazi hierarchy took a keen and often competitive interest in the performing arts. Propaganda Minister Goebbels fancied himself a writer-producer and oversaw big projects, while Field Marshal Göring was more of a state patron dispensing favors. Goebbels was also a notorious enthusiast of the casting couch, while Göring took pride in his buxom wife, Emmy, best known as a stage actress who had appeared in several movie roles. The couple enjoyed hobnobbing with the film community.

In fact, Herbert and Ingeborg Engelsing owed their marriage to Field Marshal Göring and his wife. Ingeborg, a petite gamine with tousled hair and a charming grin, came from a distinguished family of lawyers and scholars. She was also a *Mischling* (half-Jew). When the couple got engaged in 1936, Ingeborg, just twenty years old, was instructed to report for her *Rassenmerkmale* (race characteristics) assessment, to be "examined, weighed, and medically measured."

"I can only remember that my upper lip was judged to be too short," she wrote later. Her photographer found a special lamp that lightened her hair and helped portray her as "tall, slim and blond."[9] Nonetheless, the permission to marry failed to come through. The couple began to look for every possible string to pull.

Fortunately, Engelsing found an advocate in one of Tobis's leading ladies, a dark-eyed soubrette named Käthe Dorsch. Hermann Göring had been smitten with her as a young (and slender) World War I flyer. Dorsch wed another, but Göring sustained his affection for her through his two subsequent marriages. The actress took advantage of his attachment to help a long list of acquaintances, many of them Jews, who were being hunted by the Gestapo. (Göring was fond of saying, "I'll decide who's a Jew and who's not.")[10] Now Käthe Dorsch took up the cause of the Engelsings. Finally, in September 1937 came the welcome news: Göring had placed the Engelsing request on Hitler's cake plate one day and emerged with his permission for the match.[11]

Göring's wife Emmy sometimes joined Käthe Dorsch's efforts, pleading special cases of Jews and leftists, winning a concentration camp release here, an exit permit there.[12] German Jews began to pass the word that the actress disapproved of their persecution, and was at heart a "good soul."[13] Emmy Göring played her cards carefully. Even if she intervened, it was in everyone's interest that she never appeared to do so.

Herbert Engelsing was one of the producers who approached Kuckhoff about filming his novel. He was surprised to find an author who resisted making a film version of his work. Engelsing's wife later described Kuckhoff's principles: "His political convictions meant more to him than prestige and profits," she observed. "So he made do with writing dialogue for apolitical films. My husband worked off and on with this talented writer, without having any idea that both Kuckhoffs were committed Marxists. He only knew that they were no Nazis, and that meant that the Schulze-Boysens [the other guests] would please them."

At that point, Greta Kuckhoff was in need of a pleasing experience. The evening, which would lead to such momentous events in their lives, began in disaster. Greta had felt nervous about the dinner from the start, and had taken special pains with her appearance. She was still a working-class girl from the factory town across the river, going to dine with the Grunewald elite. But her husband insisted on saving money by setting out for the Engelsings' elegant suburb on foot. Their path ended suddenly at a garbage dump, leaving them no choice but to climb over it, at which point they were surrounded by a pack of barking dogs. They finally gave up and took a taxi. "A fine economy measure," Greta fumed.

Ingeborg Engelsing recalled their entrance with amusement: "So they arrived, not only late, but quite tattered. Their droll descriptions of the various obstacles made us all laugh."[14] Greta was less amused, grumbling, "They'd already started eating without us.

"Adam told them the story of our odyssey partly at my expense. It was looking like one of those evenings that was going to pass without consequence." But the after-dinner conversation took a different turn. In Greta's words, it was "one that wouldn't be forgotten."[15]

The Engelsings' other guests, Harro and Libertas Schulze-Boysen, specialized in the unexpected. This was their first actual meeting, but the Kuckhoffs may have heard of Harro from Arvid Harnack, who had met him in 1935. At that point Arvid had not pursued the connection, describing it as "too dangerous."

Harro Schulze-Boysen was just entering his thirties, and cut a striking figure as a Luftwaffe lieutenant with his pale coloring and chiseled features (a friend once said he had "a head like a greyhound"). His extraordinary facility with languages led him to a position in the intelligence division of Göring's Air Ministry, analyzing foreign press reports in French, English, Swedish, Norwegian, Danish, Dutch, and Russian. In a society that was glutted with propaganda and starved for information, Harro's access to foreign news placed him among a narrow elite.

Like the Kuckhoffs and the Engelsings, Harro Schulze-Boysen was a committed antifascist, and his animosity was even more visceral. He had been born to privilege, the scion of a distinguished Prussian military family. His great-uncle, Admiral Alfred von Tirpitz, had prodded the kaiser into building up the German fleet to rival the British, helping to create the conditions that led to World War I. Harro's education included a long stay with a British family in Liverpool and tramps through the Scottish Highlands, where he perfected his English and expanded his international perspective.

Harro inherited the daring of a military man without the attendant discipline. As a teenager he was briefly imprisoned by the French for agitating against their occupation of the Ruhr. He then entered a quixotic phase that led him to various youth groups, ranging from left-wing Nazis to a congress of "revolutionary European youth." He enrolled in the university in Berlin, but soon dropped out of classes to spend more time on politics. (His family had long accepted that their boy was less likely to study for grades than to serve as a "spirited leader for his older schoolmates.")[16]

In 1931, Harro took part in a decisive political encounter in the great hall of the university. Someone had cut off the swastika ribbons from the wreaths on the student memorial, and the Nazi students were furious. The two political camps staked out their positions, one side of the hall held by Socialists, Communists, and a few centrists; the other side by the Nazis and their brownshirt supporters, who screamed insults against "Jews" and the administration. The rector, "a helpless old man," stood wringing his hands and pleading ineffectually for order. Harro Schulze-Boysen, still enrolled as a student of political science, boldly intervened. "Harro appeared with a good-natured expression, hands in pockets, and strode back and forth between the enraged parties," a friend recalled. He approached "the decent guys among the misguided Nazi fanatics, trying to bring them over to the Left to talk."[17]

The polarization made it impossible to focus on school. In 1932, at the age of twenty-four, Harro joined the staff of a magazine called *Gegner* (*Opponent*) with a circulation of about three thousand. The magazine corresponded to a movement which, like Harro himself, was marked by youthful exuberance and haphazard leftist politics. Its closest ties were with a French trade union movement supported by the visionary architect Le Corbusier.[18]

Harro laid out his position in a March 5, 1932, editorial. His belief system was actually an anti-ideology, a condemnation of the rash of doctrinaire movements surrounding him. It was also anathema to the strict, intolerant dogmas of the KPD:

> The battle cry arises from all sides. To add a new one would be absurd. Thousands of people speak a thousand languages, screaming their "isms" in each other's faces, and are willing to go to the barricades for their opposition movements. We stand at the door to a new era. But we believe that nobody holds the single key. Arrogance leads us nowhere, it runs contrary to real life. . . .
>
> People here ask what party we serve, what doctrine we proclaim. We serve no party. We serve an invisible confederation of thousands, who may be present in every camp and know that the day is approaching when all must unite. We have no program. We proclaim no truths written in stone. The only thing that is sacred to us is life—the only thing that appears to be of value to us is movement.

Harro ran his magazine on energy and sheer charisma. His political meetings, held in Berlin cafes, overflowed with spirited debate going in all directions. But when the Nazis seized power in March 1933, they took him seriously. Harro was detained in the initial March arrests and spent the night in jail. He returned to work the next day not too much the worse for wear.

A month later storm troopers broke into the *Gegner* offices not far from the university, where the editors were discussing plans for an antifascist protest march.[19] The Nazis seized the staff, including Schulze-Boysen and his coeditor Henry Erlanger. The two were dragged off to a "wild camp" in a dank cellar, stripped, and forced to run a gauntlet as they were flogged with lead-weighted whips, a sadistic reference to an old Prussian military tradition. Erlanger, who had the added liability of being half-Jewish, was beaten to death. Schulze-Boysen made it through the ordeal three times, then defiantly chose to run a fourth. The Nazis were impressed. One of them remarked, "Man, you really belong with us." They left a calling card of swastikas carved into his thigh.[20]

Schulze-Boysen's mother was a Berlin socialite married to a high-ranking naval officer. She worked every possible connection to obtain her son's release, and persuaded family friend Magnus von Levetzow (an admiral who had become chief of police) to send a squad to raid the cellar. Harro was rescued, but Levetzow was soon fired. Some claimed it was for helping Harro, but others said it was because he declined to persecute Jews.[21]

After the three days of torture Harro was finally delivered to his mother, bound and flanked by two SS men, "like some terrible criminal." Frau Schulze-Boysen found her son looking "pale as a corpse, with deep black shadows under his eyes, hair chopped off with a garden shears, no buttons on his suit."[22] One of Harro's kidneys was so badly injured that he had to be hospitalized. Harro was under orders to remain silent about Erlanger, but he could not forgive the storm troopers for his friend's death. His mother returned to the police to report Erlanger's murder, and Harro was rearrested and taken to police headquarters. His mother succeeded in freeing him once again.[23] A friend who saw him shortly after his second arrest didn't recognize him. Part of an ear was missing and he was still bleeding from wounds on his face.

By this point even Harro could see the futility of open defiance. He told a friend, "I have put my revenge on ice."[24]

The following year Frau Schulze-Boysen's wayward son made an about-face. He enrolled in a flight academy for pilot training, and began to look for a job. Germany was still forbidden to have an air force under the terms of Versailles, but the Nazis were quietly assembling a new Air Ministry under Hermann Göring, and Harro's father had connections to the principals. And so began Harro's extraordinary double life.

In 1934, Harro was assigned to air force intelligence. Göring, always eager to ingratiate himself with high society, was willing to overlook Harro's past infractions. This was not the case for everyone. Others on Göring's staff, including his personnel officer, nervously pointed out Harro's previous anti-Nazi journalism. Göring's reply was brusque: "That's yesterday's news. Let it go."[25]

Harro was less than thrilled with his new career, with its tedious paperwork, cramped working conditions, and officious colleagues. He still aspired to be a journalist, and eventually he won a slot as a contributor to the Air Ministry's magazine, *Luftwehr*. He simultaneously wrote for underground publications under a pseudonym. One of these, *Wille zum Reich* (*Will to Rule*) enlisted a broad cross-section of antifascists, ranging from quasi-Communists to lapsed Nazis.[26]

Harro set about forming his own circle. His initial meeting with Arvid Harnack had gone poorly, but he had no problem attracting others into his lively crowd of artists and performers who liked to combine a good party with their fulminations against the regime.

In 1934, Harro fell in love with a vivacious young aristocrat named Libertas Haas-Heyes. Libertas's mother, the daughter of a Prussian prince, had raised her children in the family castle on a property near Hermann Göring's estate. In 1935, Libertas had joined a hunting party with Göring, who enjoyed her flirtatious attentions. She used the occasion to argue for Harro's promotion.

Libertas confided in Ingeborg Engelsing about her slightly scandalous past. Her mother had eloped with her tutor, an art professor, to the great horror of her aristocratic father. The couple had divorced when Libertas was nine, and "this lively, lovely girl lived like a migratory bird, first with her father, then with her mother," doted upon by both.[27] Libertas's father taught in the fashion design department of the state-run School of Industrial Arts and Crafts, housed in the elegant edifice at 8 Prinz-Albrecht-Strasse. Libertas often romped in its grand hallways as a child. But those days were long over. The academy had been commandeered by the Nazis in 1933 as the new Gestapo headquarters, and the basement, which once housed spacious ateliers for sculptors, had been carved into a warren of tiny torture and interrogation cells. John Sieg and his colleagues had numbered among its early inmates.

Libertas was not overly concerned with politics. Her childhood had been a dazzling round of finishing schools in Switzerland, luxury hotels in Paris, and horseback riding on the family estate. Her choice of career was similarly diverting. In May 1933—the same month that Goebbels burned books on the Opern-Platz—she landed a job down the block in the Metro-Goldwyn-Mayer office at 225 Friedrichstrasse.

It should have been a banner year for MGM in Berlin. The company had just won the Academy Award for Best Picture with *Grand Hotel*. The story, told from the point of view of a shattered German World War I veteran living in a Berlin hotel, was written by a popular Berlin journalist. It featured Greta Garbo, who had been a film star in Berlin only a few years earlier, and the "Grand Hotel" itself was a fictionalized version of the Hotel Adlon, a few blocks north of MGM's Berlin office.

But the original "Grand Hotel" was also near Goebbel's book-burning site, which was more to the point. The author of the story, Vicki Baum, was a Jewish feminist. Baum had left for Hollywood in 1932, and now it was clear she would not return. Her novel and play had triumphed in Weimar Germany, but the movie closed in Berlin shortly after its February 1933 premiere. "Nazis Halt 'Hotel' Due to Race of Vicki Baum," Hollywood's *Variety* reported.[28]

Libertas chose not to dwell on such contradictions, perhaps because she stood to benefit. Like several of her prominent relatives, she had joined the Nazi Party and its girls' auxiliary (the *Bund Deutscher Mädel*) after the takeover, once it became socially expedient.[29] Now the nineteen-year-old had a chance at a plum position in the film industry, thanks in part to the Reich's Film Chamber's purge of "every Jewish film man employed in all of the American film offices and branches." Jews had accounted for over fifty percent of the Hollywood representatives in Germany, so there were many vacancies to fill.[30]

Libertas celebrated her new position by having her picture taken behind her typewriter, wearing a dark dress accented with a prim white color, and a broad smile. Wildly attractive (if not conventionally beautiful) she was an outrageous flirt. She had a bold gaze, a full mouth, and wavy blond hair bobbed into a *Bubikopf*. Libertas enjoyed shocking her elders, and often posed for snapshots with a cigarette or pipe dangling from her lips. She and Harro shared a sense of adventure and a love of the movies.

The couple lived together for a year before they finally bowed to parental pressure and wed in 1936.[31] First, of course, it was necessary to fill out the obnoxious official "race" certifications. There had been rumors that Libertas had a Jewish great-grandmother in France, and Harro complained that he didn't know how to prove otherwise without "digging her up to check on whatever the worms haven't eaten."[32] (Harro never lost his hostility to Nazi anti-Semitism, and claimed that the Nazis' motivation was to exploit the Jews as scapegoats for their own economic blunders.)

Harro and Libertas's wedding took place in the chapel at Libertas's grandfather's castle. Harro took on the tasks of vetting the Lutheran hymns and keeping his little brother in line: "I suggested 'A Mighty Fortress,' which Hartmut needs to learn by heart, because we have to sing at the end," he wrote to his parents. The couple honeymooned in Sweden, where Libertas's older sister Ottora was preparing to marry a Swedish count.

Within a year of her marriage, Libertas Schulze-Boysen left the Nazi Party. Hitler always said that a good wife's place was in the kitchen, and Libertas cited this reason in her resignation. In reality, she was influenced by her husband's strong antagonism to the Nazis. Harro had little interest in her learning how to cook and keep house, and Libertas had no intention of curbing her adventurous spirit. Soon after their wedding, with her husband's encouragement, she set off on a coal freighter for the seedy port city of Constanza in Romania, planning to write about the experience. Harro was content to ship his laundry off to his mother.

One of the newlyweds' few gestures toward domesticity was their frequent entertaining. Their home offered a large, comfortable living room on a quiet side street in an exclusive Berlin suburb. Over 1936 and 1937, every other Thursday night, they invited a few dozen friends over to socialize. The couple served cakes and tea to a roomful of celebrated artists and shaken concentration camp survivors (sometimes the two groups overlapped). They were often joined by friends from high society and relatives from the aristocracy. These individuals could be problematic, more inclined to harbor Nazi sympathies than the bohemians. The first requirement for any social gathering was to survey the room, then mete out one's remarks accordingly.

Libertas was the star of many of these evenings, as an enthusiastic accordion player and song-leader. The group joined in rousing campfire songs, alternating with favorites from the banned Brecht-Weill repertory. Libertas was assisted in her hostess duties by her cousin Gisella von Pöllnitz, an aspiring journalist with the United Press agency who was subletting a room in their apartment.[33]

Harro was a devoted son who wrote often to his parents, describing his sparkling social life: "Every two weeks we hold this great picnic evening at home. Everyone likes it so much that we're going to keep doing it. It's a great way to see all your friends from time to time and settle your social obligations too. It's usually about 25–30 people . . . we've got enough space. We just give them tea. The others bring biscuits, wine, etc. The first hour or so there's a good lecture, then music and dancing til 12. At 12 o'clock sharp we throw them out."[34]

Harro's boldness could rub some people the wrong way, but others adored him. Ingeborg Engelsing, the movie producer's wife, was a devoted friend, grateful for his kindness to her little son, Thomas. Harro often stopped by to keep her company while she fed him.[35] Many of their conversations centered on politics, but foundered on the question of what one could actually do to defeat the Nazi regime.

"[Harro] doesn't surrender secrets, but he makes it very clear that he has bottomless hatred for the Nazis," Ingeborg reflected. "Hitler is for him vulgar, rude, and ill-bred."[36] Ingeborg was intrigued by Harro's idiosyncratic brand of politics. "He doesn't see parties in the usual 'right and left' constellation, but as a circle, in which the Nazis would collide. His explanation impresses me in such a way that I incorporate it and still hold to it today," she wrote years later. "There was no indication that he was a Communist, but rather an aristocratic Bohemian who doesn't want anything to do with either the narrow-minded bourgeois nor pedantic bureaucrats. He dreamed of a revolution of the elite."[37]

Ingeborg realized that Harro was protecting her from the full knowledge of his activities. As a half-Jew and a young mother she was doubly vulnerable. But Harro wasted no time in recruiting other rebellious souls. The Schulze-Boysen salon of creative dissidents grew rapidly, and it seemed as though every friend brought in other like-minded acquaintances who were tired of hating the Nazis in isolation. From Harro's *Gegner* circle came a gifted sculptor, Kurt Schumacher, whose carvings graced the doors of Hermann Göring's country estate.[38] He had once attended night classes at the art academy on Prinz-Albrecht-Strasse where Libertas's father had taught, and where the Gestapo now had its headquarters.

Schumacher, like Harro, looked like an ideal Aryan beau, with thick blond hair and strong handsome features. His parents were early members of the KPD, but Schumacher himself was as much of a dreamer as a party militant. He pledged allegiance to "a peaceful community of peoples who, by the work of their own hands, could create an existence worthy of humanity."[39] Schumacher's style was influenced by his teacher, Ludwig Gies, a sculptor who reworked Christian motifs into Gothic forms. The Nazis labeled the style "decadent," and Schumacher did his own sculpture in private, camouflaging his personal work with state commissions. Schumacher's wife was another welcome addition to the circle. Elisabeth Hohenemser, an open-faced woman with blond wavy hair, had met Schumacher in art school. She was an accomplished graphic artist and photographer in her own right. Elisabeth was half-Jewish, but the couple had married in 1934 before the Nazi race laws became an impediment. However, her racial status made it difficult for her to get regular employment after 1939, and she was obliged to moonlight for income.

The Schumachers brought other friends into the Schulze-Boysen circle. One was a doctor Kurt had known since his student days, Elfriede Paul, a birdlike woman with round spectacles and a shy smile. She ran a busy medical practice in the fashionable suburb of Wilmersdorf.

Movie producer Herbert Engelsing introduced a second member of the medical profession. Engelsing met Helmut Himpel, a young dentist, through shared family connections in the Rhineland. Thanks to Ingeborg Engelsing's useful introductions around the film industry, Himpel became Berlin's "dentist to the stars," responsible for the smiles of Germany's leading performers.

Himpel's hatred of the Nazis stemmed from their race laws. He was deeply in love with a beautiful law student named Marie Terwiel, but they were forbidden to marry because she was half-Jewish. (They had no Göring connections to smooth the way.) The young couple's stand against the regime was personal, principled, and extremely dangerous.

Himpel flouted Nazi regulations on every front, illegally treating Jewish patients in his home, and forging ration cards and travel documents for them, along with his fiancée.

As Gestapo surveillance increased, doctors such as Elfriede Paul and Helmut Himpel were doubly welcome in resistance circles. Medical waiting rooms were excellent venues for underground meetings, and antifascist doctors and dentists soon acquired rafts of new "patients" who fell silent and assumed pained expressions the minute a stranger walked in.

Playwright Günther Weisenborn was another new prospect for the circle. Harro Schulze-Boysen had met Weisenborn at a rally in 1932, fresh from his triumph with *U-Boat S-4* and his collaboration with Brecht on *The Mother*. But the following year Weisenborn's novel and plays were consumed on Goebbels's pyre.

Weisenborn reacted to the Nazi takeover by going into a deep depression, and left Germany in disgust. In early 1937 he traveled to New York, where he stayed with a friend on Central Park West and found a job with the *Staatszeitung und Herold*, New York's leading German-language newspaper. But by the end of the year, Weisenborn decided to return to Germany.

Later, he wrote that Kristallnacht, the night of November 9–10, 1938, marked a personal turning point. He described the scene at a burning synagogue in Berlin, where crowds of hate-filled Nazis gloated, and indolent firefighters smoked and laughed instead of putting out the flames. Weisenborn wrote, " 'As of today,' I said, 'any means against these people are justified.' "[40]

Following Weisenborn's return to Germany, he published books and plays, many of them contributing to the growing body of "between the lines" literature indirectly critical of the regime.[41] He worked briefly as a representative of Metro-Goldwyn-Mayer, Libertas's old shop, and made two trips to England.[42] As a screenwriter, he was also part of the Engelsings' social circle.[43]

Libertas Schulze-Boysen, an aspiring writer herself, was dazzled by Weisenborn's talent and success. Weisenborn was even more dazzled by her. Later he wrote a rhapsodic description of their days at the lake. "Almost alone on the beach, we swam naked. At that time the weather wasn't hot yet. We all enjoyed it, especially Libs and Marta [Wolter], our two beauties. They always competed to see who could go home after three or four days with the best tan. They spent long hours off by themselves, not so interested in the discussions, baring their breasts to the sun."[44]

Libertas and Weisenborn soon became lovers and collaborators, with Harro's tacit permission. In 1938 he wrote proudly to his parents that Libertas had earned some money with a film treatment, "though the script still has to be written." Libertas and Weisenborn began work on a new play, based on the life of Robert Koch, the German scientist who developed a vaccine for tuberculosis.[45] They called their drama *Die guten feinde* (*The Good Enemy*).

Weisenborn's career gave him entrée into the country's highest cultural circles, which he observed with a dramatist's eye. In 1939 he attended the Day of German Art in Munich, where he was seated near Hitler. Weisenborn recorded the dictator as "an ugly malicious pasha . . . in a smoking jacket, with that modest brutality that our people so loved in him."[46]

Before Weisenborn could join Harro's resistance activities, he had to pass a screening process. Members of the group always started out gingerly, planting conversations with a new prospect to discern his true leanings. After a few weeks' scrutiny, Weisenborn was summoned to confer with Harro and two co-conspirators. Weisenborn later described the meeting and its participants. Walter Küchenmeister, Elfriede Paul's lover, was a former Communist journalist, battered by his recent sojourn in the Sonnenburg concentration camp. Weisenborn saw him as "a small, dark-haired man with glasses and a young, intelligent worker's countenance." Sculptor Kurt Schumacher had "a bright young artist's face with short blond hair and a certain fanaticism in his eyes."[47] Harro looked on intently, Weisenborn wrote, "as though I were his son taking a school exam."

Schumacher put the matter squarely on the table. "If you're against something, don't you have to actually *do* something to oppose it?" Weisenborn agreed, though with a certain fatalism. He knew that their prospects for success were slight, and the risks were unthinkable.

Nonetheless, the four young men sealed their trust over the tea table and shook hands. By the time they left, they were calling each other by the familiar "*du*" instead of the formal "*Sie.*"

Günther Weisenborn introduced friends from the theater world to the group, including actress Marta Wolter, recently emerged from the concentration camp. Marta was awaiting her fiancé Walter Husemann's release from Buchenwald in September 1938. He would become another liaison between the Schulze-Boysen circle and John Sieg's Communists in Neukölln.

The camp survivors' eagerness to rejoin the resistance was both admirable and worrisome. Not every victim was a saint. One heard uplifting reports from the camps of prisoners' self-sacrifice and solidarity, but there were also accounts of inmates who militated against each other—Stalinists against Trotskyites, politicals against Jews. Former concentration camp inmates posed special problems for the resistance groups. Many political prisoners were released on the condition that they seek out their old networks and inform on them. It was only reasonable for newly freed prisoners to be shunned as probable stool pigeons by their old contacts.

These crises of confidence made Schulze-Boysen's circle all the more unusual. In Harro's "Party of Life," old friends were welcome, especially if they had been persecuted. Members were judged as individuals, not by political affiliation. Harro was determined to live life as he pleased, socializing and debating with anyone he liked. But some of Harro's political contacts whispered that his circle had grown too quickly, with a membership that had spun dangerously out of control.

\ \ \

CHAPTER 13

The Birthday Party

1938–1939

As the Spanish civil war approached its climax, Harro and his friends grew increasingly incensed by the Nazis' support for the Spanish fascists.

Spain was everyone's laboratory. Harro's Air Ministry executed the Nazis' experiments with aerial bombardments of civilian populations, devastating the Basque village of Guernica in April 1937. Stalin used Spain as a testing ground for his blood purges, ravaging the ranks of Spanish Republicans, their foreign supporters, and Soviet officials in the field. Harro had inside knowledge of German actions, but if he was exposed to accounts of war crimes on the Loyalist front, he may well have dismissed them as Nazi propaganda.

In late 1937, Harro was ordered to report to the Gestapo. The summons was a result of a contact with an old friend from the *Gegner* days, a photographer named Werner Dissel. Dissel had come to Harro unbidden, with an important piece of military intelligence: two Panzer tank regiments had been dispatched to the nearby town of Neuruppin, en route to Spain. That fall Dissel was arrested for "organized activities and communist demoralization" against the army, and his interrogators linked him to Schulze-Boysen. Harro arrived at Gestapo headquarters without knowing how much Dissel had already revealed.

Dissel managed to hand Harro a pack of cigarettes that contained a hidden message: "*Extra Fontana Terra Incognita.*" Harro deciphered the code as: "*Unknown territory* [to the Gestapo that I told you about the two

Panzer regiments being deployed to Spain, currently] *outside* [the town of Neuruppin (the birthplace of popular German writer Theodor)] *Fontane*. This permitted Harro to fashion a cover story that allowed him to escape detection.[1]

Harro's social life presented an additional peril. One of his salon's aristocratic guests was a Hapsburg count named Karl von Meran, who doubled as a Nazi informer. Meran told the Nazis that Harro was a "skillfully disguised Communist." Harro's colleagues at the Air Ministry came to his defense, and it is unclear how far the investigation proceeded. But Harro and Libertas brought their living room soirees to an abrupt halt by the end of 1937.[2]

Nevertheless, Harro stepped up his activities against his employers. In February 1938 he learned of plans to infiltrate German agents into Spain for a sabotage operation in Barcelona. Anxious to warn the Republicans, he wrote a report that included secret details on the men and munitions that the Luftwaffe was transporting to Spain.[3] Libertas's cousin Gisella von Pöllnitz was commissioned to drop the document into the mailbox of the Soviet trade representative in Berlin. Harro hoped he would forward it to the Soviet embassy in Paris, to pass along to the Spanish Republicans. But a Gestapo agent observed the young woman making the drop, and she was arrested at her workplace in the United Press office in Berlin. The Schulze-Boysen apartment was searched, and the Air Ministry was once again informed that they had a security risk on their hands.

Harro and his closest collaborators panicked. They made plans to flee to Cologne, and from there on to Amsterdam, where Libertas's brother worked in the United Press office.

Fortunately, Gisella stonewalled her interrogators, and the house search failed to produce incriminating evidence. Furthermore, the Air Ministry resented the Gestapo meddling. Luftwaffe officers frostily informed the secret police that they could handle their own internal affairs. Harro got off with a warning, and his next letter home was as breezy and affectionate as ever, he was careful not to worry his parents.[4] But he shared his broader concerns with them, describing the tensions among the Nazi hierarchy and speculating on how the coming conflict could ripple throughout Europe and the Far East.

When German troops marched into Austria in March 1938, Harro's prediction came a step closer. The disparity between Nazi propaganda and the information he possessed created an unbearable tension. Harro and Libertas joined Kurt and Elisabeth Schumacher in a meeting with Dr. Elfriede Paul to discuss what to do. They could not tolerate the idea that the Nazis could bury all public objections to their war crimes and aggression, and decided to produce a flyer denouncing the war in Spain. Harro and Paul's partner Walter Küchenmeister, who had worked on several Communist newspapers in the 1920s, went to work drafting the text. The authors presented Harro's descriptions of the fascists' "animalistic behavior" in Spain, hoping they would stir the German public to opposition.[5]

Soon Dr. Paul's waiting room was transformed into a clandestine print shop, where some fifty copies of the document were painstakingly reproduced by typewriter and carbon paper.[6] As always, distributing the flyers was the biggest problem, since the authorities kept a close watch on anyone buying multiple stamps and paper in bulk or sending mass mailings. Dr. Paul traveled around the city on the pretense of making house calls, mailing disguised flyers from remote locations.

Few glimpses of the day-to-day operations of the underground survived the war. One was offered by one of the few surviving participants, who wrote a memoir about his experiences in one small group within the network. Hans Sussmann had been a member of the Communist underground since 1933, and started out working on clandestine newspapers in the southeast district of Berlin. He also raised money for persecuted Communists and their families, and helped smuggle fugitives out of Germany.

Sussmann's memoirs illustrate how the lines blurred between political and religious interest groups. The first stop for his group's underground railroad was a nursing center run by the Sisters of St. Mary in Neukölln. There, a sympathetic Dr. Höllen had set up an operation to smuggle Jews out of the country. The fugitives were taken to Höllen's parents' home in the ancient city of Trier to the west, then smuggled over a border to Belgium, Switzerland, or France. Another way station was a monastery on the Bavarian-Swiss border. Sussmann recounted how Dr. Höllen's network also rescued two Communists from his circle.

Sussmann's resistance activity included writing articles for clandestine newspapers in his home. He made certain to blast loud music from the radio to cover the sound of his typewriter from the neighbors. His friends brought large packets of Persil (Germany's leading laundry powder), emptied the boxes, inserted the newspapers, then refilled the containers with detergent, carefully resealing the packages. Then they nonchalantly carried their soap packets in grocery bags to clandestine meetings.

By 1936, Sussmann's original group had broken up. One member was arrested, another went underground, and a third succumbed to a drinking problem. This was when a friend directed him to the heterodox Schulze-Boysen circle as a way to remain active.

For Sussmann, the psychological impact of resistance work was like a chronic illness. "If you're fighting an opponent that you hate from the bottom of your heart, you don't take it lightly," he wrote. "It's as though you're possessed, and the urge to fulfill it is an indispensable obligation. One constantly lives in fear—in fear of death."

Sussmann met Elfriede Paul, Walter Küchenmeister, and the Schumachers, though not under their real names. They asked him to resume his production of illegal flyers, which included messages from the KPD Central Committee, news of the outside world, and updates on the fates of Communist, Socialist, and other antifascist leaders. Sussmann and his wife, Else, distributed some of the flyers on evening walks, placing them in telephone booths, public toilets, subway stations, and movie houses. Others would go into Persil boxes to unknown destinations.

Sometimes unidentified strangers appeared at Sussmann's meetings with Dr. Paul and Küchenmeister, introduced only by a first name. Sussmann believed they were connected to a larger group, but he was given no further information. Paper supply was a constant headache. "The regime made it impossible to purchase such materials in bookshops, because you had to present your identity card with every large purchase." Kurt Schumacher came to the rescue—as an artist he could get stencils and paper from wholesalers without attracting attention.[7]

Harro Schulze-Boysen may have been one of the pseudonymous strangers at the meetings, and he was almost certainly involved with the flyers. But as the breakup of Sussmann's first group showed, it was safer to keep contacts and activities compartmentalized.

The Schulze-Boysens resumed their social life on a much-reduced scale. When weather permitted, they migrated out of doors, to the patchwork of lakes west of the city or the sandy beaches of the Darss peninsula on the Baltic coast. There they hosted cookouts and sailboat rides for their regulars: the Engelsings, Marta Wolter Husemann, and Günther Weisenborn from the movie industry; the Schumachers, Elfriede Paul and her partner Walter Küchenmeister from Harro's student days. The group, accompanied by Libertas's ubiquitous accordion, greeted the furtive German spring with an outing at Pfingsten on Pentecost (a holiday just after Easter). Their snapshots show them huddled together in shorts and swimsuits, pale bodies exposed to the sun, their brave smiles showing strain about the eyes. It was a brief respite in a country hurtling toward war.

Personal relations were beginning to fray. Harro and Libertas, a thoroughly modern couple, had elected to have an "open marriage." It is not clear which of them strayed first, but Libertas, needy of attention and admiration, embarked on a series of affairs (that included her involvement with Günther Weisenborn). Harro tolerated the situation without reproach, and pursued his own romantic interests.[8]

As the German conflict broadened, Harro stepped up his anti-Nazi journalism. In October 1938 he coauthored a new flyer with Walter Küchenmeister, denouncing the German occupation of the Czech Sudetenland. The Schumachers helped to reproduce and distribute about fifty copies.[9] International contacts became more crucial than ever. Elfriede Paul's medical practice gave her the means and the excuse to travel outside the country. Over 1938 and 1939 she made a series of trips to Paris and London to assist in the emigration of Jewish friends.

In the spring of 1939, Dr. Paul and the Schumachers accompanied her companion, Walter Küchenmeister, on a trip to Switzerland. Küchenmeister suffered from a serious case of tuberculosis, aggravated by his concentration camp sentence, and Dr. Paul recommended alpine air as a remedy.[10] But the agenda also included a meeting with a member of the German Communist Party in exile, Wolfgang Langhoff. Dr. Paul and her companions wanted to offer the services of their Berlin network to the international struggle against fascism.

Langhoff, an old theater friend of Günther Weisenborn's, was an international celebrity. A prominent actor and producer of agitprop theater before the Nazi takeover, he had suffered through a succession of Gestapo torture chambers and concentration camps. He spent a year in slave labor hauling peat at Börgermoor, one of the first concentration camps for political prisoners. Langhoff channeled his experience into the lyrics to a haunting song called "*Die Moorsoldaten*" ("We Are the Peatbog Soldiers"), which quickly became an anthem of suffering and defiance in the camps and soon traveled to the world beyond.[11] In 1935, Langhoff published a book about his experiences, subtitled *Thirteen Months in a Concentration Camp*. It became an international sensation as one of the first major exposés of Nazi abuses.

Langhoff welcomed his visitors from Berlin to his new base in Zürich, but he could not be encouraging. He was only a way station to the KPD party leadership that was now scattered across Europe, with bases in Paris, Stockholm, and Moscow.

Furthermore, Langhoff's comrades-in-exile were ludicrously out of touch. In January 1939 the German Communist Party marked its twentieth anniversary with a conference outside Paris, which included leaders from France and the cross-border operations. But members from the underground in Germany were notably absent. From their seemingly safe distance, the exiled leaders outlined their bold visions for reactivating Germany's mass organizations, as though they had not been thoroughly infiltrated and smashed by the Gestapo several years earlier. They exhorted their beleaguered counterparts inside the country to build up their regional and factory leadership base, although many members of their cells were now either residents of concentration camps or Gestapo informers. One conference participant angrily responded that "the speakers displayed complete ignorance of the conditions in Germany."[12]

Langhoff listened carefully to Küchenmeister and Dr. Paul, and dutifully conveyed their offer of assistance to his superiors. But the KPD's Paris Secretariat, already crippled by Stalin's purges, dismissed the idea. They pointed out that the unorthodox band of Berliners was "ideologically dubious."[13] Few among their unruly artists and intellectuals had ever bothered to join the party. Even worse, one member of their group, Walter Küchenmeister, had been thrown out of the KPD in 1926 for pilfering from the party till. But at least the Paris Secretariat responded. KPD officials in Moscow and Stockholm didn't even favor Langhoff with a reply.[14]

Schulze-Boysen's group was acquiring new members all the time, but they could achieve little in isolation. The dogged Dr. Paul returned to Switzerland in June to try again, this time with Gisella von Pöllnitz in tow as her tuberculosis patient. The trip was a failure on both counts; the doctor failed to find new contacts, and young Gisella died shortly afterward.[15]

Between the near-disaster of the letter drop at the Soviet embassy in Berlin and the disappointment of Dr. Paul's Swiss expeditions, Harro's group was blocked at every turn. This was intensely frustrating. Over the course of 1939, Harro's work brought him increasingly intimate knowledge of the Nazis' military planning, while his zeal spurred him on to ever more daring action.

In early 1939 the Nazis began preparations to invade Poland. Air force intelligence was directly involved in the process.[16] That spring Harro wrote an analytical paper comparing Germany's air force capabilities to that of Britain and France. The report conveyed Harro's longstanding view (perhaps a product of wishful thinking) that the two democracies could soon overtake Germany's aircraft production. Hermann Göring, head of the Luftwaffe, panicked at the result, and ordered Harro's defeatist analysis to be destroyed.

On April 20, 1939 (the Führer's birthday), Harro was promoted to lieutenant, and the following month he was placed in the new press office of the air force intelligence division.[17] Harro's superiors, impressed with his linguistic abilities, assigned him to review foreign press reports, which gave him a rare grasp of international events at a time when Germans viewed the world through a scrim of propaganda and censorship.[18] Harro was eager to share the benefits of his privilege, and offered foreign news briefs to Dr. Paul and the Schumachers, who secretly retyped and copied them for their information-starved friends.

In August, Harro initiated an even riskier venture. Kurt Schumacher was using his sculpture studio as a hiding place for Rudolf Bergtel, a political prisoner who had just escaped from a concentration camp, and Harro volunteered to help him flee the country. He asked Bergtel to memorize a large amount of military intelligence, including German aircraft and tank production figures, as well as plans for a new submarine base in the Canary Islands. Bergtel was instructed to recite the information to the KPD representatives in Switzerland on his arrival. Harro dressed Bergtel in a Luftwaffe uniform and took him to the central train station, walking him past wanted posters displaying his own face. Harro put the escapee on a train to Austria and Schumacher took a seat nearby. They got off the train at the Austrian-Swiss border, and Schumacher, an accomplished mountaineer, guided Bergtel over the Alps into Switzerland.[19]

Once again, their effort was futile. The KPD representatives distrusted the source of the information because Schulze-Boysen and his circle were outsiders, not party regulars. Bergtel's information, which three men had risked their lives to convey, was never even passed on to Moscow.[20]

In late August the German public awoke to the startling news that the Nazis had reached an agreement with the Soviets, known as the German-Soviet Nonaggression Pact. The two countries would refrain from attacking each other and, under the secret protocol, would carve up and divide Finland, the Baltic republics, and Poland as spoils. Expanding on their secret military collaboration after World War I, the Soviets would supply the Germans with raw materials in exchange for advanced military technology.

Stalin was jubilant, convinced that the alliance with Hitler would guarantee his survival. The Germans would help him rebuild the Soviet military institutions he had just destroyed, and together the two dictatorships could face down the Western democracies.

The political discourse in both countries was turned upside down. Prisoners in Soviet reeducation camps were ordered to avoid the word "fascist" in favor of the friendlier term "German National Socialists." European Communist Party leaders were informed that their adversary was no longer German fascism; it was imperialism, which made Britain the new archenemy.[21] Stalin began to ship massive trainloads of raw materials to augment the German arsenal.

One of Stalin's first gestures of friendship was to round up the suspected German and Austrian dissidents he had been holding in Soviet camps and prisons. These included Communists, other German antifascists, and Jewish refugees.[22] German Communists accounted for about 570 of the prisoners. They were herded over the bridge at Brest-Litovsk to German-occupied Poland, where Soviet and Gestapo agents checked their respective lists, sorting out the candidates for interrogation, concentration camps, and execution.[23]

One of the prisoners at the bridge was the widow of KPD official Heinz Neumann, who had been executed by the Soviets in 1937. Greta Buber-Neumann, the daughter-in-law of Martin Buber, had been sent to a slave labor camp in Kazakhstan. Now the Soviets delivered her over to the Gestapo. The Germans dispatched her to the Ravensbrück concentration camp, where she spent the rest of the war.[24]

The events of 1939 continued to unfold rapidly. For months tensions had been building on the German-Polish border. Poland, which had been reconstituted under Versailles, had few admirers abroad. The country had failed to achieve political stability, due to a long history of internal power struggles, extreme poverty, and a bitterly contested border. In 1938, *Life* magazine published a major feature under the headline "Poland: Misery, Pride and Fear Call the Tune." The author described the country as "almost friendless in Europe," and criticized Poland's land grabs in Lithuania and Czechoslovakia as the actions of "a jackal to Germany's lion."

"Polish politics is a mess," the article went on. "There is ample excuse ready to hand for intervention [by Germany and Russia]." The piece highlighted the country's ethnic divisions, reporting that Poland's six million Russians were restless. One million ethnic Germans were "scattered thinly all over Poland and many of them are anti-Nazi." Poland's three million Jews, who had suffered repression under various regimes in different countries, "continue to wear the dress and haircuts the Tsars forced on them . . . the most miserable, submissive and hopeless people in all Poland."[25]

British and French diplomats attempted to stave off Poland's rapacious neighbors, but Hitler's forces were ready to move, and no one was prepared to prevent them. The Nazis launched a series of pseudoterrorist incidents, blaming them on the Poles. These actions culminated on the last day of August, when German SS units, disguised in Polish-style mustaches and sideburns, staged attacks on three German targets, including a radio station in the border town of Gleiwitz. German radio audiences listened breathlessly to a live broadcast of the station's "takeover" by "Polish militia," complete with gunshots and a ranting speech in Polish. Once the Germans "retook" the station, they found a "Polish" corpse slumped over the transmitter. This was an unfortunate prisoner who had been dragged out of the concentration camp at Sachsenhausen, dressed in a Polish uniform, drugged, shot, and dumped on the scene. Hitler proclaimed that this vicious pantomime provided the justification to invade Poland, and a million and a half German troops stood ready at the border.

As Harro Schulze-Boysen saw it, the escalation was Germany's only way out: things had to get worse before they could get better. He could even see a bright side to the Hitler-Stalin pact. The last week in August, Kurt Schumacher had invited Harro to address a roomful of young working-class Communists. Harro, wearing civilian clothes and identifying himself only as "Hans," told them not to despair over the pact. It would help Germany in the end, he said, because the combined German-Soviet threat was the only thing that would stir the sluggish Western democracies into action against Hitler. Besides, Harro argued, Germany and the Soviet Union had by no means smoothed over their fundamental ideological antagonisms. Their fight to the death would come in good time, and the Soviets would benefit from additional time to prepare for battle. The "Nonaggression Pact," he quipped, was really a "Not-Yet-Aggression Pact."[26]

A week later Harro Schulze-Boysen traveled out to a lake in the Berlin suburb of Wannsee, where his sailboat was waiting. He met Günther Weisenborn—his friend, co-conspirator, and wife's lover—at the dock. The two sailed with a strong wind against an evening sky. Harro was in a pensive mood. "Tomorrow night we move against Poland," he told Weisenborn. "So far Hitler's had room to maneuver, but now he will start to box himself in. Now the real world history will be made, but not by him alone. We're all going to play our little part, everyone around us and we ourselves. It will be the biggest war in world history, but Hitler won't survive it."

On September 1 the Germans invaded Poland at dawn. Soon the air force was obliterating Polish roads, bridges, and cities with the world's first large-scale aerial bombardment. The Polish armed forces were no match for the Germans. By the end of the day, the British and French governments informed Berlin that unless German troops were withdrawn from Poland immediately, they would declare war. The Germans declined, and on September 3, Hitler's latest act of aggression was transformed into a regional conflict.

If Hitler was expecting the German capital to hail him as a conquering hero, he was disappointed. The stubborn Berliners remembered the miseries of World War I all too well. Some even recalled that in *Mein Kampf,* Hitler himself had written that going to war against the British was the kaiser's fatal error. American diplomat George Kennan recorded the city's response:

> The Berliners themselves—the simple people, that is—were, of all the major urban or regional elements among the German population, the least Nazified in their outlook. They could never be induced to give the Nazi salute. They continued to the end to greet each other with the usual "*Guten Morgen*" in place of the obligatory "*Heil Hitler.*" Nor did they evidence any particular enthusiasm for the war.
>
> I can testify (because I stood among crowds of them on the Pariserplatz, outside our embassy, on that particular day) that they witnessed with a reserved, sullen silence the victory parade of the Polish campaign. Not even the most frantic efforts of professional Nazi agitators could provoke them to demonstrations of elation or approval.[27]

Harro spent the day following the invasion with a group of friends at the Engelsings', celebrating his and Herbert Engelsing's joint birthday. Harro was turning thirty. Wine flowed freely, and the Engelsings used the last of their gas ration to fetch Libertas's accordion. She played the old songs from the lake as the company sang along, but then, stirred by the events of the day, she played "The Marseillaise" and "It's a Long Way to Tipperary."

Then, perhaps in his cups, Harro led a loud chorus of the Polish national anthem, a nineteenth-century hymn that had once rung across Europe:

Poland is not yet lost, as long as we still live,
What foreign aggression has stolen, we will reclaim with sword
    in hand . . .
Neither German nor Russian can triumph over us, once we take
    up our weapons.
Unity will be our watchword, and our Fatherland will be ours.

The song was a daring choice for September 2, 1939. Ingeborg Engelsing nervously circled the house to make sure no one was listening. The party went on until dawn, and Harro's mood darkened, burdened with knowledge. Hitler, he said, would try to conquer England, but the outcome was questionable. The Western Europeans couldn't defeat Germany on their own, and the Soviet Union's position was still in doubt. Only the entry of the United States could secure an outright victory. But he believed it would be a long time before the West could unite in a full counterattack.

In the meantime, Harro mused, their own prospects were not good. Hitler's dictatorship will only grow madder and more reckless, he said. No one would escape the inferno.[28] One of his friends later described Harro's mood that evening.

This slender flight officer, with his sharply drawn profile and blue eyes full of life and energy, cut an unusual figure in Grunewald. There were writers, actors, painters, film producers, doctors, lawyers, and beautiful women present. Would the Thousand-Year Reich last only through 1939, or until 1940?—that was the reigning question. Only the Luftwaffe officer, whose chin trembled with hatred when he spoke of the Nazis, disagreed. He didn't want to destroy their optimism, but clearly Hitler was leading them into an unavoidable catastrophe. Things were not so simple. That was Schulze-Boysen.[29]

Harro fell silent. As though weary of his own sense of doom, he started to dance—expertly, elegantly, enchanting all the women. And just as abruptly, he tired of his spectacle and stopped.

\ \ \

CHAPTER 14

The Inner Front

1939–1940

HARRO SCHULZE-BOYSEN WORKED IN A SPARE, MODERN OFFICE in Göring's Air Ministry, a large gray slab of a building across the street from Hitler's chancellery. If Göring's ministry had been constructed slightly farther down the block, Harro might have looked out on the Gestapo headquarters on Prinz-Albrecht-Strasse, where his father-in-law had once taught art classes, and where political dissidents were now brutally interrogated.

A few blocks west, next to the U.S. ambassador's residence, an even larger set of granite slabs loomed over a central courtyard. This was the Bendler Block, a complex that once included the vast quarters of Harro's great-uncle, Admiral Alfred von Tirpitz. Now it served as the command center for both the Joint Chiefs of Staff and German military intelligence.

Admiral Wilhelm Canaris, the white-haired chief of military intelligence, belonged to the same military caste as Harro Schulze-Boysen, but with different leanings. Canaris had served under Harro's great-uncle as a young submarine officer. Harro's father, a decorated naval officer, was friendly with Canaris, and Harro's younger brother Hartmut would soon become a submarine officer himself.

But the two men approached politics from opposite ends of the spectrum: Harro was a thirty-year-old leftist romantic rebel disguised as an air force lieutenant, while Canaris was a conservative Catholic monarchist. Both men became notable figures in the resistance. But Harro had opposed the Nazis from the start, and joined the military only to attack them from within, while Canaris had initially favored the Nazis and took several years to recognize their menace.

The Nazis had promoted Canaris soon after the takeover, perceiving him as a sympathetic and easily manipulated ally. Their ambitions meshed neatly in Spain, where Canaris had spent years and maintained close ties. As a Catholic, he strongly identified with the Spanish Falangist cause, and hung a picture of his good friend Francisco Franco over his desk. When Franco joined the revolt against the Spanish Republicans in 1936, Canaris was one of the first people he called. Canaris successfully argued the general's case before both Hitler and Mussolini, winning him arms, air strikes, and intelligence support.[1] During the Spanish civil war, Canaris and Schulze-Boysen worked at cross purposes. Canaris infiltrated German agents into Spain, while Harro took measures to disclose their identities to the Republicans via the Soviets.

But as the Spanish civil war wound down and Nazi abuses gathered momentum, Canaris began to catch Harro's consuming hatred of Adolf Hitler and his party. Canaris watched in dismay as the Nazis subverted the church, the military, and the legal system, every institution Canaris held dear. He was certain that their adventurism would destroy the nation as well as the German armed forces. By the late 1930s the admiral was doing everything he could to slow the onset of war. On the day the final orders were given to invade Poland, he pulled an associate aside, into a dimly lit corridor of the command center, and told him, "This means the end of Germany."[2]

Canaris was also sickened by the atrocities that accompanied the invasion of Poland, and supported fellow officers' attempts to court-martial soldiers who committed war crimes. But the Nazis took no notice of their protests. Instead, they informed Canaris and his colleagues of their secret plan for mass executions in Poland. The murders were given the sanitized Nazi code name of "Extraordinary Pacification Action," and Jews were to be given "special" treatment. According to one post-war account, Canaris received an eyewitness report of one massacre and went to Hitler to protest. "You're getting too soft, sir!" Hitler answered. "I have to do it, because after me no one else will."[3]

A small group of dissident officers began to collect around Canaris, but others were torn. Hitler's land grabs had been popular with army personnel, who were still smarting from the territorial losses under Versailles. Furthermore, after 1934, the traditional pledge of allegiance to the German nation was replaced with an oath of loyalty to the Führer himself, required of every member of the armed forces:

> I swear by God this sacred oath that I shall render unconditional obedience to Adolf Hitler, the Führer of the German Reich and people, supreme commander of the armed forces, and that I shall at all times be ready, as a brave soldier, to give my life for this oath.

German soldiers, steeped in religious discipline and the cult of military honor, did not take their vows lightly.

Yet some officers, like army conspirator Henning von Tresckow, held a different definition of patriotism. In the summer of 1939 he told a fellow conspirator that "both duty and honor demand from us that we should do our best to bring about the downfall of Hitler and National-Socialism, in order to save Germany and Europe from barbarism."[4]

Tresckow's view was fervently shared by Admiral Canaris's right-hand man, army Lieutenant Colonel Hans Oster. Oster was outraged at the Nazis' offenses against German military tradition, and tormented by the crimes against Germany's Jews. Oster lamented that the Jews were being "driven to their destruction," and took dramatic action to help them, at great personal risk.[5]

A massive military conspiracy began to form, with army intelligence at its heart. Hans Oster ran the day-to-day logistics, reaching out to political leaders to help shape a transitional government once Hitler was deposed. Canaris provided essential cover. The Oster conspiracy ran parallel to Harro Schulze-Boysen and Arvid Harnack's efforts, but there were many points of contact.

One of Oster's most trusted allies was Arvid Harnack's cousin, Hans von Dohnanyi, a justice official and architect of the thwarted 1938 coup attempt. Another cousin, Ernst von Harnack, convened his own overlapping circle of conspirators. Like most Social Democrats, Harnack had lost his government position in 1933. Over the winter of 1938–39 he summoned Dietrich Bonhoeffer's brother Klaus and other prominent Social Democrats to his home to plot the regime's overthrow. They drew up a plan for a "Unity Front" of civilian and military groups, which would unite German antifascists without regard to party background.[6]

Although many of the conservatives in Oster's group had staunch anti-Communist backgrounds, there was a tacit understanding that different groups would try to cultivate different sources of foreign support. It was a ragged process with many intermediaries. One of them was historian Egmont Zechlin, a friend of Arvid Harnack's since his student days, who connected Harnack to a number of participants in the military plot.

The Harnack clan was also responsible for informal connections between the two resistance networks. Arvid's cousin, Social Democrat Ernst von Harnack, was placing himself at great risk by simultaneously helping Jews escape to England and participating in the Oster conspiracy. He remained in touch with Arvid, promoting the theory that in order to succeed, the "opposition must spin their web through the whole machinery of the regime . . . and at the same time try to make contact abroad."[7]

Arvid and Mildred never wavered in their political convictions, but they personally questioned how far they were willing to go. In 1939, as the wider war loomed, Arvid became increasingly anxious about Mildred. She was prone to nervous depression. Although she longed for a child, she had little hope for the immediate future in Germany, and debated returning to America.

In October 1939, Mildred applied for fellowships from both the Rockefeller and the Guggenheim Foundations, to work on a book on American literature. Both applications were rejected; the Guggenheim committee dismissed her as a "beginner."[8] Arvid had experienced a similar disappointment two years earlier when he applied for a Rockefeller grant, hoping to use his time in America to lobby for the German resistance. The foundation responded that it was limiting its work with Germans because "foreign experience might decrease the willingness of the beneficiary to adjust himself to German conditions on his return."[9]

The Harnacks lived in a constant state of anxiety. They refused to have a telephone or hold meetings in their home for fear of surveillance.

They limited their visits to the apartments of their less conspicuous contacts, where they could exchange news and secretly monitor foreign broadcasts.[10]

There was good reason to fear. By 1939 the Nazis had made great progress in wiping out the opposition. In April the Gestapo reported that over their first six years in power, the Nazis had placed 162,734 people in "protective custody," which usually meant concentration camps. They added that 112,432 prisoners were sentenced by trial, and 27,369 were awaiting trial. In the month of May 1939 alone, 1,639 people were executed for political offenses.[11] (Under the Weimar Republic, capital punishment had been virtually abolished. Only three executions took place in Germany between 1928 and 1930.)[12]

Despite these alarming signs, Arvid continued to smuggle information out of the Economics Ministry. He had lost contact with the Soviets in 1938 as a result of Stalin's purges of the embassy staff, but over the course of 1939 he frequently met with U.S. diplomat Donald Heath to pass on economic intelligence.[13]

Arvid believed that economics was the key to understanding the German crisis, granting him a unique role. Heath disapproved of Harnack's connections to the Soviets, but Harnack believed that both the Soviets and the West were required to ensure a victory over the Nazis. Heath's young son Donald Jr. once overheard Arvid tell his father: "I can be a bridge between the United States and the Soviet Union here in Germany. I understand you, you understand me, and I can be helpful to both sides."[14]

Heath sent carefully worded summaries of Arvid's analyses to his superior, Undersecretary of State Sumner Welles. A brilliant analyst, Welles shared Franklin Roosevelt's elite social background and was informally known as the architect of FDR's foreign policy.[15] But Welles also had powerful rivals at the State Department, and his career suffered from a campaign of innuendo regarding his homosexual activity. Welles was receptive to Donald Heath's reports from Arvid Harnack and other Germans dissidents, and understood the urgency of Heath's communiqués. But he was far from an ideal advocate within the bureaucracy.[16]

It was still utterly unclear what role, if any, the United States would assume in the European conflict. But Heath's German sources held on to the hope that the United States would help them avert catastrophe. One of Heath's letters to Welles quoted a prominent anti-Nazi, referred to only as "our friend": "President [Roosevelt], in the desire to bring the world back to sanity, must endeavor to exert an influence not only on the governing circles in Great Britain but also on Germany as well."[17]

As the Nazis stepped up their preparations for a broader war, opposition figures increased their international efforts. The young diplomat Adam von Trott was the strongest link between the German resistance and British officials. He was connected to Arvid Harnack through their mutual friend Egmont Zechlin. As a Rhodes scholar at Oxford, Trott had made many influential friends among the British elite. He had joined the German foreign ministry with the intention of pursuing resistance activities from an international base.

Trott embarked on an ambitious program of one-man shuttle diplomacy, enlisting the support of influential friends from his student days. But Trott had also made an influential enemy at Oxford by running afoul of literature professor Maurice Bowra. The malicious don took it upon himself to discredit Trott with his contacts at the British Foreign Office. Despite Trott's many distinguished references, the British government wrote him off. The Foreign Office considered the idea of a diplomat trying to overthrow his own government to be "traitorous"—even if the goal was to save millions of lives from his government's policy of mass murder.

The British government passed the discouraging word on to the Roosevelt administration. Trott traveled to Washington and New York in the fall of 1939, almost overlapping with Arvid Harnack's summer trip. He, too, was granted only inconclusive meetings with low-level American officials. Trott's storehouse of information and contacts offered Washington a tremendous advantage in dealing with the Nazis, but the Roosevelt administration dismissed him without a hearing, and the FBI shadowed him as a spy.[18] In early 1940 the disappointed diplomat finally returned to Germany by way of Japan.[19]

The various German resistance groups erratically divided up the world. Arvid Harnack reached out to Washington and Moscow. Trott shuttled desperately to London and Washington, in hopes that a peace could be negotiated that would avert a world war and leave Germany intact.[20]

Only a few foreign officials were sympathetic to their plight. One of them was the British military attaché in Berlin, Colonel Noel Mason-Macfarlane. A man of action, he informed his government in 1939 that his apartment window offered a good bead on Hitler's cavalcade, and offered to shoot him. The British government disapproved of his plan, considering it bad form.[21]

In 1940, Roosevelt dispatched Sumner Welles to Europe to explore the possibilities of preventing war. Welles's office commissioned young diplomat George Kennan, an expert on both Germany and the Soviet Union, to write a policy paper for his review. Kennan took a shortsighted view of the situation, warning against "the siren songs" of German dissidents "who held out the hope of overthrowing Hitler and setting up a government of 'reasonable men.' " Kennan lived to regret his analysis.[22]

Stalin, taking advantage of the diplomatic lull, pursued his own aggressive campaigns. After digesting their half of Poland, the Soviets invaded Finland in late November, taking advantage of the Hitler-Stalin pact and the momentary paralysis of the Western democracies.

Stalin trusted Hitler and assumed the alliance would hold. In late 1939 he took the astonishing step of cleaning out his German intelligence networks. Soviet intelligence services contacted their leading undercover agents across the globe and informed them that their efforts were no longer necessary. These included the Polish communist Leopold Trepper, who was building up his network in Western Europe from his base in Brussels, and master spy Richard Sorge, who transmitted a wealth of detailed intelligence from Toyko under cover as a German journalist. The agents were told to suspend their intelligence operations and come back to Moscow at once. Reading between the lines, Sorge and Trepper found ominous hints that they could expect some difficult conversations about suspected Trotskyite tendencies.[23]

Both agents managed to disobey orders and remain abroad, thus surviving the purges. They maintained their covers and continued to build up their operations, convinced that no matter what Moscow said, the confrontation between Germany and the Soviet Union was inevitable. For the moment, their priority was to keep a low profile.

Other Soviet intelligence agents were less fortunate. All over the West, the Soviet *residenturas,* offices charged with in-country intelligence oversight, were devastated by Stalin's purges. In Berlin, only two of the sixteen members of the Soviet intelligence staff survived.[24]

The Soviets had groomed members of the German Communist Party to backstop their intelligence, but there wasn't much to work with. Historian Michael Burleigh writes that by 1939, the party's remnants were reduced to

> informal localized networks of activists too fearful to do anything, loosely linked to a Party executive being depleted in Moscow. . . . They were so inconsequential that the Gestapo reallocated desk officers to other more pressing targets such as homosexuals, Jews and Freemasons. Arrests of Communists declined vertiginously from five hundred in January 1939 to seventy in April 1940.[25]

Thus it is little wonder that the German Communists' party-in-exile rejected the overtures of Dr. Paul and her stubborn clique of concentration camp survivors and antifascists in the spring of 1939. The KPD itself was in disarray.

For years, the Schulze-Boysen and the Harnack groups had worked to infiltrate the Nazi policy circles. Their success depended on blending into Nazi society and remaining inconspicuous. Now they were personally tested by their emotional reactions to the suffering around them. Harro Schulze-Boysen put everything at risk when he helped Kurt Schumacher's friend escape from a concentration camp. The Harnacks aided their friend, Jewish publisher Max Tau, in his flight to Norway in 1938. The couple saved food from their own scarce rations to offer their other Jewish friends, and Mildred collected documents for refugees.[26]

But their humane impulses led to internal debates. Everyone in the circles had Jewish friends, colleagues, or relatives, and all of them condemned the country's mounting anti-Semitism. But clandestine activity imposed an algebra of inverse proportion: the more effectively one worked to topple the regime, the less conspicuous one could afford to be in helping its victims.

Greta Kuckhoff insisted on maintaining contact with her Jewish friends, even if it meant attracting attention. She took her son, Ule, around for frequent visits, and offered free English lessons to Jewish families waiting for visas to Britain and America. But it was an unsettling experience. Once she went to see a couple who had a new baby boy. She entered the building, holding Ule's hand, and noticed that the couple's brass nameplate was missing. When she reached their door, she found that the family and their possessions had vanished without explanation.[27] The neighbors only shrugged: "Maybe it's for the best. This way the boy can grow up with his own kind."

Greta's Jewish friends told her they felt German to the core, and some regarded emigration as an act of cowardice. Why, they demanded, should they allow a crass Austrian usurper to evict them from their own country?

Adam Kuckhoff was sympathetic, but he warned Greta that helping a Jewish family here or there wasn't going to change the larger picture. The only real way to help persecuted Jews and other victims of the regime was to overthrow Hitler as quickly as possible.

Greta was stung by criticism from Arvid Harnack as well. Her visits to "obviously" Jewish families was attracting attention to them all, he told her, and she was only doing it to make herself feel better by proving her altruism.[28] Granted, Mildred Harnack continued to help Jews trying to flee Germany, but she did so on discreet trips abroad, not by knocking on doors and quizzing the neighbors.

The circle was experiencing its first divisions over the question of ethics and methodology. Was it proper to concentrate on overthrowing the regime or should they be helping its victims? Or should one attempt to do both, at the risk of endangering both activities? Greta, the sociologist, still hoped that setting a good example would inspire her fellow citizens, while Arvid, enmeshed in high-level intelligence activity, was deeply concerned about security.

Over the course of 1939 and 1940, members of the Harnack-Kuckhoff circle advanced their strategic positions in government. Arvid's job at the Economics Ministry continued to generate valuable information for Donald Heath. Their exchanges were facilitated by the closing of the American School in Berlin, where Heath's son, Donald Jr., had been a student. In late 1939, Mildred became his tutor in English and American literature, and the boy became a courier for messages between his parents and the Harnacks.[29] Even from his child's perspective, young Donald could recognize his family's delicate position. One day he came home early to find the family cook in the music room with a Leica poised over a photo stand, taking snapshots of his mother's diary. The cook was fired immediately.[30]

Adam Kuckhoff continued to work in publishing, but he expanded his contacts in the film community. Producers still inquired about the film rights to his novel, but he was more conscious than ever of how his words could be twisted in the interests of "false patriotism." The couple needed money, but his wife approved of his resolve. "It took more courage to turn down the film than to make a blind jump off a cliff," Greta noted.[31] Adam churned out articles on film theory, and Tobis Film commissioned him to polish dialogue for their upcoming productions, including the 1939 thriller *Die Vierte Kommt Nicht* (*The Fourth One Isn't Coming*), and *Der Fuchs von Glenarvon* (*The Fox of Glenarvon*, 1940) starring Olga Tschechowa.[32]

Greta occupied herself with their young son, Ule, and her role as her husband's secretary, but she also kept up with her own work. Her translation business was another rare opportunity to get news of the outside world. It was only through her work with Italian texts that her group learned that the Italians had adopted a variant of Nazi race policies against the Jews.[33] The Kuckhoff apartment also became an archive of illegal materials. Frightened friends appeared at regular intervals with banned literature to drop off as they tried to sanitize their own households. Soon the Kuckhoffs' bookshelves were lined with the dangerous volumes. The Kuckhoffs had access to information, but few ways to disseminate it.

This was one reason they were glad to know John Sieg. John had been working at the Reichsbahn (state railways) since 1937, rising through the ranks to senior positions at important train stations. Before 1938 the railways had offered the German underground a vital artery to the opposition in exile in Prague and Paris. That period was over. Prague was now under German occupation, and the train service had become the prime conduit of men and supplies to the front. But the altered conditions also presented new opportunities: John was now well-trained in telegraph operations, signal towers, and worker oversight, an enviable battery of skills for an antifascist with the will to do mischief. John Sieg was no longer a working journalist, but every day, as he switched the engines to Prague and counted the boxcars to Warsaw, he realized that he was staring down the biggest story of his life. His Neukölln network gave him access to Germany's blue-collar antifascists and the remains of the KPD network. All in all, he was a useful person to know.

CHAPTER 15

"The New Order"

1940

ONE CHILLY SUNDAY IN THE WINTER OF 1939–40, JOHN SIEG met with some old Communist Party contacts for a walk in Treptower Park; it was now too dangerous to meet on the streets of Neukölln. They chose to ignore the proposition of the Hitler-Stalin pact that the Soviets and the Nazis were currently friends. As German Communists, they had been discounting instructions from Moscow for a while, staying focused on their resistance activities against the Nazis. But they still lacked basic facilities: a meeting place, an office, a clandestine publishing base.

John's Neukölln apartment was out of the question. As a Communist Party member, *Rote Fahne* reporter, and former Nazi prisoner he was too conspicuous. But one of the group suggested a possibility nearby—Otto Dietrich's modest home at 5 Biebricherstrasse. The gray three-story building, close by a vast cemetery, became the base of the group's activities for the next two years.

"Hot days and cold days followed one another. The thread ran invisibly through the streets of Neukölln, and the junction was in Biebricher Street," one member of the group wrote later. "The revolutionaries also followed each other—in and out of prison—but this home remained undisturbed." The young Communist printer Herbert Grasse had emerged from his two-and-a-half-year sentence in January 1939; Biebricher Street soon welcomed his friends from the concentration camp into the circle. "Whoever comes along with Herbert is welcome. We have full confidence in his friends," they said.[1] Grasse found a job printing handbills in a small shop, which gave him access to printing and paper supplies. He reached out to his old Communist Party youth contacts, and he soon activated a new network of antifascist informants and collaborators in the factories and the arms industry.[2]

John Sieg's blue-collar co-conspirators took note of his contacts among the educated elite, including the Kuckhoffs and the Harnacks. The workers never learned their names, but they were impressed that such "big shots" were linked to the cause. Rigid social divisions still prevailed in Germany, and some KPD working-class regulars doubted that privileged intellectuals could be true partners in the class struggle, especially if they lacked party credentials. University educations were regarded with a mixture of suspicion and awe.

The Kuckhoffs and the Harnacks were anxious to hear John Sieg's reports on working-class resistance. Within the confines of the propaganda-saturated state, it was easy for opposition circles to feel isolated and abandoned. Battered Communist workers watched resentfully as leftist intellectuals joined the Nazi Party and assumed comfortable positions in the Nazi bureaucracy, while intellectuals feared that the working classes were all too eager to follow orders in return for a factory job and a few beers. Only a few feeble, clandestine connections remained to suggest that anti-Nazi sentiments transcended any single class.

"John always brought questions that workers from this or that factory wanted answered," Greta recalled later. "Then he carried back the answers from the previous time, with analyses of certain Nazi projects. He also took articles that were not written for workers."[3] This last statement was somewhat defensive. Greta had been born into a blue-collar family, but schooled and married into a different class. Now she was subject to criticism for her group's impenetrable academic prose.

John's Neukölln friends cautioned him not to put too much faith in bourgeois intellectuals. They weren't as careful and disciplined as the KPD regulars, they warned. Some of them talked too much, and the Gestapo was always attentive to indiscretions. John Sieg chose to ignore the warnings, and served as a rare link between the Neukölln KPD cell and the unaffiliated Kuckhoff-Harnack circle.

John Sieg could vouch for Adam Kuckhoff, having known him for years. Harro Schulze-Boysen was new to the scene. John quietly questioned Marta Wolter Husemann, a member of the Schulze-Boysen circle whose husband was a KPD militant with the Neukölln group. Marta was fond of the artists and movie people who gathered around the Schulze-Boysens, but she confirmed to John that they were in no way comparable to a KPD cell. They lacked a "unified and single political purpose" and were in no way "oriented as uniform Communists"; in fact, their politics weren't even clearly defined.[4] In other words, Marta enjoyed their company because Harro was still campaigning for his "Party of Life."

Greta Kuckhoff did not attend the Schulze-Boysens' lake parties, and it is not clear whether she was ever invited. Greta was feeling increasingly marginalized in many regards. She contributed to the resistance efforts in a number of ways, including translating, typing flyers, arranging meetings, and transmitting information, all of which required energy, and some of which entailed risk. But she resented the way the men in the group treated her as though she were just a housewife. Her husband, Adam, was often distant and self-absorbed. Arvid Harnack had returned to the imperious manner that had been so off-putting back in Wisconsin. She had traveled to London in 1939 to help with Jewish immigration matters and meet with British trade unionists. When she returned, Arvid rebuked her for taking an afternoon to see *Snow White* at the movies.

Now she was aware that when John Sieg, Adam, and Arvid met, they would disappear behind closed doors. The official explanation was that they were "protecting" her from inside information for the sake of Ule, her little son. Greta and Adam were the only couple in their group with a child; the Harnacks, the Schulze-Boysens, and the Siegs were all childless. The others often urged Greta to spend as much time as possible with her son.

It wasn't that Greta was an unwilling mother. One of the few glimpses of her smiling is a snapshot of her gazing blissfully at her baby boy. But she was still ambivalent about parenthood. These were challenging times. She didn't know how to answer young Ule when he begged for a swastika flag, just like the other kids'. One day he proudly produced a small Nazi flag he had found on the street. His parents were upset until his father thought of a stratagem to get rid of it: "Go plant it in the ground," he told Ule, "and it will grow into a big one!"[5]

Greta supplemented her housekeeping chores with her intellectual tasks, getting up long before dawn to read through drafts of clandestine publications and make editorial suggestions. But sometimes she felt she was wasting her time. Adam, Arvid, and John generally ignored her ideas. They increasingly followed the editorial guidance of a new member of their circle, who had far more impressive journalistic credentials.

This was Johannes (known as "John") Graudenz, an older man with craggy features, deep-set eyes, and a stubborn cowlick. He had learned English as a teenage waiter in England, then drifted into journalism and a job with the Americans' United Press agency. In the early 1920s, UP posted him to Moscow, where he broke the story of Lenin's death to the world.

Graudenz wrote of Lenin in favorable terms, but his precise political affiliations were unclear. He had joined a leftist splinter party as a youth in Berlin, but he showed an independent spirit. In 1924 he organized a journalists' trip down the Volga through famine-stricken regions of the country. The Soviets were angered by his photos and expelled him from the country, but he managed to sneak his film out with him to Berlin. The United Press published his images across the United States, showing starving children under the headline "Tearing the Veil Off Russia."[6] Graudenz was popular among the foreign correspondents, and American journalists were especially grateful for his help in negotiating bureaucratic obstacles.[7] Graudenz was also a serious photographer. In 1924 one of his pictures was chosen as the subject for a "portfolio for Walter Gropius" by six master artists from the Bauhaus. It was reinterpreted as paintings by Wassily Kandinsky, Lyonel Feininger, Paul Klee, and others.[8]

In 1928, Graudenz was hired by the *New York Times* bureau in Berlin, and the *Times* hosted him on a visit to New York. But in 1932 he fell out with his new bureau chief and left the paper. After the Nazi takeover, he worked as a traveling industrial salesman, eventually marketing brake systems for heavy vehicles. He was antagonistic to the Nazi regime from the start, and open to any opportunity to prove it.

Graudenz joined the Schulze-Boysen circle through an unlikely connection. His neighbor, Annie Krauss, was a professional fortune-teller and psychic who counted Libertas Schulze-Boysen among her clients. The fortune-teller and the former journalist eagerly accepted Libertas's invitation to join her husband's underground efforts. Annie Krauss's customers included superstitious military officers, who shared details of upcoming campaigns as they asked for her forecasts, which she passed along to the group.

But she played on the superstitions of the group as well. Graudenz's teenage daughters saw them bring in plans for resistance actions for her approval. "She would lay her hand on it and say, 'Nothing will happen to you,' so they didn't take enough precautions." The girls were unimpressed. They called Krauss, a matronly woman with an ominous glare, the old *spökenkieker* (spook-spotter).[9] But Annie Krauss made a significant contribution to the group. Her living room soon acquired a printing apparatus for anti-Nazi flyers, produced under John Graudenz's expert supervision.[10]

In 1938, Krauss took in a twenty-two-year-old Jewish woman named Sophie Kuh, who was nervously awaiting a British visa. Sophie, a fragile young woman from a broken home, was deeply grateful for the haven. Soon Sophie Kuh found another source of unexpected support. "One day a tall gentleman came to visit Annie Krauss," she recalled later. It was her neighbor John Graudenz. He was kind and supportive to the young woman, even though he knew that any assistance to Jews was closely monitored by the Gestapo. Sophie called Graudenz "a wonderful friend," and he impressed her with his willingness to appear with her in public. On one occasion, she recalled,

> We were traveling in his car on the Kurfürstendamm. My passport already had a "J" stamped in it. The police stopped the car. I jumped out and disappeared into the crowd so he wouldn't get into trouble. He said later that he didn't care, I should have stayed in the car. But the Nazis did these terrible things at that time, very quietly. Someone would just disappear.

Sophie told Graudenz about her stepfather, a prominent writer and, as a Romanian Jew, a member of the highly vulnerable population of stateless Jews from the former Austro-Hungarian Empire. After their homeland was dissolved following World War I, many were unable to get alternate passports and visas. Graudenz helped him with money and food. Sophie's British visa eventually came through and Graudenz himself drove her to the train station. But there was no way to save her stepfather. He was deported and died in a concentration camp.[11]

The months between September 1939 and April 1940 passed slowly and miserably. In London, British civilians stared at the skies for the first German bombers to appear. Only the most deluded optimists believed that a shooting war could be averted now.

The antifascists working inside Germany felt the pressure mount. For Colonel Hans Oster, the anti-Nazi officer in military intelligence, the decisive moment came on November 7, 1939, two months after the German invasion of Poland. Oster asked a friend to drive him to the apartment of a Colonel Gijsbertus Sas, the Dutch military attaché in Berlin, whom he had befriended three years earlier.

When Oster returned from his conversation with Sas, he was visibly upset. "There is no way back for me," he told his waiting friend. "It is much easier to take a pistol and kill somebody; it is much easier to run into a burst of machine-gun fire than it is to do what I have done."

Oster's friend learned later that he had just given Sas the entire plan for Germany's invasion of Western Europe.[12] Sas shared the information with Danish and Norwegian officials, as well as his own government. But Oster's intelligence was undermined by Hitler's changes in plan—the invasion was postponed twenty-nine times.[13] Instead of taking advantage of the warnings to mount a defense, the Dutch commander in chief dismissed them as false alarms, suppressed the information, and accused Sas of sensationalism.[14] Oster's intelligence grew more and more detailed, yet the intended beneficiaries shrugged it off. "The people who received the message laughed about it," recalled Dutch official J. G. de Beus. "But when the time came they were not sufficiently prepared."[15]

Sas's final meeting with Oster on May 9, 1940, was like a "funeral meal." After dinner Oster stopped by his headquarters one last time to check his information, and returned full of despair. "The pig [Hitler] has gone off to the western front, now it is definitely over," he told Sas. "I hope we shall meet again after this war."[16] Oster, a career officer, fully understood that his actions could contribute to German casualties in the field. He also understood that in the eyes of many, his actions had crossed the line between dissent and treason. Yet like Harro Schulze-

Boysen and other dissident officers, he regarded his decision as the act of a patriot. He told Sas, "One might say that I am a traitor (*Landesver-räter*), but in reality I am not; I consider myself a better German than all those who run after Hitler. It is my plan and my duty to free Germany, and at the same time the world, of this plague."[17]

The German invasions were launched amid northern Europe's hazy spring. On April 9, 1940, the German army marched into Norway and Denmark. On May 10 it attacked Belgium, the Netherlands, and France. The operations went smoothly and successfully. France, Germany's traditional rival, had been complacent in the period leading up to the onslaught, confident that its defenses would hold.[18] They lasted a matter of weeks. France was vanquished on June 4.

The situation went from bad to worse. By late May the German armed forces had driven hundreds of thousands of British Expeditionary Forces to the French coast at Dunkirk. Over the next few weeks the world was transfixed by the spectacle of a massive rescue, as some 326,000 British escaped across the Channel on a motley flotilla of British motorboats and fishing smacks.

The Nazis reveled in their victory, lavishing medals on one another and parading their spoils. American correspondent William Shirer found that few Berliners around him shared a sense of triumph. "Strange, the apathy of the people in the face of this decisive turn in the war," he wrote after the conquest of Holland and Belgium. "Most Germans I've seen, outside of the officials, are sunk deep in depression at the news."[19] The circle of military resisters around Admiral Canaris and Hans Oster was devastated. They had been counting on the horrors of a protracted European war to tip German public opinion in their favor. Once again they were stymied.

The summer wore on, giving every indication that the European contest had entered its endgame. Talk of the British invasion resumed. On July 15 the Nazi-controlled press announced the German troops "now stand ready for the attack on Britain. The date of the attack will be decided by the Führer alone."[20] But the Führer refused to show his hand. Hitler expansively announced that he was ready to consider peace proposals from Britain.

The Nazi hierarchy set about imagining the future. The following week, the economics minister and the president of the Reich Economic Chamber unveiled plans for the "new order" in Europe: a population of 320 million people covering 1.5 million square miles.[21] The Reichsmark would be substituted for the gold standard, bankrupting the United States and making Germany the clearinghouse for the world economy. In this imagined empire, all roads led to Berlin.

In late July, the British spurned Hitler's offer of a compromised peace, but they knew that the Germans were far better prepared for war. The Nazis had spent years intensively building up their armed forces, militarizing their industry, and honing state-of-the-art field operations with advanced technologies. The same could not be said of the Polish, the French, the British, or the Americans.

In some cases, invisible gestures contributed to immense consequences. As German and British strategists raced to control strategic chokepoints, one obvious focus was Spain. In July 1940, the Germans sent military intelligence chief Admiral Wilhelm Canaris to convince his old friend Franco to join the Axis powers and give them control of Gibraltar.[22] It was another Nazi miscalculation. Canaris told Franco that the Nazi cause was doomed, and there was no reason for Spain to go down with it. Franco elected to maintain Spanish neutrality and Gibraltar remained in British hands, clearing the way for the Allied invasion of North Africa and Italy in November 1942.

For the Berlin circles, the way forward was unclear. Harro Schulze-Boysen was determined to continue to enjoy life amid the tension. In May 1940, as the Dutch offensive was under way, he organized a bicycle trip to Libertas's family castle with artists Kurt and Elisabeth Schumacher and writer Günther Weisenborn. Their friends Herbert Engelsing, the film producer, and his wife, Ingeborg, joined them, and Libertas brought along her accordion. To all outward appearances the group was merely relishing another spring holiday of swimming and cookouts at the lake. But, Ingeborg Engelsing wrote later, Harro had also brought secret reports from the German press agency and forbidden foreign press reports. He gathered the group to discuss plans for another round of flyers based on the information.[23]

Harro was exasperated with the Western democracies. Britain had squandered precious time, France had capitulated, and America stood idly by. As the crisis grew, his vision became more apocalyptic. As he now saw it, Hitler's military machine had overwhelmed the corrupt Western democracies. The Germans would have to plot their own course, distinct from both the West and the Soviets.[24]

Schulze-Boysen's vision illuminated another fault line running through the expanding circle. The few orthodox KPD veterans in his circle often retained their loyalty to Moscow and were offended by his irreverence. Others were more critical than Harro. Another member of his circle, cement merchant Hugo Buschmann, was so incensed at the Soviets that he turned down a trade mission to Moscow, refusing to travel in a country allied with Hitler.[25]

As of the summer of 1940, Arvid Harnack was the only member of the circle with an active, ongoing exchange with a foreign government. He continued to meet with Donald Heath from the U.S. State Department, though the encounters were increasingly difficult to arrange.

Heath's superior in Berlin, U.S. chargé Alexander Kirk, found it ever more uncomfortable to support the U.S. policy of neutrality in the European conflict. Even the reticent Kirk was moved to strong language. On July 17, 1940, he sent Roosevelt an impassioned memorandum summarizing the political and military situation in Europe. The possibility of long-term neutrality was an illusion, he argued: "There will be no place for the United States in the world envisioned by Hitler, and he will exercise his power with a view to eliminating it as a great power as soon as possible. . . ." The United States must decisively cast its lot against Hitler, Kirk wrote. "That alignment must be immediate, it must be open and unequivocal, and it must be supported by the extension of material help. . . ."[26]

Roosevelt's personal sympathies were clearly with Britain, and he took what steps he could, but he was severely limited. The idea of a war was still unpopular with most Americans, and Roosevelt was facing a tough election. Furthermore, Alexander Kirk's call for "material help" could be called an exercise in wishful thinking for the time being. At the time of his writing, the U.S. Army ranked eighteenth in the world, outnumbered by Germany, France, Britain, Russia, Italy, Japan, and China—as well as by Belgium, Holland, Portugal, Spain, Sweden, and Switzerland. The German military had 6.8 million men, compared to 504,000 in the U.S. armed forces.[27] Winston Churchill understood that part of the Americans' paralysis resulted from their intelligence deficit, and tried to fill the gap. In June 1940 he sent Canadian officer William Stephenson to New York to open a British intelligence office in Rockefeller Center. But Stephenson found the Americans less than eager for his help.

In August the war entered a new phase. On August 13 the Germans launched a massive air attack against Britain called Operation Eagle. The British responded in kind, sending bombers over German cities and facilities in occupied countries. Initially, both air forces were commanded to concentrate on military targets. But on August 23, a mission went wrong. A dozen German bomber pilots, under orders to bomb aircraft factories and oil tanks in the London suburbs, unloaded their bombs over residential areas in the heart of London instead.[28] Two nights later, the Royal Air Force retaliated for the German error by launching its first air raid on Berlin. Now both sides were committed to a policy of aerial attacks on civilians.

Berlin was in shock; Field Marshal Göring had assured its citizens that it was impossible for the British to penetrate the city's air defenses.[29] Now Berliners saw that he was wrong, deepening their misgivings about the road ahead.

For months, German troops had been poised for Operation Sea Lion, the invasion of Great Britain, but both Hitler and his high command vacillated over the plan. There were many obstacles. The Luftwaffe had not scored its expected victory in the air battle over Britain, and weather conditions were uncertain. On September 17, 1940, having lost the last of the favorable tides, Hitler called off the plan indefinitely.

As the wages of war grew more costly, so did the penalties for opposition. Capital punishment had not only become more frequent under the Nazis, it was more dramatic. As of 1934, death sentences were carried out with an ax, but in December 1936 the Nazi minister of justice decreed a shift to the guillotine. Two months later the device was installed in a shed on the grounds of the massive redbrick prison at Plötzensee. Many of its initial victims were members of the German Communist Party, such as twenty-eight-year-old Liselotte Hermann, a former biology student and mother of a four-year-old son. Hermann was beheaded after she was arrested with the floor plans of a munitions factory in her possession.[30]

Under the Nazis' standard procedure, the broken bodies were taken to be dissected at the Institute of Anatomy and Biology, just off the Tiergarten park where the Harnacks and Donald Heath took their tense, furtive walks.[31] Only a decade earlier, the medical institute worked under the direction of Adam Kuckhoff's friend, Adolf Grimme. Now its laboratories had been commandeered for a political end, to inflict a final humiliation on the remains of traitors against the regime.

\ \ \

CHAPTER 16

All Possible Foolish Rumors

1940–1941

OVER THE COURSE OF 1940 THE HARNACKS AND THE KUCKHOFFS
watched their society settle into the grim rhythms of war. As Nazi forces
stormed across Europe, they gathered momentum and swept up everything in their path. Each conquered territory became a source of manpower and supplies. Ethnic Germans in Poland and Czechoslovakia were
recruited or press-ganged into the German army, while Frenchmen were
recruited or forced into slave labor. Poles were terrorized, enslaved, or
murdered. Foreign mines and factories were retooled to feed the German army, while soldiers' wives and parents were placated with silk
stockings and Dutch cheese.

With France's June 1940 surrender, the Nazis reached the high-water
mark for domestic popularity. Many Germans saw the recent conquests
as a simple means to redress the accumulated grievances of the past thirty
years. The boundaries of Greater Germany now closely resembled a
1914 map of Europe, uniting the German-speaking peoples of Germany
and the Austro-Hungarian Empire and doing away with the notion of
Poland altogether. France's punitive terms at Versailles had been reversed (and the penalties exacted many times over). With Germany's old
enemies crushed, the Reich appeared invincible.

The resistance circles in Berlin were stalemated, and the production
of anti-Nazi flyers dropped off sharply. They had lost their audience. For
the moment, the antifascists were at a loss for new arguments that could

shatter mass delusions of the Nazis' success, and they concentrated on communicating within their circles.

The German generals realized that the prospective Russian invasion was a different matter. Hitler was asking them to commit their forces to a two-front war, going into the harsh Russian winter. But at least in its earliest conception, this was not an impossible undertaking. The generals reasoned that if the German army could conquer Russia before winter set in and the United States remained aloof, the British would have no choice but to sue for peace. Hitler would win, and a massive slave nation with a staggering supply of natural resources would be added to his arsenal.

On the home front, the hardships of militarization mounted faster for German civilians than the benefits of victory. The government imposed food rationing in 1939, a few days before the invasion of Poland, to save supplies for soldiers at the front. The rationing, which grew more severe over time, made it more difficult for Jews to survive and for their German friends to help them. In January 1940 the government decreed that baths were limited to Saturday and Sunday, a harsh blow for the fuel-starved Berliners, who relied on hot baths to stay warm.[1] In August 1940, Berlin suffered its first civilian casualties from British air strikes. Berliners' routine now incorporated sirens and air-raid shelters by night, and mounds of fresh rubble in the morning.

In the occupied countries German troops stripped the land and terrorized local populations, but the German media filtered all such unpleasantness from its reports. In the Neverland of Nazi news, German troops were always welcomed with flowers by smiling children, and grateful citizens thanked the troops for "cleansing" and "pacifying" their land.

The Nazis never considered releasing the number of civilian casualties in their campaigns. But in May 1940 the Nazis stopped releasing the number and names of German military casualties as well. Hitler distinctly recalled that in World War I, the more Germans dwelled on their casualty lists, the more they questioned the war itself. That inconvenience, too, could be minimized.

But one sector of the population had irrefutable firsthand knowledge of the war. This was the front-line military itself. A number of officers had already objected to the Nazis' persecution of the Jewish and Christian communities, and had begun to explore resistance activities.

Until Poland, it was possible for many German officers to believe the rhetoric of liberating ethnic Germans and redrawing the boundaries of Versailles. The Polish campaign was something else again. This time, ad hoc units of Gestapo and SS personnel were attached to the regular army, with orders to carry out mass executions. They were known as *Einsatzkommando* units, variously translated as "mission command" or "task force" (also known as *Einsatzgruppen*). By 1940, these mobile killing units were held responsible for the deaths of 52,000 people in Poland, many of them Polish aristocrats, intelligentsia, and Jews, the sectors that were expected to lead resistance against German occupation.[2] But the presence and the activities of these death squads were deeply disturbing to many regular army officers, operating outside the traditional chain of command and violating every norm of military conduct. In the opinion of some military historians, Poland represented the turning point of the German military resistance movement.[3]

In November 1939, the commander in chief of the eastern districts, General Johannes Blaskowitz, wrote a memorandum to Hitler describing the atrocities and abuses he had witnessed, and expressing his "utmost concern" regarding their impact on the troops.

Hitler called Blaskowitz's message "childish" and condescendingly told the general, "You can't wage war with Salvation Army methods." But Blaskowitz persisted, sending another strongly worded communication to the army commander in chief, deploring the "bloodthirstiness" of the *Einsatzkommandos* and calling for a "new order." In January 1940 he told his commanding officer, "Every soldier feels sickened and repelled by the crimes committed in Poland by agents of the Reich and government representatives." Blaskowitz's protests were suppressed and he was dismissed from the eastern front in May 1940. But anti-Nazi officers circulated his reports to other commands, where they caused "great agitation."[4]

One colonel, Helmuth Stieff, cited Blaskowitz's charges in an agonized letter to his wife:

I am ashamed of being a German. This minority which sullies the name of Germany by murder, plunder and arson will prove the misfortune of the whole German nation unless we put a stop to these people soon. What has been described and proved to me by the most responsible authorities on the spot is bound to arouse the avenging nemesis. Otherwise this rabble will one day do the same things to us decent people and terrorize their own nation with their pathological passions.[5]

The regime recognized that such officers' agitation was problematic. In early 1940 the high command responded by removing SS police formations in Poland from army jurisdiction, reasoning that if regular army officers were not legally responsible for the SS, the officers would express fewer qualms and the SS would be less impeded in its actions.[6]

Many Germans smelled catastrophe in the air, but they tried to maintain a sense of normalcy day to day. Their country's fate was being driven by Adolf Hitler, a man of little education but stunning intuition, who was right just often enough to throw everyone off balance. His foreign adversaries were proving equally unpredictable. Many anti-Nazi officers believed that the West would actively oppose the Nazi occupation of Czechoslovakia over 1938 and 1939. When Britain and France responded with appeasement, they assumed that the West would stand idly by as Poland was dismembered in 1939. The conquest of Poland stirred Britain and France to action, but now, with France and Western Europe under occupation, no one could predict the actions of the Soviet Union or the United States.

Hitler's invasions had left his opponents increasingly isolated. The Nazi occupation of Western Europe shut down support from the outside world and eliminated a host of exile havens. German Communists fled the Nazi advances from one capital to another, trying to keep a step ahead of the Gestapo. Many failed. Paris had sheltered Willi Münzenberg, the German Communist media czar, who occupied a permanent spot on the Nazis' blacklist. Münzenberg was expelled from the Communist Party for suspected "diversionism" in 1938, and refused a subsequent summons to the Soviet Union. The French government put him in a camp for enemy aliens when war broke out, but released the prisoners in June 1940 as the German army advanced. Münzenberg and another internee set out for Switzerland. In October his decayed body, with face battered, was found hanging from a tree in a French forest. The other escapee had disappeared without a trace. Some called Münzenberg's death a suicide, but others saw the hallmarks of a Stalinist assassination.

Berlin's antifascists watched their city close down around them. By the fall of 1940, many of the Western press corps and embassy staff had already left. On October 8, William Shirer told his diary about yet another U.S. embassy good-bye party, hosted by Donald Heath. He reported that Heath had personal cause for celebration; a few weeks earlier a British bomb splinter crashed into his office and passed directly over his desk. Fortunately, Heath had gone home early and missed the blast.

Shirer was making his own plans to leave Berlin. Journalism as he defined it had become impossible:

> Until recently, despite the censorship, I think I've been able to do an honest job of reporting from Germany. But . . . the new instructions of both the military and the political censors are that they cannot allow me to say anything which might create an unfavourable impression for Nazi Germany in the United States. . . . You cannot call the Nazis "Nazis" or an invasion an "invasion." You are reduced to re-broadcasting the official communiqués, which are lies, and which any automaton can do.[7]

Many Berliners had given up reading newspapers. When the radio propaganda became too much for them, they turned off their sets muttering "*Quatsch!*" Not even the movies guaranteed an escape. They opened with *Deutsche Wochenschau* (German Weekly Show) newsreels showing Polish peasants as they happily harvested potatoes and SA troopers in Poland who passed their time reading newspapers in the library.[8] The few remaining Western correspondents were allowed to listen to foreign broadcasts, but only on the condition that they did not share the contents with their German acquaintances. Foreign radio was the only reliable source of news; if a foreign newspaper arrived, it was usually months old.

Arvid Harnack's younger brother Falk succeeded in getting him a powerful shortwave, to give him and his wife access to foreign news. They carefully noted developments and shared them with a small circle of friends, as part of their limited resistance activity over the summer of 1940. Harnack also continued to meet with Donald Heath from the U.S. embassy, though with ever greater precautions. Despite his straitened circumstances, Harnack never asked Heath for money. Sometimes Harnack asked Heath to provide him with paper, whose bulk purchase was carefully monitored by the Gestapo. "He needed a lot, and he couldn't buy it himself," Heath's son recalled later. "My father didn't feel good about it, and soon stopped. If he had known about the propaganda, he would have been upset. Before he came to Berlin he had received training in ground rules: you don't mix political activism with intelligence work."[9] These were ground rules that Harnack violated at every turn. He knew that his clandestine newsletters represented a liability for his intelligence work, but they offered his circles of friends an antidote for despair.

Harro Schulze-Boysen spent much of 1940 expanding his circle of contacts. The new members included artists, students, KPD militants, and dissident officials working inside the Nazi ministries. Their beliefs and their backgrounds were diverse, and this could set off sparks. Some of the disputes involved old political baggage. In the autumn of 1940, Walter Husemann introduced a KPD official and former *Rote Fahne* editor named Wilhelm Guddorf to the circle. He arrived at a meeting of the Schulze-Boysen circle only to find that the group included Walter Küchenmeister, the companion of Harro's friend Dr. Elfriede Paul. Guddorf was appalled. He protested that Küchenmeister had been expelled from the KPD in 1926 for helping himself to party funds. The party condemned him as a deserter and he could well be a Gestapo informer.[10] Guddorf demanded that they cut off relations with Küchenmeister at once.[11]

Harro Schulze-Boysen was impatient with this old Communist grudge. He had nothing against the party, but he had no use for KPD militants who were more interested in party vendettas than the crisis at hand. Harro had known Küchenmeister from his *Gegner* days, and Dr. Elfriede Paul brought him into the group in 1935. Like Guddorf,

Küchenmeister had served time in a concentration camp, where he had barely survived a severe case of tuberculosis. In Harro's view, the man had paid his dues. With his usual willfulness, Harro went out of his way to strengthen his ties to Elfriede Paul and Walter Küchenmeister, and distance himself from Guddorf. If his group needed a way to communicate with the KPD, there were plenty of other routes. Kurt Schumacher came up with a fellow sculptor with party connections, and Guddorf's protests were ignored. Harro Schulze-Boysen enjoyed annoying his family by calling himself a "Communist" and throwing around Marxist jargon, but it is doubtful he would have been welcome in the KPD. The party took a dim view of chronic insubordination.

Harro encouraged the new members of his circle to infiltrate the Nazi bureaucracies to gain access to information. In July 1940 he drove his friend Günther Weisenborn to a job interview at the state radio company, the Grossdeutscher Rundfunk. Weisenborn was hired as an editor on the news desk at a crucial juncture in German broadcasting. The previous month Goebbels had launched a new schedule, coordinating daily nationwide programming with civil defense reports on air raids.[12] Weisenborn's job was to review reports of what was actually happening, and recycle them into stories that conformed to the propaganda.

Harnack, Kuckhoff, and Schulze-Boysen were frustrated. They pursued every possible avenue to oppose the regime, but their actions were desultory and indirect, and it was hard to argue that they did any real damage to the Nazi war machine.

A stunning new opportunity arrived, quite literally on Arvid Harnack's doorstep, on September 17, 1940, the same day that Hitler called off the British invasion. The surprise visitor spoke fluent German with a slight accent. He informed Arvid that he brought greetings from an old friend at the Soviet embassy, which immediately aroused Arvid's suspicion. He had not communicated with the Soviets for the two years since Stalin's purges had eradicated his embassy contacts. This man could well be a Gestapo agent sent to entrap him. The Russian invited Arvid to the Soviet embassy as proof of his bona fides, then asked him to renew his contact with the Soviets. Arvid was reluctant (his visitor described him as "mistrustful and tense") but following a long conversation, he agreed.

The visitor turned out to be Alexander Korotkov, an officer of the

Soviet intelligence agency NKVD. Korotkov was a sleekly groomed thirty-one-year-old with a bold, ironic gaze. He also had an eye for the main chance. He had begun his career at the age of nineteen, after striking up an acquaintance with an intelligence official at a soccer match. That meeting led to a job as an elevator operator, and a few years later he was posted abroad as an agent. He worked for several years at the Soviet trade mission in Berlin, where Gisella von Pöllnitz made her ill-fated drop of Harro Schulze-Boysen's Spanish intelligence in the trade mission mailbox. (There is no evidence that the Soviets passed the warnings on to the Spanish Republicans, while young Gisella endured a Gestapo interrogation for her pains.)

Korotkov ran into his own difficulties in 1939, when members of his wife's family were accused of treason, but he appealed directly to Lavrenty Beria, Stalin's notorious head of intelligence, and was reinstated. He returned to Berlin under diplomatic cover in the summer of 1940 and sought out Arvid Harnack soon after. Korotkov had been handed the difficult task of putting the Soviets' intelligence network in Berlin back in order.

Since Arvid Harnack's initial encounter with Soviet agents in 1935, the residencies, or the Soviet agents stationed abroad, had experienced constant upheaval. NKVD personnel had served as Stalin's executioners for countless Russians, Ukrainians, and ethnic minorities. Hundreds of NKVD officers had themselves fallen victim to the purges. In the process, Soviet intelligence also lost its most astute and experienced officers. The Berlin office was especially disupted. Harnack's first intelligence contact, who was recalled to Moscow and executed, was replaced by an agent who died on the operating table within a year. The next agent was appointed through nepotism, with no foreign experience and no German language.

Korotkov was a more effective choice, since he had worked illegally in Western Europe since 1933 and spoke fluent German. Now Korotkov had been sent to ask Harnack to reestablish his intelligence link with the Soviets. Korotkov found Harnack reluctant, but he agreed in the end. There is no record of the conversation from Harnack's perspective, but Korotkov made a careful entry about the meeting in his file.

Harnack, he reported, was not motivated by money and did not "see himself in the role of an agent with us as his chiefs." Harnack did not hide the fact that he had his own agenda, which concerned the future of his own country. Korotkov dutifully told his superiors that Harnack considered the Soviet Union "a country with whose ideals he feels connected and from which he awaits support." (This was not the entire story. Harnack repeatedly told his friends of his aversion to Stalin and the Soviets' bullying methods, and warned Adolf Grimme that they would need "a fist in order not to become a puppet of Moscow.")

Korotkov described Harnack as "an honest person, a truly moral person, who says what he means," and recognized that he had scored an intelligence windfall.[13]

He and his circle possessed extraordinary access to classified information and excellent covers. This was made clear from their first meeting, when Arvid informed Korotkov that Hitler planned to break his agreement with Stalin and invade the Soviet Union.[14]

Over the following nine months, Alexander Korotkov and Arvid Harnack engaged in an exotic minuet—although under less dire circumstances, it could have been considered a comedy of errors. Moscow's file on Harnack lacked context and was out of date. It was well and good for Korotkov to field abundant intelligence, but he also had some explaining to do. Over the coming months, Moscow demanded to know who Harnack really was. What was his relationship with the KPD? Who exactly were these friends of his? What was their motivation?

The only surviving records of Korotkov's meetings are those sent by Korotkov, written to ingratiate himself with the home office. Nonetheless, they offer a fascinating glimpse into the period between September 1940 and June 1941.

Korotkov recognized that, as an agent, Harnack was far from the Soviet ideal. His antifascist principles were considered a liability. The best amateur agents were the most easily controlled, usually motivated by greed or blackmail, weathering the bizarre shifts of international politics without scruples. The perfect spy was dedicated to the single narrow function of espionage, and rejected any political activity or relationship that could attract attention. This model supported more traditional Soviet agents, such as Richard Sorge in Tokyo and Gestapo officer Willy Lehmann, one of Korotkov's paid contacts who had begun reporting to the Soviets in 1929.[15] But Arvid Harnack made it clear to Korotkov, as he had to Donald Heath, that he would not allow his intelligence work to extinguish his resistance work.

Korotkov's first brief outlined his September meeting with Harnack, who was assigned the code name "Korsikanets" ("Corsican"). He quoted Arvid's report from an unnamed army staff officer at the high command that Germany would go to war against the Soviet Union the following year.

> A preliminary step for the military action against the USSR will be the occupation of Romania, which is currently under preparation and will take place over the next few months. . . . [It was suggested that] the general operations against England were going to be postponed.[16]

Korotkov's report ran directly counter to Stalin's convictions about Hitler. When Stalin received the information, he called in his intelligence chief (and Korotkov's boss), Lavrenty Beria, and asked him his opinion. Beria had recently intervened on Korotkov's behalf, but he had also just inherited his position from the executed former chief of secret police. Beria told Stalin what he wanted to hear: "I will drag this Korsikanets [Harnack] to Moscow and jail him for disinformation," he responded.[17]

Both Alexander Korotkov and Arvid Harnack saw the need to regroup. Arvid realized that his economic reports would be useful to the Soviets, but updates from Kuckhoff's new friend at air force intelligence would be far more critical. He called a meeting. Over the past five years, Arvid Harnack, Adam Kuckhoff, and Harro Schulze-Boysen had all met one-on-one, but now, over October and November of 1940, they gathered as a group for the first time.

For Arvid, a cautious man by nature, the meetings must have come as a jolt. At Arvid and Adam's prompting, Harro ran through his alarmingly long list of activities. He started with his professional duties. He was supplementing his work at air force intelligence with some university courses, and he had just been asked to teach a class for young officers at the school of foreign affairs. Harro's resistance work was even more expansive, and he cheerfully mixed it up with his day job. He gave daily press conferences for his friends, briefing them on the information he gathered from the foreign newspapers he analyzed in the office. His information was passed along to other discussion groups or published in clandestine newsletters for small circles of like-minded friends. Harro found new recruits for the resistance everywhere, including the air force, the university, and his social circles.

All in all, he was a security nightmare. Arvid Harnack told Harro that if he was going to be of any real use in fighting the Nazis, he'd have to rein himself in. It was particularly important for him to break off contact with Walter Küchenmeister's Communist exiles in Switzerland. These circles were rife with informers. Adam Kuckhoff was unsurprised by Harro's haphazard activities. Harro's wife, Libertas, had told Greta that she was concerned by the way her husband got "carried away" by his temperament, and hoped that Arvid's sober approach would be a moderating influence.[18]

Korotkov returned to headquarters for further instructions. Whatever Stalin's reaction to his initial report, Moscow was hungry for more. In December 1940 the Soviet deputy director of foreign intelligence, Pavel Sudoplatov, drew up a ten-point shopping list for Korotkov to present to Arvid Harnack. First, Sudoplatov wanted Harnack to acquire military intelligence through his ministry connections. Second, Harnack was asked to gather information about the conservative German resistance to Hitler (to address Soviet concerns that the German generals and Social Democrats would join forces with the British and the Americans against the Soviets).[19]

Later that month, Harnack officially brought Harro Schulze-Boysen into the operation. He was assigned the code name "Starshina" (a Russian military rank).[20] Korotkov asked Adam Kuckhoff to serve as the third of his direct contacts, with the code name "Starik" ("old man"). Kuckhoff was described as an old friend of Korsikanets who could report on the opposition to Hitler and assist in communications.[21] For the time being Arvid Harnack would serve as the sole contact to Korotkov.

Korotkov's reports from Berlin provided an early warning of the Nazis' plans to invade Russia, and offered the Soviets ample time to mount a strong defense. But Stalin's trust in his fellow dictator was unperturbed, and Hitler took imaginative measures to lead him on. On

New Year's Eve 1940, Hitler sent Stalin a holiday greeting, accompanied by a reassuring message. If the Soviet leader happened to hear any rumors about a possible German invasion, he confided, it was part of his deliberate smokescreen.

"I especially want to warn you of the following," Hitler added.

The agony of England is accompanied by feverish efforts to save it from its inevitable fate. For this purpose they are fabricating all possible foolish rumors, the most important of which can be crudely divided into two categories. These are rumors of planned invasions by the USSR into Germany and by Germany against the USSR. I do not wish to dwell on the absurdity of such nonsense.

However, on the basis of information in my possession, I predict that as our invasion of the [British] Isles draws closer, the intensity of such rumors will increase and fabricated documents will perhaps be added to them. I will be completely open with you. Some of these rumors are being circulated by appropriate German offices.[22]

Hitler closed his letter by suggesting that the two leaders get together sometime to discuss the disposal of England's remains and plan the new world order. Hitler was a little busy at the moment, he said, but he expected his schedule to free up around the "end of June." As it happened, his June invasion would keep both men fully occupied.

It is possible that Stalin discounted Arvid's initial report as vague, but once Harro Schulze-Boysen joined the effort in December, the information became extensive and detailed. Harro's office was directly involved in implementing Directive Number 21, signed into effect by Adolf Hitler on December 18, 1940. Known as "Operation Barbarossa," it stated: "The German armed forces must be prepared to crush Soviet Russia in a quick campaign before the end of the war against England. Preparations are to be completed by May 15, 1941."[23]

Arvid Harnack met with Alexander Korotkov again in January 1941, the first of dozens of meetings that would occur over the first half of the year. Arvid reported that his network had grown to some sixty people.

Among the military officers from the German army, navy, and air force were Baron Wohlzogen-Neuhaus from the technical department of the German army, assigned the code name "Grek" ("Greek"), and young officers from Harro's classes. Other members worked in critical areas of the defense industry. These included Karl Behrens, code name "Luchisty" ("ray of light"), an engineer for the giant electrical company AEG, and Hans Rupp, a high-ranking economist at the chemical giant I.G. Farben.[24]

But Harro Schulze-Boysen was the prize. In January 1941 he was transferred to the Wildpark-West complex near Potsdam, where Göring had built his underground command center. Harro's new post gave him the perfect vantage point for observing the preparations for war. The headquarters included both air force communications and intelligence operations, and his duties included writing up the reports from air force attachés at various foreign embassies.[25] Twice a week, Harro made the short trip into Berlin to teach his young officers at the university's Institute of Foreign Affairs.[26] If the invasion went forward as planned, he could offer an unparalleled intelligence perspective.

That month Harro wrote to his parents about his new situation in breezy, telegraphic prose:

> Things good here. Really nice gentlemen I'm dealing with. Work from early morning until *late* at night—but interesting (and that's the main thing). Strange feeling: suddenly life has entered into a new phase . . . Air is good. Food's good. Time to study is unfortunately *very* limited. I'll be in Berlin on Sunday. Today the main thing is my new address.[27]

A different limitation affected Harro Schulze-Boysen's reports. Stalin's intelligence service was unfamiliar with German air force terminology (and, for that matter, so was Arvid Harnack). Much of the information that Schulze-Boysen offered was never correctly translated.

But this confusion was dwarfed by another factor. Stalin was a prisoner of his own denial. Certain that Hitler would not invade the Soviet Union until he had dispensed with Britain, Stalin filtered every bit of information through his flawed prism, despite concrete evidence that invasion plans were under way.

The German reconnaissance flights, predicted by Harro in October 1940, were already producing a massive collection of aerial photographs of Soviet military targets. Soviet intelligence informed Stalin that between March and December 19, 1940, there were fifteen German violations of Soviet airspace. These increased with time. On March 20, 1941, the Soviet foreign ministry protested to the German ambassador that thirty-seven violations had taken place between October 1940 and March 1941, but the complaint was ignored. Other German authorities blandly noted that there were "many military flying schools" near the border, and their "student pilots easily become disoriented."[5]

Anxious officials brought the intelligence reports directly to Stalin's desk, but he continued to accept Hitler's word. Having eliminated his best intelligence officers, the dictator distrusted those who survived. He had no interest in the analysis of experts. Stalin demanded the raw data, which he interpreted through ideological blinders, without benefit of experience in the world beyond. Marxist-Leninist doctrine held that fascist Germany had to go to war against the capitalist nations before it attacked the Soviets. Stalin made executive decisions based on his bias, ignoring all evidence and arguments to the contrary.

Step by step, Harro continued to monitor the Germans' secret plans. A March 9 update stated:

> The photographic reconnaissance flights were underway at full speed. German aircraft were operating from air fields at Bucharest, Königsberg, and Kirkenes in northern Norway. Photos were taken at a height of 6,000 meters. . . . The photos are well

\ \ \

CHAPTER 17

The Road to Barbarossa

January–June 1941

OVER THE NEXT FEW MONTHS, HARRO SCHULZE-BOYSEN PROVIDED the Soviets with a play-by-play account of the plans for the coming German invasion.[1] In early January, Harro announced that the formal preparations had begun. The air force had been ordered to start large-scale photographic reconnaissance flights over the Soviet border, and Göring reassigned the Russian experts at the Air Ministry to the operations planning staff. Arvid quickly passed the information on to Korotkov, who encoded it and sent it to Moscow.[2] A few weeks later Arvid told Harro that his information had reached its destination.[3]

On January 9, 1941, Arvid sent news from the Economics Ministry. The German high command had ordered the Military-Economic Department of the statistics administration to prepare a map of Soviet industrial flights.

The German resisters thought the implications were clear, but the Soviets continued to have doubts. Some of them were inadvertently sown by Harnack himself. There was nothing clear-cut about German foreign policy, and Harnack provided an overview of the competing viewpoints. Korotkov's files over January and February reflected the tangle of Harnack's leads. While Hitler was preparing for war, Hermann Göring was putting out feelers for a peace agreement with England and America. Donald Heath told Harnack that other German generals had approached the United States for a separate agreement.[4] The Nazi monolith was never as solid as it seemed.

executed. The collected photographs are evaluated in the staff's 5th reconnaissance unit. The head of this unit is Col. Schmidt.[6]

Arvid's report added comments from his friend Egmont Zechlin. Zechlin's Nazi sources had said that they hoped to complete a surprise attack that spring, before the retreating Russians could set fire to their ripening wheat fields. The harvest could be gathered to feed the Germans.[7]

On March 20, Arvid Harnack sent a meticulous report on logistics:

In addition to the occupation forces there was only one active division in Belgium, thus confirming the postponement of military action against the British Isles. Preparation for an attack against the USSR has become obvious. This is evident from the disposition of German forces concentrated along the Soviet border. The rail line from Lvov to Odessa is of special interest because it has European-gauge tracks.

The following week, Hitler ran into an unexpected snag. The Germans had been counting on the cooperation of reactionary governments in the region, including Hungary, Romania, and Yugoslavia. On March 26 the government and prince regent of Yugoslavia were overthrown in a coup. The new government was cautiously antifascist. It offered to sign a nonaggression pact with Germany but retracted a previous offer of support. In Belgrade, angry crowds spat on the German minister's car. Hitler threw a tantrum.

The following day Hitler informed his astonished generals of his sudden decision to postpone the Soviet invasion by four weeks in order to first crush Yugoslavia. The country would be parceled out to Hungary, Romania, and Italy, with the exception of a small, collaborating slice of Croatia. Earlier, Hitler's leading commanders had balked at the idea of a Soviet invasion. Now they feared that a delay would push their operations into the fearsome Russian winter, which had cost Napoleon his army and his empire over a century earlier. Hitler was not interested in his generals' practical objections.[8]

Soviet intelligence was running into a snag of its own. Alexander Korotkov's superiors in Moscow recognized the extraordinary nature of his reports, but they were disturbed by their provenance.

Korotkov was suggesting that the Soviets should base radical policy decisions on information from a shadowy economist with no party credentials, an "air force officer" he had never met, and their vast network of unknown "sources." This would be uncomfortable under normal circumstances, but with Stalin in power, every step led to a different minefield. In Communist party terms, Korotkov's sources came out of nowhere. The Soviets wanted to check them out as quickly and thoroughly as possible.

On March 12, Soviet intelligence officials sent a letter to the executive committee of the Communist International. Their questions contained so many errors that they must have further perplexed the recipients. Who was "Johannes" Harnack? (There was no "Johannes"; they meant Arvid.) And what about this Harro Schulze-Boysen, who published the *Gegner* and was "imprisoned for two years"? (Harro was detained for days, not years.) The letter appended a list of Harnack's friends and relatives, speculating (often erroneously) which ones had belonged to the Communist Party before 1933.

German Communist official Walter Ulbricht tried to help, but he was clearly improvising. He soberly replied that "Johannes" Harnack was the secretary of a writers' organization, but it was "unknown whether he was a KPD member or just a sympathizer." Harro's magazine *Gegner*, he added, represented the "Dadaist" movement, which would have come as a surprise to Harro.[9]

More queries went out to foreign Communist residents in Moscow. Georg Lukacs, a prominent Hungarian literary critic, did a little better. He could speak on behalf of Arvid Harnack, whom he had known from literary circles in Berlin before 1933. Lukas described "HARNACK (Arvid?)" as "(not openly) a member of the KPD, and still burdened by bourgeois beliefs, which he worked earnestly to overcome."[10]

Korotkov was under pressure to clarify the sources of his reports. For months, Arvid Harnack had served as the go-between, but now Korotkov pushed for a face-to-face encounter with the young air force lieutenant. On March 27, 1941 (the same day Hitler decided to delay the

Soviet invasion), Schulze-Boysen arrived at Harnack's home to meet the Soviet.

Korotkov carefully noted his observations:

> Last Thursday Korsikanets brought us together with Starshina. Starshina is fully aware that he is dealing with a representative of the Soviet Union, and not the [Communist] Party. He gives the impression that he is fully prepared to tell me everything he knows. He answered my questions without trying to evade or hide anything. Even more: he was well-prepared for our meeting, and brought a piece of paper with certain points noted on it to convey to us.

Now that Arvid had made the commitment to provide intelligence to the Soviets, he wanted to make sure it was put to good use. This meant that he had to define himself and Harro to Soviet intelligence in terms they could understand. The web of relationships became more complex. Korotkov struggled to describe Arvid in Marxist terms that his bosses would approve (even though they had already been warned of his "bourgeois tendencies"). Arvid, in turn, tried to explain Harro's colorful politics without damaging his credibility. He chose to compare his colleague to the "Decembrist" officers of czarist Russia, who revolted in the effort to establish a constitutional government. Kororotkov passed along the description to his baffled superiors in Moscow, adding his own psychological insight:

> Korsikanets urgently asked us to accept that Starshina was, as he expressed it, a passionate Decembrist. In no case should he be given the impression that his political work, which he highly values, should degenerate into pure espionage.
>
> In contrast to Korsikanets, who forges great plans for the future and whose people are preparing for a communist takeover, Starshina is an energetic man who concentrates on the concrete actions that are necessary for the changes that Korsikanets only dreams of.[11]

On April 2, Harro reported that the invasion plans were complete. Korotkov informed Moscow that the German air strikes would start with economic and military targets. He gave a list of the four rail lines and junctions that were going to be paralyzed in the first wave of attack: "The initial objectives of the attack will be industrial targets, especially in the Donetsk basin, and engine works, ball-bearing factories, and aircraft factories in Moscow." He added that there were already German troop concentrations on the Romanian side of the Soviet border.

On April 6, Hitler made good on his threat to invade Yugoslavia and Greece. He decided that Greece was to be occupied and Yugoslavia was to be destroyed. In an operation with the code name "Punishment," German bomber pilots carried out more than five hundred missions over Belgrade in three days, killing five thousand civilians.[12]

The Germans were still indecisive, Harro reported, and updated their shifting positions. On April 17, 1941, he stated that the German victories in North Africa led the German generals to hope that they could still triumph over Great Britain. Nonetheless, he cautioned, "The general staff is continuing its preparations against the USSR with its previous intensity, as can be seen in its detailed designation of bombing targets."

Soviet intelligence now took measures to increase the flow of information from Berlin. In mid-April, Moscow ordered Korotkov to create an independent Berlin operation under the direction of Arvid Harnack, which would include direct radio contact. Arvid Harnack was asked to run the radio operation. He initially hesitated, then refused. The Soviets urged him to select his own radio operator, and suggested several candidates. Harro Schulze-Boysen nominated sculptor Kurt Schumacher.[13] Arvid acquiesced, but he was keenly aware that the presence of a Soviet radio operator among his circle could compromise them all.

Arvid was also worried about Harro Schulze-Boysen, who spent much of the spring preoccupied with his personal life. In March his younger brother Hartmut was diagnosed with tuberculosis of the bone. That crisis had hardly abated when Harro threw himself into a new love affair. In the wake of his wife's affair with Günther Weisenborn, Harro found romance with Stella Mahlberg. A young actress with dark curls and a sulky pout, she was just starting to win small roles on the Berlin stage. Harro nicknamed her "Fix," and sent her a blizzard of fond and foolish letters.[14]

But Harro's other relationships caused greater concern. On April 18, Korotkov sent a panicked alert to Moscow:

> We have just discovered a tie between Starshina and the [Communist] Party and await your guidance. What should I do? A hard line against Starshina could endanger the connection to him at a critical juncture and reduce his willingness to provide further information.[15]

The Soviets had instructed Korotkov to pressure Schulze-Boysen, Harnack, and Kuckhoff to break off all involvement with Communist Party affairs as well as any kind of political activity. Harro was the immediate concern, since his large circle now included a number of individuals with KPD ties, among them Walter Küchenmeister and Wilhelm Guddorf. Arvid Harnack and Adam Kuckhoff were also problematic, since they were still working closely with John Sieg and engaged in many kinds of political activities. The Berliners' answer to Korotkov is not recorded, but they clearly ignored his direction.[16]

As Harnack, Schulze-Boysen, and Kuckhoff increased their intelligence work, their wives were implicated as well. Korotkov told Moscow that Mildred Harnack was "fully informed about our contact," and sometimes carried messages. The wives were enlisted to trail their husbands' meetings in parks or wooded areas, to make sure they weren't being followed.[17]

Arvid and Mildred Harnack continued to see Donald Heath at the U.S. embassy when they could, but he was not long for Berlin. On May 8, 1941, a State Department official inquired whether the Treasury Department "had any objection to Donald Heath being transferred from Berlin," since his "services were required in a Latin American capital." After all, the official noted, Heath "had been in Berlin for some time."[18] Neither the State Department nor Treasury raised any objection. This was a stunning decision on Washington's part.

Heath's position as "monetary attaché" had been improvised as a response to the U.S. vacuum in intelligence, and he had become one of few American officials with extensive contacts within the German resistance. After three years in Berlin he knew the situation and the personalities well, and had won the trust of a broad range of figures in influential business and government positions. Washington's queries had reflected far more interest in the Nazis' currency policy than in their human rights violations or plans of armed conquest. Now, in May 1941, as Western Europe groaned under occupation and Britain braced itself for an invasion, the State Department prepared to transfer its most informed analyst of the German opposition—to Santiago, Chile.

Greta Kuckhoff was aware that the stakes were rising, but she was not happy with her role. Her husband, with one breath, withheld operational details to "protect her," only to ask her to take public risks without letting her know the substance of the event. She knew that the Soviet invasion was rapidly approaching, yet neither the Soviets nor the German public seemed to take it seriously. The Nazi newspapers were filled with daily threats against the British. Germans were aware that there was a buildup of tanks and troops on the eastern front, but they shrugged it off as a response to the Polish resistance. Or maybe, rumor had it, Hitler planned to take a southern route through the Soviet Union, to strike the British in India.[19]

"A lot of people find it easier to look Death in the eye than the Truth," Greta observed. Greta privately questioned whether the Soviets appreciated the value of elite assets such as Schulze-Boysen and Harnack. Was it possible that Moscow was writing off their reports as the mere "daydreams of self-important busybodies"?[20] The Soviets certainly gave no signs of preparing for war. On the contrary, Stalin continued to fulfill every commitment to build up the German arsenal. In April the Soviets assigned additional trains to deliver two thousand extra tons of rubber to Germany.[21]

Greta complained about feeling sidelined, but when she was finally given an opportunity to act, she balked. One day in May, Adam told her that Korotkov had asked for her to meet him at the Thielplatz subway station, where he was going to hand her "a small suitcase." Moscow had sent two transmitters by diplomatic pouch, he said, and now it was necessary to deliver them. Greta knew that the risk was tremendous. As her husband told her of the request, she observed that she had never seen his face "so full of sorrow."

But Greta resisted the assignment. She was far from convinced that radio communications were either workable or worth the risk.

"Let's stop playing cat-and-mouse," she demanded. "When I fetch this 'little suitcase'—is that what you're calling it?—I'm just sticking my head into the noose. It's not safe. You know that as well as I do. You need to guarantee me that it makes sense. So first: are there enough sources of information? Second, can the transmissions take place safely? Those are two simple questions, and I want simple answers."

Adam responded brusquely. First, he said, there were plenty of intelligence sources, and every detail was important. Second, every minute she spent arguing over the means of transmission meant less time for technical training and practice to make it work.[22]

Greta had to acquiesce, and began to prepare for her mission. She was anything but a natural. Her first step was to buy herself a bright yellow rain cape, the latest fashion. Her reasoning was that everyone thought of the underground people as gray and dowdy, so she would look less suspicious if she was stylishly dressed. Once she received the suitcase, she was supposed to transfer it to some friends who would hide it in a shed in their yard.

When Greta met Korotkov at the station, she was glad to see him looking cheerful and relaxed. They shared some casual conversation, then took a stroll to admire some new architecture nearby. Greta was still nervous. The street was full of SS men.

And then, along the way, Korotkov dropped the suitcase.[23]

Greta had barely recovered from this mishap when Korotov startled her with new instructions. "Take it home and put it inside your air-raid suitcase," he told her. "That way you can grab it if there's an alarm. I'll come pick it up in a day or two."

This was not part of the agreement, and Korotkov noticed her discomfort. She was to hold the suitcase because he needed additional time to convince his comrades of the validity of the Berlin reports. "You have to understand, we only go by proven facts. We bear a great responsibility," he added with a measure of self-importance.

Greta tried not to panic on her way home. Adam and little Ule were out when she got there. She stashed the suitcase in her closet, then went for a ride on the bus, "mumbling some foolish womanly nonsense: 'This is all unnecessary.' "

Once she got home again her nerves completely gave way, and she started to cry. Then she placed the case, unopened, inside her air-raid suitcase—stocked with the required water, matches, and zwieback crackers—beside the bed.

Adam examined the radio when he got home. After Korotkov's clumsy accident, it didn't work. Back it went to Korotkov for repair. Then it was delivered to a young member of the group named Hans Coppi in another subway handoff.

The radio was a portable transmitter-receiver. The battery-powered device was mounted into an ordinary-looking suitcase, equipped with a diagram and instructions. It operated at a range of up to six hundred miles, and its battery power lasted up to two hours.[24] Korotkov's second radio was taken to the apartment of sculptor Kurt Schumacher and his wife, Elisabeth, where it was also collected by Hans Coppi.

Now Adam Kuckhoff gave his wife a new assignment. They knew the plan of attack, village by village. Greta was to memorize the names of a dozen Russian towns, then meet with other members of the circle and repeat them. It was too dangerous to hand them around in writing. But Greta was too rattled, she couldn't make the names stick in her head. Adam asked Libertas Schulze-Boysen over to help, and together they completed the task.

Libertas returned to see Greta the next day. Greta invited her to the rooftop, and the two women took deep breaths of the spring air over coffee and cognac. Libertas was tired and shaky, too. Her family had a history of delicate nerves, and now she was in the thick of a conspiracy. But she carried an additional burden. Through Harro and her other connections she had been exposed to classified news from the front, and it was shattering. Years ago she had joined the Nazi Party as a lark, but now terrible things were happening in Poland and spreading beyond. "In my deepest heart," Libertas told Greta, "even though I've seen the reports and the photos, I can't believe that German people are capable of committing such horrible deeds. I know what Harro went through [in 1933]—and Hans Otto, and Ossietzky, and countless others. But this murder of entire peoples! I can't take it anymore!"[25]

At the beginning of May, Harro informed the Soviets that "the question of the German campaign against the Soviet Union has been definitely decided, and can be expected at any time." This message caused Arvid and Harro's Soviet contact in Moscow grave concern, and he forwarded it to several branches of the Soviet government and intelligence service. Schulze-Boysen's May 9 report was even more ominous.

> It is necessary to warn Moscow seriously of all the information pointing to the fact that the question of an attack on the Soviet Union is decided, the jump-off is planned for the near future, and with it the Germans hope to resolve the question "fascism or socialism." Naturally, they are preparing the maximum possible forces and resources.[26]

Now, at the end of his report, Harro described how the Luftwaffe had responded to the Soviets' objections to the surveillance. They simply increased their altitude: "Despite the note of the Soviet government, German aircraft continue their flights over Soviet territory for the purpose of photography. Now the pictures are taken from a height of 11,000 meters and the flights are undertaken with great care." Harro's report of May 11 provided another update:

> The First Air Fleet will be the main component for operations against the USSR. It is still a paper organization except for units of night fighters, anti-aircraft artillery, and the training of components specializing in "hedge hopping." Its status on paper does not mean, however, that it is not ready to move, since according to the plan everything is on hand—the organization is prepared, aircraft can be moved in the shortest possible time.
>
> Up to now the headquarters for the First Air Fleet was Berlin but it has been moved to the Königsberg area. Its exact location, however, has been carefully concealed.[27]

There were at least some officers in Soviet intelligence who were anticipating war. They were concerned that once hostilities broke out, they would be cut off from their informants in Berlin, making the radios a growing concern. As May wore on, Soviet intelligence devoted an increasing amount of its traffic with Berlin to secure the link. Harro Schulze-Boysen had tapped Kurt Schumacher as radio operator, but in early June he was drafted into the German army. On June 6, Schumacher's *Landes-Schützen* (territorial defense) company was sent to Poznań to guard French forced laborers.[28]

Schulze-Boysen scrambled to find a replacement, finally settling on Hans Coppi, the young Communist who had helped with the radio handoff. Coppi was a twenty-six-year-old machine operator, a tall, lanky man with dark eyes magnified behind thick spectacles. He, too, had served time in prison and a concentration camp for distributing Communist underground flyers. He was engaged to marry a slender young woman named Hilde, who also had ties to the Communist underground.[29] Coppi had no experience with radios, but Schulze-Boysen hoped he could learn quickly.

Arvid Harnack took on the task of encoding the messages. One of his wife's night-school students, Karl Behrens, volunteered to deliver the coded messages to Coppi and serve as backup operator.[30] Behrens was another young German whose politics were driven by personal grievance. After an early stint in the Nazi Party, Behrens joined the KPD. In 1939 he was arrested for forging exit papers for his sister's Jewish husband, Charly Fischer.[31] His efforts were in vain; Fischer was sent to Sachsenhausen and executed.[32]

As Hans Coppi and his friends struggled to master radio communications, Schulze-Boysen accelerated his reports to Moscow. At the beginning of June he told the Soviets that air bases in Poland were being readied for aircraft. He had seen the plans for a German pincer movement to surround the Red Army, moving in from West Prussia and north from Romania. Arvid Harnack added a list of the quartermasters who had been assigned to oversee occupied Russian territory.[33] But Harnack's group was concerned. Korotkov implied that the Soviets still saw room for doubt.

In early June, Adam and Greta Kuckhoff confronted Korotkov head-on. The Soviets had been handed the exact date and extensive details of the invasion. Were they prepared or not? To the couple's immense frustration, Korotkov dodged the question.

Harro's reports from the Luftwaffe reached a climax when, on June 11, he told the Soviets that Göring planned to advance the preparations by moving to new headquarters in Romania within the week: "According to senior officials in the Aviation Ministry and on the air staff, the question of an attack on the USSR has definitely been decided. One should consider the possibility of a surprise attack."[34]

On June 13, Harro's alert was reinforced by Soviet agent Richard Sorge in Tokyo, who warned: "I repeat: Nine armies with the strength of 150 divisions will begin an offensive at dawn on June 22."[35] Sometime on June 15 or 16, Schulze-Boysen and Harnack provided Korotkov with a final memorandum on the imminent German attack. Korotkov immediately passed it on to Moscow.

Stalin arrived at his office on June 17 to unwelcome news. Vsevolod Merkulov, the head of the NKVD state security service, presented Stalin with the stunningly detailed report. It included Arvid Harnack's description of the future German civilian administration for occupied areas of the Soviet Union. These were to be led by Alfred Rosenberg, a principal architect of the Nazis' notorious race policies. Harnack quoted Rosenberg's speech at the Economics Ministry stating that "the very idea of the Soviet Union must be wiped off the map."[36]

Harro Schulze-Boysen laid out more strategic specifics:

All of the military measures in preparation of the armed attack against the USSR are completely finalized. The attack can be counted on to begin at any time. . . .

The primary targets of the German Air Force are: the electrical power station SWIR 3, Moscow Enterprises, various airplane parts manufacturing facilities (for electrical equipment, ball bearings, and aircraft bodies) as well as KFZ repair workshops.

Hungary will take an active part on the German side in the military operations. German planes, mainly combat aircraft, can already be found on Hungarian airfields.[37]

Stalin had no patience for such nonsense. He scribbled his reaction in the margin of the document: "Comrade Merkulov, you can send your 'source' from the headquarters of German aviation back to his much-fucked mother. This is no informer, this is a disinformer."[38]

On June 22, 1941, all of the predictions came to pass. Operation Barbarossa, "the greatest land invasion in modern warfare," began at dawn, a mere five days after Stalin received Harro's final report.

On the eve of the attack, a German officer had gazed through his binoculars at his targets across the border in Brest-Litovsk, marveling at their utter lack of military preparedness. Most of the fortress's defenders appeared to be on leave, and those who were left behind were relaxed. The only visible activity involved some Chechen recruits who were practicing a march formation to music.

In the final hours before the invasion, the Soviet government continued to nourish the German war effort. Sometime after midnight on the morning of the attack, a Soviet train full of grain rolled across the border en route to Berlin.[39]

The Nazis deployed over three million troops: seventy percent of the German field army, plus 600,000 soldiers of other nationalities, including Croats, Finns, Romanians, Italians, Slovaks, and Spaniards. They met little resistance from the Soviet army. Stalin's most capable army officers had been shot in the purges. The Soviet intelligence services had been forbidden from providing any advance warning to units in the field, so these were taken by surprise, without the opportunity to concentrate their troops on the border. Many of their troops were on leave when the attack took place. Communications systems collapsed, leaving divisions isolated, with no means of receiving orders, and there were few orders to follow. The Kremlin had neglected to create a high command or confirm a commander in chief. (Stalin's appointment was pending.)

The Luftwaffe reconnaissance flights described by Harro Schulze-Boysen provided detailed instructions for German pilots, who handily destroyed networks of Soviet roads and railways.

The Soviet air force presented another fat target. The Soviets had concentrated over half of their air divisions in the western border districts, easily within striking distance. Fighters and bombers, old and new, were jammed together on the same airfields, without enough pilots to man them.[40] On June 19, three days before the invasion, a last-minute Soviet government decree went out, calling for "camouflage of aircraft, runways, tents and airfield equipment," but there was not enough time to implement the order.[41] Antiaircraft defenses were slight, and the Luftwaffe knocked out the Soviet airfields on schedule, with minimal effort.

German tanks and troops raced through the countryside at up to fifty miles a day. The Russian towns, whose names were so painstakingly memorized by Libertas Schulze-Boysen, were also defenseless. They quickly fell to the Germans, and many of them went up in flames. German forces broke Soviet army formations into small pockets that were easily captured or killed by a second-wave assault.[42]

In the first ten weeks of the invasion, the Germans captured 3,800 tanks, 6,000 artillery weapons, and 872,000 prisoners.[43] German newsreels showed guards channeling an ocean of Soviet POWs westward, blond Russian teenagers staggering alongside impassive Mongols and Muslim Chechens.

Stalin bellowed and raged at his generals, but the situation he had created was beyond their repair. He fell into a deep depression. Eventually he emerged from his funk and swung into action.

Stalin's first move was to eliminate the witnesses to his monumental error. He rounded up many of the Soviet air force and intelligence officers who had futilely alerted him to the intelligence provided by Schulze-Boysen, Harnack, and others. On October 28, 1941, fourteen of the most competent officers in the Soviet armed forces were executed without trial. They were joined in death by four civilian officials and two officers' wives.[44]

Back in Berlin, the members of the circle were full of consternation. Greta Kuckhoff worried about her husband, who sat at home day after day puzzling over the catastrophe. "Adam would stare at the big map of the Soviet Union that he had put up on the wall, hidden behind a curtain. . . . He compared the news reports with the information that he had conveyed, and couldn't grasp how it could have had so little effect."[45]

Together the group sifted through possible explanations. Had they been too cautious in their reports? Were the Soviets suspicious of them because their group was politically heterodox?

With the outbreak of war, Germany and the USSR broke off diplomatic relations. Alexander Korotkov and other members of the Soviet embassy staff packed their bags and waited to be shipped home in exchange for the Germans stranded in Russia. Korotkov managed to make a final contact with Harnack and Kuckhoff, to offer a small contribution in support of their activities. Arvid Harnack received some 12,000 marks for expenses (worth about $5,000 in 1941 U.S. currency), which he parceled out to his collaborators. Small amounts went to Adolf Grimme, the Social Democrat working with the dissenting Lutherans, and three members of the makeshift radio team. Harnack kept 1,000 marks ($400), for his own expenses, while Adam Kuckhoff received 1,500 marks from Korotkov in a separate payment.[46]

The Soviets settled on a coding system for the Berlin radio operations, based on a 1939 novel, *Der Kurier aus Spanien* (*The Courier from Spain*). One copy of the book was allegedly sent to Moscow and the other entrusted to Hans Coppi.[47]

Korotkov had one last request, and called a meeting with Adam Kuckhoff to convey it just before he left Germany for good.

Moscow wanted the group to help out, Korotkov reported, by scattering nails on the roads east of Berlin to slow the military vehicles heading for Russia.[48] Kuckhoff was incredulous. After all of their efforts to secure the highest-level military intelligence, after the risks they had taken to convey it to Moscow—the Soviets had come back and asked them to puncture some tires? Adam Kuckhoff, shaking his head, returned home to stare at his map. Korotkov filed his last report from Berlin on June 24 and prepared for return to Moscow the following week under diplomatic protection.

On June 26, 1941, newly appointed radioman Hans Coppi finally coaxed his balky apparatus into action. He tuned it to the agreed-upon frequency and tapped out a traditional salutation in halting Morse code: "*1000 Grüsse an alle Freunde*" ("A thousand greetings to all friends"). An operator in Moscow promptly replied, and told Korotkov, "We have received and read their test message." In the future, they planned to communicate through a primitive code.

But there would be no further radio communications from Coppi to

Moscow.[49] The subsequent transmissions failed, whether it was due to defective radios, inexperienced operators, or both.

This did not deter German military intelligence. They made a priority of tracking clandestine radio transmissions out of occupied Europe to Britain. The German operators assigned code names to the operations they detected, applying their own wry logic to the task. Because the operators sent their messages by tapping out the Morse code on a key, the Germans called the apparatus a "keyboard," or *klavier*. A network of radios was a "chamber orchestra," or *kapelle*. (The transmissions from occupied Europe to Britain were said to emanate from a *Wald Kapelle*, or "orchestra of the woods.")

The German military was also monitoring transmissions from Western Europe to Moscow. One of the Soviets' most active networks was based in Brussels, led by Polish Soviet agent Leopold Trepper. German army radio operators had systematically monitored and recorded their traffic to Moscow long before they could locate the source, break their codes, or identify their authors.

The standard terminology was extended to the Soviet "Reds," assigning the name *Rote Kapelle* to the Soviets' Brussels operation. Through a strange maze of circumstances, this name would be applied to the Berlin group as well, even though the two groups had little in common and virtually no contact.

Hans Coppi, the struggling amateur radio operator in Berlin, would have been particularly confused by the designation. He was the opposite of what the Soviets looked for in a spy. He was a conspicuous German Communist, born into a blue-collar KPD family and educated at a left-wing "school farm" whose students gravitated toward party organizations. Coppi's past, which included terms in prison and a concentration camp for his KPD activity, put him on all the wrong lists.

But Harro Schulze-Boysen saw no problem in reaching out to such individuals. They had met in 1939, as Coppi's circle of young Communists struggled to comprehend the Hitler-Stalin pact and what lay ahead. Coppi recalled the evening when Harro, calling himself "Hans," appeared at one of their meetings and told them not to ⟨…⟩ Soviet Union and the Nazis were on an unavoidable colli⟨…⟩

he told them, and when they finally clashed, the Nazis were sure to fall.

When Harro had to replace his radio operator, his thoughts turned to the young mechanics and metalworkers he had met that evening. Hans Coppi and his friends had no knowledge of Soviet operations in Brussels or Leopold Trepper. Like the other members of the Berlin circles, they had never heard of anything called the Rote Kapelle.[50] The idea that Coppi belonged to such an organization would have astonished him.

CHAPTER 18

Other Worlds

1941

THE SOVIETS HAD UTTERLY FAILED TO HEED THEIR WARNINGS. This was incomprehensible to Harro Schulze-Boysen, Arvid Harnack, and Adam Kuckhoff. But there was more to the story than they would ever know.

Stalin had received additional warnings from across the globe as an uncertain world began to coalesce against the Nazis. Harro Schulze-Boysen's intelligence had been the most detailed, but his information was reinforced by a remarkable array of sources across a broad political spectrum. These included the State Department in Washington, the Tory government in London, a German-Russian Communist agent in Tokyo, and a German Lutheran exile in Lucerne. Many of them were conduits for anti-Nazi dissidents inside Germany. All of them believed that it was in their interest to warn the Soviets of the German invasion.

Washington's alert resulted from the efforts of Erwin Respondek, a German economist who was well-connected in Nazi circles but secretly offended by their anti-Semitic and anti-Catholic policies.

Respondek shared his secrets with a U.S. embassy official in Berlin named Sam Woods, whose modus operandi was to buy two reserved seats at the movies and send one ticket to his German source. Over the winter of 1940, Respondek offered the Americans extensive details of the plans for the Soviet invasion, provided by members of the German military conspiracy against Hitler. The U.S. mission in Berlin was now openly hostile to the idea of gathering intelligence. As the Nazis advanced their scenario leading to world war, the U.S. chief of mission stated that it was improper for American diplomats, as he put it, to "run around Berlin digging up secrets."[1] Woods managed to forward the information on to Washington nonetheless.

Undersecretary of State Sumner Welles was among the few who took it seriously. On March 1, 1941, Welles passed along Respondek's warning to the Soviet ambassador to the United States, Konstantin Oumansky, an agile Stalinist who had come through the recent purges unscathed. The Soviet's reaction to Welles's assistance was to place a call to the chargé at the German embassy, and tell him that the Americans were spreading ugly rumors designed to damage German-Soviet friendship.[2]

On April 3, 1941, Winston Churchill instructed his ambassador to Moscow to deliver his personal note to Stalin. The message described the massive troop buildup on the Soviet border, which the British had learned about by intercepting coded German messages.

Soviet agent Richard Sorge, the Russian-German working for the Soviets in Tokyo, sent Moscow an even more precise alert, pinning down the date of the invasion as June 22.

Sorge's June date was confirmed to the Soviets by yet another intelligence source. This was Rudolf Roessler, who has been called the most effective anti-Nazi agent of the entire war. Roessler, a nondescript journalist from Bavaria, had student ties to a group of young men who became career officers in the German military. Roessler moved to Berlin in the 1920s and was appointed as a public arts administrator in the field of theater. His publications quoted Adam Kuckhoff, and he worked under the ministry of Adam's friend Adolf Grimme.[3]

Roessler's department was purged by the Nazis in April 1933, and he fled to Switzerland the following year. There he established contact with Swiss intelligence, and began to pass information from his military friends in Germany to the Swiss, who shared it with French intelligence. As war approached and the Swiss remained neutral, Roessler turned his attention to the Soviet Union.

Roessler's operation, which the Soviets called "Lucy," sent its own detailed descriptions of the plans for Barbarossa to Moscow. Roessler's information was delivered to Soviet army intelligence, while Arvid Harnack's and Harro Schulze-Boysen's reports were routed through the

NKVD. But all of them pointed in the same direction, and all were ignored.[4] Over a hundred warnings from various sources reached Moscow before the German invasion took place.

The final alarm was sounded on the eve of the attack, when a German soldier deserted and crossed the lines. He informed his Russian interrogators that the invasion would be launched at three o'clock the next morning. Stalin received the report three hours later—and responded by ordering the German deserter to be shot.[5]

Once the invasion was launched, Soviet intelligence was frantic to get more news from Berlin. But now the Soviet embassy route was closed. Arvid Harnack and Harro Schulze-Boysen continued to diligently gather information and divide the necessary tasks among their supporters, who encoded the messages and delivered them to the designated radio operators. What none of them realized was that, due to defective radio transmitters and novice operators, their efforts were in vain.

But intelligence for the Soviets was only one arena of opposition. The Berlin circles stepped up their activities on other fronts, viewing the situation as more urgent than ever. Western Europe had submitted to Germany, and now the German army was racing toward Moscow.[6] The German public seemed to be lulled into a propaganda-induced stupor. Every victory was easy, every German soldier was heroic, every Nazi cause was noble. The Schulze-Boysens, the Harnacks, and the Kuckhoffs were burdened by their privileged knowledge to the contrary.

Much of their secret information concerned the ongoing humanitarian catastrophe. The German military had been carrying out large-scale atrocities in Poland ever since the 1939 invasion, and members of the Berlin circles were shaken by whispered reports from the front. Now another horrific calamity was occurring in Russia. The Berlin groups realized that the Soviet Union was of absolute strategic importance; if Hitler conquered the Soviet Union, little else could stand in his way.

But the massacres on the Soviet front also affected members of the group on a personal level. The Harnacks had visited the Soviet Union and had friends there. Greta Kuckhoff loved Russian literature and avant-garde Soviet cinema. John Sieg was a steadfast Communist Party member, and Harro Schulze-Boysen had his own odd, uninformed attachment to his notions of the Soviet Union and Marxist ideals. They were also aware that the Germans were targeting Jews, and all of them had Jewish friends and colleagues.

Millions of Soviet soldiers had been captured in the initial German onslaught. The early reports received by Greta Kuckhoff and her friends suggested a disaster of epic proportions. Europe had known horrific wars before, but previous European conflicts had produced a shared military code known as the "laws of war." The Geneva Conventions and other agreements held that civilians should be protected and prisoners of war were entitled to certain rights. But in the period leading up to the Soviet invasion, Hitler issued orders that released German soldiers from the requirements of the Geneva Conventions, based on the argument that international law was not applicable to the "subhuman" Slavs.[7]

Hitler's "Commissar Order" abandoned all notions of civilized warfare. In the struggle against Bolshevism, "The troops must be aware that in this battle, mercy or considerations of international law with regard to these elements is false. They are a danger to our own safety and to the rapid pacification of the conquered territories."

Any Soviet prisoner who was believed to be a Communist Party official or commissar was to be shot on sight. Any Soviet soldier found in civilian clothes was to be shot on sight. Any civilian who resisted any aspect of the occupation was considered a "partisan," to be shot on sight.[8]

German soldiers were granted immunity for abuses committed on Soviet soil, unless they involved sexual excesses or other actions that were considered detrimental to troop morale. Some German officers objected to the murderous orders as an offense to their code of honor. They feared, correctly, that German atrocities against the Soviet population could inspire revenge if the tables were ever turned. But these concerns were ignored. Many German soldiers who objected to the orders were shot for insubordination.[9]

Events on the eastern front were far away to most Germans, unfolding in alien places with unpronounceable names. But sometimes the news struck close to home. In 1939, economist Franz Six was appointed dean of the university's school of foreign affairs, where Mildred Harnack and Harro Schulze-Boysen taught. But Six was also a prominent Nazi and notorious anti-Semite, and as the plans to invade Great Britain advanced, he was instructed to create *Einsatzgruppen* to execute British intellectuals, resisters, and Jews. After the Germans decided to invade the Soviet Union instead, Six was appointed chief of *Vorkommando* Moscow, and served in Smolensk from July 25 to the end of August 1941.

Franz Six participated in the execution of tens of thousands of Soviet civilians. An August field report described his units' operations: "*Vorkommando 'Moskau'* was forced to execute another 46 persons, amongst them 38 intellectual Jews who had tried to create unrest and discontent in the newly established Ghetto of Smolensk."[10]

The legions of Polish and Soviet prisoners of war required a wholesale repurposing of Germany's concentration camps. Dachau, near Munich, and Sachsenhausen, outside Berlin, had been established in 1933 as permanent versions of the Nazis' improvised "wild camps" and later expanded into "reeducation camps" for Communists, Socialists, criminals, and "social deviants." Some were executed, some worked to death, and some released. During the Kristallnacht violence of 1938 the sites were used as holding camps for nonpolitical Jews. But the camps were not yet the scene of mass executions.[11]

This began to change with the invasion of Poland, where large-scale executions of Polish civilians and prisoners of war occurred from the start. On May 3, 1940, twelve hundred Polish prisoners arrived at Sachsenhausen, where they were subjected to brutal conditions. A year later, on April 4, 1941, camp commanders authorized euthanasia for prisoners who were too ill or weak to work (echoing the domestic policy instituted for the mentally and physically disabled two years earlier).

Soviet prisoners of war began to pour into the camp in August 1941. Many were immediately designated "commissars." The Germans shot ten thousand Soviet prisoners over eight weeks in September and October. In the town of Oranienburg, just outside Sachsenhausen, local residents complained about the smell of burned flesh.[12] In May 1940 the Germans had repurposed some old army barracks as a concentration camp outside Auschwitz, a small town in the newly annexed Polish territory. Heinrich Himmler ordered an adjoining camp to be built in October 1941, to hold Soviet prisoners as slave labor for major German industrial corporations. The POWs were also designated as subjects for experimentation. In September 1941, camp commandant Rudolf Höss and his assistants selected six hundred Soviet prisoners of war to test a new method of execution—a gas called Zyklon B, delivered in a sealed chamber.[13]

In October 1941, a shipment of over ten thousand Soviet prisoners arrived at Auschwitz. Within six months, only a few hundred of the prisoners were still alive, and camp commandant Rudolf Höss began to seek new uses for the camp.

Many of the practices that would later become infamous were first applied to the Soviet POWs. Camp officials divided them into four categories: "fanatic Communist," "politically suspect," "not politically suspect," and "suitable for reeducation." Most of the prisoners were identified by numbers written on their chests with indelible ink, but "fanatic Communists" were labeled with chest tattoos, reading "AU" (for Auschwitz) followed by a number. The tattooing system was eventually extended to the rest of the Soviet POWs, as well as to Jews, Gypsies, and other inmates.[14]

By September 1941 the Nazi regime had drastically cut back the food rations for Soviet POWs, in some cases down to 600 calories a day. By February 1942, 2 million of the 3.3 million Soviet prisoners in German custody had perished of starvation, exposure, disease, or execution.[15] Over the course of the war, the Soviet POW deaths would rise to 3.3 million, a number exceeded only by the Holocaust of the Jews, representing over half of the Soviet POW population. (The death rate for the 231,000 British and American POWs in German custody was, by comparison, 3.6 percent.)[16]

There was no way for the resisters in Berlin to know the full extent of the catastrophe. But thanks to Harro Schulze-Boysen's position in air force headquarters and Arvid Harnack's in the Economics Ministry, they had a more detailed perspective than most. They had already taken a principled stand against the growing violence and abuses committed against the Jews, and risked their own safety to help Jewish friends escape persecution. In September 1941 they saw evidence that the fate of the Russians and the Jews had begun to converge.

That was the month when Hitler ordered that German Jews would be required to wear a yellow Star of David on their clothing. Greta Kuckhoff experienced the event through the eyes of her son. One day when she took Ule out for a walk, she watched as he ran over to a Jewish boy. Ule gave the child a big hug and asked, "Could you give me a golden star too?"[17]

Until this point, much of the regime's public discussion of the "Jewish problem" had centered on their removal. The Nazis had devised lucrative schemes to let Jews buy their way to England, America, and Palestine, provided they could produce the visas and the cash. From 1940 to 1942, some members of the Nazi hierarchy seriously considered a proposal to export all of Europe's Jews to the island of Madagascar, off the coast of southern Africa. Over 1941 the Berlin circle continued to help persecuted Jews and anguished over the mass murders taking place. But there was no way for them to foresee the full scale of the Holocaust.

The Berlin circles continued to expand, and the Harnacks, the Schulze-Boysens, the Kuckhoffs, and the Siegs' contacts rippled in all directions. One participant, language professor Werner Krauss, called the resisters "The Catacomb Society," after the winding underground passages where early Christians escaped Roman persecution. Most of the Berlin resisters knew only one member of another group at most, and very few of the groups were aware of one another.

The circles radiated out from unlikely hubs, attracting odd assortments of neighbors and friends. One group centered around the dentist Helmut Himpel and his fiancée, Marie Terwiel. Himpel's friendship with the Engelsings had given him a glittering list of German movie stars as his clients.

But 1941 was a stressful time for dentists in Berlin. They were required to spend half their time working for the armed forces, and the rest of their clientele suffered from the effects of a poor diet and twelve-hour workdays without sunlight. (Berliners' "teeth are decaying . . . all at once almost like cubes of sugar dissolving in water," wrote American correspondent Howard K. Smith.)[18] Himpel postponed his regular patients' appointments to make room for underground meetings, and continued to treat his Jewish patients, illegally, without charge.[19] Himpel and the other doctors in the group also helped conscientious objectors, writing out medical waivers for soldiers and defense industry workers to certify them as "incapacitated for duty."

Under other circumstances, Marie Terwiel would have been judged as blessed by fortune: a beautiful dark-haired musician, looking forward to a career as a lawyer, betrothed to a man she adored. But her future had collapsed under the Nazi race laws. Because of her Jewish-born mother, she was forbidden to marry Himpel, even though she and her mother were practicing Catholics. She was barred from completing her law degree or practicing a profession on the same grounds. Instead, she moved in with Himpel and found work as a secretary to a textile firm.

Marie was deeply worried about her mother, and provided secret assistance to other Jews in the form of ration cards and identity papers.[20] She found comfort in Catholic bishop Clemens von Galen's courageous stand. Galen, an anti-Communist aristocrat, had been critical of the Nazis from the start. In the summer of 1941 he gave a series of sermons denouncing the Gestapo and the Nazi Party, culminating in an attack on their euthanasia policy for the mentally ill. Word of the bishop's condemnation traveled quickly through Catholic circles, but the regime would not allow his statements to be published. Marie typed multiple copies of the sermon for distribution as flyers. Other German Catholics did the same, and the sermon was soon secretly circulating across the country. It created such a stir that Hitler was obliged to reverse the official euthanasia policy (though the practice continued unofficially until the end of the war).

Himpel and Terwiel recruited others to their underground publishing operations. One was journalist John Graudenz, another of Himpel's patients. Another was a member of their social music circle, young pianist Helmut Roloff. A political conservative, Roloff was motivated by the Nazis' mistreatment of his Jewish friends. He was especially stirred by the plight of one of his parents' neighbors, a Jewish architect named Leo Nachtlicht, who was forbidden to practice his profession and reduced to taking in boarders. One day Nachtlicht told Roloff about a young woman who had been renting one of his rooms. When she was told to prepare for deportation, she had turned on the gas rather than submit.

Roloff befriended several struggling Jewish families, including some neighbors named Kuttner that he had met in 1939. He was especially kind to their teenage daughter, a delicate girl with large frightened eyes. After the war, Annemarie Kuttner wrote that Roloff "came almost every day, bringing us provisions and helping us in every imaginable way. He hid a suitcase of ours in his room so the Gestapo wouldn't find it. He was a great psychological support to us in our years of most desperate need."[21]

These experiences drove the young pianist to join Himpel's resistance activities, with no particular interest in ideological debates.

The resistance circles acquired a note of glamour with the recruitment of Ina Lautenschläger, a member of Hans and Hilde Coppi's Communist circle. The statuesque brunette worked as a model at Annemarie Heise's fashion salon, one of the most exclusive in Berlin. At that time, salon models also served customers and rang up sales. Ina was popular with both the salon's owner and her clientele. "I knew wives of the big Nazis, high-ranking officers, artists and movie stars," she recalled. Her customers included Hitler's mistress Eva Braun and Goebbels's wife, Magda.[22] The salon staff competed for the privilege of serving Eva Braun. The salesgirl and the trunk of new dresses were transported by attentive SS drivers to Hitler's residence in Munich or his country house in Berchtesgaden.

Nonetheless, the shop's owner took a dim view of the Nazis. Frau Heise was a close friend of the film star Joachim Gottschalk and his family. She confided in Ina that Goebbels was trying to force Gottschalk to divorce his Jewish wife, which would soon lead to tragic consequences.

In late September 1941, Ina was asked to model in a series of fashion shows to promote German styles in occupied Brussels and Antwerp. Shortly before her departure, Hans Coppi arranged a meeting for her with Harro Schulze-Boysen at a downtown coffee stand. Harro questioned her about her travel schedule, and a few days later Coppi handed her a small package, no larger than a pack of cigarettes, with instructions to deliver it to an address in Brussels. When Ina arrived, a woman answered the door and took the packet without a word. Ina never learned the identity of the recipient.[23]

One of the most charismatic new resisters was a spirited twenty-year-old artist named Cato Bontjes van Beek, an acquaintance of Libertas Schulze-Boysen. Cato was the daughter of a well-known Dutch ceramicist and his dancer wife. A gifted ceramicist in her own right, Cato also had a good head for business, and was virtually running the family ceramics works before she was out of her teens. After she witnessed the arrest of Jewish neighbors, Cato started raising money and collecting ration cards to help other Jews. She was impatient at the Germans' passivity toward the repression. "Everyone's talking about it, but nobody's doing anything about it!" she complained to her family.[24]

After the Nazi invasions of Western Europe, Cato and her sister Mietje took up the cause of French forced laborers and prisoners of war. The two young women would position themselves in the Berlin subways, waiting for the Frenchmen to be herded past; then they would jump into the same subway car at the last minute. The prisoners soon learned that they could slip the girls notes listing their most urgent needs. At their next meeting the girls would sneak supplies into their pockets, including warm gloves, soap, and cigarettes, often bundled with flyers from the Schulze-Boysen group.

The two girls filled sketchbooks with drawings of the prisoners, sometimes casting grateful glances in their direction. Like Helmut Roloff, Cato was an artist with little interest in political affiliations or ideology. (Earlier she had managed to dodge membership in the Nazi girls' organization.) Cato recruited a number of family members and art students, most of them free spirits with compassionate hearts like herself.[25]

For some of her friends, participating in resistance activities was a way to withstand the cruelties of the regime. One day Cato was visiting the art academy when she noticed that one of the students was near tears. Katja Casella was a beautiful, vibrant, and immensely talented twenty-year-old painter who had just received a stipend from the Nazi Ministry of Culture for her studies. She was also Jewish, but she had managed to hide this fact from the regime. Katja was deeply in love with her fiancé Karl, a Jewish student who was sent to Sachsenhausen after Kristallnacht, then ransomed to England by relatives. It was impossible for Katja to communicate with her fiancé, but she remained close to his mother and fourteen-year-old sister Evalin, who still lived in Berlin. One day when she was on her way to visit them, she noticed that the flowers had disappeared from their balcony. The two had been deported to the camps. Katja was distraught.

After she told her story to Cato, the young woman looked at her gravely and said, "You should not be alone today. I want you to meet my group."

Cato took Katja by streetcar to a comfortable apartment in a Berlin suburb. When they entered the living room, Katja saw a dozen women sitting quietly, listening to a Bach chaconne on the gramophone. Cato left her for a moment. When she returned, Katja was shocked to see that she was accompanied by a very tall young man in a German officer's uniform.

The lieutenant soberly asked Katja what had happened to her fiancé's family. Then he folded his arms around her and gave her a strong embrace. "This barbarity has to stop," he told her. "We all have to work together to stop that devil." She found his voice warm and reassuring, and she took heart. Around seven p.m., men began arriving at the apartment, carrying their briefcases. Cato and Katja left them to their work.

Katja Casella had just been granted a rare glimpse of Harro Schulze-Boysen and his circle as they prepared to meet. She departed, uncertain of what she had seen, but reassured nonetheless. Here was proof that it was possible not to surrender. She joined Cato's circle of friends and co-conspirators, and recruited her best friend, Lisa, to work with her. The two pretty girls delivered clandestine messages and sheltered fugitives in Katja's small studio.[26]

Katja learned not to ask questions, but one day Cato explained her position. "Look," she said, "imagine a stone, that's how you can understand the whole group. I throw a stone in a pond and it makes circles, and in one of the circles, there sit you and Lisa."

By the end of 1941 the circles had spread and multiplied in many directions. There was never a way to count their members, since no roster could be kept, and knowledge of other groups was kept to a minimum for security's sake. But the groups extended to the medical profession, the military, academia, and the arts. Politically, they were made up of Conservatives, Communists, Social Democrats, and former Nazis. Their religious affiliations included Catholics, Lutherans, Jews, and a professional fortune-teller. Their ages ranged from teenagers to elderly grandparents, their status from aristocrats to slum dwellers. Their activities were concentrated in a few neighborhoods in central Berlin, but their contacts extended across the country.

The group still depended heavily on foreign broadcasts for news, but the BBC was inadvertently making it harder for them. In 1941, a British intelligence officer came up with the idea to mount a Churchill-inspired "V for Victory" campaign, with the goal of encouraging anti-Nazi sentiments in Europe and convincing the Nazis they were surrounded by enemies. BBC broadcasts began with the first notes of Beethoven's Fifth Symphony—ta-ta-ta-*dum*—which was also the Morse code signal for the letter "V." The broadcasters invited their audiences in Germany and Occupied Europe to echo the rhythm wherever they could, knocking on doors, blowing train whistles. But the BBC's clandestine listeners were not entirely enthusiastic. They found that Beethoven's sonorous theme traveled all too easily through apartment walls to the ears of eager informers.

Over 1941, the circles stepped up their production and distribution of underground publications. These were generated by scattered cottage industries, whose workrooms were determined by the locations of typewriters, hectographs, and supplies. John Sieg, the journalist-turned-railway worker, ran one publishing operation from a shed in Neukölln in partnership with the young Communist printer Herbert Grasse.

Sieg and Grasse published a number of irregular periodicals, including *21 Seiten* (*21 Pages*) and *Vortrupp* (*Frontlines*). In 1941 they launched a new underground newspaper called *Die Innere Front* (*The Home Front*), with Walter Husemann as a contributor. The paper offered political updates, listed the frequencies for Soviet broadcasts, and offered encouraging reports of the Soviet army's fight against the Nazis. It urged German soldiers and foreign laborers to distrust the propaganda about an impending Nazi victory, and seek ways to sabotage the regime.[27] At least fifteen issues of *Die Innere Front* were published over two years in both German and French.[28]

John Sieg's Neukölln was only blocks away from the Kuckhoffs' and the Harnacks' apartments, but it still represented another world. Only a few years ago it was a neighborhood of tenements, factories, and sprawling cemeteries. Now, just a few blocks east of John's apartment, the old

National Cash Register factory was converted into the "NCR" munitions plant. Hundreds of slave laborers were imported from Poland, Russia, and France, some Jewish, and many female, to work there.[29] Soon additional slave laborers were imported from across the eastern front. Dozens of crude barracks were thrown up around the neighborhood, some of them on the cemetery grounds. John's daily walk to the subway took him past sheds crammed with hundreds of Russians, Poles, and Ukrainians, frozen, starved, and beaten. Some residents of Neukölln slipped them bread and potatoes as they passed.[30] John's circle also handed them flyers with messages of solidarity, many of them translated into Polish by his wife, Sophie.

John Sieg coordinated his publishing efforts with his former editor, Adam Kuckhoff, and Greta welcomed him to the house often. "He never arrived empty-handed, and he never left empty-handed either," she recalled.[31] "He would always bring something along for us. . . . Either flyers or banned literature or information about other resistance cells."[32] John liked to transport his clandestine literature pasted between the covers of *Andersen's Fairy Tales.*

Adam and John disappeared behind closed doors for their intense conversations, following the unwritten code of illegal activity: information was shared on a need-to-know basis to minimize collective risk. But Greta still bristled at her exclusion, doubting that the Nazis would accept her ignorance as a defense if the group was betrayed.

She also worried that the group was overextending itself. Each month brought word of new pockets of antifascists who hoped to connect to a larger effort. But their efforts seemed paltry: soap and gloves slipped to some slave laborers, scant rations and foreign currency scraped together for Jewish friends, a few flyers stuffed into the mailboxes of frightened German bureaucrats. Did their work make any real difference?

The leaders at the center of the activity believed that sending intelligence to the Soviets was the most effective way to oppose the Nazis. Their information-gathering capacity improved all the time, but transmission remained a nightmare. Every night Arvid Harnack came home from the Economics Ministry for a second shift of encoding messages. These were delivered to Hans Coppi to relay to Moscow, but the radio continued to fail. Crucial information was not getting through.

The intelligence officers in Moscow were impatient. The intelligence that was arriving from Richard Sorge in Tokyo and from Rudolf Roessler in Lucerne was making a real difference. They knew that another critical body of intelligence could be provided from the group in Berlin, but the broken radios placed it out of reach.

This technical difficulty propelled the fate of the Berlin circles into the orbit of a man they would never meet: Leopold Trepper, the Polish Communist who ran the Soviets' Brussels operation. Trepper had been working for Soviet intelligence in Europe for years, and had narrowly escaped Stalin's purges by keeping a low profile.[33] Now, as the Soviets labored to reconstruct what Stalin had destroyed, they ordered Trepper to assemble a radio intelligence network across Western Europe. He stayed on in Brussels by posing as a Canadian industrialist.

"I became Adam Mikler," Trepper wrote later. "So Adam Mikler was from Quebec? I could talk for hours about the charms of Montreal." Trepper, of course, had never set foot in North America.[34]

Trepper launched his Brussels operation by acquiring a raincoat manufacturing company with the unlikely name of Au Roi du Caoutchouc (House of the Rubber King). He soon expanded it into an import-export business called the Foreign Excellent Trenchcoat Company.[35] Trepper's raincoat business enlisted unsuspecting salesmen across the continent. His espionage partners represented a wide spectrum of committed antifascists. A considerable number of them were Polish Zionists he knew from his early days in Palestine. Others were German Communists who had honed their forgery skills in Berlin. One of Trepper's most heroic partners was a Parisian art collector named Suzanne Spaak. The beautiful socialite combined her intelligence work with humanitarian missions, and smuggled scores of Jewish children to safety.[36]

Before the war, Trepper also lacked radios. He wrote that eventually his network accounted for three in Berlin, three in Belgium, and three in the Netherlands. But until June 1941, his agents sent their information through the Soviet military attaché in Vichy France. Trepper's group invented an ingenious system for smuggling documents across borders.

The first step was to reserve a berth in a sleeping car. Another member of the network would independently reserve a compartment, which would remain empty—preferably it would be one that communicated with the first. After the ticket-taker had passed through, the agent would leave his sleeping car, go into the compartment, unscrew an electric light fixture, place the fountain pen in which the microfilm was concealed inside the fixture, and return to his own place.

At Moulins, for instance—the station at the line of demarcation between Occupied and Unoccupied France—our courier and his baggage would naturally be searched. Then the German police would open the compartment, see that it was empty, and go on without stopping. After that the agent had only to retrieve the pen with its storehouse of information.[37]

The Soviets insisted on sending two of their own agents to support Trepper's efforts, and perhaps to keep an eye on him as well. Trepper was unimpressed by his new colleagues from the start. One Soviet agent, who called himself "Carlos Alamo," was an impetuous amateur who had recently returned from assisting the Republican air force in Spain. Alamo was fond of boasting about a valiant solo mission he had flown there. The only problem with his story, Trepper noted, was that Alamo was a mechanic, not a pilot. Trepper was further dismayed when Alamo missed both his first and his second outdoor rendezvous, because he panicked and decided that the Belgians strolling in the park were enemy agents. Trepper complained that Alamo's three months' training in radio operation wasn't adequate preparation. When he was put in charge of the raincoat shop, he was so inept that Trepper had to hire another manager to back him up.[38]

The Soviets redoubled Alamo's incompetence with a second agent, named Anatoli Gourevitch, whose idea of an effective cover was to pose as a Uruguayan national, with the code name "Kent" (chosen from a British spy novel). Kent, like Alamo, was delighted to be living in Belgium instead of the Soviet Union. An aspiring roué, he wore his hair in a flattop and habitually puffed on a pipe. He soon acquired a blond mistress, while his colleague Alamo indulged his expensive taste for fast cars.

In Trepper's eyes, Kent's tradecraft was even more feckless than Alamo's: "When Kent, fresh out of his 'academy of espionage,' went into a working-class bar in the Paris suburb and ordered tea, he aroused ridicule but, above all, he attracted attention. For an intelligence man, this is against the rules. At school they forgot to teach Kent to be inconspicuous." The situation became even more serious when Trepper needed help for two of his lieutenants from the Jewish underground in Palestine.

> I asked Kent to find each of them a very safe hideout, but he did nothing of the sort. Sophie was staying . . . in a rented house we used for broadcasting, and Kamy was living with Alamo. The most elementary requirements for security had not been respected. If we had deliberately set out to bring on a catastrophe, we would not have acted otherwise.[39]

Trepper contrasted the Soviet bumblers with himself and his friends, who had spent half a lifetime evading pogroms in Poland and arrest by British colonial officers in Tel Aviv. "This irreplaceable experience was worth all the courses in the world."[40]

By late summer 1941, as the German army raced toward Moscow, the Soviets ordered their Brussels operation to help them reestablish radio contact with their prime sources in Berlin. On August 26, 1941, intelligence officers in Moscow sent a radio message to Brussels, ordering Kent to drive to Berlin and find out what the problem was. The coded message was excruciatingly detailed:

> Go to Berlin to Adam Kuckhoff or his wife in Wilhelmstrasse 18,*
> tel. 83 62 61, second stairway to the left, upper story and explain
> that you were sent by a friend of Arvid's and Harro's, that Arvid
> knew as Alexander Erdberg. . . . Suggest to Kuckhoff that he
> arrange a meeting with Arvid and Harro.

---

*This was a Soviet error. The Kuckhoffs lived at Wilhelmshöherstrasse.

If possible, find out from Kuckhoff:

1. If the radio connection is there and why isn't it working?
2. Where are the friends and what is their situation? Italijanes, Lutschisti, Leo, Karl and the others?
3. Let them be informed about the transmission to Erdberg.
4. Suggest the connection to Istanbul, through a Soviet businessman, or to Stockholm, through the consul, both in the name of von Strahlmann.

In case you can't meet with Kuckhoff, go to the wife of Harro Schulze-Boysen, Libertas, Altenburger Allee 19, tel. 99 58 47. Explain that you come from someone who met with Elisabeth (Schumacher) in Marquardt (near Potsdam). This order also applies if you meet Kuckhoff.[41]

Moscow also ordered Gourevitch, or "Kent," to get detailed information from the group to transmit back to Moscow once he was back in Brussels, and to instruct them to prepare a safe house near Berlin to receive sensitive visitors.

When Trepper heard that Moscow had broadcast the actual names and addresses of the contacts in Berlin, he was incredulous. "It's not possible. They have gone crazy!" he exclaimed.[42] The messages were in code, but Trepper knew that the Germans were advancing their code-breaking capabilities by the day.

Trepper could not be certain of catastrophe, but he suspected it. The German army's radio service had indeed begun intercepting and recording messages from Trepper's outpost two months earlier, only days after the Soviet invasion, and was already hard at work deciphering the code.

As the German army moved in on Moscow in autumn, the atmosphere in Berlin began to change. With the shortwave radio procured by Arvid Harnack's brother Falk, Harro and Arvid could now monitor the German exile radio broadcasts from Moscow. This showed them how their intelligence reports might have benefited actual field operations, and added to their frustration when their transmissions failed.[43]

One night, Adam Kuckhoff asked his wife to follow him to the rooftop, even though she balked at exposing herself to the bone-freezing rain.

He spoke quickly. Arvid Harnack had insisted that he inform her that Moscow had been in touch by way of Brussels. Furthermore, the radio transmission had included their names.

"Addresses, too?" Greta demanded.

"How else can they find us!" he answered.

Greta was not placated. "Why so many names? Wasn't one enough?"

Adam tried to calm her. If someone was sent to work on the radios, he would be more likely to go to Mildred's or Libertas's apartments, which were more conveniently located. The most that would probably be asked of Greta would be to give him directions.

Once more, Greta suspected that she was the last to know. Perhaps she was only being informed because the visitor was already in town, about to arrive on her doorstep. She resented the men for giving her only half of the pertinent information, when she shared equal risk. But she was getting used to not asking questions.[44]

It took Kent two months to make his way to Berlin. He arrived on October 29, 1941, and touched base with other Soviet agents in town.[45] Then he called Schulze-Boysen at the home number sent by Moscow. Libertas answered and agreed to meet him in a subway station. She explained the problem with the broken radio and arranged a follow-up meeting with her husband. The couple brought Kent back to their apartment for a four-hour meeting.

Kent's arrival came as an utter surprise, but Harro did not focus on the breach of security. He was pleased by the Soviet's appearance. He had been trying to undermine the Nazis for months with his transmissions of intelligence, with no evidence that it was getting through. The German army was now closing in on Moscow, and it appeared that the next few months could determine the outcome of the war.

Harro hoped that Kent would make good use of his information. The two men sat down in the living room and Harro offered his visitor a long menu of military intelligence, which Kent carefully recorded in his notebook.

Kent was under pressure from Moscow to get more information and wanted to arrange another meeting, but Harro was wary. He had already endured one Gestapo investigation and assumed that he was still under surveillance. If Kent visited or called again, the Soviet's thickly accented German would arouse further suspicion. The two men traded proxy addresses.

Kent returned to Brussels and prepared a series of transmissions to Moscow with Harro's information. Over the month of November 1941, he reported the location of Hitler's headquarters in East Prussia, known as the Wolfsschanze, as well as information on Germany's preparations for chemical warfare.[46] He let the Soviets know that the Germans were planning to move on the Caucasus, the gateway to Soviet oil fields, before they attacked Moscow. Harro passed along the additional news that the Germans were facing severe shortages in oil and field provisions; their supply lines were badly overstretched. Kent also conveyed Harro's crucial data on German aircraft production and losses sustained in combat.[47]

Harro had handed the Soviets a mother lode of invaluable intelligence and Kent transmitted it from Brussels in marathon sessions, breaking every possible security precaution by staying on the air for long sessions every night, for seven days straight. This offered the German counterintelligence operators an easy means of homing in on the signal. They tracked the transmissions and carefully recorded the coded content.[48]

As of October, the German army had still appeared unstoppable. But over the next two months, their luck began to turn. The Soviets' additional intelligence was part of the equation, and became a factor for the British as well.

In late June 1941, the British and the Soviet governments had sent military missions to each other's headquarters in London and Moscow to set up intelligence exchanges. (Britain sent Noel Mason-Macfarlane, the attaché in Berlin who had sought permission to shoot Hitler from his window.) The British had initially advised the Soviets to prepare for the German victory by destroying everything of value and sinking the Soviet fleet.[49] But over the summer and fall of 1941, Churchill decided to reinforce the Soviets, supplying them with high-grade intelligence obtained from British code-breaking operations.[50] (This included highly sensitive material that had not been offered to the Americans.)

The Soviets' agent in Tokyo, Richard Sorge, provided other crucial information over the same period. In October 1941, Sorge informed Moscow that the Japanese had decided not to invade the Soviet Union from the east—they had an entirely different offensive in mind. In his last dispatch before his October 18 arrest, Sorge pinpointed the date for the Japanese attack on Pearl Harbor, which would trigger the war in the Pacific (and, together with Hitler's declaration of war on the United States, another world war). Sorge's information allowed the Soviets to transfer fresh, winter-ready troops from the east to fight the Germans. Intelligence began to flow between London and Moscow, benefiting both.

The Americans were still trying to steer clear of a war, but their neutrality was rapidly eroding. Roosevelt feared that an absolute Nazi victory in Europe would leave the United States isolated and exposed. In March 1941 he initiated support for the British through the Lend-Lease Program. After the Nazis invaded the Soviet Union in June, Roosevelt decided to extend the support to Moscow. The United States completed an aid agreement with the Soviets in October 1941, and the Americans began to ship critical military vehicles and supplies eastward.

Now the Soviets gained an additional strategic advantage. The German army was already literally bogged down in the Russian winter. By November their tanks and trucks were crippled by mud, and snow was on the way. The Germans' overtaxed supply lines meant that their troops were running short of food and fuel, preparing to fight a winter campaign in the heart of Russia with the same uniforms they had brought in June.

The Nazis demonstrated this vulnerability in December, when Hitler asked the German people for donations of warm clothes for their soldiers in Russia. Joseph Goebbels offered a detailed list of needed items on an evening radio broadcast. The German public reacted angrily. They had bought the idea of an invincible German war machine. Now they were told that their loved ones were stranded on a freezing, treacherous front without even hats and gloves.[51] By December 4, 1941, German troops had fought their way through worsening weather to the outskirts of Moscow. But winter hit full force, with temperatures falling to thirty-two degrees below zero Fahrenheit.

Then, on December 6, 1941, the Soviets mounted a massive counterattack.[52] The Germans faced 100 Soviet divisions over a 200-mile stretch (including the 18 fresh divisions from the east), equipped with 1,700 tanks and 1,500 planes.

Hours later, on the other side of the world, another event transpired to tip the balance: the Japanese attacked Pearl Harbor. The strike was a calamity for the United States, but European antifascists hailed it as a ray of hope. Once the United States entered the war, with its untapped resources and manpower, the fascists could be defeated.

Americans were so focused on the war in Europe that some believed there were German pilots in some of the planes at Pearl Harbor. This was not the case, although Hitler did greet the event as a cause for celebration. The United States declared war on the Axis powers the following day, and Hitler judged that Japan would be more effective as a partner than the United States would be as an enemy.[53] As he often had, he was indulging in wishful thinking, based on a notion of America that was vague and out of date. He imagined that German-Americans would lead a powerful pro-Nazi movement, and he totally underestimated the ability of American industry to convert to wartime demands.

Winston Churchill was more astute. He later wrote that his nation's fate hung on two eventful days in 1941. The first, he said, was the Germans' June 22 invasion of the Soviet Union. On that day, Churchill recalled, "I knew we would not lose the war."[54] The second date was December 7.

As the tide continued to turn against the Nazis, Harro Schulze-Boysen took satisfaction in watching his predictions coming to pass, relieved at the prospect of Allied reinforcements.[55] He continued to write to his parents from his Luftwaffe post in Potsdam in guarded terms. "The war is flooding over an ever-greater part of the globe," he wrote in December.[56] A week later he updated his father, a high-ranking naval officer, couching his analysis in official language: "On the Eastern Front the Russians appear to be bringing in some additional reserves. This endless front, where we're now on the defensive, is already a very serious problem."[57]

Berlin shrank once more. In the days following Pearl Harbor, the last remaining American embassy officials burned their files and prepared to receive Hitler's declaration of war. Then they were packed onto a train and sent to an internment camp near Frankfurt, where they languished for five months, until an exchange could be set up for their German counterparts.[58]

As British bombs rained down on German cities, the Kuckhoffs, the Harnacks, and the Schulze-Boysens tried to balance their personal lives with the demands of their situation. They still had possession of Hans Coppi's Soviet radio. To be discovered with it was tantamount to a death sentence, whether the radio was working or not. Some members of the group were high-profile government officials. Others were Communists, subject to surprise searches by the Gestapo. The group reviewed its members, trying to identify the most innocuous individuals to house the device. One candidate was Oda Schottmüller, a modern dancer who participated in the German army equivalent of USO tours to entertain the troops. At other times the radio was stored with Greta's neighbor, Erika von Brockdorff, a blond secretary who worked in a government industrial safety office with Kurt Schumacher's wife, Elisabeth.[59]

One night Greta Kuckhoff dashed into a shelter during an air raid and was shocked to see Brockdorff carrying the telltale radio suitcase. Greta quickly realized that bringing the radio was safer than leaving it in the apartment during the raid. Besides, it wasn't as conspicuous as she feared. Once it was stored away, the radio looked like the air-raid suitcases that every mother in Berlin now kept packed and ready.

Air raids had become a quotidian nightmare for Berliners, especially for parents of young children. Greta hated pulling her little son out of bed to shelter from the bombs, which often came three or four times a night. She would sit up with him in the cold cellar, telling stories until it was safe to go back. Sometimes after she put Ule back to bed, she and Adam would venture out into the night, stumbling over the rubble and counting the buildings in flames. Berlin was not yet extensively damaged, but on one family visit, the couple witnessed a devastating raid on Adam's ancient home city of Aachen. They were filled with rage, less at the British bombers, Greta wrote, than at the German fascists whose war was leaving so many cities in ruins.[60]

It threatened to be a dismal Christmas. That winter Mildred Harnack suffered an ectopic pregnancy. At the age of thirty-nine she feared she would never have children.[61] Libertas Schulze-Boysen lost her grandmother in December, and she and Harro spent a melancholy weekend attending the funeral at the family castle.[62]

Greta and Adam Kuckhoff longed to show their son a world that was different from the travesty outside their door. When Greta thought of her own meager childhood, she fondly remembered the toys her father crafted by hand. Her favorite was a Noah's ark filled with tiny animals. When she got pregnant, she had started a collection of miniatures for her child. By Christmas 1941, Greta and Adam had gathered more than twelve hundred pieces. They included little bicycles and families of pigs and geese. There was a small farm with cattle, a village with houses, and a forest with rangers and their dogs. After the Kuckhoffs told their friends abroad about the project, they started receiving exotic additions from Africa, France, Britain, and the United States.

At first the couple had decided to keep the gift packed away for their son's sixth birthday, still two years off. But that winter their resolutions broke down. It was a bad day. They had been trying to send a transmission to Moscow, but the radio kept breaking down. They had just run off a new set of anti-Nazi flyers, but people were hesitant even to accept them. Arvid Harnack had come over to the apartment for a tense meeting on the freezing roof. They stood there grimacing and shivering as the storm clouds threatened to open up.

Back downstairs, Adam and Greta looked at each other and decided it was time to recover some joy. Soon they had lost themselves in their miniature fantasy. In one corner of their living room they attached a moon and tiny stars to the ceiling, then laid down silver wool to make a winter landscape. They found a mirror for the duck family's pond, and fashioned a hilltop for the mill. Villages, forests, and farms sprang up across the floor, a tiny world without Nazis, bombs, or concentration camps. Greta realized that it was no longer for their child. "Now we were building it for ourselves."

They stood up and saw it was good. The couple couldn't bear to pack it away again. When Ule beheld their creation, he was openmouthed with joy. Greta was glad that they didn't wait for another Christmas, glad that they were both able to share the moment with their son: "My husband always used to say, 'If you don't do something too early, you usually do it too late.' "[63]

\ \ \

CHAPTER 19

"Distress About Germany's Future"

1941–1942

ON NOVEMBER 1, 1941, HARRO'S WIFE, LIBERTAS, THE FLIRTA-
tious aristocrat and former MGM press agent, started a new job at the
Reich's Kulturfilm central office. In the new order, this position was as
coveted as her old spot was at MGM. It was also politically sensitive.
Kulturfilm was an important division of the Nazis' movie empire, and
this was the undisputed domain of Joseph Goebbels, minister of propaganda and public enlightenment.

Libertas's family connections led to Goebbels's rival, the portly air
minister Hermann Göring, whose enthusiasm for the dramatic arts
waxed with his marriage to actress Emmy Sonnemann. But he had limited influence in the world of film. Joseph Goebbels had a stranglehold
on cinema that even Göring couldn't break.

By the time Libertas got her job, the Nazis had nearly completed their
consolidation of the entire German movie industry. At the center of their
efforts was the giant company Universum-Film AG, better known as
UFA.

UFA had gone through many metamorphoses since its founding as a
propaganda film agency in World War I. The Kulturfilm department,
where Libertas worked, was launched at the end of the war to create
uniquely German educational documentaries. Many dealt with war-
related health problems such as tuberculosis and venereal disease. "The
wounds of war can only be healed if we devote ourselves to the tasks of
humanity," its catalog stated.[1]

In its early days, UFA was a freewheeling player in Weimar culture, employing left-wing artists such as George Grosz and John Heartfield, and releasing such daring films as Fritz Lang's *Metropolis* and *Dr. Mabuse*. But a 1927 financial crisis delivered UFA's management into the hands of right-wing press baron Alfred Hugenberg, who worked closely with the Nazis. After 1933 the studio terminated the contracts of Jewish employees. It was impossible to continue the old ways of doing business, as leading artists left the country and export revenues were slashed by foreign boycotts of German films. The country's smaller movie companies went out of business, allowing UFA to fill the gap. Again, consolidation of ownership helped the regime tighten its grip, until its hold on the machinery of filmmaking was absolute.

In 1940, UFA's Kulturfilm division was placed directly under Goebbels's control. Two years later the Nazis completed the consolidation of all of Germany's remaining film production companies (including Herbert Engelsing's Tobis Films) into a massive UFA conglomerate.

Libertas Schulze-Boysen's new job had her working on films dealing with "art, German peoples and lands, and other peoples and countries."[2] The subject matter had ominous new overtones. The Nazi propaganda machine was aggressively promoting the new map of Europe. Conquered lands with ethnic German populations were depicted as lost relations happily restored to the Fatherland, not desperate nations shattered by bloody occupation.

Libertas Schulze-Boysen gathered footage and worked on scripts. She made certain to share the fruits of her success with her friend Adam Kuckhoff. She recommended him for her former position as Berlin film critic for the Nazi newspaper *Essener Nationalzeitung*, where she had spent the previous year, writing reviews that met Nazi requirements. She also helped get Adam freelance assignments as a UFA screenwriter, script doctor, and field producer.[3]

Libertas found herself at the center of a dangerous world full of secrets and contradictions. The regime had instructed German filmmakers to keep the public inspired and amused. As the war dragged on, they were under increasing pressure to project a cheerful patriotic façade. But many of Libertas's colleagues were undergoing personal and professional torment.

Goebbels's constant meddling ruined both projects and careers. In 1938 he had flung himself at the beautiful Czech movie star Lida Baarova, declaring that he would abandon his job, his wife, and his children to run away with her. Hitler was greatly displeased, since he often pointed to the smiling images of Goebbels, his wife, Magda, and their brood of blond children as evidence of the Nazis' family values. Hitler finally ordered Goebbels to go back to his wife, and commanded Baarova to disappear.[4]

Renate Müller was another artist whose life was blighted by the regime. As a young actress she had overlapped with Adam Kuckhoff at the Staatstheater, and became a popular ingenue in a number of films, including the 1933 cross-dressing comedy *Viktor/Viktoria*. She was a good friend of the Engelsings and enjoyed playing Ping-Pong with them on summer holidays.[5] But she, too, ran into political difficulties. Some people said her difficulties arose from her anti-Nazi sentiments; others suggested that her problem was a Jewish lover. In 1937, Müller checked into a Berlin clinic with a serious but unnamed health problem. Shortly afterward the thirty-one-year-old actress fell to her death from a third-floor window. Witnesses reported that Gestapo agents had arrived on the scene slightly earlier, and there was disagreement as to whether she jumped or was pushed.

In 1940, Goebbels oversaw the production of *Jud Süss*. He decided that the actor Ferdinand Marian, whose dark good looks often cast him as a Latin lover, was perfect for the part of the Jewish villain. Marian was horrified by the idea, but Goebbels forced him to comply by threatening the safety of his half-Jewish stepson. Marian acquiesced at the cost of a nervous collapse.[6] Once the shoot was completed, Goebbels declared that Marian's depiction of "Jew Süss" wasn't vile enough, and he took over the editing himself to address the problem.[7]

Jewish actors were barred from working altogether. Cabaret and film stars Paul Morgan and Fritz Grünbaum, who compounded the crime of being Jewish with their political satire, had already perished in Buchenwald and Dachau.[8]

Other popular figures occupied a gray area. One of these was Joachim Gottschalk, a matinee idol known for his portrayal of calm, sensitive characters. (He was called the "German Leslie Howard.") Gottschalk's liabilities were his long and happy marriage to Jewish actress Meta Wolf and their young son, Michael. After Kristallnacht, the regime pressed him to divorce his wife. Gottschalk refused. He wanted to flee the country with his family, but his possibilities for flight were limited by his high profile and UFA contract. He continued to appear in highly popular films, while his wife disappeared from public view.

One night in April 1941, Meta Gottschalk succumbed to the temptation to attend the premiere of her husband's new film *Die Schwedische Nachtigall* (*The Swedish Nightingale*). There, she charmed prominent Nazis in attendance—until they learned she was Jewish. Goebbels ordered her and eight-year-old Michael to register for deportation to the concentration camp at Theresienstadt. Gottschalk begged to go with them, but the officials refused, and told him instead to report to the army. The couple spent the next few months in an agony of indecision. Gottschalk was banned from working on further films, but he made a few appearances on Germany's nascent television service. Then those, too, ceased.

On November 6, 1941, Gottschalk, thirty-seven, and his wife, thirty-nine, sedated their son and turned on the gas in their apartment, killing all three. *Time* magazine reported that Gottschalk willed his skull to the Deutsches Theater, where he had often appeared as Hamlet, "so that I can continue to act in the play, although in another role, and by my personal presence inspire my successors to do their best."[9]

The Nazis forbade the German press to mention the incident, but word of the event spread quickly and created a public uproar.[10] For the Schulze-Boysen circle, the news hit close to home. Gottschalk's only other starring role that year was in the film adaptation of Günther Weisenborn's novel *Das Mädchen von Fano* (*The Maiden from Fäno*, released in January 1941). His death occurred only five days after Libertas Schulze-Boysen started her new job at UFA, Gottschalk's studio.

Some situations were more complicated than they seemed. Formerly leftist actors Heinrich George and Gustaf Gründgens were harshly criticized for selling out to the Nazis. Nonetheless, they helped old friends with political problems that no one else would touch. When Heinrich George was named director of the prestigious Schiller Theater, he appointed Günther Weisenborn chief dramaturge, even though he had long been banned from writing under his own name. As a darling of the Nazi regime, George was in a position to do his old friend a favor.

Gustaf Gründgens employed the actress Pamela Wedekind, daughter of the banned author of *Lulu* and *Spring Awakening,* and offered parts to a number of actors who had been threatened with blacklisting because they had Jewish wives.[11] But their private lives showed the strain. Heinrich George's drinking got seriously out of hand. Gründgens worked anxiously under Göring's protection, but it was rumored that Goebbels was seeking ways to have him eliminated for his "unconventional lifestyle"—he was bisexual.[12]

The Schulze-Boysens' and Kuckhoffs' friend, lawyer, and film producer Herbert Engelsing worked at the heart of this maze of loyalty and betrayal. Between 1937 and 1944 he served as producer or executive producer for thirty-four films, featuring Germany's leading stars and directors. He oversaw his own division of Tobis Film, which maintained its brands even after it was consumed in the UFA consolidation. In short, Engelsing was a major player in the industry, escorting his lovely (half-Jewish) wife to gala premieres, surrounded by the bedazzled Nazi hierarchy.

Ingeborg Engelsing enjoyed the glamour. Her life, she wrote, was "a constant round of movies and parties." But she struggled with the protocol. At one film opening Goebbels made a sudden entrance, and the gathered company greeted him with a "Heil Hitler" salute. Ingeborg was dismayed. She had sworn never to give a Nazi salute out of allegiance to her Jewish family members. (She also considered it "unfeminine" and particularly unattractive in evening dress.) Ingeborg managed to finesse the moment by raising her arm to fidget with her hair.[13]

The Nazi hierarchy was so thirsty for cinematic glory that the film community was often allowed to stretch the rules. The Nazis were particularly stung by the desertion of Weimar stars like Greta Garbo and Marlene Dietrich for Hollywood, exacerbated by Dietrich's public contempt for Nazism. But UFA found other stars to promote, sometimes ignoring inconvenient details from their past. One of them was Olga Tschechowa, the beautiful German-Russian actress. Engelsing appreciated her work, and 1939 was their banner year, when Tschechowa starred in Engelsing's productions *Bel Ami* and *The Fox of Glenarvon* (which included dialogue by Adam Kuckhoff).

But 1939 was notable for Tschechowa in other respects as well. That was the year she was photographed in a spectacular evening gown leaning against Hitler himself at a diplomatic reception. Tschechowa declined to inform the Führer that she had a brother in Russia working for Soviet intelligence, or that she was serving as a go-between for the Soviets and German military officers who opposed war with Russia.[14]

Herbert Engelsing was close to many members of the Babelsberg film community who opposed the Nazis and helped victims of the regime. He worked with Heinrich George and Gustaf Gründgens, and wrote contracts for Olga Tschechowa. The Engelsings were forever grateful to musical star Käthe Dorsch for lobbying Göring to make their marriage possible, and supported her ongoing efforts to rescue Jews from persecution. They grew so close that they named their daughter after her.

It is not known how far Herbert Engelsing pursued political discussions with his stars, who were frequent dinner guests and cocktail companions, but the circumstances encouraged intimacy. Ingeborg wrote that friendships blossomed quickly when the glamorous company had to flee the dinner table and spend the evening squatting in cramped air-raid shelters. On the other hand, it was always risky to show one's hand. One might be excused for trying to help an old friend, but the wrong joke at the wrong time could mean a concentration camp or worse.

Engelsing's shadowy figure could be detected in many areas of the Schulze-Boysens' resistance efforts. Their friendship ran deep, in both political and personal terms. One night in November 1938, the Engelsings and the Schulze-Boysens were on the way to dinner with a Swedish diplomat when they suddenly glimpsed a synagogue going up in smoke. It was the onset of Kristallnacht, and the two couples shared their anger and distress. Over the summer of 1940 the Engelsings were guests of the Schulze-Boysens at the lake. Herbert was photographed on a sailboat with Libertas, every inch the lawyer on holiday in his swimming suit and bathing cap worn with horn-rimmed glasses.

The Engelsings remained close to the Kuckhoffs as well. In December 1941, Ingeborg Engelsing brought her little boy, Thomas, to see the miniature world Greta and Adam had created for their son. It was the Engelsings who had engineered the meeting of the Schulze-Boysens and the Kuckhoffs, and the Engelsings who recruited additional members of the circle, such as their dentist friend Helmut Himpel and his fiancée, Marie Terwiel.

Herbert Engelsing offered the group material support as well. According to one account, he rented a room for Harro's underground activities at 2 Waitzstrasse in Charlottenburg, near the Schulze-Boysen apartment.[15] The group typed the leaflets in the Waitzstrasse room and stored them in Kurt and Elisabeth Schumacher's cellar.

Engelsing and his wife were particularly close to Harro. Like many of his friends and relations, they could be exasperated by his inchoate politics, but they admired his courage and sense of justice. He was especially kind to their children. Engelsing carefully maintained a state of deniability regarding the Schulze-Boysens' resistance activities, but he also created space for them to expand.

The individual who was best positioned to take advantage of this space was Libertas. When the Nazis decided to groom her to be a documentary producer, they inadvertently exposed her to shocking raw material.

After the invasion of the Soviet Union in June 1941, Harro, Libertas, and their friends were exposed to internal reports of atrocities committed by German troops. Over the following months, the news only grew worse. Libertas resolved to use her position to create an archive documenting the atrocities. Initially she intended to use the material to dissuade young Germans from joining Nazi organizations, but as time passed, her purpose evolved. Someday, she reasoned, the Nazis would be brought to justice, and the prosecutors would need hard evidence of their misdeeds.

Libertas set to work gathering the information and filing the results. The primary sources of her photos were the soldier perpetrators themselves. They returned to Berlin from the front, bearing snapshots from the field. (Soldiers were forbidden to photograph executions, but photographs were taken nonetheless.) Libertas, through a combination of flirtation and flattery, coaxed them into giving her photos to copy in the UFA facilities. Greta Kuckhoff later wrote that Libertas's images showed "cynically grinning torturers" posing with their victims. "The men were proud of their crimes. Some of them were youthful, others had graying temples.

"It was a strange collection," Greta continued.

There were pictures from the Röhm massacre and—here the number of photos grew enormous—pictures of interrogations, "special treatment" [torture] and the liquidation of Polish, Jewish, and Soviet civilians. Libertas had a skillful way of asking the men the reasons for their actions, whether they had children who loved them, and what their professional plans were. Names and addresses were collected as well. Everything was carefully recorded. She sometimes brought us the evidence. It made for a shattering picture of the relapse into barbarism.

There was one man who spoke in lyrical terms of the beauty, habits, and usefulness of certain insects. He was incapable of harming a potato beetle. Then he displayed a photo of himself with a tiny baby that he was about to hurl against a wall.

Another one, from the countryside, began by showing pictures of his five kids with skinny legs, and then, without hesitation, produced a snapshot from "the East." It showed him pulling his bayonet from the body of an old bearded farmer. Libs, as we always called Harro's wife, suffered agonies from this work. But she accomplished it consistently, because we considered it necessary.[16]

The Kulturfilm office was the perfect staging ground for her efforts. The educational film division shared offices with the hard-line propaganda filmmakers, who received a constant flow of material from the front. Libertas was surrounded by military files and film, meaning she could hide her archives in plain sight. Rarest of all, the office held a wealth of cameras, typewriters, and supplies, providing the technical means of copying materials inconspicuously.

By December 1941 it was clear that Hitler's military plans had gone badly awry. German troops were stretched across Western Europe, many of them occupying hostile countries. Erwin Rommel, one of his best generals, was tied down in North Africa attempting to bolster Hitler's wobbling Italian allies. The German forces in Russia were now hopelessly stranded, facing the Soviet counterattack and the brutal Russian winter. Then the Americans entered the war.

Some German officers had doubted Hitler's plans from the start, but had been deterred by the early string of victories. Now they sought ways to control the damage. As the military situation grew more difficult, Hitler became more erratic, behaving less like a military strategist than a sociopath pursuing private vendettas. At the heart of his mania were the Jews.

Historians disagree as to exactly when the Nazis made the fundamental decision to exterminate Europe's Jews. Some believe that their prolonged discussions of a Jewish colony in Madagascar indicate that the decision was made after the war began. Others argue that Hitler's anti-Semitic diatribes in *Mein Kampf* revealed his ultimate intentions over a decade earlier.

Whichever the case, once genocide was decided, the Nazi hierarchy took great pains to conceal the plans from the German public. For the past eight years, Germans had known that "concentration camps" functioned as horrific prison and labor camps with high mortality rates. For years they had witnessed political prisoners and common criminals who served out their sentences, and were then released or given a furlough in their weakened states. Many concentration camp prisoners died suddenly, often under mysterious conditions. But before the war there was no reason to connect the term "concentration camp" with the concept of industrialized mass murder.

In other words, as the deportations began, it was impossible for Germans to avoid the conclusion that something very bad was happening to Jews. But few of them possessed the means, or the desire, to learn exactly what.

On December 18, 1941, Heinrich Himmler met with Hitler and recorded in his notebook, "Jewish question—to be exterminated as partisans."[17] The plan was elaborated on January 20, 1942, at an elegant villa in Wannsee, a Berlin suburb graced by lakes where Harro Schulze-Boysen liked to sail. There, fifteen top Nazi military and civilian officials met to discuss the "final solution" to the "Jewish question," chaired by thirty-eight-year-old SS officer Reinhard Heydrich.

Together, the group formulated a plan that integrated the full range of barbarities already visited upon Polish intellectuals, Soviet prisoners, mental patients, and Eastern European Jews. Ranged around a table in a gracious, light-flooded room, the meticulous bureaucrats spent eighty-five minutes assembling the basic architecture of the Jewish genocide. Historians do not know exactly which officials received copies of the Wannsee Protocol that resulted from the meeting, but it is believed that thirty copies were produced, and that each one reached at least five to ten officials.[18]

Greta Kuckhoff wrote that Harro Schulze-Boysen caught a glimpse of documents from the Wannsee conference and conveyed their content to "reliable people in various countries," who took no action.[19] Some scholars question this claim, and no independent evidence has established that it took place. But if the transcript of the Wannsee meeting was indeed viewed by 150 to 300 officials from a dozen different ministries, it is possible that Harro could have caught sight of it and reported its contents to foreign contacts.

As the Berlin circle learned more about the atrocities taking place on the eastern front, Harro and Libertas felt compelled to step up their actions. Harro began to clip articles from Nazi newspapers that quoted party members bragging about their crimes.[20] Libertas continued to collect snapshots and filmed evidence from the East, and started a file of information she heard from the soldiers who brought them back. As the atrocity archive grew, Harro began to hold small meetings in his house to review the materials and discuss what action to take.

The Schulze-Boysens were not the only ones gathering evidence. A similar archive was being accumulated by Arvid Harnack's cousin, lawyer Hans von Dohnanyi, a leading figure in the Hans Oster conspiracy. After the war, Allen Dulles wrote that Admiral Wilhelm Canaris's papers had included Dohnanyi's chronology of Nazi crimes from 1933 on. Canaris maintained his own card file of Nazi leaders and their crimes and kept a diary "to inform Germany and the world once and for all of the guilt of those people who were guiding the fate of Germany at this time."[21]

In January 1942 the Schulze-Boysens added a new couple to their circle. John Rittmeister was a melancholy psychotherapist who had studied with Carl Jung. The doctor described himself as a "leftist pacifist," and shared the Schulze-Boysens' antagonism to the Nazis and anger at the persecution of the Jews. He and his wife, Eva, a former nurse, had gathered their own small group of dissidents. Rittmeister was heartened by Harro's reports of German military setbacks on the Russian front, and wanted to let Germans know that the tide had turned. He convinced Harro Schulze-Boysen to join him in drafting a flyer that would reach an influential audience and explode the myths of Nazi propaganda.

On February 23, 1942, Berlin police recorded a disturbing occurrence in their blotter. It concerned

> a large number of six-page inflammatory pamphlets . . . written under the title *"Die Sorge um Deutschlands Zukunft geht durch das Volk!"* ["Distress About Germany's Future Runs Throughout the Land"]. The typed flyers were sent to various Catholic dioceses and to a number of people in intellectual professions such as professors, doctors, engineers, etc. through the post office.[22]

The pamphlet denounced the culture of lies the Nazis had foisted upon the German people, stating

> Minister Goebbels strives in vain to throw ever more sand in our eyes. . . . But no one can deny that our situation worsens from month to month. . . . No matter what lies the High Command puts out, the number of war victims is rising into the millions.[23]

The authors argued that the Nazis' policies had created a vicious cycle of conquest and want: "The struggle for raw materials for the war effort only leads to ever-new theaters of war; that is, to new fronts and new mass graves." Hitler had assured the Germans that England would break down. But the British had stiffened their resolve, and support was flooding in from America. Germany's army was utterly overextended, and by summer it would deplete its last reserves. German soldiers would die senseless deaths in the ice and snow by the hundreds of thousands, and the entire continent would be left a field of rubble.

The pamphlet urged the "stupid people" in Germany to heed the anti-Nazi warnings of the Catholic bishop of Münster and the Lutheran bishop of Württemberg. Hitler was going to go down in defeat, just like Napoleon, and the Germans must find a way not to go down with him.

"Write to soldiers in the field," the authors urged. "Let them know what's going on at home. Tell them that Germans are no longer willing to submit to the yoke of the Nazi Party bosses. . . . Let the SS know that the people abhor their murders and their betrayal from their deepest souls." The flyer turned the principle of the "Führer Oath" on its head: "Each of us should do exactly the opposite of what this government demands."

·The pamphlet was signed "AGIS" in homage to an ancient king of Sparta who rallied his people against corruption. The document was drafted by Harro Schulze-Boysen, John Graudenz, and John Rittmeister. John Sieg may also have contributed.

The production and distribution of the pamphlet required a small army. The twenty-year-old ceramicist Cato Bontjes van Beek and her boyfriend, Heinz Strelow, typed the master copy.[24] Marie Terwiel reproduced it on her typewriter, five copies at a time, and located mailing addresses in the phone book. John Graudenz manned the hectograph. He and Helmut Himpel ran off and distributed between three hundred and five hundred copies.[25] Himpel's friend Helmut Roloff, the classical pianist, helped stuff the envelopes, wearing gloves to prevent fingerprints.

The addressees represented an extraordinary range of powerful and influential figures. They included anti-Nazi religious leaders, Hitler's half-brother Alois, and Johannes Popitz, former finance minister and a conservative anti-Nazi. An even more noteworthy name appeared on the list: Roland Freisler, the bloodthirsty state secretary for the Ministry of Justice, who had just returned from the Wannsee conference on the "final solution."[26]

Most of the recipients declined to circulate the flyers as requested, and immediately sent them to the Gestapo. The police registered receipt

of 288 copies by mid-March.[27] This was not surprising. The mere possession of the flyers was a criminal offense.

Gestapo agents fanned out across the city, trying to trace the origin of
the flyers. They sought the authors and the hectographs, scoured the
post offices where they were mailed, and questioned shop owners who
sold paper and envelopes. But they failed on every count. Harro's friends
had covered their tracks.

CHAPTER 20

The Antiwelle

1941–1942

AT THE SAME TIME THAT THE GESTAPO WAS RACING TO TRACK down the originators of the AGIS flyers, the circle was working on an even bolder document, this one produced at the initiative of John Sieg. Recently Sieg had been working at the railroad telegraph office in Tempelhof, and continued to link the Communist and trade union resistance circles with the Schulze-Boysen intellectuals. He drafted articles for both groups' underground publications.

John was also tending his wife, Sophie, who was shattered by her family's recent sorrows. Her sister's husband in Poland had been shot by the SS, and her nephew was deported to Sachsenhausen. Sophie comforted herself by helping with her husband's articles for flyers and the underground newspaper *The Inner Front*, intent on getting her Polish translations into the hands of Polish slave workers and prisoners of war.[1] The group was also publishing editions of one hundred to two hundred copies in Czech, Italian, and French. Russian was more complicated, since they couldn't lay hands on a Cyrillic typewriter. Max Grabowski had to copy the letters on the plate by hand. One member of the group, Kurt Heims, had become a firefighter. As the bombs fell on Berlin, he was able to acquire knapsacks full of paper from burning businesses. (His friends noted that his uniform gave him an advantage.)[2]

In early 1942, John Sieg told Adam Kuckhoff that he had a new document to share. It was called "Letter from Captain Denker to His Son." (The captain's name translates to "thinker" or "philosopher.") The letter described the emotions of a former Social Democrat who has just visited a military hospital full of soldiers returning from the eastern front.

The origins of the letter are obscure. Greta wrote that Sieg, along with her husband, took material that Libertas Schulze-Boysen coaxed from soldiers on leave and elaborated on it,[3] supplementing the information with their own research. The letter's narrator speaks about police matters and medical facilities in impressive detail, no doubt obtained from some of Sieg's resistance contacts, which included some members of the Schutzpolizei (civil police), who remained tacitly antifascist. The resistance circles also included several doctors with access to hospitals, as well as soldiers who had recently returned from the front. John Sieg had seen a picture of a child in the situation described, in Libertas Schulze-Boysen's archives.[4]

Adam Kuckhoff responded to the idea with enthusiasm, and assumed his old role as editor to help Sieg shape the eight-page document. Whether or not there was an actual Captain Denker, the "Open Letter" is a rare and accurate depiction of the German war crimes that were taking place, and reflects their psychic impact on a man whose "mental illness" represented his last flicker of humanity.

The letter merits quotation at length. It demonstrates the authors' determination to shine a light on the massive human rights violations that were occurring without the possibility of public investigation or disclosure. The style of the letter is also striking. It reflects John Sieg's eye for detail and ear for dialogue, developed as a reader of American realism and a reporter on the streets of Berlin. But the story also unfolds with the benefit of Adam Kuckhoff's literary sensibility, progressing from the banality of the hospital wards to its devastating conclusion. Despite its passages of clichéd propaganda, the work emerges as an aching and compassionate treatise on the madness of war.

The letter opens with the narrator expressing shock that his correspondent has joined the military police at the eastern front, given his background as a sober and professional civilian police officer. He then continues:

> In the state hospital in —— I've recently visited some comrades
> from the police who have been transferred from the eastern front,

all of them as a result of nervous breakdowns. You know the atmosphere of a hospital, that special kind of quiet. They had cheered up the rooms with flowers; the patients have to listen to music. To these ridiculously simple means of raising their spirits they have added, as if in a novel, a few rays of sun.

There is also one ward there, which the comrades told me about with almost shy relief, where even worse cases of nervous collapse are housed. There, once strong, really tough district officers hop around continually like kangaroos, you know, and others crawl around on all fours, shaking their heads deliberately the whole time, their hair falling disheveled over their faces, with an expression, someone swore to me, like that of a St. Bernard. I have learned many shocking things from the comrades. The quiet of those rooms was deceptive; the furies were raging in there. In whispers, not looking me in the eye, hoping for me to offer some redeeming justification, they told me of mass executions of Russian civilians, of elaborate cruelties, of limitless blood and tears, of the brutal orders of the SS, of the unfathomable equanimity of the helpless victims, and yes, of course, they told me a lot about the struggle of the partisans, which was something that greatly interested me from a political and tactical point of view.

Of course I didn't offer a word of comfort to any of these sick men, nothing that would have helped them in the ghastly horror of the darkening hours of evening as they told me all the more eagerly of their deeds. Am I really supposed to exorcise the spirits of those who have been struck down? Am I supposed to offer some kind of absolution to those who went on to tell me (even if they were blushing) that they carried out orders, month after month, as a kind of routine task, to shoot as many as 50 people a day?

One of these nonetheless deplorable executioners—and this will interest you as an expert in criminality—can't shake off the memory of a small, dirty rag doll. Moreover, he told me, in haste and confusion, one of his fingers stiffened up as the result of being badly bitten. You must forgive me for passing along this detail, since of course it now simply drowns in the everyday sadness of the hundreds of thousands of details of the terrorism practiced by the organs of those who are today in power—even just those that are committed here in Germany. Do you still remember all the horrors you told me about right away in 1933, the countless bestialities committed in the dungeons of the SA and the SS, in the cells and torture chambers of the Gestapo, the accursed marshes, and the other hellish concentration camps? . . .

According to his account, this comrade had to carry out executions with his revolver. The victims had to kneel. Then he walked along the row behind them, shooting each one in the back of the head at close range. When I asked him about the pools of blood, about the way in which the bodies had fallen and piled up, he answered in the matter-of-fact fashion of an anatomist—no, rather with the flat tone of a slaughterhouse worker—without, as far as I could see, any awareness of the gruesome particulars of what he'd done, let alone the meaning of the "National Socialism" of his bosses. But at last there was one thing that made him crack: he was told to execute a young woman, a peasant, and her three children. "Why?" I asked. He shrugged his shoulders. "It was an order."

The woman was holding an infant in her arms. It was bitterly cold, and she was trying vainly—for the two minutes of her life that remained—to shelter the crying child warmly in her pitiful rags. With a helpless demeanor of apology she explained that this was all she had; everything else had been stolen from her. The woman's six-year-old son was kneeling on the woman's right; to her left was her two-year-old daughter, who was groping around behind her as she knelt down to find her doll. So—"the doll too." As I said, it was a ridiculous, pathetic scrap of a rag doll. And after the child knelt down, in that awkward childish way, she fussed with the doll until it too was kneeling in the snow beside her.

"Who did you shoot first?" I wanted to know. "The woman or the baby?"

"Oh, I'd never have shot the baby first."

"I see, so you spared it, thinking that perhaps you'd give it to someone later?"

No, he said, there were more and more cases of disobedience among the police. On this occasion an SS man had been lurking behind him in the background, and suddenly the six-year-old boy had jumped to his feet and thrown himself at the gunman. According to his account, there must have been a fierce, bitter struggle between the boy and the officer, only for a few seconds of course, but that's when his finger was bitten—the one that had stiffened up—so he had to fire twice at the boy. The first shot missed and the second one turned the boy's eye into a dripping, bloody pulp. The girl meanwhile remained very still and simply fell over without a sound next to her doll. There's nothing more to be said about this insignificant doll, except that it became our murderer's little obsession—his "tic"—according to the other comrades. That doll, the last wretched leftover, had become the focus of his "illness," and soon he would be sent "downstairs" to be with the "kangaroos" and the "St. Bernards."

Adam Kuckhoff suggested to John Sieg that they rework the Captain Denker letter 'to send to soldiers on the eastern front. According to Greta, her husband had an activist agenda, hoping that the document could "appeal to the morality shown in former times. The former Social Democrat captain could offer the soldiers—or if possible, whole companies and regiments—insights that will lead them to proper conduct."[5]

The sculptor Kurt Schumacher was now stationed near Poznań, a major way station to the Russian front. He clandestinely circulated the letter among the soldiers. Sieg and Kuckhoff prepared a second version of it specifically for military distribution a few months later. There is no evidence of its effect, but producing the letter was an important gesture in itself, as an attempt to alert Germans to acts that the Nazis energetically concealed. Over the second half of 1941, the barbaric nature of the German occupation on the eastern front was grossly misrepresented to the German public.

On July 11, 1941, days after German troops rolled across the Soviet border, *Einsatzgruppen* squads received a confidential order to execute male Jews between the ages of seventeen and forty-five who were "convicted" of looting. The soldiers were required to carry out the executions in secluded places and forbidden from taking photographs. The victims were noted in official registers as "Bolsheviks," "partisans," and "looters," distorting the official records in case they fell into the hands of outsiders.[6]

The mass killings of Jewish and other civilians were further disguised, even within internal German military communications. Executions were labeled "special duties," "pacification," or *Aktion nach Kriegsgebrauch* ("actions according to the custom of war").[7] In a July 16 meeting, Hitler was pleased to announce that the Soviets issued a call for partisan resistance behind the lines, which to his mind offered a justification to execute at will.[8]

The German public was further misled by the mass media. Government newsreels presented clean-cut German soldiers comporting themselves bravely on the battlefield, executing dangerous "criminals" only to assure orderly occupation conditions. The "Open Letter" from Captain Denker was rare in circulating, in however limited a fashion, a different version of reality.

The second revelation of the "Open Letter" was the depth of trauma experienced by German soldiers who carried out atrocities. This information had also been suppressed by the regime. By 1940, Heinrich Himmler was already aware that his orders to massacre civilians could have damaging psychological effects on police forces.[9] In 1942, SS leader Erich von dem Bach-Zelewski was hospitalized in a condition similar to the one described in the Captain Denker letter. In the opinion of the chief SS doctor, the officer suffered a nervous affliction that was partly brought on by the executions he had conducted. Laid up in an SS hospital in Berlin, he was tormented by flashbacks of the shootings of Jews he had overseen.[10] Such conditions were closely guarded secrets. Kuckhoff and Sieg's Captain Denker letter reflected the contents of classified reports arriving from the eastern front, but conveyed the information to an entirely different readership.

Harro Schulze-Boysen's new target audiences, foreign slave workers and soldiers at the front, represented risky ventures. His group often had the sense that they were risking their lives to reveal urgent truths to a passive society, without any proof that their efforts made any difference.

But Harro Schulze-Boysen told his associates that their actions would resonate in the future: "If the Russians come to Germany (and they will come) and if we are to play some role in Germany, we must be able to show that there was a meaningful resistance group in Germany. Otherwise the Russians will be able to do what they want with us."[11]

Over the same period that John Sieg and Adam Kuckhoff were working on the Captain Denker letter, related flyers were emerging from a different source. In early 1942, several exiled German Communists secretly returned to Germany in the effort to revive their old networks. One of them, Wilhelm Knöchel, made his way to Berlin from Amsterdam and established contact with underground Communists. His connections indirectly extended to some members of the Schulze-Boysen circle with Communist ties. Knöchel soon launched his own hectographed publication, *Der Friedenskämpfer* ("The Fighter for Peace"), offering detailed accounts of German atrocities across the eastern front. The flyers quoted German soldiers and SS personnel who were "disgusted and horrified" by the actions committed by their units.[12]

In a remarkable "special edition" published in June 1942, Knöchel's group detailed the mass executions of French, Czechs, Germans, and Norwegians across Europe. They went on to list specific companies that carried out mass shootings of Soviet POWs in Leningrad and civilians in Lvov. The publication referred to a collection of incriminating photographs from the front.

Like John Sieg, Knöchel lacked the technology to reproduce photographs for publication, but the flyer used line drawings to present shocking images of mass murders at execution pits. These images correspond closely to photographs taken at the front by soldiers, which became public only after the war. At the time, the Nazis forbade soldiers to disseminate testimony or images of the mass killings, under the strictest penalties. Knöchel's flyer represented something close to real-time reporting on one of the largest-scale human rights crimes of the period.

It is not known whether Knöchel ever met John Sieg or saw his "Inner Front" flyers, but Knöchel's and Sieg's groups established contact and exchanged microphotocopies of materials through intermediaries Elisabeth Schumacher and Wilhelm Guddorf. This raises the possibility that some of Knöchel's line drawings could have been based on photographs from Libertas Schulze-Boysen's archives.*

---

*Knöchel was arrested in 1943 and executed in Brandenburg prison in 1944.

Although the Russian front provided much of the breaking news, Poland also remained a pressing concern. The province of Poznań lay in the heart of the territory Germany had ceded to Poland after World War I, and had then retaken in 1939. In the summer of 1941, Kurt Schumacher was drafted and sent to guard French laborers there. When his wife, Elisabeth, traveled east to visit him the following spring, she was stricken to see the conditions of prisoners of war and Jews in Poland. The experience only compounded her fears for her Jewish relatives in Germany.

A few weeks later Elisabeth learned that her elderly Jewish uncle, a leading musicologist named Richard Hohenemser, and his wife had stopped answering their door. She contacted a close friend, an eminent China scholar and Communist named Philip Schaeffer, to help her break into their apartment. Schaeffer tried to lower himself into their window from the roof, but the rope did not hold. He fell to the street and was badly injured. It turned out that the old couple was already dead, having turned on the gas to avoid deportation. Elisabeth was also unable to save her uncle Moritz, who had bankrolled her through art school, from deportation to Theresienstadt.[13]

Schulze-Boysen's group knew that terrible events were transpiring in occupied countries, but they needed proof in hand. In early 1942, Libertas Schulze-Boysen used her influence at the Kulturfilm center to get a job for Adam Kuckhoff directing a short documentary called *Poznań—Stadt im Aufbau* (*Poznań—City Under Construction*).

Adam's official task was to document the Nazis' ambitious program to reshape the city as Germany's gateway to the east. At the same time that Jewish and Catholic Poles were being shot en masse elsewhere in the district, workers in the city center were unloading trainloads of rare marble. Hitler planned to refit Poznań's castle as his personal palace, perfectly situated to greet victorious troops coming home from the front. But Kuckhoff traveled east with his own agenda of gathering material for the atrocity archive and forging contacts for the circle. Greta wangled permission to visit him, and was shocked at what she saw.

On her return, she promptly drafted a report on "all of the inhumane treatment, of both Jewish and Polish citizens." She described how "the kiosk, used under martial law to post death sentences carried out for the

smallest infractions or cases of insubordination, was plastered with no-
tices."[14] Anyone with eyes in their heads, Greta wrote, could see that this
was a site of mass murder.

But Arvid Harnack informed her there was no way that the group
could publish her report as a flyer. It would be too easy for the Gestapo
to track the information—too few people had access to it. Circulating
her report would give them away instantly.

Over early 1942, the resistance circles struggled to find new avenues
for action. The intelligence work was stalemated. Both the U.S. and the
Soviet missions were now shuttered, and radio contact had failed. Harnack, Kuckhoff, and Schulze-Boysen continued to infiltrate members of
their groups into the Nazi bureaucracies. Harro was pleased with the
progress of writer Günther Weisenborn, who had joined Goebbels's
Reich Broadcasting Company in July 1940.

Within a year Weisenborn was sitting in on the company's secret
conferences and passing the reports on to Schulze-Boysen. One of the
benefits of his job was privileged access to speeches by foreign leaders.
He would take them home overnight and copy them, then hand off the
typescript to another member of the circle for reproduction. Within
days, statements by Roosevelt, Stalin, and Churchill were secretly circulating in Berlin.[15]

Weisenborn also tried his hand at sabotaging the news. He was
harshly chastised for his "mistakes," but he was promoted nonetheless,
first to chief of correspondents, then to cultural editor.[16]

The circle continued to churn out leaflets. Ceramicist Cato Bontjes
van Beek drove much of the effort, writing and typing out originals, with
John Graudenz at the helm of the hectograph. Cato's artist friends and
other members of the group participated in the distribution, discreetly
leaving the flyers in subway stations and telephone booths.

The bombs were falling faster now. By night, large areas of the city lit
up in flames. The ruins were still smoking in the morning, as neighbors
and rescue workers pulled bodies out of the rubble. Anxiety and opportunity went hand in hand. On blackout nights the circle would assemble:
soldier-scholars in mufti, pretty young art students, blue-collar workers
from the Communist cells. Taut with nerves, they would pad their clothing
and load their bags with flyers, then fan out across the city. They learned

how to avoid attracting the attention of passersby, disguising themselves as girlfriends having a casual chat or a young couple locked in a shadowy embrace. The next morning, puzzled policemen would be ordered onto the streets to gather up leaflets and scrape anti-Hitler flyers from the walls.

The members of the circle were driven by zeal, hurling themselves into noble actions one day and preposterous escapades the next. "For use at night the group also constructed a contraption which looked like a suitcase," Weisenborn reported. "When it was set down in the street it stamped some anti-Nazi slogan on the pavement."[17] It is hard to imagine the appeal of such a device, which courted death for the meager return of a slogan on a sidewalk.

In May 1942 the Nazis launched a new propaganda effort that struck the circle as a personal affront. Joseph Goebbels had designed a major exhibit called "The Soviet Paradise" to occupy most of the Lustgarten, the vast public space directly in front of the downtown cathedral. Massive photo panels depicted Russian Slavs as subhuman beasts who lived in squalid villages where the sun never shone. German soldiers, on the other hand, were portrayed as the innocent victims of terrorists. Once again, anti-Semitism and anti-Bolshevism went hand in hand. Visitors were handed official booklets that read:

Marxism and Bolshevism—The Invention of Jewry.

Early on, Jewry recognized unlimited possibilities for the Bolshevist nonsense in the East. This is supported by two facts:

1. The inventor of Marxism was the Jew Marx-Mordechai;
2. The present Soviet state is nothing other than the realization of that Jewish invention. The Bolshevist revolution itself stands between these two facts. The Jews exterminated the best elements of the East to make themselves the absolute rulers of an area from which they hoped to establish world domination.

According to the GPU's figures, nearly two million people were executed during the years 1917 to 1921. A direct result of the revolution was the terrible famine that demanded 19 million victims between 1917 and 1934. Over 21 million people lost their lives through this Jew-incited revolution and its consequences. . . .

Further proof that the Soviet state belongs to the Jews is the fact that the people are ruthlessly sacrificed for the goals of the Jewish world revolution.[18]

The exhibit's most distressing feature was an installation about SS measures against "partisans." Greta and her friends were horrified by the images. "There were photos showing the firing squads, and bodies of young girls, still half-children, dangling horribly from ropes like their comrades," she wrote. Greta knew that many of the Nazis' "partisans" were Russian and Jewish civilians. She and her husband stayed at the exhibit for two hours, watching the dense crowds and wondering what they were really thinking.[19]

The circle decided to act. They decided to base their protest on an unexpected technology. A couple in the group, Fritz and Hannelore Thiel, had come across a child's rubber-stamp set. Soon it was put into action, printing tiny wax-coated stickers that could be attached to walls and phone booths. The couple delivered the stickers to the young people for a *Zettelklebeaktion* (sticker-pasting operation).

The stickers mocked Goebbels's rhetoric with the words:

> Permanent Installation
>
> The NAZI PARADISE
>
> War Hunger Lies Gestapo
>
> How much longer?

Harro Schulze-Boysen led the charge. He believed that the public needed a bold, public demonstration to show them that the opposition had not been extinguished in Germany. He was opposed by many of the older members of the group. John Rittmeister, Adam Kuckhoff, Günther Weisenborn, and Arvid Harnack all argued that the action was not worth the risk. But Harro was determined. He assembled a team, starting with regulars John Graudenz and Marie Terwiel. They were joined by Hans Coppi, the young machinist–radio operator, and his wife, Hilde. Harro also invited a band of young students, including some of Cato's art school friends and Liane Berkowitz, the nineteen-year-old daughter of a Russian-Jewish symphony conductor, who had joined the group with her boyfriend.[20]

On the night of May 17, 1942, Schulze-Boysen donned his Luftwaffe uniform, seized his pistol, and led his motley band into the streets. He stood guard, pistol cocked, as they moved through the broad boulevard and down narrow alleyways, plastering hundreds of stickers on walls darkened by the blackout. They took special care to cover the surfaces of posters advertising the "Soviet Paradise" exhibit. Liane Berkowitz was handed a hundred handbills and sent to the Kurfürstendamm thoroughfare with a young soldier. The two were told to behave like young lovers wandering from lane to lane, leaving a trail of handbills in their wake.[21]

Only blocks away from Harro's handbill operation, a dark-haired young electrician was nursing plans to take the protest a step further. Herbert Baum was a Jewish Communist, born in Poznań, who had been pressed into labor at a Siemens plant. He and his wife, Marianne, had collected a number of Berlin's young Communist and leftist Jews. They hosted meetings in their house, helped with immigration where possible, and maintained links with other leftist underground circles, especially in the factories. One of his contacts was Walter Husemann, Marta Wolter's husband and a Communist member of Harro's circle.

Herbert Baum was even more reckless than Harro. On May 18, he and his group delivered bags containing incendiary bombs to the exhibit at the Lustgarten square. The bombs injured eleven people and damaged part of the exhibit, but the government managed to hush it up. Four days later the Gestapo started the roundup. Some 250 Jews were arrested in retaliation for the act, of whom around a hundred were shot at Sachsenhausen.[22] Twenty-two members of Baum's group were sentenced to death and executed. Baum himself spent several days in the Gestapo torture cells and died in custody. Officials described his death as a suicide.

Shortly after the "Soviet Paradise" action, Arvid Harnack asked the Kuckhoffs to revisit the exhibition and see what marks were left by the actions. Greta was depressed to report that little evidence of the fires remained. The word on the street, she learned, was that "the Jews had attacked the exhibit because they can't stand the truth."[23]

Nerves were beginning to fray. Following the "Soviet Paradise," some members of the circle began to distance themselves from Harro. How could he risk their lives for such a modest return? One potential deserter was his own wife. Libertas Schulze-Boysen told Günther Weisenborn that she wanted out. She wasn't a political animal, and some members of the circle hadn't accepted her from the start. She had supported her husband for the past five years and didn't want to leave him in the lurch. But she was frightened. It felt as though "every action led them closer to Death."[24]

Harro, on the other hand, seemed to gather energy from the risk. On May 19, two days after his group action, he started a long, spirited letter to his parents about his plans for their annual Pfingsten outing at the lake. The weather was summery and he hoped it would stay that way. "When you're working hard, you forget whether it's summer or winter for weeks at a time," he wrote.[25] Libs had just spent four days in Vienna in film meetings, which had gone well. It seemed, he wrote, that the trip had done her good.

Harro and Libertas got their splendid weather for the spring holiday. They spent it with members of their circle, which had been woven into a web of genuine friendship. Earlier that month Harro cataloged his fascinating friends for his parents:

> There's J[ohn Graudenz], an old journalist, already over 40, with a lively wife and two cheerful daughters. . . . He's a salesman now and has a sweet little villa near Stahnsdorf. . . . Then comes Rittmeister, somewhat older than me, a well-known psychiatrist. He lives in our neighborhood. His little artistically-gifted wife recently visited us. . . . Then there's 19-year-old Horst Heilmann, for the past year and a half my best student in international relations at the university. . . . He's a radio operator at the High Command and listens to the radio every free minute. And then we have a dentist [Himpel] with his girlfriend [Marie Terwiel], who's like Libs in so many ways. . . .
>
> And there are also the old friends. Walter [Küchenmeister], and the doctor E[lfriede Paul], whose practice, in times of war, keeps growing. . . . Kurt Schumacher, the sculptor, guarding prisoners in

Posen [Poznań]. At first he was really unhappy, but we've introduced him to some acquaintances in Posen [Poznań], and now he's
doing better there. Weisenborn is now a big man in radio. . . .

Harro's antic good humor masked his growing frustration. That
spring he had discovered that the Germans had captured some British
codebooks, which enabled them to chart the course of Allied convoys between Iceland and northern Russia before they had even sailed.[26] These
convoys extended the critical lifeline of the Lend-Lease Program across
the Arctic Ocean to the Soviet Union. From late 1941 through 1942, the
"Murmansk Run" supplied the beleaguered Soviets with 7,000 tanks,
350,000 tons of explosives, and 15 million pairs of boots from the United
States. The Germans recognized the importance of the supplies, and organized a massive attack on the British, Canadian, and U.S. vessels, de-
ploying U-boats, aircraft, and battleships, among them the massive
Tirpitz (named after Harro Schulze-Boysen's great-uncle).

Schulze-Boysen was anxious to alert British intelligence to the danger. In June 1942 he and John Graudenz traveled to the mountains south
of Frankfurt for several weeks, and stayed in the imposing castle of Stet-
ten, which belonged to a friend, in the village of Kocherstetten. The trip
was described as a vacation, but the two men had a more urgent purpose.

At Kocherstetten they met up with Marcel Melliand, a friend of Graudenz's. Melliand, a textile manufacturer and secret antifascist, was planning to travel to Switzerland on business. Schulze-Boysen convinced
Melliand to convey his information to British intelligence in Switzerland.
But Melliand was ultimately unable to get a visa, and his trip was canceled.[27] Had Harro's mission succeeded, he might have averted a devastating outcome. German submarines and aircraft ravaged the Allied
convoys over the summer.[28]

There was a poignant underlying reality to the group's activities.
Harro Schulze-Boysen's beloved younger brother Hartmut was in the
German navy, and Arvid Harnack's brother Falk was in the army. Adam
Kuckhoff had a son in the armed forces. They could not escape the
thought that their actions, undertaken to counter the ravages of Nazism,
could also endanger their loved ones.

Harro Schulze-Boysen used the rest of the summer to prospect for new allies. One important contact was Arvid Harnack's friend Egmont Zechlin, a prominent history professor and Bismarck scholar. In the thirties Zechlin had often debated Harnack's notion that a Soviet-style planned economy could be an answer to the global depression. But these differences did not alter their mutual respect, and the two men grew closer over the war years. By mid-1942 they found common ground. Zechlin, who was maimed in the trenches of World War I, wrote:

> We were of one mind that this senseless war must be brought to an end, and that no one should have any dealings with Hitler and his people, since the atrocities in the Ukraine had denied them any moral standing. This had become the overriding and decisive issue—that the war had been lost morally as well.[29]

They agreed that Germany could only be saved by people who were willing to treat the Nazis not as unsavory compatriots, but as foreign enemies. With Zechlin's help, Harro and Arvid met with Albrecht Haushofer, a professor and politician who had once been popular with the Nazis. Haushofer had experienced a change of heart and had joined the military conspiracy against Hitler that would come to be known as the 20th of July movement.[30] Zechlin later stated that he was hoping to create "a functional coalition," and that Haushofer "was in favor of backing the Harnack group with their focus on the East, in order to facilitate negotiations with the British." Zechlin had the impression that Harnack and Haushofer "understood each other very well."[31]

Harro Schulze-Boysen and other members of the group made frequent attempts to communicate with the armies of foreign workers who had been shipped into Berlin. They sometimes went drinking at the Bärenschenke bar on Friedrichstrasse, looking for foreign recruits. They tried to persuade skeptical French laborers to join "legions" that would rise up against the regime when the time was ripe. Germany's population of forced laborers would eventually number over twelve million, and there had been sporadic outbreaks of rebellion, especially among Poles and Ukrainians.[32] Harro's drinking companions were dubious about his plans.

But Harro's energy was usually contagious. Somehow his wife got a second wind, and she decided to reenter the fray. In July 1942 she summoned a young man named Alexander Spoerl to her office at the Kulturfilm center. Spoerl, a tousle-haired youth of twenty-three, was puzzled. He had received an excellent offer as a script editor for Kulturfilm, completely out of the blue. His father was a well-known writer, but his own background was in mechanical engineering. Spoerl explained all this to the dazzling, slightly older woman: he had no experience as a script editor, and the mission of the Kulturfilm center was actually a mystery to him.

Libertas listened calmly, then suddenly asked him, "Are you still operating your Antiwelle?" Spoerl had no idea why he felt he could trust this stranger, but he answered in the affirmative. The Antiwelle, or "anti-wave," was an anti-Nazi organization run out of the film industry. This was another project that bore the fingerprints of producer Herbert Engelsing. The Antiwelle's name had been coined by Tobis cameraman Heinz Landsmann, who had been working with Herbert Engelsing on the feature films *Philharmonik* and *Die Grosse Schatten* over 1942, and Engelsing was the one who told Libertas about Spoerl and his Antiwelle involvement, arranging for him to be transferred to her office.

Libertas quickly outlined her plans for their collaboration. It was to be both artistic and political in nature. Libertas wanted to try to expand the influence of the Kulturfilm center to make an impact on the entire production of documentaries in Germany. At this point Spoerl decided that Libertas was simply an idealist, and he had no idea that she was part of a group. But he was excited at the prospect of getting involved in a larger effort than the Antiwelle. He found Libertas "enchanting"—"the instinct of a woman, with a woman's naiveté and ardor, and a very strikingly male intellect." The two of them began an enthusiastic collaboration, experimenting with filmmaking with the goal of making "great, innovative films together once the Nazi period was over."

Gradually Spoerl realized that Libertas belonged to a larger organization. She introduced him to Harro and other friends, usually out at the lake or at afternoon teas at the Schulze-Boysen apartment. In July 1942, Spoerl received his first assignment for the resistance. Leica films were coming in to the office from the eastern front, showing atrocities committed by the SS. As a well-trained amateur photographer, Spoerl was asked to develop and enlarge the images. Libertas took the initiative of equipping a darkroom at the center and procuring a photocopying machine, where they could duplicate newspaper clippings, reports, and flyers. Libertas told Spoerl how she had brought Adam Kuckhoff into the center, and that he was traveling back and forth to Poznań on a regular basis.[33] Spoerl took the stills of SS atrocities home to his apartment at night and enlarged them for the archives.

The campaign on the eastern front had bogged down, offering the Berlin circle moments of hope and euphoria. It was clear that the tide had turned; the only question was how long it would take for the regime to go down. Spoerl felt in retrospect that the group became too outspoken in public, preparing for an open struggle far too soon. Members of the circle weren't even sure how to define an "open struggle," and Harro Schulze-Boysen wasn't able to explain it to them. They supposed that the eastern front would collapse and take the regime down with it. Some members of the group planned to grab weapons that they had stockpiled in Teupitz, a tiny town twenty-five miles south of Berlin where the Schulze-Boysens had bought a plot of land with some of Libertas's inheritance.[34] The arms would be used to occupy post offices and town halls. Looking back, Spoerl judged their plans to be honorable but naïve.

"If I speak so critically of our hopes, I don't want it to sound in any way as if I'm disparaging what we did," Spoerl wrote later.

> We unfortunately underestimated the obedience of the soldiers and the capacity for suffering of the German people, and with the best will in the world it was impossible to predict what form the collapse would eventually take. The most important thing is that a group existed, without any help from the population and at a time when Germany was still at war, and took action simply as a result of the dictates of conscience.[35]

As the group continued to try to enlighten the German public, it pursued more direct action as well. John Sieg, working for the state railway, served as the linchpin for opposition groups in German factories and plants. Later Kurt Hess, a member of his group, recounted their attempts to make mischief: "War munitions trains and army transports were misdirected, or [Sieg] caused them to be held up for hours, without anyone knowing who was directly responsible."[36] Sieg's contacts included defense workers in the Hasse & Wrede engine plant, the AEG electric company, and the Alkett armaments manufacturer. Their efforts included work slowdowns, assistance to forced laborers, and the distribution of illegal literature.

But the Soviets were still focusing on their critical need for radio communications. Over the summer of 1942 the Germans mounted a second offensive across southern Russia, aiming for the oil fields of the Caucasus, just as Schulze-Boysen had indicated. The Soviets wanted more such intelligence, and decided to take drastic measures. They recruited two German Communists in the Soviet Union to return to Germany, one a veteran of the International Brigade in Spain, the other a German prisoner of war. In early August 1942 the Soviets dropped the two into East Prussia by parachute, bearing a new radio.[37] The two made their way to Berlin, pretending to be German soldiers on leave. They were supposed to stay in a country house Mildred Harnack had prepared for them, but they ended up staying at the Schumachers' instead.[38] The parachutists sent a radio message to Moscow that they had met with Schumacher and made contact with Harro. "The anti-Fascist group has grown considerably and is actively working," they reported. "Their radio apparatus is functioning but for some reason cannot make contact."[39]

The Soviets were set on directing the groups' energies back into intelligence. They saw the antifascist activities as counterproductive, serving only to endanger their intelligence work. But the flyers, the stickers, and the relief efforts persisted, no matter how much the Soviets discouraged them.

From the perspective of the regime, every activity undertaken by the group, from assembling atrocity archives to misdirecting Reichsbahn trains, was enough to warrant a death sentence, or at the very least consignment to a concentration camp. But ironically, the group was not compromised by Harro Schulze-Boysen's audacious street actions, John Sieg's defiant publications, or Greta Kuckhoff's unceasing concern for her Jewish friends. When the Berlin circle was finally apprehended, it was through the careless incompetence of the Moscow "professionals."

\ \ \

CHAPTER 21

Crime and Punishment

1942–1943

ONE DAY IN EARLY SEPTEMBER 1942, LIBERTAS SCHULZE-BOYSEN'S young assistant, Alexander Spoerl, realized that Adam Kuckhoff had gone missing. He was still on assignment to produce the documentary on Poznań, working out of the branch office in Prague. But he had suddenly stopped communicating with the home office, and Libertas's telegrams to him went unanswered. The company production chief showed up from Prague, tense and tight-lipped. Then Libertas called Spoerl to her office and started agonizing about a missing suitcase. Spoerl had no idea what was in the suitcase, but it was obviously something dangerous. "For the first time since I'd met her," he wrote later, "Libertas lost control."

Libertas had planned to visit her sister Ottora in Sweden, where she lived grandly as the wife of a Swedish count. Göring had promised to help her get permission to travel, but at the last minute she learned that her permit had been canceled.

Libertas still hadn't gotten over the puzzling telephone conversation with Harro's secretary a few days earlier. Harro had been summoned urgently from his office near Potsdam to report to his senior officer, the secretary said, something about a courier mission to the front. He ran out of the office and didn't come back. But he had left behind his hat, his gloves, and his insignia.

The danger signals mounted. The woman who delivered Libertas's mail at her apartment stopped her on the staircase and told her that her letters were being monitored by the Gestapo. Libertas called the Engelsings and told them that she believed that Harro had been arrested, and that she was being shadowed. They asked her to come stay with them, but Libertas rejected the idea. Herbert Engelsing tried to contact Adam Kuckhoff, but there was no answer. Their dentist friend, Helmut Himpel, was missing, too.[1]

Libertas and Alexander tore apart their darkrooms at the Kulturfilm center and Alexander's home, destroying the archives, emptying wastebaskets, and burning rolls of film that Alexander had hidden in an old radio set. Then they set about fabricating evidence of their "innocence," copying personal snapshots and writing fake letters to each other about their undying loyalty to Nazi ideals. These were placed strategically around the room.

Libertas had already ransacked her apartment's hiding places for Harro's political papers—flyers, notes, drafts of essays—and stuffed them into a suitcase. She parked the suitcase at the home of an actress friend for a few days, but the actress lost her nerve and called a director friend. She asked him to send the suitcase on to his friend Günther Weisenborn.[2]

Weisenborn's first hint of disaster arrived with a confused call from the director. A young soldier had left behind a suitcase, he said. It contained strange writings and he was a little concerned about it. Weisenborn agreed to take a look. When Weisenborn opened the suitcase, he immediately recognized Harro's handwriting and realized that the group had been compromised. Weisenborn went to a phone booth and tried to call Schulze-Boysen's office at the Luftwaffe. He was not there, and they couldn't say when he'd be back. Weisenborn hung up the phone, and joined in sounding the alarm. He had last seen Harro the day before his disappearance, when thirty members of the circle had converged on Wannsee for a day of sailing. It had seemed a Sunday like any other, with music, a cookout, and long talks about the future.

Link by link, the members of the circle cleared their homes of incriminating evidence. One Soviet radio was bundled into a pram and shoved into the River Spree. John Graudenz put another radio set in a large suitcase, locked it, and bound it with wire. He intended to leave it with Helmut Himpel, but Himpel knew that if Harro was under arrest, he wouldn't be far behind. Himpel approached his neighbor, pianist Helmut Roloff, who agreed to hide the suitcase in his apartment.[3]

And then—silence.

Libertas moved in with Spoerl for a few days. The two of them moved about the city like ghosts, convinced they were being followed and watched at every turn. Finally, her nerves gave way. She announced that she was going to take a three-week vacation in an area of the Black Forest where Harro's brother was staying. She could try for the French border—or perhaps she could make a dash for Switzerland. Libertas asked her mother to take her to the train station.

A few days later, Alexander Spoerl contacted her hosts in the countryside. They were surprised to hear from him. Libertas? She had never arrived.[4]

Harro's father, a career naval officer, was currently stationed in the Netherlands. After relatives informed him that his son and daughter-in-law had disappeared, he rushed to Berlin, and then to military intelligence headquarters to consult his fellow officer Admiral Canaris. The admiral was on the road, but the colonel in charge told Schulze-Boysen that his son's situation was serious. The Gestapo was in charge. At Prinz-Albrecht-Strasse, Schulze-Boysen learned that Harro had already confessed to subversive and treasonous activity. He wasn't able to see his son until September 30, when two Gestapo agents accompanied him into the room, "emaciated, pale, with deep shadows under his eyes."[5]

The arrests were the result of a chain of gross errors committed by Soviet intelligence. The disaster had been set in motion a year earlier, on August 26, 1941, when Moscow had wired the encoded names and addresses of Adam Kuckhoff and Harro and Libertas Schulze-Boysen to their agents in Brussels. This action provided the Gestapo with the text, although they were initially unable to interpret the code.

The next bungle came a few months later, when Leopold Trepper's agent Anatoli Gourevitch (code name "Kent") returned to Brussels from his October trip to Berlin. He had stayed on the air transmitting material from Harnack and Schulze-Boysen for seven nights in a row, for hours at a stretch. This allowed the Germans ample time to locate the source of his signal.

On December 13, 1941, German agents had broken into Trepper's Brussels quarters. There they discovered compromising materials and arrested those present, including the Belgian housekeeper Rita Arnould and the young Polish encipherer Sophie Poznanska. Trepper and Gourevitch ("Kent") fled, but they were tracked down in Paris in less than a year.[6] Sophie Poznanska, who had met Trepper through Jewish circles, underwent months of torture and committed suicide to avoid compromising her associates. But Rita Arnould talked, giving away names and critical information about their communications system.

Each piece of intelligence yielded a harvest of arrests. The Germans spent months assembling the data and honing the techniques they needed to break the Soviet code. Eventually, by midsummer 1942, they met with success. The Germans painstakingly worked their way through stacks of intercepted messages. Among them was a transmission from Moscow, providing the names, addresses, and telephone numbers of Adam Kuckhoff and Harro and Libertas Schulze-Boysen.[7]

The German names were a shocking revelation. These were not their usual blue-collar KPD malcontents; they included members of the Prussian elite. But identifying these individuals was only the first step of the investigation. The Gestapo placed them under tight surveillance to identify additional collaborators, and took careful note of their contacts.

At the end of August a protégé of Harro's forced their hand. Horst Heilmann, a young mathematician who worked in military intelligence, caught sight of a document incriminating Schulze-Boysen. He called his mentor to warn him, but failed to get through on the phone. He left a message, and when Harro unwittingly returned the call, Heilmann's superior answered and realized that the game was up. He moved quickly to control the damage. On August 31, 1942, the Gestapo made its first move, arresting Harro Schulze-Boysen in his office. No one in his family was notified.

Other arrests followed swiftly. On September 7, the Gestapo tracked the Harnacks down at the seaside, where they were on a holiday with history professor Egmont Zechlin and his wife. (Zechlin later speculated that the Harnacks might have been seeking a fishing boat to Sweden.)[8]

On September 9, Gestapo agents arrived at a Berlin station in time to locate Libertas Schulze-Boysen on a westbound train and escort her off.

Greta Kuckhoff was first alerted to the risk on August 31. She was getting ready to celebrate her husband's birthday with his mother, their son, and his two former wives. Adam came home looking more serious than usual, and told her that Harro Schulze-Boysen had disappeared from his office. The couple tried to assess the danger without arriving at any conclusion. A few days later, Adam followed through with a planned business trip to the film center in Prague, and Greta went on with her chores, unaware of what was happening to her friends.

After her arrest, Libertas Schulze-Boysen was taken to Gestapo headquarters at Prinz-Albrecht-Strasse, the stately building where she once played outside her father's classrooms. Libertas languished in detention, certain that her relative lack of involvement and her aristocratic pedigree would free her in the end. One day she met a pretty redhead who was present in the office in some uncertain capacity. Libertas and the young woman, whose name was Gertrud Breiter, struck up a casual conversation. Libertas was convinced that she had found a friend.[9] "I have only one favor to ask you," she said. "I can't tell you the address, but will you warn Hans Coppi?"

Gertrud Breiter was actually the secretary of Libertas's police interrogator. She immediately reported the conversation to her superior and came back for more. As a result of the exchange, Hans Coppi, who had recently been drafted into the military and posted to a town outside Poznań, was arrested that night, and his wife, Hilde, was seized in their Berlin home. Libertas's conversations with the obliging Gertrud continued, and the names began to flow: the Kuckhoffs, the Schumachers, John Graudenz, and others.[10] "She was very intelligent," Gertrud Breiter observed later, "but very, very unstable."[11] For her patriotism, Breiter was rewarded with 5,000 reichsmarks, a medal, and a personal letter from Heinrich Himmler.

The Coppis were only two of the Gestapo's arrests of September 12. That same day Adam Kuckhoff was picked up in Prague and Greta was tracked down at home with her son, Ule. She asked the Gestapo agents if she could leave her child in the kindergarten downstairs until his grandmother could pick him up. The agents followed them, but before they could stop her, Greta told the teacher that she was under arrest. The agents intervened. "Frau Kuckhoff is mentally ill," they told the confused teacher. "We're taking her to an institution. Forget all the nonsense she's telling you, it's a symptom of the disease."[12] Greta was taken to police headquarters at Alexanderplatz. Other prisoners from the group who saw her there noted that her face looked drawn and white.[13]

Kurt Schumacher was seized in his army barracks in Poznań; his wife, Elisabeth, was arrested at their Berlin home. The Gestapo attacked their apartment and studios, smashing Schumacher's work. The destroyed works included Schumacher's gypsum model for a sculpture entitled *Antiwar Relief* and a wood carving called *Dance of Death*.[14]

They came for John Graudenz at his cottage in Stahnsdorf. He tried to escape through the basement, but the Gestapo had the house surrounded. He was taken in along with his wife and two teenage daughters.

The dentist Helmut Himpel and his fiancée, Marie Terwiel, were arrested together in his home on September 17, the same day as their friend, pianist Helmut Roloff. The Gestapo quickly located the suitcase containing the Soviet radio stored in Roloff's house, but it was still locked. Roloff told the police that he was just storing it for his friends and had no idea what was inside.

On the twentieth they came for Cato Bontjes van Beek and her father at his house. (Katja Casella and Lisa Egler-Gervai, the two young Jewish art students, were alerted by a panicked phone call from Cato's boyfriend. They jumped on a train for Poland and miraculously avoided arrest.)

Günther Weisenborn and his wife heard a knock at the door at five o'clock in the morning on September 26. He answered it to find four men in civilian clothes on the doorstep, their hands in their pockets.

The cellars at Prinz-Albrecht-Strasse were filling up. Weisenborn counted over a hundred members of the groups: doctors, professors, writers, artists, former government officials.[15] Most of the women were held across the river in the Alexanderplatz jail. Radio operator Hans Coppi's wife, Hilde, and nineteen-year-old Liane Berkowitz was pregnant.

Over the fall of 1942, German authorities detained over 120 people in connection with the case. Treatment of the prisoners varied a great deal, as did the prisoners' responses. Officials were required to apply in writing for permission for "intensified interrogation." Torture was meticulously monitored by an SS doctor to gauge the effect on the prisoner's state of health. Official records showed that Harro Schulze-Boysen's questioning began with twelve blows of an ax handle. Arvid Harnack, John Graudenz, and Adam Kuckhoff were beaten with rubber truncheons.[16] Remarkably, the three men withstood the first round of torture and stubbornly maintained a common front: they were friends, that was all. Sometimes they spent their holidays together.

Each prisoner was painstakingly photographed for the files: first a side view (with the head stabilized against a metal brace); then full face; then three-quarter profile, sometimes with added accessories like hat or glasses. Harro and Arvid looked relatively fresh when their pictures were taken, but Helmut Himpel and Kurt Schumacher's faces already showed signs of abuse. A number of the prisoners wore German army uniforms. Mildred Harnack was pale and gaunt, while Liane Berkowitz looked ready to burst into tears.

The record is contradictory as to which of the prisoners gave way under interrogation and named names. It is clear that the members of the circle tried to hold out as long as possible to give their friends time to escape. In October the police took Arvid Harnack and Adam Kuckhoff to the "Stalin room," which featured whips and thumbscrews. Some reports state that at that point, Kuckhoff gave up the names of Adolf Grimme and John Sieg.[17]

A few days later, on October 11, one of John Sieg's underground contacts went to pick him up from work at the Tempelhof train station in Berlin. Sieg was uncharacteristically late. When he finally appeared, his friend noticed that he looked unusually pale and that two men were following close behind. Sieg walked straight past him without a word, offering only an intense stare as a warning that he was under arrest.[18] His friend kept walking, and never saw Sieg again. Sieg's wife, Sophie, was arrested at her job the following day, and the Gestapo called for Grimme and his wife at their home around the same time.

Greta Kuckhoff was devastated to hear that her husband and Harnack had succumbed. "Finally they told everything and gave away all the names in the belief that people had made themselves scarce. I was speechless when I heard that Adam had confessed."[19]

It was reported that eventually, under harsh interrogation, Kurt

Schumacher told the police about the German Communist agents who had been dropped by parachute bearing new radios, one of whom had stayed with his wife. Soon the Gestapo was on the trail of the KPD parachute agents, as well as the succession of Germans who had sheltered them in their homes.[20] Many of the hosts had been members of Schulze-Boysen's leafleting circle, with no knowledge of or involvement in his links to the Soviets. Others were KPD loyalists who had no ties to Schulze-Boysen, Harnack, or Kuckhoff, other than the shared misfortune of Moscow's carelessness.

Elisabeth Schumacher's friend Philip Schaeffer was one of the outsiders arrested in the roundup. Schaeffer was the friend who tried to help her rescue her Jewish uncle and aunt from suicide. He was still in the hospital with the injury he sustained in the attempt. Schaeffer, a major China scholar and KPD member, had little to do with the Schulze-Boysen circles, but he had been in and out of concentration camps for contributing to anti-Nazi publications in the past. Schaeffer and his wife joined the ranks of prisoners in the Gestapo interrogation chambers.

The more experienced members of the KPD underground were prepared to guarantee their silence. On October 15, after three days of torture at Prinz-Albrecht-Strasse, John Sieg hung himself in his cell. Well before his arrest, Sieg had told his friends that he would kill himself if he was ever interrogated, as the only way to ensure he wouldn't betray others.[21] Sieg's friends credited his suicide with saving many lives. Remarkably, several members of his Neukölln circle survived the war.

The young printer Herbert Grasse followed Sieg's example by throwing himself out of the fifth-floor window of the police headquarters at Alexanderplatz the day after his arrest.[22] Guards foiled Walter Husemann in the same gesture, prying him away from the interrogator he had grabbed in an attempt to take him along.

Mildred Harnack attempted suicide as well. It was not clear whether she was tortured or not, but she was deathly ill and full of despair. She tried to kill herself by swallowing pins, and was punished with solitary confinement.[23]

Libertas, who had long feared for her delicate nerves, clung to the hope that her family and their Göring connections would save her in the end. From the beginning, she seemed to be getting favored treatment.

Unlike the other prisoners, she was allowed to exchange letters with her mother. She was permitted to hang pictures on her wall, listen to the radio, read magazines—and, from time to time, have coffee with her interrogator and his charming secretary. Alexander Spoerl brought her suitcases filled with food, sprigs of violets, and her favorite cigarettes. Her mother went to Göring to plead his favor as she had in the past.

But those days were over. "I regret nothing more than being dragged into this business, and that I promoted your son-in-law into the officer corps and brought him to work in the Ministry," the field marshal told her brusquely. "I have no intention of being of any assistance to you."[24]

Surprises emerged along the way. The prisoners learned through their interrogation that the Gestapo had been closing in on them for months. The police even had a name for their unruly association: the Rote Kapelle (Red Orchestra). This notion was all the stranger because the group had never thought to create a name for themselves.

There were other revelations as well. Most of the circles had only included five or six contacts, few of whom overlapped with other groups. Now friends, neighbors, and professional colleagues passed each other in the hallway, startled at the possibility that the familiar faces might be connected to their secret activities.

By mid-October the Gestapo was satisfied that its investigation was complete. It was time to move toward the trials, and there were many legal niceties to pursue. In order to secure a death sentence, the prosecution had to produce either a confession or two witnesses' testimony against the accused. A strange arithmetic ensued.

Günther Weisenborn learned that one accusation had been made against him by an unnamed "young woman." If it stood alone, he might escape with a prison sentence. Then he learned that he had also been incriminated by sculptor Kurt Schumacher, who occupied the cell next to his. The second statement meant death.

Weisenborn's first move was to take precautionary action, slitting his bedsheet so he could fashion it into a quick noose if he needed to. Then he began to try to communicate with Schumacher, through the crude alphabet of knocks that prisoners have utilized throughout history. He finally managed to let Schumacher know that his statement constituted a death sentence against him, and Schumacher immediately promised to take it back. Weisenborn asked what he could offer in return. A pencil, Schumacher responded. The next day, on the way back from his daily walk around the courtyard, Weisenborn managed to slip a forbidden stub of pencil into the opening to Schumacher's cell.[25]

Most of the women remained at the prison at Alexanderplatz. (This was usually a men's facility, but the sudden influx of prisoners had created space problems.) Soon the women were given the fifth floor to themselves, where their conditions were less harsh than the men's.[26] The women were allowed to sing and talk into the night. Greta Kuckhoff had the opportunity to get to know some of the other women in the group for the first time. She and Marta Wolter Husemann would talk late into the night. Greta admired the young Communist actress, "a slim woman in black pants and turtleneck sweater, with really pretty blond hair."

Cato Bontjes van Beek kept her hands busy darning socks for the male prisoners. She worked out a system to lower consoling notes to Walter Küchenmeister's frightened teenage son, imprisoned on a men's floor below.

Greta also grew close to Elisabeth Schumacher, whom she had known before the arrests. The two women usually talked after the lights were turned out. As Christmas approached, Elisabeth's family sent her an advent wreath, which she installed in her window to cheer up the other prisoners.[27]

The Nazis had a difficult time absorbing the shock, which traveled all the way to the top. Hitler had no difficulty comprehending an act of sabotage from a Jewish Communist such as Herbert Baum, who had led the attack on the "Soviet Paradise" exhibit. In fact, such actions confirmed his worldview. But the Schulze-Boysen group was something else again. It was led by the great-nephew of Admiral von Tirpitz, riddled with uniformed military officers, and guided by high-ranking officials from a half-dozen ministries. Most of its prominent, educated members stood to gain from the regime, if they would only play along.

The Führer was "highly indignant," an aide reported. He wanted "the Bolshevists within our own ranks" to be executed immediately and without mercy.[28] But no aspect of the case was to be disclosed to the public under any condition. The prisoners' families were forbidden to discuss it under threat of concentration camp.[29]

By late October, the Gestapo was in the final stages of the arrests and investigation. Now came the question of the trial. Most sedition cases were directed to the *Volksgerichtshof* (People's Court), known for its swift judgments and frequent death sentences. However, the involvement of Harro Schulze-Boysen and other uniformed defendants argued for this case to go before a *Reichskriegsgericht* (Reich Court Martial).

Hermann Göring understood that, as the man who brought Harro Schulze-Boysen into his air ministry, he needed to choose his prosecutor carefully. On October 17, 1942, he summoned judge advocate Manfred Roeder, chief legal officer for Luftwaffe Air Fleet IV, to the command car of his special train. They met near the Ukrainian town of Vinnitsa, where Hitler and Göring had both recently established field headquarters.

It was a devastating year in Ukraine. Luftwaffe Air Fleet IV was pounding the region in thousands of bombing missions. The Nazis had scheduled the extermination of three million Ukrainian Jews over 1942, and some 80,000 were shot in the infamous extermination pits that October alone. One surviving photograph in the U.S. Holocaust Memorial Museum shows a lone man kneeling in front of a pit full of bodies, while a member of *Einsatzgruppe* D prepares to shoot him in the head. The back of the photo bears the inscription: "The last Jew in Vinnitsa."*

Part of the job description for military judge advocates such as Manfred Roeder was to prosecute soldiers who balked at their orders, among the three million Germans serving on the eastern front. The Nazis made an example of those who challenged their authority, such as Michael Kitzelmann, a twenty-five-year-old lieutenant who had won the Iron Cross second class for bravery. Kitzelmann, a Catholic from Bavaria, wrote agonized letters from the Russian front to his parents and told his fellow officers, "If these criminals should win, I would have no wish to live any longer." He was denounced, tried by field court martial, and convicted of *Wehrzersetzung* (damage to military capability). Kitzelmann was shot on June 11, 1942. Göring could trust that Roeder, as a judge ad-

---

*Vinnitsa had also been the site of major massacres by Stalin's agents over the late 1930s. The German occupiers would conduct an investigation in 1943 into the mass graves of Stalin's Russian and Ukrainian victims there, who numbered up to 10,000.

vocate on the eastern front, was unlikely to sympathize with any human-itarian motives expressed by Rote Kapelle defendants.[30]

The forty-two-year-old Roeder was a veteran in the military justice system, known for his aggressive courtroom style and his handsome pro-file. (He bore a passing resemblance to Dirk Bogarde.) His new assign-ment led him to combine creative legal arguments with political expediency. He would decide which of the 117 Rote Kapelle prisoners in custody would be tried, aware that Hitler had reserved the right to over-rule the more important sentences, regardless of the court's decision.[31] Within the legal maze lay a political minefield, and the only fatal error was leniency.

Roeder was frustrated by the Gestapo's delay in sharing its inves-tigation. Finally, in early November, he received the files of Harro Schulze-Boysen, Arvid Harnack, John Graudenz, and Hans Coppi. The Schumacher files arrived a few days later. But Roeder had a hard time understanding the case, given that he hadn't seen the files on Leopold Trepper's lieutenant Anatoli Gourevitch ("Kent"), who was undergoing Gestapo interrogation over the same period in Belgium. Gourevitch was the Soviet piece of the puzzle.

Shortly afterward, Gourevitch's files arrived on Roeder's desk, and were followed by the delivery of Gourevitch himself at the Prinz-Albrecht-Strasse interrogation center. Then Roeder (or, as Greta Kuck-hoff called him, "the bloody judge") set to work.[32] Gourevitch nervously told the Gestapo the dates and details of his meetings with the Schulze-Boysens, and identified their pictures from a photo album. He added a de-tailed overview of Soviet intelligence operations in Western Europe.[33]

Roeder immersed himself in the files, piecing together a narrative that sought to explain how members of the Reich's gilded youth could partake of such treasonous affairs. Unsatisfied with the Gestapo interro-gations, he questioned the prisoners himself, playing, for the moment, the "good cop." Helmut Himpel commented that he "seemed like a nice guy."[34] But Roeder was using his interviews to fashion a prurient soap opera of corruption and vice.

Harro Schulze-Boysen, Arvid Harnack, and Adam Kuckhoff had al-ready confessed to their work for the Soviets, so those basic facts were no longer in dispute. Military espionage was classified as "high treason" and the penalty was death. That much was settled.

But Roeder had to address their motives, and in doing so, he decided to take a moralistic high ground. Harnack and Kuckhoff, he charged, had received money from the Soviets. This was true, though it had been early on, and in negligible amounts. Nonetheless, Roeder presented this as evidence that the men were traitors for hire. Some members of the group had affairs out of wedlock, not an uncommon phenomenon. Roeder relished this evidence for his sex angle. The Gestapo found nude photos of Libertas taken by one of the Schumachers. Although Libertas's father was an art professor and both Schumachers were professional artists, Roeder decided that this was hard evidence of depraved lives.

Curiously enough, Roeder took a more tolerant view of the working-class members of the KPD. His true vindictiveness was reserved for traitors to their class and to polite society, namely the Schulze-Boysens and Arvid Harnack.[35]

Roeder determined that of the original 117 cases, 76 would stand trial; the rest were released for lack of evidence. The list was broken down to be tried in groups. The trials were a legal travesty. Prisoners were not allowed to read the cases against them, and in some instances, they met their lawyers for the first time five minutes before the trial began.[36] Most of the trials lasted only a few hours, and a verdict was produced the same day.

The families of the Schulze-Boysens and Arvid Harnack tried to help. They still occupied influential positions throughout German government and industry. Harro's father was a high-ranking naval officer, while Arvid's cousins served in half a dozen different ministries. The arrests came as a shock, but the families held firm. Harro's parents lobbied energetically on his behalf, while Arvid's younger brother Falk wrote reams of letters and struggled to get his brother legal representation. Falk asked his cousin Klaus Bonhoeffer to defend Arvid, but he had to refuse. He was too deeply involved in his own resistance work, and raising his profile would damage them all. In the end, only four lawyers were found to represent some eighty defendants in over twenty trials.[37]

On December 16, 1942, a trial was called to order for thirteen major

Rote Kapelle defendants, among them the Schulze-Boysens, the Harnacks, and the Schumachers. Other defendants included journalist John Graudenz, radio operator Hans Coppi, and Erika von Brockdorff, Greta's neighbor who had helped to hide the radios.

Roeder's prosecutorial style was aggressive and bombastic, even by the standards of the time. He spent much of the trial haranguing the defendants and often cut them off before they could even answer his questions. The judges were privately critical of his legal arguments, and remarked on the dignity of the defendants. One by one, in statements that ranged from calm to impassioned, the prisoners declared that they had been motivated by common decency and hatred of the regime—not by money or sex.[38]

Only Libertas Schulze-Boysen broke ranks. Up to the end, she trusted in her connections. She broke down in the courtroom and started to shout that everything was Harro's fault. She wanted a divorce. Her defense counsel asked for an adjournment.[39]

The verdicts were delivered on December 19. Most of the defendants were sentenced to death. The court declared that Harro Schulze-Boysen "never honestly served the National Socialist state." Harro's younger brother Hartmut heard this statement with pride.[40]

Arvid Harnack's relatives reported that when he heard his death sentence, he was "radiant with joy," because he was told at the same time that his wife, Mildred, had been spared the death penalty.[41] She and Erika von Brockdorff were sentenced to ten and six years hard labor, respectively. Mildred, in the view of the judges, "had acted more out of loyalty to her husband than of her own volition."[42]

But Hermann Göring exploded when he heard the news, stating that Hitler would never settle for imprisonment. He was right. When Hitler received the two women's files, he sent them back without signature or comment, a clear sign that they were to be retried until the court came up with the desired result.

Now the Nazis faced scheduling problems. German tradition held that all executions were suspended between Christmas Eve and the Day of the Epiphany on January 6. They needed to hurry. There were also complications regarding the manner of execution. The Nazis had escalated the number of death sentences many times over since they took power, and the guillotine shed at Plötzensee had dispatched thousands of members of the German, Czech, and Polish undergrounds, as well as common criminals. Now Hitler decided that the leaders of the Rote Kapelle required a more degrading form of execution.

The firing squad was the method of choice for military men, affording them a measure of dignity. The guillotine was quick and relatively kind, suitable for young people and ladies. Hanging was the least honorable end, reserved for partisans and spies. With certain modifications, it could also be a particularly slow and painful way to die. Laborers set to work installing a long steel beam with eight meat hooks in the execution shed at Plötzensee prison. Designed especially for the men of the Rote Kapelle, it would be called into use many times in the future for other resisters.

Over the course of his trial Arvid asked his cousin Adolf von Harnack to represent him on personal matters. Later, Adolf wrote,

> Arvid performed one last valuable service for the family in the face of death. He got the message to me through his lawyer and the prison chaplain, Dr. Poelchau, that in a number of his interrogations he was intensely questioned about my brother Ernst and advised him immediately to go abroad, though there was only the slightest evidence against him. I passed along this very serious message immediately. Since my brother was not involved with Arvid Harnack's trial in any way, he did not follow this warning.[43]

Arvid's Social Democrat cousin Ernst would pay a terrible price for dismissing Arvid's counsel. Deeply involved with the Oster-Bonhoeffer conspiracy, he would meet his end on the same beam as Arvid only weeks before the Allies took Berlin.

On the evening of December 21, 1942, the condemned prisoners were conveyed to Plötzensee and allowed to write their farewell letters. Harro Schulze-Boysen told his parents, "This death suits me." It was, he said, what he had always expected.

Arvid Harnack's thoughts returned to his childhood, and he asked for his execution to be accompanied by an early Christmas celebration. He was supported by prison chaplain Harald Poelchau, himself secretly involved in the rescue of Jews and resistance activity. Arvid, with the help of the minister, recited the story of the Nativity according to Luke, then sang his favorite hymn, "I Pray to the Power of Love."[44]

The court official who observed the executions said that the hangings took place without incident. "As far as I could see, complete unconsciousness came at the very instant when the noose tightened."[45] The women were guillotined. Most went quietly to their deaths. Only Libertas Schulze-Boysen struggled to the end, screaming, "Let me keep my young life!"

Friends and family were generally aware of what was happening, but they were not apprised of the schedule. At Christmas, Herbert Engelsing informed Alexander Spoerl that the Schulze-Boysens had been sentenced to death. The following day, Libertas's mother told him that her daughter had already been executed.[46]

After Christmas the cases of Mildred Fish Harnack and Erika von Brockdorff were reviewed, applying more stringent standards, a smidgen of fresh evidence, and a keener understanding of Hitler's wishes. The court sentenced both women to death.

It is not certain how much the prisoners learned of developments beyond the prison walls, but they would have found some of them heartening. One was a long overdue acknowledgment from the Allies. On December 17, 1942, the United States, Britain, and ten governments signed the Allied Declaration, confirming and condemning Hitler's extermination policies toward the Jews. The BBC's European service read the document over the radio several times a day for a week. Only a tiny minority of Germans possessed both the radios that could receive foreign broadcasts and the secure conditions in which to hear them. Nonetheless, historians believe that this alert saved lives by urging some Jews to hide and by prompting non-Jews to help them. Many of the members of the Rote Kapelle group awaiting execution had been involved in these activities for years, without the need for outside encouragement.

The Royal Air Force dropped some 1.2 million flyers about the Nazi extermination program over the course of January. About 150,000 copies of it were dropped on Berlin alone. Perhaps some even fell within the prison walls.[47]

Beyond their borders, the German armed forces were experiencing humiliating military setbacks. In late October, they were defeated by the British at El Alamein, and the following month British and American forces landed in North Africa. In the Soviet Union, the Germans were being beaten back, pounded by winter and Soviet reinforcements, and cut off from their supplies. The hand of the German resistance could be perceived on both fronts. The North Africa campaign benefited from German Admiral Canaris's trip to Spain a few years earlier, when he advised Franco to remain neutral, depriving the Germans of the choke-point of Gibraltar. The Allies were also aided by intelligence about the Soviet campaign flowing in from a number of antifascist Germans, including Rudolf Roessler in Switzerland, who helped them ward off the Nazi offensive.

If the Harnack and Schulze-Boysen group had been able to hold out a few more months, they might have encountered a more favorable opportunity to help. In November 1942, only weeks after the mass arrests, an American lawyer named Allen Dulles landed in Bern. He described himself as "the last American to reach Switzerland legally before the German invasion of southern France cut the Swiss off completely."[48]

Dulles, a high-ranking OSS officer, established the first serious American intelligence presence on the scene, and immediately forged contacts with a broad network of German exiles. His best source was an antifascist German government official named Fritz Kolbe, working inside Germany. Kolbe contacted Dulles after he had been turned away by the British. (When Kolbe offered his documents to the British attaché in Bern, the officer answered, "I don't believe you. And if you're telling the truth, you're a cad.")[49] Kolbe went on to provide Dulles with over two thousand official documents over the next two years, including plans for major offensives and secret aircraft designs.[50]

Only six months earlier, Harro Schulze-Boysen and John Graudenz traveled toward the Swiss border, searching for a route to smuggle military information to British intelligence in Switzerland.[51] Dulles might have been easier to reach than the British, and he was certainly more open to collaboration.

The second mass Rote Kapelle trial took place over several days in mid-January 1943. Its nine defendants included many of the young peo-

ple recruited by Cato Bontjes van Beek and her boyfriend, Heinz
Strelow, a noncommissioned officer in the army. Others were Friedrich
Rehmer, a factory worker and army conscript, and nineteen-year-old
Liane Berkowitz, his half-Jewish fiancée. Berkowitz, whose forlorn face
peered out beneath a tangle of dark curls, was six months pregnant.
Rehmer had been seized in a military hospital, where he was recovering
from grave wounds sustained on the Russian front. He may have been
severely traumatized as well; in the hospital he was reported as ranting,
"Anyone who has seen what we have done in Russia must think it an eter-
nal disgrace to be called a German!"[52]

The students had taken part in an extensive anti-Nazi propaganda
campaign, distributing leaflets and pasting stickers on phone booths, but
they had no involvement in Soviet espionage. Nonetheless, state prosecutor Roeder sought the death penalty for them, in retaliation for their
"aid and comfort to the enemy." In most cases, he was successful.[53]

Shortly after the second round of death sentences were handed down,
some of the judges had second thoughts. They had attempted to maintain
at least a semblance of legality, and they recognized that Roeder was
rewriting the legal definition of espionage before their eyes. The Reich
court-martial recommended a pardon for nineteen-year-old Liane Berkowitz and twenty-two-year-old Cato Bontjes van Beek.

The request reached the desk of Hitler himself, who vehemently denied the motion. His ruling was countersigned by Wilhelm Keitel, head
of the armed forces high command. The precedent had been set. Putting
up anti-Nazi stickers was now legally equated with Soviet espionage.

Over the next two weeks, dozens of defendants rotated through the
courtroom, and the death sentences were handed down in profusion:
Hans Coppi's wife, Hilde, the mother of a newborn, who had helped to
hide a radio. The dentist Helmut Himpel and his fiancée, Marie Terwiel,
whose solidarity with persecuted Jews led them to produce anti-Nazi flyers and store a radio. Philip Schaeffer, the China scholar and librarian
who had tried to help Elisabeth Schumacher rescue her Jewish uncle and
aunt.

Greta and Adam Kuckhoff were tried at the beginning of February in
a group of eight defendants. The couple was allowed a few minutes together before the trial "to talk about personal issues, children and stuff

like that," their guard told them. But Adam was intent on enlisting Greta's help in clearing Adolf Grimme, the Social Democrat minister who had been his friend since student days, who was also in the group.[54] The eight prosecutions were completed in a single day.

Afterward the defendants were shown into a waiting room and allowed to talk among themselves. They traded excited rumors of a stunning German defeat just a few days earlier, in a frozen city on the Volga called Stalingrad. The guards paid no attention. "The SS people were enjoying their free time too, joking among themselves and ignoring us," Greta recalled grimly. "For them we were nothing but dead people on vacation."[55]

On February 2 they were called back to the court for the last time and asked if they wanted to make any final statements. Adolf Grimme reminded the court that he was a man of substance. As the Prussian minister of culture, he had received the Goethe Prize from Field Marshal Hindenburg himself. He was never a Communist, he was a religious socialist who had fallen under the sway of Adam Kuckhoff.

Then came the verdict: Greta and Adam were both among the condemned. Adolf Grimme was not. Greta was amazed at her husband's reaction of happiness and relief that his friend had been spared. Greta had found Grimme's self-defense to be shabby and inappropriate. To make things worse, Greta's last precious moments with her husband were interrupted by his exchange with Grimme.

"I didn't like the way Grimme was cleaning his glasses all the time, so he didn't have to look Adam in the eye," Greta wrote angrily years later. "He also made sure to change the subject as soon as possible and told my husband how sad he was that he hadn't been able to finish his writings. For one precious moment my husband let go of my hand to shake Grimme's hand, and asked if he would be willing to take care of his unfinished writings after his death."[56] Adam Kuckhoff may have known that he could not escape a death sentence, and decided to do what he could to protect his old friend. Still, it was a hard choice for his wife to accept.

Greta returned to the prison and prepared to die. She thought obsessively about Grimme, who, in her opinion, had regressed to his spineless Social Democrat ways, even if there was nothing in Grimme's power that could have saved Adam. She wrote letters full of longing to her parents and her son, and dreamed of food—her mother's herring and pancakes; the oysters of New England, raw and fried; and the barbecued pork chops she had savored at the frozen lake in Wisconsin.

Greta filed an appeal for clemency, as the others had done before her, with little hope of success. Time passed slowly. On February 16, 1943, Mildred Harnack was led to the execution shed at Plötzensee. Although she was only forty, her hair had turned pure white, and she had the thin, stooped frame of an elderly woman. She had spent her last days translating verses by Goethe and holding deep conversations with the prison chaplain, Harald Poelchau. As she approached the guillotine, hair cropped, her last words were: "*Und ich habe Deutschland so geliebt!*"— "And I have loved Germany so much!"

Seventy-nine defendants linked to the group were tried in a total of nineteen trials in the seven months between December 15, 1942, and July 1943. Forty-five were sentenced to death, twenty-nine were sent to prison, and two were acquitted for lack of evidence.[57] One of these was John Sieg's wife, Sophie. The investigators were unable to find enough evidence to indict her, but she was sent directly to Ravensbrück concentration camp without trial.

The parachutists who had been sent from Moscow also went untried. Albert Hoessler, a German Communist veteran of the Spanish civil war, died early on in Gestapo custody at Prinz-Albrecht-Strasse. Two others were captured and executed.

The case of the fourth parachutist, Robert Barth, was far more complicated. A German Communist typesetter for the *Rote Fahne* in John Sieg's day, Barth served a year in Plötzensee in 1933 and joined the resistance upon his release. He was drafted into the German army, captured by the Soviets in 1942, then recruited as a Soviet agent out of a POW camp. After he parachuted into Germany, he was arrested by the German police at his wife's hospital sickbed and taken to Prinz-Albrecht-Strasse. The Gestapo succeeded in "turning" Barth, and he collaborated in the transmission of fake radio messages to Moscow for the next two years. After the war the Soviets placed him under arrest and sent him back to the USSR. He was court-martialed in the summer of 1945 and executed by a Soviet firing squad.[58]

Another prime source of Soviet intelligence fared no better than the Berlin group. Richard Sorge, the Soviet agent in Tokyo, was arrested by the Japanese in October 1941. The Japanese held him long after his trial, assuming he would be valuable in a prisoner exchange, but the Soviets abandoned him. It is said that Stalin's response to the offer was, " 'Richard Sorge.' I do not know a person of that name."[59] Sorge was hung in a prison outside Tokyo on November 7, 1944.

Some of the Rote Kapelle defendants escaped with prison sentences. Adolf Grimme and Günther Weisenborn were both given three years for "failure to inform the authorities" of the conspiracy. They were sent to the penitentiary in Luckau, southeast of Berlin. The former Prussian minister of culture and the screenwriter were put to work gluing paper bags.

Falk Harnack, Arvid's devoted younger brother, soon found himself directly in the line of fire. In 1934 he had started an antifascist student group in Munich, which carried out leafleting campaigns. He eventually made contact with siblings Hans and Sophie Scholl and joined their protest circle called the White Rose. After Falk was drafted in 1941, he was posted to Chemnitz on the Czech border. In the winter of 1942, Hans Scholl and his friends traveled to meet him there. Falk told the Scholls about his family's resistance activities. Arvid had already been arrested, but Falk hoped to introduce them to his Bonhoeffer cousins.

But in February 1943 (shortly after Mildred Harnack's execution), the students were betrayed by an informer. They were tried by Judge Roland Freisler, a participant in the Wannsee conference on the "final solution," and a recipient of Harro Schulze-Boysen's AGIS flyer only a few months earlier. Freisler sentenced most of the students to death, including Hans and Sophie Scholl. The authorities were convinced of Falk Harnack's guilt, but they decided to release him as a decoy to lead them to other resisters.

Falk was posted as a corporal to Greece, where he made contact with the Greek resistance through a relative. On December 20, 1943, his commanding officer received a secret order signed by Himmler himself, bearing the instructions that Falk should be discharged from the army and delivered to the SS. Falk was informed only that he was to fly back to Chemnitz. The next day Falk arrived at the airport with his lieutenant, with whom he had been friendly. He was awaiting departure, his luggage already loaded on the plane, when his lieutenant called him aside.

"Is it good or bad?" Falk asked. "Not good," the lieutenant answered. He allowed Falk to escape into Athens, a city he knew well. As Falk saw it, "it was a choice between a certain, horrific death in Germany, or a chance for survival in Greece." Still wearing his Wehrmacht uniform, he stole from house to house by night, aware that those who sheltered him were risking their own lives as well as those of their families. Eventually he made his way to the mountains and spent the rest of the war fighting alongside the Greek partisans. There he continued in the family tradition, drafting flyers that told German troops to refuse to die for Hitler, and live for a free Germany instead.[60]

The spring of 1943 passed slowly for the condemned women in Berlin. Greta savored her scant rations of winter sun, and worried about little Liane Berkowitz. Still a teenager, she was frantic with worry about her unborn baby. In April she gave birth to a little girl in the women's prison and named the baby Irene. The baby was taken away. Liane would remain mercifully ignorant of her baby's death a few months later, which occurred under mysterious circumstances in the midst of a government euthanasia operation.[61]

In May, as another round of executions took place at Plötzensee, Greta was put to work making paper butterflies to decorate Nazi rallies. Sometimes she was allowed precious family visits from her parents, and on one occasion from her son. At the end of August, Greta heard her prison door open slowly, unlike the usual sharp motions of the guard. It was the prison chaplain. "Now they are all dead," he told her. "Your husband, and the girls. All of them."[62]

Sixteen prisoners had been guillotined on August 5, 1943, between 5:00 and 5:45 p.m., at precise three-minute intervals: Greta's husband, Adam, died at 5:06, followed by Marie Terweil, Hilde Coppi, Cato Bontjes van Beek, and Liane Berkowitz.[63]

Many of the women's bodies were delivered to Dr. Hermann Stieve, a gynecologist and anatomist at the University of Berlin. Dr. Stieve was obsessively interested in the impact of terror on the female reproductive organs. When the women were notified of the date of their executions, Dr. Stieve began to monitor their menstrual cycles in order to "observe the effect of highly agitating events on female sexual organs." An execution was timed to allow Stieve to perform a gynecological examination while the woman was still alive; upon death, her pelvic organs were removed for examination. Stieve boasted in one of his books that the "materials" arrived in his laboratory within ten minutes of availability. His subjects included Elisabeth Schumacher, thirty-eight; Libertas Schulze-Boysen, twenty-nine; Cato Bontjes van Beek, twenty-two; and Liane Berkowitz, twenty. Prison authorities noted that the arrangement with Dr. Stieve saved the state from dealing with "difficulties with respect to burial."[64]

The previous February, Mildred Harnack's body had also been delivered to the medical institute for dissection. But through a strange twist of fate, it turned out that Dr. Stieve knew the Harnacks through family connections. He recognized Mildred's remains and delivered them to the family, allowing them to cremate her and bury her ashes in a cemetery in Berlin.[65]

Mercifully, Greta knew only that her friends were gone. She had a sudden vision of her survival as its own exquisite form of torture, leaving her as the last tree standing in the forest. But these thoughts were disrupted by the memory of her son. Wasn't she supposed to stay alive for his sake?

On September 27, Greta was summoned back to court. She felt defiant—they had killed her husband and condemned her to death. What more could they do to her? To her astonishment, she learned that her death sentence had been revoked the previous May. With the principal executions carried out, Roeder had been transferred to other cases and Hitler's attention had turned elsewhere. The army judges grilled her for four hours, and then informed her that she was sentenced to ten years in prison.

And then another odd thing occurred. Shortly after her court date, Greta was told she needed to return for some formalities. The guard who picked her up told her they would not go by car; this time they would walk to the court. She was initially suspicious, but once they were outside, the guard took her aside. "I had to take your husband and some of your friends to Plötzensee, and it was very difficult for me," he confided. "How can people behave like this? Now I'm very happy to accompany you—and not to Plötzensee." He took her to a quiet bar where she could make some phone calls, and handed her his wallet.

Greta called her friend Hans Hartenstein. He listened to her soberly, then advised her to hold on until the war was over and to stay as healthy as she could.[66] Hartenstein convinced the officials to give Greta a brief leave before she started serving her sentence, and she spent the day with him and his family outside the city. Then Greta was transferred to a prison in Cottbus, east of Berlin. Over the following months she spent many long hours on a prison assembly line, making gas masks for the front.

\ \ \

CHAPTER 22

The Survivors

1943–1950

THE 1942 ARRESTS EXTINGUISHED THE ACTIVITIES OF GRETA
Kuckhoff's circle, but they did not end the German resistance. For the
next two years the conspiracies expanded on several fronts. As the German army suffered relentless defeats in Russia, military men gravitated
toward the officers' conspiracy to assassinate Hitler. Hans Oster and his
inner circle maintained contact with prominent civilians who were laying the groundwork for a democratic post-Nazi government. One of
their first actions was going to be the liberation of the concentration
camps.

Many members of Arvid Harnack's family were deeply involved in
the conspiracy, including Harnacks, Dohnanyis, Bonhoeffers, and Delbrücks. They lamented Arvid's arrest and tried to help where they could,
but had no choice but to keep their distance.

Nonetheless, the fate of the resistance circles began to converge. On
April 5, 1943, as the Rote Kapelle executions were well under way, Luftwaffe judge advocate Manfred Roeder made an unwelcome visit to the
office of Admiral Wilhelm Canaris. Roeder's prosecution of the Rote
Kapelle was considered to be unusually brutal, even by government in-
siders. Now he came to inform Canaris that he was pursuing a new investigation, based on suspicions of a vast conspiracy to overthrow the
regime.

It was natural enough for him to pass the word on to the admiral as
head of military intelligence. But Roeder was approaching the white-

haired officer not as a colleague, but as a prime suspect. Canaris was put on notice that he was under investigation. His deputy, Lieutenant Colonel Hans Oster, was suspended from office and placed under surveillance.[1]

The two anti-Nazi officers had been skirting calamity for years. The previous month, in the wake of the disaster at Stalingrad, Oster and Hans von Dohnanyi had made two separate assassination attempts against Hitler. Their massive network of conspiracy came to be called the 20th of July movement, named after its final and most ambitious attempt to overthrow the regime. Four of its civilian leaders were Harnack cousins: Hans von Dohnanyi, the Bonhoeffer brothers Klaus and Dietrich, and Ernst von Harnack.

Over the previous months the military plotters had somehow managed to hide the evidence of their many assassination attempts. Their downfall came through different means. For years, the Oster group had been assisting persecuted Jews, intervening in arrests and secretly channeling resources to help the victims leave the country. In 1942, Oster, Dohnanyi, and Bonhoeffer devised a plan they called "Operation U-7" to help a group of thirteen Jews and Jewish Christian converts escape to Switzerland. They designated the refugees as "intelligence agents" and provided them with foreign currency and false documents. Hans Oster personally accompanied one Jewish family to the train station and put them on the train to Switzerland.[2]

These escapes required large amounts of cash in foreign currency, which was tightly controlled by the regime. One of Hans von Dohnanyi's couriers was caught, and implicated him under interrogation. The Gestapo arrested Dohnanyi, on suspicion of illegal currency trading. He was tried and sent to the concentration camp at Sachsenhausen.[3] The Gestapo followed the trail to Hans Oster, who was caught redhanded as he attempted to destroy evidence of Dohnanyi's transactions. He was discharged from his office and placed under house arrest.

Dietrich Bonhoeffer was arrested in March 1943. Manfred Roeder conducted his prison interrogation, only three months after the execution of Arvid Harnack. Bonhoeffer stayed true to his calling as a Lutheran pastor, and wrote a series of prison letters and essays agonizing whether it was ethical to lie under interrogation in order to protect his collaborators. (He decided that it was.) Bonhoeffer remained serene in the belief that the plot to overthrow Hitler would proceed without him, and that the Germans would soon be approaching the Allies for peace talks.

With many of his closest associates under arrest, Admiral Canaris stepped up his efforts to communicate with the Allies. In April 1943 he approached FDR representative Commander George Earle in Istanbul, seeking ways to bring the war to an end quickly. That summer he reportedly met with the head of British intelligence and U.S. intelligence chief William Donovan in Spain. Roosevelt disapproved of the meeting and refused to respond to Canaris's overtures.[4] Adam von Trott continued to reach out to the British at enormous personal risk, trying to explain that millions of lives could be saved by killing Hitler and brokering an early peace—first, by liberating the concentration camps, and second, by sparing the German civilian victims of British air raids. But the British were even less interested in dialogue than the Americans.

One of Trott's close British friends worried that his clandestine diplomacy was exposing him to excessive danger, and wrote to the Foreign Office in concern. But Foreign Office official Geoffrey Harrison had made his position clear in July 1942, when he circulated a memo downplaying the value of the German opposition. He followed it with a statement that he saw no need to take precautions on Trott's behalf. Trott's "value to us as a 'martyr,' " he wrote, "is likely to exceed his value to us in post-war Germany."[5]

Despite their harsh interrogation, Bonhoeffer, Oster, and Dohnanyi said nothing to betray the conspiracy to the Gestapo. But other damaging evidence mounted. The Nazi investigators learned that instead of merely embezzling money for personal gain, the truth was far more serious: the funds were actually being used to help Jews. The three men had also exploited their official travel privileges for antiregime activities and helped dissenting Lutheran clergy avoid military service.

As Bonhoeffer, Dohnanyi, and Oster waited out their detentions, the military conspiracy drew to a climax. Even before the coup attempt, 9,523 German soldiers and officers had been executed by the Nazis on charges of mutiny and political opposition.[6] Now the coup leaders reached out to civil society, religious circles, and the military. Dozens of individuals had stepped forward to volunteer for further assassination attempts, by carrying loaded guns to official ceremonies and strapping themselves with explosives as would-be suicide bombers. One after another, the attempts failed, often by the narrowest of margins. Hitler still had the luck of the devil; he called it *Vorsehung*, pronounced with his extravagantly rolled Austrian "r." The dictator's infamous intuition led him to chop and change his itinerary constantly, foiling the most elaborately planned attempts.

The conspirators scheduled their final move for July 20, 1944, armed with what they believed were watertight plans. But the plans went terribly wrong. One of the coup leaders, Colonel Claus von Stauffenberg, left a bomb in a briefcase next to Hitler in a room where he was meeting with his officers. It was speculated that an aide, seeking leg room, moved the briefcase behind a portion of the thick wooden table, which absorbed the shock when the bomb detonated. A single random moment determined that Hitler was wounded and enraged, but not killed.

The military conspirators mistakenly assumed success, and moved to take over the government. But Hitler's forces reacted rapidly, and maintained control. The Gestapo arrested six hundred suspects, and rounded up thousands of additional opponents the following month.[7] Judge Roland Freisler, who had tried Falk Harnack and the students of the White Rose movement, was put in charge of the trials. Some two hundred prisoners were immediately executed. A number of the July 20 resisters met their end in the shed at Plötzensee, consoled in their last hours by Harald Poelchau, the same minister who comforted Mildred Fish Harnack. They were suspended from the same meat hooks that were installed for Arvid Harnack and Harro Schulze-Boysen.[8]

Arvid's cousin, Social Democrat Ernst von Harnack, died in the same small chamber at Plötzensee where Arvid and Mildred were executed some months earlier. Once, long ago, newlyweds Arvid and Mildred Harnack had visited him in his official castle, where Mildred was haunted by the ghost of a headless page.

Other Harnack cousins involved in the plot, including Hans von Dohnanyi and Klaus and Dietrich Bonhoeffer, were sent to a concentration camp. For a long time, the investigators failed to prove their links to the July 20 conspiracy. As the war drew to a close, their families cherished hopes of seeing them again. But then a hidden copy of Admiral Canaris's diary was discovered, providing the evidence the Gestapo had been seeking. Now they could prove that Canaris and his intelligence officers had been early instigators of the conspiracy. Nazi officers arranged an impromptu trial, and the men were executed in the final hours of the war, after Soviet troops had already surrounded Berlin.

Greta Kuckhoff saw the dawn of 1945 from a prison fortress in the tiny Saxon town of Waldheim. She and the other women prisoners worked on an assembly line by day, and spent nights in a crowded attic. They tried to make out the progress of the war through forbidden glimpses out the window, to the menacing sound of aircraft overhead.[9]

Finally, one morning in May, the Soviet army arrived. The soldiers went from door to door releasing the prisoners, who rushed out to fill their stomachs with the guards' abandoned bread and jam. Greta had no idea of the devastation that was taking place in Berlin, where the final battle had flattened every structure in sight and vengeful Soviets subjected girls and women to mass rape. Greta found some salvaged fabric and pieced together a semblance of a dress, cutting it narrow. In prison her weight had dropped from 118 to 97 pounds.

Outside the prison walls, Greta encountered a strange new world. She walked for days. Trains were erratic, bridges were down. It was a glorious spring and blossoms hung heavy on the bough, but her attention was drawn to decaying corpses strewn by the roadside. She passed farmhouses that had been oddly bypassed in the assault, and breathed the aroma of coffee and potato pancakes wafting from their tidy kitchens. But when she got to Berlin, the air of normalcy vanished. Her city was a field of rubble stretching in all directions. Berliners called it *Stunde Null* (Zero Hour).

Greta's first concern was to join her parents and her son, Ule. But she was also anxious about the orphaned children of her executed codefendants. She located Hans and Hilde Coppi's baby son, Hans, born in prison ten months before his mother was executed. The toddler had his mother's fine features and his father's searching eyes. Greta became a kind of godmother to him, and looked out for him for the rest of her life. Greta also sought out the little daughter of her neighbor Erika von Brockdorff, who had been guillotined for hiding one of the radios. Saskia, a sweet-faced child with long blond braids, couldn't understand why her mother had abandoned her. Saskia later recalled how Greta made friends with Jewish American GIs, and included her in jeep rides to birthday outings.[10]

Greta also searched for John Graudenz's two daughters, Karin and Silva. The two pretty teenagers had been arrested and interrogated at the same time as their parents, then released and sent back to the family cottage to live on their own. (Their father was executed; their mother served part of her prison sentence and was then granted a mysterious early release.) It was too late for Greta to help Liane Berkowitz's daughter, Irene, who had died in Nazi custody shortly after her birth.

Greta closely observed the aftermath of the war, and took every possible aspect of it personally. She noted grimly that the Nazis' surrender was signed by General Wilhelm Keitel, the same man who had signed the death sentences for Arvid Harnack, the Schulze-Boysens, and the other members of her group. Keitel was also the officer who issued the infamous "Commissar order" authorizing the mass murder of Russian civilians, telling his soldiers that "any act of mercy is a crime against the German people."[11] Keitel was tried at Nuremberg the following year. When he received his death sentence, Keitel requested a firing squad, but the court assigned him a less honorable death by hanging. His punishment was inadvertently exacerbated by the American GI hangman who botched the job. Like the hapless German antifascist resisters hung from the meat hooks at Plötzensee, the general took over twenty minutes to die.

The surviving members of Greta's group had dispersed. For Günther Weisenborn, the writer, liberation came in the form of a Soviet soldier in a sheepskin cap. Weisenborn had spent the end of the war in the Luckau penitentiary, not far from Berlin. As the Russian troops approached the city, the Gestapo rounded up groups of political prisoners and took them away to be shot. But the Soviets arrived before it was Weisenborn's turn, and it fell to the writer to bring order to the chaos that ensued. Starving prisoners stormed the kitchen, breaking open kegs of syrup and sucking the liquid up from the floor. Weisenborn joined a committee of six that called the desperate horde to order.

The Soviet captain gathered the surviving political prisoners and appointed them mayors of the surrounding towns. Weisenborn, the bespectacled, pacifist playwright, set off for the nearby village of Luckau and presented himself to the Nazi mayor. The nervous official reviewed his papers and quickly ceded his office to the newly sprung convict. Mayor Weisenborn supervised the villagers in restarting the mill, opening the school, and burying the bodies that lay scattered across the fields.[12] Then he set off for Berlin.

That summer Weisenborn returned to the site of his interrogation at the Gestapo headquarters on Prinz-Albrecht-Strasse to look for any remaining trace of his friends. When he examined Cell 2, where Harro Schulze-Boysen had awaited his interrogations, he found a piece of paper wedged into a crevice. It was a poem in Harro's handwriting, dated November 1942, the month before his execution. The final stanza read:

> The final argument
> Won't be left to the gallows and the guillotine,
> And today's judges don't
> Represent the judgment of the world.[13]

With the end of the war, German antifascists could finally come out of the woodwork. No one could tell, then or now, exactly how many there were, but some tried to extrapolate the figures. For example, several thousand Jews called "U-Boats" survived the war, most of them hidden by non-Jewish citizens of Berlin. The German writer Peter Schneider estimated that every Jew who survived under such protection required the collaboration of an average of seven non-Jewish Germans.[14]

One interested observer was Eric Boehm, who had fled the country as a German-Jewish teenager and returned as a U.S. Army interrogator. After the war he began to document the German resistance. He tried to tally the number of Germans who had suffered the consequences of taking a stand against the regime, and wrote:

> Over a period of twelve years almost 3,000,000 Germans were in and out of concentration camps and penitentiaries for political reasons—sometimes for as little as a remark critical of the gov-

ernment. About 800,000 of these had been arrested for overt anti-Nazi acts; only 300,000 of them were still alive after the war—so that among the "illegals" alone 500,000 gave their lives.[15]

Boehm realized that the very idea of a German resistance would be startling to his American audience. But, he reminded them, the machinery of propaganda had made it impossible for them to get an accurate picture of what had happened in Germany.

> In the newsreel shots of Nazi pageantry we saw the masses marching and heiling their Führer. We read of 99 per cent plebiscites. But of course we saw no newsreels of anti-Nazi opposition, of concentration camps, of surreptitious distribution of leaflets, or of arrests at night by apparently harmless civilians—the Gestapo. Only the fanatic supporters and the masses giving their whole-hearted or conditional support were in evidence.[16]

The survivors of this devastated population looked to the Allied occupiers, and to the Americans in particular, to carry out "the judgment of the world" against their Nazi persecutors.

Günther Weisenborn and Greta Kuckhoff were among those who waited impatiently for justice from the International Military Tribunal at Nuremberg. In 1946 they joined Adolf Grimme in submitting a brief that accused Manfred Roeder of crimes against humanity, based on his use of torture in interrogation and his brutal prosecutorial methods. Arvid Harnack's younger brother, Falk, recently returned from fighting with the Greek partisans, joined in the effort. He called Roeder "one of the bloodiest and cruelest persecutors of the German anti-Fascists."[17]

The survivors were certain that the case against Roeder would be straightforward. The Nuremberg prosecutors took a special interest in pursuing the German judges and lawyers who had corrupted their nation's legal system, and made a public example of their trials. In the celebrated "Justice Trials" of 1948, sixteen Nazi judges were tried, and ten of the sixteen were convicted and sent to prison.[18] One of the court's strongest denunciations was directed at a judge who had sentenced a Jewish man to death for an alleged offense that was usually punished with a prison sentence.[19] Manfred Roeder easily fell under the same category. He had aggressively pursued death sentences for a number of victims, including the half-Jewish, pregnant nineteen-year-old Liane Berkowitz, guillotined for attaching some stickers to a wall. By any authentic legal standards, and certainly by Nuremberg's, Roeder was ripe for punishment.

But unfortunately for the Rote Kapelle survivors, other political forces were now at work. When American correspondent William Shirer returned to Berlin in 1945, he noticed some disturbing trends, such as "a certain American lieutenant colonel . . . who stoutly declares that our official denazification policy will drive the Germans to Communism and who therefore opposes our denazification whenever he can."[20]

By November 1945, Shirer wrote, there was already a pronounced change in the U.S. military personnel in charge of the process.

> The magnificent American Army which landed on the Normandy beaches and swept to the Elbe in less than a year is deteriorating at a frightening pace. Officers and men have but one thought: to get back home. Those who stay are pretty inferior. They know nothing of Germany or Germans and they are not fit to govern our zone. Too many of them have already been taken in by German propaganda. Few of them have the faintest idea of what Nazism was. Most of them therefore either are opposed to denazification, even though it is a military order that they are supposed to carry out, or are uninterested in doing anything about it.[21]

Among those headed for home were many of the Jewish GI's who had befriended Greta and shared her desire to see the Nazis brought to justice.

Writing in the spring of 1947, Shirer noted that the Germans themselves were turning hopefully toward a democratic socialism. "If in space they were caught between the United States and the Soviet Union, so were they in their ideas. They wanted neither our unbridled capitalism nor Russia's totalitarian communism. They sought something in between."[22] Here Shirer captured the ideological spirit of Greta's circle in Berlin, both the living and the dead. But the occupation would not make this course easy. Shirer was disgusted at the way the American military government cut deals with notorious Nazis, hounded survivors of the Communist resistance, and sabotaged Eisenhower's decrees: "Already what the Germans had done was being rapidly forgotten. A new enemy and a new war was beginning to be talked about. Russia! The Bolsheviks! Gotta fight them bastards next."[23]

These phenomena would have a profound impact on Greta's future.

On May 8, 1945, only a week after Adolf Hitler's suicide, Manfred Roeder had been taken into U.S. custody as a witness for the Nuremberg trials. When the three Rote Kapelle survivors called for him to be tried as a war criminal himself, they aroused the interest of the U.S. Army's Counterintelligence Corps (CIC). But the CIC regarded Nazi prosecutions as yesterday's news. Roeder told the American Army intelligence agents that he could help them root out Soviet spies, and they believed him.

Once again, the chaotic nature of Allied intelligence led to a fumble. The CIC agents might have saved themselves considerable trouble by conferring with their British colleagues. British intelligence had already carried out an extensive investigation of the Rote Kapelle, and quickly concluded that the Berlin group had been driven by anti-Nazi motives, with little relevance to professional Soviet postwar espionage. But the American CIC had no idea the British investigation had taken place.

The Nuremberg prosecutors were continuing on their own parallel, equally uncoordinated, track. By January 1947 they reached the decision that Manfred Roeder should be prosecuted for war crimes. In May the Office of the Chief of Counsel for War Crimes reclassified him from mere witness to "Defendant A" (a prisoner who is to be indicted and tried).[24] The following month Roeder was interrogated at length by Robert Kempner, a Jewish lawyer from Berlin who had fled the Nazis and returned as a Nuremberg prosecutor.[25]

Kempner invited Rote Kapelle survivor Adolf Grimme to attend the interrogation and confront Roeder in person. Grimme was now fully restored to his former stature in West Germany, serving as both minister of culture in Hanover and as educational adviser to the British occupational authority.[26]

Greta Kuckhoff couldn't understand the delays in the Roeder prosecution. She knew that the Nazis were taking every opportunity to destroy incriminating files, and she feared that the records of Roeder's orders for torture could disappear before he reached trial.

Beyond her frustration over Roeder, Greta was smarting from a cold bath of postwar politics. The German public was shockingly unrepentant. Richard Cutler, an OSS officer stationed in Berlin after the war, recorded that many German army officers still viewed their country's mistakes in terms of tactics, holding that

> Success is right. What does not succeed is wrong. It was, for example, wrong to persecute the Jews before the war since that set the Anglo-Americans against Germany. It would have been right to postpone the anti-Jewish campaign and begin it after Germany had won the war.

Cutler was startled that "no German ever mentioned to me that the war resulted from a clash of principles."[27]

But Greta found that discussions of principle were lacking on the American side as well. On August 5, 1947, she was invited to speak on Radio Berlin on the fourth anniversary of her husband's execution along with eleven women from the group.[28] Greta used the occasion to take issue with Allen Dulles's recently published book, *Germany's Underground,* which praised the 20th of July movement at the expense of other resistance efforts.

Dulles's brief passage about Greta's circle dismissed it as "an interesting plot in 1943." He missed the most salient points of its history, and managed to make major factual errors in nearly every sentence. Dulles had little interest in Lieutenant "Harold" Schulze-Boysen and his circle. "Always wearing a black sweater, he went around with revolutionaries, surrealists, and the rag-tag and bobtail of the 'lost generation.' "[29]

Dulles added that "Otto" Harnack was a member of the group, but omitted Arvid's service to the Americans, as well as the role of his American wife. He made no mention of the group's many actions on behalf of persecuted Jews.[30] Greta, still grieving for a husband and friends who sacrificed their lives fighting the Nazis, could not live with their depiction as "rag-tag and bobtail." Greta told her Berlin radio audience that her group had "only noble motives."[31] But by 1947, with the cold war under way, no one was interested in the noble motives of the past.

On August 28, 1947, an officer in the U.S. Army counterintelligence office in Berlin reported on a "telephone intercept" between Greta Kuckhoff and an unknown person. Greta repeated her criticism that Allen Dulles's book "did not give a true picture of the Rote Kapelle" and characterized it as "just a small unimportant group of espionage agents."[32]

A few weeks later, as Nuremberg prosecutors were interrogating Manfred Roeder, Greta opened her door to two Americans with a different set of questions. One of them, whose misspellings suggest that he was not a native English speaker, boasted that he found Greta an easy mark:

> On 10 October 1947, this agent using the cover name Conrad and [Special Agent] Jonston, using the name of Brown, visited Greta Kuckhoff at her apartment located at 18 Wilhelmshöherstrasse, Berlin Friedenau. Posing as two strong leftists, dissaffected with the way the US is handeling its foreign affairs and especially Germany, Kuckhoff's confidence was soon obtained and most important and touchy political subjects were freely discussed and aliased. GK is one of the few survivors of the Harnack-Schulze-Boysen subversive movement.

The agents wrote that Greta "openly stated that she was a strong radical socialist advocating German unity the Soviet way, whereby united Germany under a socialist government is the sole hope for survival and reconstruction."

The CIC agent also recorded Greta's drive to stir the conscience of the German people, and to honor the memory of her husband and their friends:

> K[uckhoff] is still interested in making the Germans, especially those in the Soviet sector . . . conscious of the great sacrifices and hardships endured by the Schulze-Boysen group and uses readily every opportunity to propagandate the entire matter.

Army CIC agents "Conrad" and "Brown" were pleased to report that they were able to trick Greta into naming "Soviet agents."

> It is believed by the undersigned agent that Mr. Hans F. Johnston has the full confidence of Greta Kuckhoff and this is proven by the fact that she gave him for his "study" a lot of documents and printed material pertaining to the activities of the Rote Kapelle. This material was returned to Greta Kuckhoff after photocopies had been made.[33]

But there had been no need to trick her. Greta was always proud to name the people close to her who had died fighting the Nazis. She never hid the fact that they had given information to the Soviets as one of their myriad activities.

As it turned out, this information was of no value to Allied intelligence. The names that Greta provided were the same ones that appeared in the 1943 Gestapo report, which had been in the possession of British intelligence for over a year.[34] However, based on this supposed "breakthrough," the CIC opened an investigation of the Rote Kapelle, rooted in the belief that there were still survivors at large in Germany working for Soviet intelligence. And no one was better qualified to help track them down, the army officers reasoned, than Manfred Roeder.

On December 23, 1947, the Army CIC took custody of Roeder, effectively placing him out of the reach of the Nuremberg prosecutors. Bestowed with the code name "Othello," Roeder proceeded to spin his new hosts a tale. Roeder told the gullible Americans that his bloodthirsty prosecutions were a matter of just following orders—an excuse that was not supposed to hold up in the Nuremberg proceedings.

Roeder expanded on his argument to explain the death sentences he had demanded for marginal figures in the case. "The Führer decreed that everyone who took part in the Rote Kapelle was to be sentenced to death immediately," Roeder stated. This was demonstrably false. A number of defendants had been convicted and sentenced to prison terms, especially those who had been tried in the months after Roeder left the case. Others who had been swept up from Leopold Trepper's operations were kept alive to convey false intelligence to the Soviets.[35] In fact, Hitler reserved his personal interest for representatives of Germany's elite. Most of the other sentences were left in the hands of the court. Roeder's prosecution drove the death sentences of most of the minor defendants.

The CIC housed Roeder with another notorious prisoner who had been borrowed from the war crimes authorities. Walter Huppenkothen, a senior Gestapo official, had served as the liaison with the murderous *Einsatzgruppe I* squad during its first wave of Polish massacres. Toward the end of the war, he was the officer who ordered the executions of Dietrich Bonhoeffer, Hans Oster, and Wilhelm Canaris. After Germany's defeat, Huppenkothen's Gestapo chief had advised him to lie low for as long as possible. "It's only a matter of time until the Americans will want you in their coming fight against the East," he told him.

Once in detention, Huppenkothen volunteered to enlist his Gestapo contacts to help the Americans. They offered to round up the German Communists they had sent to concentration camps, but only if the Americans could give them "some assurances."[36]*

Benno Selke, the deputy director of the Evidence Division for Nuremberg, was angered by the U.S. Army Intelligence's recruitment of Roeder and Huppenkothen. He wrote:

> This office finds it hard to believe that CIC would knowingly enlist the aid of two such notorious, unscrupulous opportunistic Nazis who would sure have been tried [at] Nuremberg, had the scope of the Nuremberg trials been greater. It seems that their only selling point could possibly be the fact that they are presumably anti-Communist and have knowledge in connection with Russian underground methods.[37]

Like Huppenkothen, Manfred Roeder sensed what the Americans wanted to hear. He gave the CIC the names of "Soviet agents": specifically, Greta Kuckhoff, Günther Weisenborn, and Adolf Grimme, the

---

*Neither Roeder nor Huppenkothen could be called the most egregious CIC recruit. This was surely Gestapo officer Klaus Barbie, known as the "Butcher of Lyon" for his zeal in tracking down French Jews and sending them to their deaths. In 1947 the CIC recruited Barbie as a paid agent to infiltrate the German Communist Party on their behalf, and paid him $1,700 a month. Over the next four years, army intelligence shielded him from numerous French attempts to extradite him for war crimes.[38] When this was no longer possible, the CIC presented him with a set of false documents and packed him off to Bolivia.

very same individuals who had filed charges against him. The list was as unlikely as it was suspect. Greta Kuckhoff was the only one of the three who had ever had any contact with a Soviet intelligence officer. That contact was minimal, and took place only through her late husband. Günther Weisenborn was neither a Communist Party member nor did he have Soviet ties. Adolf Grimme, far from being a Communist, was a leading member of the rival Social Democrats. He was also a prominent figure in the Confessing Lutheran Church and a trusted liaison to the British occupational authority.

The CIC was understandably confused by the welter of information about the various Soviet spy networks described in the Nazi files. The Nazis had intentionally fabricated parallels between the Brussels operation run by paid Soviet agent Trepper and his associates, and the Berlin circles that established only a late and haphazard connection to the Soviets amid many other resistance activities. U.S. Army intelligence hoped that Roeder would help them untangle the relationships between Moscow, Brussels, Paris, and Berlin, and the possible Soviet networks that could follow in their wake. But Roeder's goal was to deflect his own prosecution for war crimes by obscuring the facts.

The cold war that stirred into existence in postwar Berlin was an early chill of McCarthyism. A May 13, 1948, CIC memorandum pointed to a suspicious article in the University of Wisconsin alumni magazine "glorifying Mildred Fish-Harnack as an American woman who had died as a member of a German underground movement." Greta Kuckhoff, the memo noted, was a University of Wisconsin alumna and may have been a source for the article praising Mildred. The author suggested pursuing an inquiry at the University of Wisconsin for pro-Soviet activities in the United States.

But the memo also acknowledged that Manfred Roeder's accusations were wearing thin. "No concrete evidence has been obtained through Othello's interrogation that any one of the survivors of the R/K is presently engaged in espionage work for Soviet-Russia." The CIC agents reluctantly reached the same conclusion as their counterparts in British intelligence—"The Rote Kapelle, as such, is not active today"—and moved to distance themselves from Roeder. There was now no official obstacle to his prosecution.

But then the Americans found a new sticking point. "If Othello [Roeder] was ever hard pressed," the officers worried, "he might reveal his relationship with the CIC in order to protect himself." Therefore, the CIC requested, "If and when [Roeder] is released, his release [should] be arranged in such a manner that he will not come under the control of Soviet or Soviet-sponsored authorities." No such assurance could be made if an international trial was pursued.

Roeder was returned to the Nuremberg prosecutors, but now he confidently refused to answer their questions. He didn't need to, he said, because he was working for the CIC. Nuremberg investigator Benno Selke, clearly frustrated with Roeder's manipulation, protested in an August 4, 1948, memorandum to the commanding general at army intelligence:

> The interrogation and investigations in the case of Roeder are seriously hampered, if not completely stalemated, by the fact that he steadfastly refuses to give information, stating that he was so directed by a C.I.C. officer, Lt.-Col Hayes of Regensburg, for whom he is presently working according to his statement. . . .
>
> Roeder, one of the most hated men in Germany at the present time, who could well qualify as Public Enemy No. 1 in any German democracy, is a notorious former Air Force Judge, whose brutally harsh and bloodthirsty methods earned him the right to act as "investigating officer and prosecutor," not only in the "Rote Kapelle" case but also in other cases involving members of the German underground.[39]

In a recent review of the surviving files on the case, the Interagency Working Group at the National Archives in Washington, D.C., concluded that the Allies were unwilling to include the Rote Kapelle in their dispensation of postwar justice:

> It is clear from the contents of the file that Allied intelligence officers were interested, not in possible Gestapo misdeeds (use of torture) in eradicating the Red Orchestra, but rather in what information about Soviet military intelligence practices might be

gleaned from German files and from interrogating those Germans involved with the case. . . .

Despite evidence of Gestapo mistreatment of Red Orchestra agents, there was apparently little interest on the part of the western Allies in prosecuting German officials connected with the Red Orchestra investigation. Indeed, as differences between East and West grew greater in the postwar period, American intelligence officers showed more interest in the Red Orchestra case as a source of information on Soviet intelligence trade craft and methodology, rather than as a case for possible prosecution in the wake of Germany's defeat. The U.S. Army file on the Red Orchestra clearly reflects this state of affairs.[40]

Irony was heaped on irony. It is hard to imagine anyone less qualified to comment on espionage tradecraft than the amateurs of the Rote Kapelle, whose every action was marked by zealous ineptitude.

After Manfred Roeder was released, he settled in a small town near Lüneberg, in northern Germany. The Nuremberg officials turned the case over to German courts in October 1948, but the local German prosecutor did not exert himself in pursuing the charges. Greta Kuckhoff and Falk Harnack doggedly provided evidence and interviews for the proceedings, but in November 1951 the investigation was suspended.[41] (One of Roeder's successful arguments was that he had acted according to the laws of 1942. If this defense had been honored at Nuremberg, the top Nazi leadership would have gone free.)

By this time, Roeder had regained public prominence as a supporter of a West German party on the radical right. He used his platform to revive his charges of wartime treason against the Red Orchestra. In an April 25, 1951, speech he attacked two survivors who had achieved distinction in West Germany. Social Democrat Adolf Grimme was now director of Northwest German Radio. Helmut Roloff, a political conservative who had joined the conspiracy through his efforts to help Jewish neighbors, was an acclaimed concert pianist and music educator.[42] Neither man had the stomach to pursue Roeder, but they were also tired of defending themselves against his calumny. (After the war, it was said that the well-rewarded Communist survivors of the resistance in East Germany remembered "more and more" of their wartime activity, while survivors in the West, battered by defamation, remembered "less and less.")

Roeder fired yet another salvo in 1952, when he repeated his attacks in a book entitled *Die Rote Kapelle: Europäische Spionage* (*The Red Orchestra: European Espionage*). The cover showed the dastardly hand of Moscow suspended over Europe, pulling strings in a dozen different countries. Roeder repeated his attacks on the West German official Adolf Grimme, who he said had been "ninety percent convinced by Adam Kuckhoff's Communist ideology." Roeder expressed scorn for those who complained about the forty-four death sentences he won in the Nazi court: "How many German soldiers were direct or indirect victims of their deeds will never be known."

Roeder argued that German troops fighting for their country had been betrayed in the field. For Roeder, the struggle was not between Nazism and its millions of victims, it was between patriotism and treachery.

> It was a struggle which the German soldier led against an enemy
> in disguise, that ambushed him with novel but malicious methods,
> paying lip service to the words "freedom, love of humanity, and
> patriotism." His real language traveled through the ether—and
> that was treason.[43]

Roeder lived for a time on his wife's family estate, then moved to what was described as a "California-style villa" in a picturesque town called Glashütten, outside Frankfurt am Main, where he was elected to the town council.[44] There he entertained visiting journalists, dropping anti-Semitic remarks and boasting about his good friends in the CIA.[45] Manfred Roeder never stood trial, and lived until 1971.[46]

Roeder's colleague Walter Huppenkothen, who had presided over the concentration camp "trials" and death sentences of Dietrich Bonhoeffer and Hans Oster, also escaped lightly. He was tried in Munich in 1950, but the verdict was set aside for two years. He was finally convicted of the concentration camp executions in 1955 (for violating procedures), and was sentenced to seven years in prison. He never stood trial for his murderous Gestapo activity in Poland.

The Nuremberg trials of 1945–46 won wide publicity, and "Nuremberg" became a synonym for the idea that war criminals will ultimately face retribution. In the initial round, eleven high-ranking Nazis were sentenced to death, and on October 16, 1946, ten of them were hung at dawn. (Hermann Göring cheated the executioner by taking poison the previous day.) There were subsequent Nuremberg trials for groups of Nazi doctors, judges, and *Einsatzgruppen*, accompanied by widespread publicity suggesting that justice was being served.

That was not how it looked to the German resisters. Some six million people had belonged to the Nazi Party, and the expansive crimes of the Third Reich required the participation of hundreds of thousands. But from its beginning in November 1945 until its end in June 1948, the Nuremberg process initiated only 3,887 cases (many involving groups of defendants). Of these, 3,400 cases were dropped. A mere 489 cases—thirteen percent of the total—went to trial, involving a total of 1,672 defendants. Of these, 1,416 were found guilty.

Fewer than 200 of them were executed. The judges sentenced 279 of them to life imprisonment, but by 1955, only about 40 convicted Nazi war criminals were still behind bars (including those with life sentences or commuted death sentences).[47]

In late 1945, the Allies gave German courts the power to try Germans accused of crimes against fellow Germans and stateless persons, and after 1950 German courts were authorized to try all Nazi crimes. This process was also disappointing. Up to 1992, German prosecutors initiated proceedings against 103,823 individuals, but they resulted in only 6,487 convictions. The Nazis were a powerful presence in the postwar legal system, and tens of thousands of cases bogged down, then completely disappeared.[48]

Soon after the war, the Allies began to facilitate the reentry of notorious Nazis into public life, including Gestapo agents and concentration camp personnel.

The Nazis had terrorized German democrats, Jews, and leftists for twelve years, and had organized a machinery of mass slaughter across Europe. They had placed millions of individuals in prisons and concentration camps, and executed 4,980 people for their connections to the failed 20th of July plot alone. The insults rippled through the generations. The widows and children of Gestapo and SS officers were considered the survivors of patriots. Widows and children of the executed resisters of the 20th of July movement were deprived of their pensions and called traitors.

Greta Kuckhoff moved back into the apartment she had once shared with her husband. Now Greta shared her home with seven-year-old Ule and a roommate named Grete Wittkowski, a Jewish Communist who had escaped the Holocaust by fleeing to England. (Wittkowski would become East Germany's highest-ranking female official.) A neighbor described Greta's living room as a museum to her past, full of "mementos and overstuffed, scraped leather furniture . . . the darkened buff walls covered with pictures and framed photos. No trace remained of the Gestapo family who moved in after Greta and Adam were arrested."[49]

Nevertheless, everywhere she looked, Greta saw signs of "renazification."

CHAPTER 23

Life in a Cold Climate

1945–1981

BERLIN WAS IN LIMBO. IT WAS RECKONED THAT A THIRD OF ITS buildings had been razed, and displaced persons flooded into the city with nowhere to live and almost nothing to eat. Over five million German soldiers returned from the front, and some thirteen million German and ethnic German refugees arrived from the east.

Berlin was technically divided into four occupation zones, but in the early days people still moved easily between sectors. Even amid the rubble, the town was starting to recover its old spirit. Prisoners from concentration camps and penitentiaries joined returning Jewish and leftist exiles, all bent on reclaiming remnants of their past lives. Günther Weisenborn wrote, "No one believed that the division of the city would last. . . . We lived a reckless life, full of hope and with a critical eye in this strangely unnerving city."[1]

Theaters were among the first buildings to be refurbished and heated, and Berliners flocked to their warmth, drawing on the power of theater to interpret the nightmares of the recent past. Rote Kapelle survivors were among the earliest authors to reemerge. Günther Weisenborn was one of the first. His 1946 play, *Die Illegalen* (*The Illegals*) portrayed the world of the Schulze-Boysen group in a series of short, deft scenes. Weisenborn published it within a year of leaving prison, and the play was performed extensively in Germany over the following decade. *Die Illegalen* dramatized the anxiety of parents who opposed the Nazis but feared for their children in the resistance, and depicted the shy embraces of young people assigned to play lovers in order to paste anti-Hitler stickers on the walls. Weisenborn's program notes commented on the complexity of postwar culture:

> Among the audience there are courageous and indifferent people; refugees, returnees from the front, former traitors and secret Nazis; indifferent bourgeois and young hopeful people. There are widows of fascism sitting next to people of good will, villains next to desperate people, those who are exhausted and those who still have hope.[2]

Three years later Weisenborn published a slim volume called *Memorial*, which he had begun in prison, writing on paper bags. The book was a collage of his reporting days in New York, his underground work with Harro Schulze-Boysen, and his ordeals in prison. Its epigraph stated: "It surprises me that we still have the same faces that we had three thousand years earlier, after so much hatred and suffering has been dragged over them."[3]

Weisenborn gradually resumed his work in German cinema, but he was not always welcome. The Allies, and particularly the Americans, were unenthusiastic about artistic explorations of the recent past. U.S. authorities initially forbade the production of new German films, even by proven antifascists, and fed German audiences a diet of light Hollywood entertainment.

Weisenborn and Falk Harnack struck up a collaboration with Wolfgang Staudte, a veteran of Piscator's Volksbühne who had been banned from working in theater under the Nazis. Staudte directed the first feature to deal with the Nazi legacy, the 1946 film *Die Mörder sind unter uns* (*Murderers Among Us*) starring Hildegarde Neff. It told the story of a concentration camp survivor who returns to Berlin after the war to find her apartment inhabited by a traumatized veteran. American officials refused Staudte permission to produce the film, so he took it to the Russians and made it at East Germany's new DEFA film center, built on the ashes of the UFA in Babelsberg. The film became a postwar classic.

A few years later Staudte made *Rotation,* an ambitious film depicting a resistance group similar to Weisenborn's. The plot concerned a printer who is torn between his brother-in-law's commitment to the antifascist underground and his son's loyalty to the Hitler Youth. He joins an underground leaflet campaign, is arrested by the Gestapo, and narrowly misses execution. The film shows non-Communists and Communists working together against the fascists, watching in silent agony as their children's minds are warped by Nazi propaganda. Western occupation authorities also judged this film as unsuitable for postwar German audiences.[4]

German playwrights had dealt with World War I through the *Heimkehrerdrama* (homecoming drama) that portrayed a soldier's returning to "face the difficulty, or impossibility, of reintegrating into a society which rejects them as symbols of a recent past that it wishes to forget." Now many of the same writers faced an even more difficult task. This time they were not just reflecting the horrors of war back to their countrymen, but the horrors that had enveloped the entire society. This task would consume Günther Weisenborn for the rest of his life.

German books about the resistance were also discouraged. After the war, Rosemarie Reichwein, the widow of a 20th of July conspirator and leading Social Democrat, hungered to know more about her husband's fate. "Above all, I tried to get hold of literature on the *Widerstand* [resistance]—a difficult job," she told an interviewer.

I found the first book on the subject in Sweden; the diaries of Ulrich von Hassell. At first this book could only be published in Switzerland . . . since the Allies did not like to see this kind of literature. They just did not want it to be known that there had been any resistance at all.[5]

There were even greater efforts to erase the record of the Communists. "To this day the Communist resistance is misunderstood," Reichwein stated in the 1990s. "To be sure this is not surprising in light of the fact that the GDR was our neighbor. We were afraid and wanted nothing to do with Communism. But despite all this we should not overlook that the Communists lost more lives."[6]

Reichwein had a special appreciation for the women in the Communist resistance circles.

There was a distinction between us wives whose husbands were active and the Communist wives in the city. There, the wives themselves took a very active part, distributing leaflets or establishing underground links. They probably did more than us; we stood in the background, approved of what our husbands were doing and supported them but weren't active ourselves.[7]

Freya von Moltke, whose aristocratic husband was executed as an anti-fascist, praised Greta Kuckhoff's circle in an interview.

I always felt there was nothing I could do, although I found the whole National Socialist development dreadful. That was the difference between me and the women of the "Red Orchestra." They were people who wanted to do something, who couldn't put up with nothing being done. To write off all the Red Orchestra people as Communists misses the truth.

I regret not having gone as far as they did and regard it as a weakness. But that was what I was like. I regret it but perhaps if I had acted like them I would no longer be alive, and I am a sufficiently normal woman to have wanted to stay alive for the sake of my two sons.[8]

The Western occupiers had political reasons for suppressing the history of the Communist resistance in Germany, but some officials admitted their errors regarding the German resistance as a whole. In his 1947 book, Allen Dulles frankly acknowledged that the United States and other Allied governments had failed to give German antifascists the support they deserved.

Before the war the West did not take too seriously the pleas of those anti-Nazi Germans who tried to enlighten it. . . . After Hitler went to war and Western eyes were finally opened to what

Hitlerism meant, no one would have anything to do with any German, whether Nazi or not. All were suspect.[9]

Neither the occupiers of West Germany nor those of East Germany possessed a political vocabulary that encompassed Greta and her group, and the survivors were unwelcome in both worlds. Arvid Harnack's younger brother, Falk, was an example. After the war, he had a successful career in German theater, which led to projects for the East German film company DEFA. In 1949 he directed another feature film that directly confronted the Nazi past, called *Das Beil von Wandsbek* (*The Axe of Wandsbek*), based on the true story of a humble butcher who agreed to fill in for an executioner, beheaded four Communists, and committed suicide out of remorse. After its initial critical success, the East Germans pulled the film from the theaters for being too sympathetic to the moral struggle of the butcher. It was Harnack's first and last film in East Germany. He departed for West Germany, where he resolutely continued to produce films that dealt with the Nazis and the resistance, even though they ran counter to the cultural tide. In 1955 he and Günther Weisenborn collaborated on the screenplay for *Der 20. Juli* (*The 20th of July*), which Harnack directed. One of the first films to deal with the military conspiracy, the feature won a West German Film Award as "outstanding feature film promoting democratic values."

Falk Harnack and Günther Weisenborn resumed their collaboration in 1974 on a television movie version of Weisenborn's novel *Der Verfolger* (*The Pursuer*), another depiction of life in the underground. Weisenborn died in 1969, Falk Harnack in 1991, both in West Germany. Neither man ever abandoned his mission to defend the memory of the resistance. In his later years, Falk used to brood for days about the unsettled past, then telephone Manfred Roeder in the middle of the night to berate him.[10]

Greta Kuckhoff was also haunted by her legacy. By the fall of 1945 she was at work on a book called *Adam Kuckhoff zum Gedenken: Novellen-Gedichte-Briefe* (*In Memory of Adam Kuckhoff: Novels, Poems, Letters*). The slender volume was published the following year, printed on cheap postwar paper with a blurred photo of Adam in the frontispiece. Greta was only four months out of prison when she completed her lengthy introduction. For the first time in twelve years, Greta could write without fear or Nazi censorship. For the last time in her life, she published writing that did not have to pass a Communist litmus test.

As a young widow, she described her husband's struggles of conscience. He was an artist who lived in the world of the senses, responding ecstatically to the beauties of nature. He was a moralist who wrestled with the ideals of truth and justice. His natural form of expression was fiction and poetry. He loved her and their son, Ule. Why then had he risked everything—and lost—in his quixotic vendetta against an all-powerful enemy? She answered,

> Kuckhoff was glad to be alive, but he loved liberty and truth more than his life. He was deeply imbued with the knowledge that there was no possibility to serve this truth searchingly as long as the barbaric false teachings of National Socialism maintained their tyrannical rule.

In 1933, Greta recounts, Adam had received many invitations to leave Germany and resettle in a place where he could "breathe freely and write." But he felt obliged to decline. "Of the small group of politically engaged writers, Kuckhoff was among the few who were not politically or 'racially' under attack," Greta explains. "He was able to stay, and therefore he had to stay."[11]

The most striking aspect of Greta's essay is what it omits: it makes no mention of Communism, Marx, or the Soviet Union. Instead, she writes of God, freedom, and the influence of American writers Theodore Dreiser and Sinclair Lewis. Even the murdered Hans Otto is cited only as an in-law and fellow artist, with no reference to the Communist Party. Greta's selections from her husband's writings include passages of aesthetic theory, lyrical poetry, and moving letters of farewell. There are no Communist calls to arms or works of Marxist theory. Perhaps this brief moment is the closest that posterity can come to hearing Greta's true measure of her husband.

Berlin's freewheeling postwar period was coming to an end, and the cold war loomed unmistakably on the horizon. Even most militant German Communists resented the Soviets' excesses. They had extirpated German civilian populations from regions of East Prussia they had inhabited for centuries, and stripped Germany of every bit of industrial material they could carry, including the wherewithal for food production.

But Greta's disillusionment with the Americans was also growing. Instead of prosecuting Roeder, they investigated her. While the Soviets commemorated her group's resistance activities, the Americans derided them. She was shocked by the Americans' lackadaisical approach toward the Nazis as they reinstated many local officials and recruited others for intelligence work.

In 1948 matters came to a head. The United States and its Western Allies, frustrated by the Soviets' grabs for power and refusal to cooperate in reconstruction efforts, decided to launch a new currency system in their zones to jump-start the economy. There was an exchange of hostile gestures, culminating in the long-term division of Germany and the city of Berlin.

Greta's apartment was in the American sector, but she had been employed as a social worker for the municipality of Berlin, which was run by the Soviets. Now her paychecks, issued in the old currency, were worthless outside the Soviet sector. She packed up her belongings and moved. There were many advantages to her action. In East Germany the resistance was honored, and survivors were granted ample rewards. Greta's benefits would eventually include a handsome villa in Pankow, the Berlin suburb favored by the party elite, and a dacha in the country.[12] As a member of a privileged class, she benefited from access to state stores and scarce goods.

But Greta's choice was based on emotion as well as expedience. In 1949 she publicly announced that she was giving up hope that Roeder would ever be brought to justice. "Conditions in West Germany are such that no equitable outcome can be expected," she wrote.[13]

Greta soon found that life in East Germany subjected her to other pressures. The difficulties were traceable to April 30, 1945, the day Hitler died, when the Soviets transported Germany's Communist Party leader Walter Ulbricht back to Berlin. Ulbricht had a long and ugly history. As a Comintern official in the Spanish civil war, he was instructed to identify "politically unreliable" German leftists in the international brigades and mark them for execution. He had sat out the war as Stalin's guest in Moscow, looking the other way as Stalin murdered hundreds of his fellow German Communists in Soviet prisons and concentration camps.

Now Moscow's surviving guests rejoined the KPD members who had stayed in Germany and others who had found refuge in the West. Often their political perspectives varied according to their experience. Many KPD members who stayed in Germany had worked alongside non-Communists: Christians, Jews, and Social Democrats. Together, they had faced prison, concentration camps, and execution.[14] Under Moscow's new rules, any resulting heterodoxy in their outlook made them second-class citizens.

Ulbricht set to work reshaping East German society and the German Communist Party according to the dictates and needs of the Soviets. In West Germany, the Marshall Plan would help to prevent economic crises that could drive more political upheaval. But in the East, factories, vehicles, and art collections were dismantled and shipped off as compensation for the Soviet Union's terrible losses.

The Soviets had captured over three million German prisoners of war, and demanded that many of them remain in the Soviet Union as forced labor. Other soldiers who had made it home against impossible odds were sent back to join them. Some of the Soviets' POWs were held well into the 1950s, and over a million German POWs died in Soviet captivity.[15]

One of the most tragic Soviet abuses involved the persecution of members of the non-Communist resistance. East German intelligence official Markus Wolf later wrote how his Soviet masters used the denazification process as an excuse to purge political rivals:

> When Soviet occupation officials carried out mass arrests of ex-Nazis and assorted opponents of Stalin, thousands of Social Democratic opponents of Nazism were swept up, and some ended up in labor camps that, ironically, had only recently been Nazi concentration camps. We knew very little about that, and what we did know we viewed as cruel Western propaganda.[16]

One of their victims was Arvid Harnack's cousin Justus Delbrück, a member of the 20th of July conspiracy who had narrowly escaped execution by the Nazis. He was liberated by the Soviets from the Lehrterstrasse Prison at the end of the war, only to be rearrested shortly after.[17] Delbrück reportedly died of diphtheria in Soviet captivity in October 1945. Michael Burleigh writes that some 122,600 German prisoners were detained in the Soviets' Special Camps immediately after the war. "Some of these people were discreetly murdered. The low figure for deaths in these camps 'as a result of sickness' is 42,800."[18]

East Germans who had only recently escaped the enveloping lies of Nazi propaganda were now blindsided by the Soviet version. Greta's neighbor from New York, Edith Anderson, was struggling to remain a loyal Communist, but early on she realized that the average East German periodical was less a newspaper than a "smokescreen and cattle prod." One of the most closely held secrets was the story of Stalin's purges, including his persecution of German Communists before the war. Only a handful of returnees from Moscow knew the terrible truth before it was revealed in Khrushchev's "secret speech" of 1956. Edith Anderson later speculated that Berlin's Moscow crowd was so standoffish because they were shamed by what they knew.

Ulbricht and his government took measures to co-opt the Social Democrats by transforming the German Communist Party (the KPD) into the German Socialist Unity Party (SED). When the new party faltered in early postwar elections, the regime responded by banning the other parties and making East Germany a one-party state. (The East Germans stated that the KPD and the Social Democratic Party had "merged.") Ulbricht's regime subjected East Germany to disastrous economic policies and repressive police state measures. Soon his government was facing waves of opposition from disaffected workers, frustrated intellectuals, and dissenters from the party itself. East German officials were especially distrustful of German Communists who had spent the war in Britain and the United States. Intellectuals were high on their list, routinely suspected of treason and ties to Western intelligence by the Moscow contingent. Intelligence chief Markus Wolf wrote, "In East Germany, the word 'intellectual' had a disparaging ring in both the Party and the Ministry of State Security. Many tried to defend themselves from accusations of 'elitist thinking' or 'immodesty' by stressing their acceptance of the leading role of the working class and biting their tongues about the idiocies perpetrated in its name."[19] Nonetheless, over the following decades many of them were purged, tried, imprisoned, or worked to death.

One early attack affected the prominent actor and director Wolfgang Langhoff. This was Günther Weisenborn's friend, the Communist concentration camp survivor who had tried to help Harro Schulze-Boysen's group from his exile in Switzerland. After the war Langhoff was appointed director of the prestigious Deutsches Theater, where he employed Falk Harnack and hosted a 1946 memorial service for actor Hans Otto, killed by the Nazis in 1933. In August 1951, Langhoff was accused of vague connections to Noel Field, an American Quaker Communist who had worked for the OSS. The East Germans stripped Langhoff of his position and the episode blighted his career. (Even less fortunate individuals were expelled from the party and public life altogether, making them "nonpersons," while others were imprisoned under harsh conditions.)[20]

Greta Kuckhoff, struggling with survivor's guilt, fixed her attention on the mission of honoring the memory of her husband and friends. Initially, East Germany offered Greta Kuckhoff many of the opportunities she craved. She became an iconic fixture at the commemoration and naming ceremonies. Rote Kapelle orphans and survivors' children remembered her pale, grave face as she bent over them to ask after their lives and their studies.

But now her own personal history was trapped in the pincer of cold war politics. The West Germans, under the tutelage of the Americans, were not eager to admit that German Communists had led a spirited resistance movement through the Nazi period, after many other political parties had sold out or given up. The heterodox nature of the Harnack/Schulze-Boysen group, mixing Communists with every other political description, made them doubly uncomfortable.

West Germans who believed that the war had been lost from "poor timing" saw the group as traitors responsible for the deaths of Germans on the Russian front, rather than as citizens who were trying to save their country from tyranny and disaster. The history of the anti-Nazi resistance was suppressed and the West German legal system upheld the convictions of Germans executed for resistance activities. Widows of the officers and statesmen who gave their lives in the 20th of July coup attempt were denied government pensions until the 1960s. Dietrich Bonhoeffer, the Lutheran pastor who rescued Jews and campaigned tirelessly against Nazi abuses, was not publicly exonerated of his legal conviction until 1996.[21]

The East Germans, on the other hand, were reluctant to admit that the German resistance included anyone but Communists. They expropriated the history of the Harnack/Schulze-Boysen group and rewrote it to their own purpose. The official East German accounts conveniently omitted the involvement of many of the non-Communists in the group, and inflated the roles of the Communists. The members' many ties to Social Democratic and religious institutions were ignored wherever possible.

Furthermore, the East German version of history was extremely elusive concerning the Jews. In many regards, it was a question of omission. Many monuments to the victims of the Nazis were dedicated to "antifascists," which was treated as a synonym for "Communists." The memorials at Sachsenhausen and other concentration camps honored German Communist inmates, and largely ignored Jews and other populations. When officials in East Berlin erected a plaque in memory of the Herbert Baum group, they labeled them "Communists" but neglected to add that they were also Jewish resisters awaiting deportation to the camps. The East Germans' versions of the Harnack/Schulze-Boysen story gave no weight to the many chapters concerning Jews, half-Jews, and Jewish rescue efforts. These were not areas of interest.[22]

Greta's benefits in East Germany came at a high price. For the rest of her life, she was torn between passively enjoying the rewards of party privilege, and bitterly defending her concept of the truth.

Once she moved east, Greta was rewarded with official positions that required membership in the Communist Party. This led to an early compromise. East German records show that Greta actually joined the Communist Party after the war, but party officials backdated her membership to 1935.[23] The record needed to be bent to conform to the myth.

Another compromise may have occurred in the direction of intelligence. In 1947, the year in which Greta realized that U.S. authorities were tapping her phone and sending agents to investigate her instead of Manfred Roeder, she made contact with East German intelligence. Assigned the code name "Cannes," she stated that she had ties to Americans and British in West Berlin. A 1966 "top secret" review stated that in 1948 her file was "withdrawn" without explanation. In 1950, according to her file,

> the connection to "Cannes" was restored, but there are no materials about working with her in the file. The file also lacks the materials which described when and under what circumstances Cannes was enlisted, and to what extent the materials she delivered in the years 1947–1949 were accurate and valuable. Also missing in the file is its comprehensive and accurate personal information.[24]

Was Greta's intelligence connection active, or an unspoken requirement for working in the East? Did Greta actually inform against the Americans and the British, or did she target the Nazis in her midst? How much actual intelligence against the West could someone moving to East Germany actually offer? (Wouldn't East German intelligence prefer an informant who stayed in the West?) Greta's file raises more questions than it answers.

Greta rose quickly in the East German bureaucracy. She won a place in the country's first trade delegations to neighboring Eastern European nations and the Soviet Union. In December 1950 she was appointed to serve as president of East Germany's Central Bank. Two years later she presided over a plenary session for a trade conference in Moscow. The East Germans boasted that "this is probably the first time that such a conference was presided over by a woman.[25]

As an uneasy equilibrium was restored in both East and West Germany over the next decade, the reconstructed histories of the Nazi period took root. In the West, the story of Greta's group was largely suppressed. Arvid Harnack's assistance to the Americans and Harro Schulze-Boysen's attempt to help the British went forgotten. Donald

Heath, Arvid's contact at the U.S. embassy, mourned his friend for the rest of his life, but his government discouraged him from publicizing Arvid's services to the United States.

Despite her early success, Greta Kuckhoff soon experienced political difficulties. The troubles began in the early 1950s. Stalin died in March 1953, to Greta's relief. (She told one of her young protégés that "Stalin was bad for socialism.")[26] But East German strong man Walter Ulbricht gambled that, in the aftermath, the Stalinist hard-liners would prevail. He tried to impress them with a policy of "accelerating socialism" by imposing onerous taxes, limiting the production of consumer goods, and repressing church communities. On June 17, 1953, angry workers marched on the government ministries in Berlin. Hundreds were shot and killed, many directly in front of the former Air Ministry where Harro Schulze-Boysen had worked.[27]

Bertolt Brecht, recently returned from America, acidly wrote that since "the people had forfeited the confidence of the government," the Communist government should "dissolve the people and elect another."[28]

Instead, the East German government initiated a series of sweeping investigations and arrests. By 1958 a growing number of "soft" German Communists protested Ulbricht's hard-line tactics, calling for economic and political liberalization. Many sympathized with the reformist movements in Eastern Europe.

One of East Germany's leading voices for change was a high-ranking Communist official named Karl Schirdewan, who had spent eleven years in Nazi prisons and concentration camps. In 1958, Ulbricht struck again, purging Schirdewan and his followers and going on to remove legions of suspect party and government officials. The *Washington Post* reported that the number reached as many as thirty thousand.[29] For days, East German schoolchildren recited condemnations of Schirdewan from the party newspaper and attended classes devoted to criticizing the fallen official.

Greta Kuckhoff was among the thousands who lost their posts. A few years earlier, she had been magically transformed from a political prisoner to a high-ranking government official. Now, even more abruptly, she was "retired" from her position as president of the Central Bank.

In November 1958, she was included in a list of "persons who fell from grace in the Party purge that started in February of this year, e.g. Schirdewan . . . Greta Kuckhoff and Grete Wittkowski, all tarred with the brush of hostility to Ulbricht or of preference for 'excessively soft' planning targets, cultural policy etc." The report was compiled by an analyst for the U.S. government's Radio Free Europe.[30] The abrupt departures of Greta Kuckhoff and Grete Wittkowski were especially noteworthy because they were the only two high-profile female officials in the *frauenlose welt* ("women-less world") of East German politics.[31]

The East Germans strongly encouraged their deposed officials to cite "reasons of health," and Greta dutifully announced that her asthma had flared up. But her friends privately commented that her health seemed unchanged, and she remained active for decades to come.[32] Some victims of 1958 (such as Greta's roommate Grete Wittkowski) were eventually restored to high position, but Greta spent the rest of her career working in organizations of lesser influence, notably the German-British Relations sector of the German Peace Council.

Greta never abandoned East Germany, but she never entirely conformed to its demands. She presented the Rote Kapelle orphans with mixed messages. She chided young Saskia von Brockdorff when she decided to emigrate to the West. But Hans Coppi recalled that for all her bitterness over the handling of Roeder, she always spoke warmly of the United States and described Wisconsin as "the happiest time in her life."

Greta's struggle to define her legacy was not over. As researchers delved into records from the war, troubling accounts boiled to the surface. In 1967, French author Gilles Perrault published a book called *The Red Orchestra: The Anatomy of the Most Successful Spy Ring of World War II*. He built his narrative around the Nazi manhunt for Soviet agent Leopold Trepper in Belgium, but his story necessarily wound back to the circles in Berlin. Perrault's passages about Greta's circle were generally sympathetic.

But 1970 brought a West German rebuttal in the form of a book called *Codeword: Direktor*. Greta was shattered to learn that the author, journalist Heinz Höhne, had based his account largely on Nazi sources, quoting extensively from Gestapo interrogations, the trial transcript, and interviews with Manfred Roeder himself. Höhne interviewed many important sources firsthand, and wrote scathing passages about the Nazi abuses and Roeder's prosecution. But at the same time, he echoed the Nazis' depiction of Harro Schulze-Boysen and his associates as traitors who worshipped at the altar of "crazy fanaticism."[33] They "cannot be included in the ranks of German resistance," Höhne argued. They were only "an unfortunate aberration."[34]

Höhne repeated Nazi accusations against the group in great detail, including Roeder's innuendos, fabrications, and outright slander. The charge: that Schulze-Boysen's group had sent "500 messages to Moscow containing primarily military information."[35] Not one such message had been conveyed by the faulty radios, and Korotkov only sent a total of a few dozen reports to Moscow over the entire period of contact. Höhne also quoted the Nazis' spurious charge that the group was driven by mercenary motives, listing phantom payments as "wages of treachery."[36]

Manfred Roeder's prosecution had been marked by his prurient allegations of sexual misconduct, depicting the group as a "wanton sex-obsessed society." One member was credited with the unlikely feat of "intimate relations with four Soviet agents in a single night."[37]

Höhne reprinted Roeder's claim that Libertas Schulze-Boysen was a lesbian, adding that Adam Kuckhoff had been drawn into the conspiracy by his "passionate attachment" to her. Greta Kuckhoff was angered and wounded. She could not understand why, years after the war, the Nazis' vicious allegations against her circle should be revived to poison future generations.

At the same time, Greta was unhappy with the East Germans' distortions. The East German regime kept the actual records of the Rote Kapelle under close wraps. East Germany's foreign intelligence chief Markus Wolf wrote:

Details about [the Rote Kapelle] were more accessible for me in Western publications than in our own ministry's archives. [Stasi chief Erich] Mielke kept files about the Nazi era under his personal control in a special section of the Investigations Department, and try as I might I could not gain access to them.[38]

Nonetheless, Wolf pursued his strong personal interest in the story. His father, Communist physician and playwright Friedrich Wolf, had worked in the same theater circles as Hans Otto and Adam Kuckhoff. As a member of a Jewish family from the German Communist Party elite, Markus Wolf would have been proud to identify with the Rote Kapelle's actions. But he was honest enough to confirm that it was not the nest of Soviet Communist spies that his government made it out to be. Indeed, he wrote, while the Rote Kapelle was "one of the biggest resistance organizations," only "a few of its members were Communists, and a small portion were agents of the Soviet intelligence services." Instead, Wolf was struck by the group's lack of Communist orthodoxy.

> I was interested in how these people of such varied backgrounds and political convictions dedicated themselves to resisting Hitler. . . . What was the source of their inner strength to swim against the tide and battle an omniscient and barbaric regime? Such issues of the moral and historical responsibilities of individuals were largely passed over in publications within the GDR.[39]

For the first two decades following the war, the West German debate over Greta's group was dominated by the question of treason. There were still unreformed militarists who were looking for ways that Germany could have won the war, regardless of the consequences for humanity. The East German government was more supportive of the indivdual survivors, but uncertain of the nature of the group. Immediately after the war, the names of Harro Schulze-Boysen, Arvid Harnack, and Adam Kuckhoff were unknown to the KPD leadership, who surmised that they were part of the 20th of July conspiracy.

The ground had begun to shift in the 1960s. Gilles Perrault's and Heinz Höhne's books coincided with new initiatives in Moscow and Berlin to claim ownership of the Rote Kapelle as a Communist Party initiative. The story of the Rote Kapelle had been absent from East German history books until 1969.

Suddenly, the group was in the limelight. Erich Mielke, the notorious chief of the Stasi, decided to promote the idea that his agency was inspired by the Rote Kapelle's service to Soviet intelligence. In late 1969 the Soviet regime showered honors on members of the group, including the posthumous presentation of the Order of the Red Banner, complete with the legend "Workers of the World Unite." (A Soviet official had to travel to West Germany to deliver it to Harro Schulze-Boysen's patrician parents.)

That same year, the East Germans mounted a major exhibit on Harro Schulze-Boysen, John Sieg, and Wilhelm Guddorf, emphasizing Sieg and Guddorf as members of the Communist Party, and passing over the majority of the group who were not. Erich Mielke compiled an archive of Rote Kapelle documents and interviews that produced a vast stream of East German books, articles, and exhibits, all part of a propaganda campaign to create the fiction of the "unbroken continuity of resistance led by the KPD." The archive itself was off-limits.

Greta was deeply disturbed by the East German exhibit. She acknowledged that Sieg had been an active member of the group, even if he had "too many irons in the fire." But Guddorf was a marginal figure at best, coming late to the leafleting activity and contributing little to their circle's actions. Her strongest memory of him involved his arguments with Harro, as he tried in vain to enforce KPD orthodoxy.

Greta appealed to the Party's Institute of Marxism-Leninism, which was responsible for historical reinterpretation, and informed it that the KPD had never recognized her group's work—in fact, her husband had tried to contact the party leadership and had never been honored with a reply. There were no possible grounds to suggest that the circle had been "under the direction of the Moscow leadership of the KPD."[40]

Greta told an East German interviewer that the exhibit "sickened" her. It treated her husband and herself as "peripheral figures," which hardly reflected their level of illegal activity.[41] She decided that the only remedy was to write her own book.

But her effort was rapidly overtaken by rival efforts. Heinz Höhne was working on a West German television series based on his book. (Its racy tone was suggested by the title of one of the episodes: "The Rote Kapelle: The Game Is Up.") The East Germans rushed to create their own film version, with the eminently forgettable title *KLK to PTX* (based on the Soviets' radio call signal). Greta was chagrined that the individuals in charge of the production didn't see fit to consult her. Not even the actress playing her in the film got in touch.[42]

Now, in 1971, Greta sat down with an East German publisher to discuss the completion of her book, with renewed motivation. "Life has become so bitterly hard," she said. "I find the Höhne book disgusting."[43]

But while Greta was determined to do battle with Höhne's book, the East German publishers had an entirely different purpose in mind. They wanted a book that would give the East German Communists the moral high ground over the Nazi period. They were telling the story of how the Central Committee of the KPD led a heroic twelve-year resistance against the fascists. The problem with Greta's account was that she would not compel her life to conform to the myth.

The East German publishing house was anything but independent. Controlled by the government through the Ministry of Culture, the Office for Literature included a desk of intelligence officers who operated out of the publishing division.[44]

At the outset, Greta wasn't above making demands. "If the New Life Publishers want to take a long time and use shoddy paper, I'll have to publish in West Germany," she informed them. This was probably an empty threat. But Greta's travails had just begun. The guardians of the state found her memories politically unacceptable.

Greta's editor objected to the tone of her manuscript, and fought her on it, line by line, over large political points and quibbling details. When Greta wrote that her father was a "musical instrument maker," her editor demanded to know why she was so pretentious. What was wrong with the proper Marxist term, "worker"?

The complaints went on and on. Greta refused to show proper deference to the Soviet Union and the German Communist Party. Why did Greta need to bring up "the destruction of the Trotskyite opposition in Russia"?

Why did she write with such warmth about her friends Hans Hartenstein and Adolf Grimme, both Social Democrats, while her treatment of Communists and the Party was always "critical" and "generalizing"?[45]

Greta was told to compensate for the utter lack of evidence that either her husband or Arvid Harnack had ever joined the Communist Party.

(The most they could say about Arvid was that he had "worked with Communists" before 1933.)[46]

German Communists had certainly been active in the resistance, but for the East Germans, this meant the denial of other resisters. Greta wrote that after her arrest, there were plans for "other large-scale resistance efforts, for example, that of the Officers." Her editor replied, "The Putsch of the 20th of July 1944 cannot be classified as a 'resistance effort.' "[47]

When Greta referred to the Baum Group as "Jewish Communists," her editor told her that the term "Jewish" was irrelevant. "They were engaged in a class struggle, not a race struggle." But Greta knew that while German Communists could elect to leave the party, Jews were not allowed a choice.

Her editor threw a tantrum when Greta wrote that the Nazis wanted a country "free of Jews, Communists, Gypsies, and above all, anyone with a little ability to think for himself."

"This is the terminology of fascism," her editor fumed. "It doesn't follow any political or party critique. The struggle wasn't about race, it was about class, and the big push was against the revolutionary working class and the KPD, not against those with the 'ability to think for themselves.' "

"Not about race" was the East Germans' way of stating that Greta had violated their historical judgment that the Jewish and Roma (Gypsy) Holocausts were negligible compared to the repression of the KPD.

When Greta criticized the Communists' wavering policies over the 1930s, her editors responded that her "understanding of the KPD policies toward the creation of worker unity and the German popular front is only presented from the standpoint of negative memories and a pessimistic evaluation of the correct strategic line of the KPD."

In mind-numbing party prose, her editor informed his superiors that the woman clearly needed to be taken in hand:

Her narrow subjectivity, through the manifold personal experiences and fixed personal opinions that mark the profile of this author, require the objectification of this book in every term that is demanded by Party literature in the Leninist sense.

Greta was unwilling to have the central drama of her life "objectified in the Leninist sense." However, this was the condition for publication. In his general comments, her editor reported, "Throughout this whole manuscript, there is an ongoing indirect polemic against the circles of the KPD that were supposedly 'hostile to intellectuals.' " Greta dared to suggest, he wrote, that these KPD militants feared that intellectuals like her and her friends would "seek to be independent (and therefore dangerous!)."[48]

At the heart of the dispute was the regime's effort to fabricate a history of unified resistance, led by the Central Committee of the KPD. Time after time, Greta's matter-of-fact account undermined the falsehood.

Greta wrote of her group's interest in the analyses of the KPD's *Auslandsleitung,* or "leadership abroad," which included the outposts in Paris, Prague, and Amsterdam. Her editor took her to task, insisting that she change the reference to the "ZK," or the Moscow-based Central Committee.

The disagreement over the role of the KPD's Central Committee had deep implications. During the 1930s, Stalin eliminated independent-minded members of the Central Committee and replaced them with his minions. He also targeted many of the leaders in exile in Prague, Paris, and Amsterdam. Stalin went on to murder hundreds of German Communists and deliver hundreds more into the hands of the Gestapo.

These murders occurred over the same period that Greta and her group were seeking new ways to oppose the Nazis: by helping Jews, recruiting diverse new members, and lobbying the United States. (At the same time, they were trying and failing to make contact with German Communist Party leadership outside the country.)

Nonetheless, the problem, according to the East German editor, was that Greta didn't offer "appropriate representation of the struggle of the Party organizations, the leadership status of the Central Committee of the KPD, and the historic place of the Schulze-Boysen/Harnack Organization within the overall antifascist struggle in Germany."

Greta had reasons to omit the Central Committee. Over the years, it had blindly followed Stalin's instructions to help the Nazis bring down the Weimar Republic, and gone along with the German-Soviet Nonaggression Pact of 1939. Greta, along with countless other German antifascists, had suffered the direct consequences of Stalin's attack on the German left and the fractured response to the Nazis' consolidation of power. Why should she prettify the forces that had devastated her life?

Greta battled with her editor over the changes. There were reports of hours of heated arguments, and one acrimonious exchange between her and her editor came to thirty pages. Greta won ground on some points, and lost on others. There is evidence of the text she was obliged to change, but there is no way to measure the extent of her self-censorship.

Every round reminded her that, as far as the regime was concerned, the purpose of her life story was to manufacture a myth. There was no monolithic block of resisters following a strategy dictated by the KPD Central Committee. This fantasy of the East Germans and the Soviets was built on the paranoid mythology of the Gestapo. The reality was far messier—but also more compelling. The German resistance consisted of many fragmented groups—including Greta and her friends, the KPD circles, and the 20th of July movement—who undertook many activities, sometimes overlapping, sometimes at cross purposes.

Greta's book, *Vom Rosenkranz zur Roten Kapelle: Ein Lebensbericht* (*From Rosary to Red Orchestra: A Life Story*), was only a partial victory. Her memoirs were published in 1972, in time for her seventieth birthday. They suggested the path of her life, but left many telling details in the shadows of censorship.

The East Germans covered Greta with prizes, and over the following years she would be invited to a host of naming ceremonies for their newly rediscovered martyrs. Adam Kuckhoff was honored with a traffic circle in Berlin. Mildred Harnack had a high school named after her in the Berlin district of Lichtenberg. John Sieg's name was attached to a technical school in the bomb-blasted neighborhood of Friedrichshain, not far from Neukölln. As a final irony, Sieg, who had been tortured for days by the Gestapo before ending his own life, was memorialized on a medal bestowed by the Stasi, East Germany's own secret police.

Greta's book remains a conundrum. As the warring voices sound within its pages, the reader must guess which passages correspond to Greta's editorial minder and which represent the thoughts of the woman herself. Read closely, Greta's book still suggests the outlines of an extra-ordinary life, devoted to her ideals, her family, and her friends. It begins with the shy young student en route to her great adventure in Wisconsin, and follows her saga until she sinks beneath the weight of her unimaginable history.

Greta Kuckhoff died on November 11, 1981, at the age of seventy-nine. The orphans of the Rote Kapelle remembered her as a woman of caring dignity and rectitude, who offered support and sustenance, but also expressed stern disapproval at their lapses. Despite his privileged upbringing, her own son, Ule, never managed to make much of himself. He committed suicide at the age of fifty-one in 1989—the year the Berlin Wall came down and East Germany ceased to exist.

Fortunately, Greta's mangled autobiography is not the only record of her voice. Another, clearer version had emerged in an earlier piece of writing. In 1947, Greta wrote an essay describing her reaction to a celebrated novel called *The Seventh Cross,* the tale of a Communist who escapes from a concentration camp in the 1930s. The novelist, Anna Seghers, was a Jewish Communist who escaped the Nazis and wrote her book in Mexico, based on interviews with recent émigrés. The novel became an international best-seller, and Spencer Tracy starred in a popular movie version in the United States.*

Seghers described the lives of ordinary Germans living under the Nazi regime, including some who risked their lives to help the prisoner. But Greta's response to the book bordered on anger. It raised the wrong questions, she said. Greta was not interested in taking credit for the actions she and her friends performed out of conviction, but she wanted to know what everyone else was doing at the time:

> Wasn't the situation such that, at least after 1945, it had to be made clear to readers that they too ought to have taken part in the struggle—there would have been fewer victims. It seemed to me—and still does—that in a book about this time every citizen must be challenged, so that he will finally see clearly it wasn't a question of the victims, it was a matter of clever, well-thought-out *deeds.* A little less fear, a little more love of life in a few hundred thousand

---

* Hollywood altered Seghers's Communist character's affiliations.

and the war wouldn't have been possible or would have been over sooner.

Sympathy for the fighters without victory only has meaning if it strikes like a bolt of insight to people who until then had been in-different or hardened: This is your concern—it ought to have concerned you then. Don't evade the issue! You don't need to feel sorry, sympathy is evasion. It is soothing, it allows one to speak an *ego te absolvo* over the evil deed one did oneself or at least allowed to happen, an absolution through which nothing is basically changed.[49]

Greta recognized that dramatic social change, for good or for ill, is often achieved by passionate minorities. Whether they succeed or not depends on whether they reach a critical mass. Greta had no time for the idle moralizing of those who waited out the regime in silence, safety, or exile. She didn't distinguish between Communist or Socialist, Catholic or Jew. For her, the world was divided into two categories: those who took action, and those who did not.

To Those Born After

THE EXECUTION SHED AT PLÖTZENSEE STILL STANDS, CONVERTED into a memorial. The guillotine has been removed, but the meat hooks still hang across the beam. The Gestapo headquarters at Prinz-Albrecht-Strasse were damaged in the war and razed soon after. The outlines of the basement interrogation cells were long visible, and their retaining walls displayed an exhibit about the prisoners who were held there, including the Harnacks, the Kuckhoffs, and their friends. It is now home to a permanent memorial.

The Bendler Block hosts a different kind of memorial. The military headquarters where the 20th of July conspiracy was launched now houses the Gedenkstätte Deutscher Widerstand (German Resistance Memorial), a massive archive commemorating the various forms of German resistance, including the Rote Kapelle. It is a daunting display of specialized scholarship, almost entirely in German, and unknown to most foreign visitors.

The Air Ministry where Harro Schulze-Boysen worked somehow escaped destruction. It now serves as the German Finance Ministry. After the war, a quote from Harro's poem (recovered by Günther Weisenborn from his cell) was carved over a bull's-eye window on an upper story:

Wenn wir auch sterben sollen
So wissen wir: Die Saat

Geht auf. Wenn Köpfe rollen, dann
Zwingt doch der Geist den Staat.

"Glaubt mit mir an die gerechte Zeit, die alles reifen lässt."

Even if we should die,
We know this much: The seed
continues to sprout. Heads may roll, but
the Spirit still masters the State.

"Believe with me in the just time that will allow all to
ripen."

Most of the survivors of the Berlin circle went on to lead productive lives. Besides Greta Kuckhoff, Günther Weisenborn, and Adolf Grimme, they included Dr. Elfriede Paul, Sophie Sieg, and Helmut Roloff. Dr. Paul served a Nazi prison sentence until the end of the war, and returned to practice medicine in East Germany. Sophie Sieg, liberated from Ravensbrück concentration camp by the Red Army in April 1945, returned to Neukölln and became a local Communist health official. The party wheeled out the tiny, bespectacled old lady many times over the years for ceremonies to commemorate her husband. She died in 1987, two years before the Berlin Wall came down.

Helmut Roloff, the young pianist, was saved by his friend, the dentist Helmut Himpel, who convinced the Gestapo that Roloff had no idea what was in the locked suitcase. Roloff was released after a few months' questioning. He became a noted concert pianist and music educator in West Berlin, and died in 2001. Herbert and Ingeborg Engelsing survived the war, but their marriage did not. Ingeborg moved to California, where she remarried, wrote her memoirs, and earned a doctorate in German literature. She died in Carmel in 2007.

The postwar years also brought many hardships. One of them was a rash of suicides among Germans who could not come to terms with the past. Stella Mahlberg, Harro Schulze-Boysen's lover toward the end of his life, killed herself in 1947, reportedly at a time she was undergoing

American interrogations.[1] Gustaf Gründgens, the leftist actor who made a devil's pact with the Nazis, took an overdose of sleeping pills in 1969.

The postwar period held no joy for many of the Soviets' wartime field operatives. In contrast to the amateurs in Berlin, the figure in the Rote Kapelle file who came closest to the technical definition of a professional Soviet spy was Leopold Trepper. He survived the war as a result of the German intelligence effort to broadcast disinformation back to the Soviets. After 1945, Trepper returned to Moscow, where Stalin incarcerated him in the infamous Lubyanka Prison for a decade. He was finally released and went back to Poland, but then fled the country in reaction to Polish anti-Semitism. He died in Jerusalem in 1982.[2]

A similar fate awaited Trepper's colleague Anatoli Gourevitch, who as the agent "Kent" had visited the Kuckhoffs and the Schulze-Boysens in Berlin. Gourevitch survived the war in custody, another beneficiary of the Germans' disinformation campaign against Moscow. At the end of the war he flew back to Russia and was taken straight to Lubyanka. After sixteen months of interrogation, the Soviets sentenced him to twenty years in a gulag. He was released in a general amnesty in 1955.[3]

The other true intelligence professional in the Rote Kapelle saga was Alexander Korotkov, the Soviet agent who recruited Arvid Harnack in Berlin. He fared better than his colleagues, escaping Stalin's purges to acquire the position of KGB resident in Soviet-occupied Berlin. Markus Wolf once overheard him reminiscing with KGB colleagues about their experiences repressing the 1956 Hungarian revolt. In 1961, Korotkov died of a heart attack as he played tennis in Moscow; he was fifty-one.

The scholars, authors, and artists of the Rote Kapelle left a remarkable literary and artistic legacy, but few of their works are currently in print. This holds true even for Günther Weisenborn, whose early book on the German resistance is widely cited by scholars, and whose play about the underground was an important marker of postwar culture.

One literary critic recently wrote,

> Today Weisenborn is virtually unknown; few of his plays have been performed since his death on 26 March 1969, and his novels have practically disappeared. He was not an experimental playwright and did not use nontraditional dramatic techniques. It is

likely that his plays will be viewed primarily as documents of the inanities and horrors of Nazism.[4]

This suggests that chronicling the "inanities and horrors of Nazism" is not a worthwhile pursuit. But Weisenborn's writing offers a firsthand glimpse into the inner workings of fascism and resistance that exiled writers could only imagine.

Members of the resistance circles, both executed and surviving, left a number of children, and they have produced books of their own. Hans Coppi was the son of Hans and Hilde Coppi. Both of his parents were executed within a year of his birth. He grew up in East Germany and was trained as an engineer, but over time he developed an avid interest in the story of his parents and their organization and became a noted scholar in the field. After German reunification he joined Professor Johannes Tuchel, director of the German Resistance Memorial, to collect, codify, and publish scholarship about the group.

The surviving documentation had been scattered across half the globe, in East and West Germany, Russia, and the United States. It took the end of the cold war to allow historians to begin to create a unified narrative. Coppi and Tuchel have done more than anyone else to assemble historical research about the group and to reverse the long history of cold war distortions and misconceptions.

In 2000, journalist Shareen Brysac published a book about Mildred Harnack, *Resisting Hitler,* based on extensive interviews and research into American and Soviet files. Brysac presented extensive evidence of Arvid Harnack's intelligence work for the Americans as well as the Soviets, casting his antifascist activities in a different light. It is clear that a great deal of documentation remains to be discovered, whether in private American collections, German attics, or in the depths of the Kremlin's files.

Artist Stefan Roloff is the son of classical pianist Helmut Roloff, who provided assistance to Helmut Himpel, Marie Terwiel, and their associates. Over 2002 and 2003 he released a documentary and a book about his father and his associates, drawing on interviews with his father and other survivors as well as his own innovative cinematic techniques. His was the first comprehensive approach to the subject of the Rote Kapelle and the postwar aftermath. He conducted exhaustive archival research about the Gestapo interrogations, the irregular legal proceedings, and the subsequent American investigations.

The name of Libertas Schulze-Boysen has been carried on in an unlikely fashion. At the time she was arrested, Libertas was hoping to find refuge with her sister Ottora, who was married to Count Carl Ludwig Douglas in Sweden. The year after Libertas was executed, the couple gave birth to a daughter, who became Libertas's namesake. Dagmar Rosita Astri Libertas Douglas grew up to become the British Duchess of Marlborough. As Rosita Marlborough, she has continued the family's artistic tradition as an accomplished painter who exhibits in London and New York.

Harro Schulze-Boysen's memory has been cherished by his younger brother Hartmut, who became a highly regarded diplomat in the German foreign service and served as the German consul in New York. He always took pride in his brother's courage, regardless of passing political currents in Germany.

If history is written by victors, fame tends to accrue to those who succeed rather than those who attempt the impossible. Bertolt Brecht, raging against the Nazis in exile, wrote a poem asking for the understanding of future generations, asking them to resist passing judgment on others' efforts if they have not shared their circumstances. His words could serve as an epitaph for Greta Kuckhoff and her friends.

> Our forces were few. The goal lay far in the distance.
> It was clearly visible, though I probably wouldn't reach it myself.
> So went the time I was granted on earth.
>
> You, who will emerge from the flood that submerged us,
> Also remember, when you speak of our weaknesses,
> The dark times that you have been spared.[5]

The last known surviving participant of the Berlin circle is Katja Casella. As a twenty-year-old art student, she joined her best friend Lisa Egler-Gervai in supporting the group. The two pretty students served as couriers and sheltered fugitives, learning not to ask questions along the way. They were among the Jewish participants in resistance activities that enlisted Lutherans, Catholics, Communists, Socialists, Conservatives, and artists without political portfolio, to work against a common enemy.

Katja narrowly escaped arrest by fleeing to Poland. After the war, she was reunited with her fiancé, Karl Meirowsky, and the two were married. A few years later, Katja organized a "surrealistic cabaret" in Berlin called *Die Badewanne* (*The Bathtub*), an entertainment that combined modernist performance art with fierce social satire. The sketches skewered craven Nazi-era officials and depicted death by guillotine and suicide. They climaxed with harsh lights shone into the faces of the audiences, as the performers demanded to know who among them was a Nazi.

Eventually Katja and Karl tired of confrontation and withdrew to the Spanish island of Ibiza. There she painted picture after picture: large, glowing canvases of abstract designs, haunting portraits of faces suffused with sorrow and light.

Sixty-five years after the Gestapo swept through the streets of Berlin making its arrests, Katja was still welcoming visitors to her modest home in a northern suburb. The painter was in her late eighties and nearly blind, but she was still vibrant and beautiful, with a bright gaze and a strong, throaty laugh. Her paintings now lined the walls of her house, some of them echoing the influence of her teacher, Marc Chagall. Every aspect of her life reflected the essence of the Rote Kapelle that ideological historians could never capture: the free spirit that reacts to injury and outrage by choosing to take action, whatever the risk.

Katja had known years of happiness married to the love of her life. After Karl's death, she stayed on in Ibiza, returning to Germany only when her medical condition made it necessary. She lived quietly in Berlin, uncertain whether the Nazis were really gone. But in trusted company, she wanted to talk about old times. She recalled every detail of her first encounter with the Rote Kapelle, that terrible day when she was crushed by the deportation of Karl's mother and sister. She remembered the women gathered quietly in the drawing room, the Bach chaconne on the gramophone, Cato sitting with her on the sofa.

And then the tall young Luftwaffe lieutenant, with a head like a greyhound, came and folded her in his arms, saying, "This barbarity has to stop. We all have to work together to stop that devil." With those words, Harro Schulze-Boysen transformed her from a victim to a resister.

Acknowledgments

\ \ \

THIS BOOK BENEFITED FROM THE GENEROSITY OF MANY PEOPLE. I begin with special thanks to my former students from Germany. Nicola Liebert tutored me in German, introduced me to Rilke, and taught me much about German history and culture. Kirsten Grieshaber did literary battle with the East German edition of Greta Kuckhoff's memoirs, and has offered me frequent encouragement along the way. Deborah Steinborn has been of immense help, offering the gifts of a close reading, a haven in Hamburg, and stolen hours with little Charlotte to cheer me on.

Others have provided timely assistance with translations. Heidi Philipsen read and assessed the novels of Adam Kuckhoff. Margit Rustow shared her recollections of the period and deciphered letters in vexing old German script. Amelie Wilmanns provided wonderfully helpful research assistance in Berlin. Bernard Pötter and his family welcomed us to Kreuzberg and befriended us in countless ways. I owe much to Erika Hall, along with her peerless mother and daughter. Erika's wartime memories informed my feel for daily life in Nazi Germany, and she also offered close readings of crucial literary works and reviewed translations.

Stefan Roloff belongs in a category by himself. I hope his book, *Rote Kapelle*, finds the audience it deserves in the United States. His companion documentary, *The Red Orchestra*, brings the resistance experience to life as no other medium can. I look forward to his next book and documentary project on Katja Casella Meirowsky and the theme of survivors. Stefan has been fearless in challenging outdated notions and flawed conventions, and infinitely generous in providing me with his expert analysis, research materials, and friendship. His mother, Inge Roloff, offered me a welcome refuge in Zehlendorf along with her musical artistry and many wise insights. I only wish I could have met Helmut Roloff as well.

Professor Volker Berghahn was uncommonly gracious in reading an early draft of the manuscript and shedding light on the vagaries of German history in our conversations. I appreciate Peter Hoffman's seminal scholarship and the time he took to discuss it with me. Hans Coppi shared his encyclopedic knowledge of the Rote Kapelle, and guided me through the formidable archives at the Gedenkstätte Deutscher Widerstand in Berlin. I also benefited from Johannes Tuchel's excellent scholarship and manifold insights. Rainer von Harnack offered many personal recollections of his extraordinary relation, Falk Harnack, as well as a priceless trove of family papers. I was inspired by a talk by Hartmut Schulze-Boysen some years ago, and admire his courage and his constancy to his brother's legacy.

It was humbling to interview the children of members of the Rote Kapelle, most of whom suffered the loss of one or both parents. Their sacrifices were exacted without their consent, but their parents surely acted out of love for them. Saskia von Brockdorff and Karin Graudenz were among those who kindly received me and answered my questions.

I am grateful beyond words for the chance to meet Katja Meirowsky, the last known survivor of the Rote Kapelle, who was located by Stefan Roloff. She is a true force of nature and a formidable painter. I hope that this book can contribute to a major revival of interest in her story and her art.

These individuals have informed my opinions and corrected many of my errors, but they cannot be held responsible for the mistakes that remain. These must be considered my own.

I have been very fortunate in my friends. Cornelia Bessie and her late husband Michael offered me much-needed advice and support from the beginning. Cornelia has been a touchstone for me regarding both the craft of writing and the mysteries of Germany. I was also grateful for the encouragement of my Columbia colleagues Seymour Topping and Kenneth Jackson. The work of Aryeh Neier sparked many of the questions explored in this book. Many other friends, including Jane Owen, Marge Sorensen, and Kevin O'Kane, have helped to keep my faith alive through their interest.

I offer my sincere thanks to representatives of the German consulate in New York, who have been helpful beyond the call of duty, and exemplary in every regard. I also thank my colleagues in the human rights community, including Human Rights Watch and the Committee to Protect Journalists. This book was born of a human rights perspective, and they helped me conceive a new framework for these historical events.

Much of this book is based on documentation that has only begun to come to light. My subject matter will be affected by material that will emerge at a later date. These are hazards of the profession, and I only hope that those who come after will recognize my good-faith effort in making sense of this complicated tale with the material I could find.

I thank my agent, Heather Schroder at ICM, and editor Kate Medina at Random House, who believed in this book from the start. Random House's Jonathan Jao improved the manuscript with his excellent notes.

This book would not have been possible without the research compiled by the Gedenkstätte Deutscher Widerstand, a remarkable institution. I hope more Americans will explore it when they visit Berlin. The Butler Library at Columbia and the New York Public Library also offered valuable materials. The McCloy Fellowship fueled my research at a crucial juncture, and the Guggenheim Fellowship supported a long and particularly thorny passage of the work. I offer my sincere thanks to the foundations, founders, and staff.

I am grateful to my family for living with me and this project over these many years. My parents—together with the countless uncles and aunts, cousins and in-laws who lived through the period—gave me a nearly insatiable interest in everything related to World War II. David and Julia have been good sports, exploring the haunts of Berlin and tolerating my conversion of the family room into a German resistance archive.

My greatest thanks go to George Black. I was immeasurably fortunate to profit from his counsel as a writer and his acumen as an editor throughout this arduous process. His assistance with translations has been indispensable. He has generously served as sounding board, critic, and companion every step of the way, from the Görlitzer Bahnhof to our own private Erwin Geschonnek film festival. Whatever is good in this book owes a large debt to him.

Notes

\ \ \

Chapter 1: **GRETA GOES TO AMERIKA**

1. Greta Kuckhoff, *Vom Rosenkranz zur Roten Kapelle*, p. 25.
2. Ibid., p. 37.
3. Ibid., p. 23.
4. V. R. Berghahn, *Modern Germany*, p. 71.
5. Otto Friedrich, *Before the Deluge*, p. 52.
6. Germany had stabilized its currency the previous year. Greta's 500 marks were now worth about US $110.
7. Kuckhoff, *Vom Rosenkranz zur Roten Kapelle*, p. 45.
8. Shareen Brysac, *Resisting Hitler*, p. 51.
9. Kuckhoff, *Vom Rosenkranz zur Roten Kapelle*, p. 83.
10. Ibid., p. 88.
11. Hans Coppi, Jürgen Danyel, and Johannes Tuchel, eds., *Die Rote Kapelle im Widerstand*, p. 97.

Chapter 2: **GRETA AND ADAM**

1. Greta Kuckhoff, *Vom Rosenkranz zur Roten Kapelle*, pp. 96, 93.
2. Ibid., p. 94.
3. Germans were deeply resentful of the French demands, but the French had not forgotten the punitive reparations Germany had exacted after the Franco-Prussian War in 1871, nor the devastation of the recent war.
4. Otto Friedrich, *Before the Deluge*, p. 174.
5. Ibid., p. 301.
6. Kuckhoff, *Vom Rosenkranz zur Roten Kapelle*, p. 98.
7. Ibid., p. 99.
8. Jessner was usually mentioned in the same breath as his principal rivals: Max Reinhardt, the genius behind the Deutsches Theater, and Erwin Piscator, who dominated Berlin's Volksbühne popular theater, bringing avant-garde theater to

factory workers and slum dwellers. Between them, these three giants revolutionized Western theater.

9. The position of dramaturge originated in eighteenth-century Germany, and only gained currency in U.S. theaters in the late twentieth century.

10. Kuckhoff, *Vom Rosenkranz zur Roten Kapelle*, p. 100.

11. Adam Kuckhoff, "Arbeiter und film," from *Fröhlich Bestehn*, p. 106.

12. Friedrich Schiller, *Wilhelm Tell*, Act II, Scene ii.

13. David Eggenberger, *An Encyclopedia of Battles*, pp. 7–8.

14. Otto Rudolf, *Memoirs*, Cologne Zentralarchiv für Kriegstheater.

15. Dieter Götze, online article "Ein Idealist der Linken: Adam Kuckhoff."

16. Details on Kuckhoff's editorship of *Die Tat* from www.luise-berlin.de, and table of contents of journal.

17. It later turned out that Diederichs was in the final months of a fatal illness.

18. Note: This is the chronology provided by Regina Griebel, Marlies Coburger, and Heinrich Scheel in *Erfasst?*, which coincides with the dates in Greta Kuckhoff's *Vum Rosenkranz zur Rotin Kapelle*. Other sources place Adam at the theater a year later.

19. Tony Meech, "Brecht's Early Plays," *Cambridge Companion to Brecht*, p. 49.

20. Ilse Brauer and Werner Kayser, *Günther Weisenborn*, p. 68; "Günther Weisenborn," Viktoria Hertling, *Dictionary of Literary Biography*.

21. See Meech, *Cambridge Companion to Brecht*, p. xix. Early editions of the play included credit for Weisenborn's contribution, sometimes as coauthor, sometimes as dramaturge. Few modern editions of the play acknowledge Weisenborn's contribution; Brecht was known for rallying collaborators to his projects, then claiming sole authorship of the results. See the introduction to *The Mother* by Bertolt Brecht, translated by Lee Baxandall. Weisenborn's earlier version had been coauthored by Volksbühne dramaturge Günther Starki. Other collaborators on the Brecht project were composer Hanns Eisler and director Slatan Dudow.

22. Martin Esslin, *Brecht: The Man and His Work*, p. 48.

23. Neher missed the opening night in order to tend her husband on his deathbed, but she was cast in the film version and Brecht used her picture on the cover of the published work.

24. The play is also known as *Luise Millerin*. It was the basis for the Verdi opera of the same title.

25. Curt Trepte and Jutta Wardestzky, *Hans Otto*. See illustration following p. 80.

26. Ibid., p. 20.

27. Ibid., p. 19.

28. Ibid., following p. 80.

29. Hans Otto, reproduced in ibid., insert following p. 88.

30. In 1932 the Soviet Communist Party decreed that "Socialist Realism" would now be the only acceptable aesthetic. Soviet theater became literalistic and pedantic, and the Communist modernists in Berlin found themselves in disgrace. Avant-garde dramatists such as Brecht had come to Communism as a form of rebellion, only to be met by Soviet philistines demanding their own brand of orthodoxy. This paradox would continue to dog Communist artists throughout the twentieth century.

31. Greta Kuckhoff, *Adam Kuckhoff zum Gedenken*, p. 11.

32. Kuckhoff, *Vom Rosenkranz zur Rote Kapelle*, p. 102.

Chapter 3: **BERLIN**

1. Mildred Fish to mother, October 18, 1930, Gedenkstätte Deutscher Widerstand (hereafter cited as GDW) archive.
2. Shareen Brysac, *Resisting Hitler*, pp. 82–87.
3. Mildred Fish to mother, October 18, 1930, GDW archive. That night Mildred saw a play called *The Caucasian Chalk Circle* by the young consumptive poet who wrote under the name Klabund. He had died an early death two years before. His wife, Carola Neher, missed playing her lead role in the original cast of *Threepenny Opera* to be at his deathbed. Klabund's play was first produced in 1925 by Max Reinhardt at the Deutsches Theater, with Brecht serving as dramaturge, and Brecht wrote his own version after the war.
4. Mildred Fish to mother, November 27, 1930, GDW archive. One of the lecturers was the editor of *The Nation* magazine, visiting from New York, who updated Mildred on the unemployment crisis in the United States. See Brysac, *Resisting Hitler*, p. 96.
5. Brysac, *Resisting Hitler*, p. 96.
6. Germany's total was 562,612, compared to only 51,000 in all of France and 46,000 in England. Gordon A. Craig, "Berlin, the Hauptstadt," *Foreign Affairs,* July/August 1998, p. 164.
7. David Clay Large, *Berlin*, p. 25.
8. Ibid., p. 26.
9. Over the 1920s Germany published some 7,000 periodicals, over 4,000 daily and weekly newspapers, and 30,000 book titles a year. Oron J. Hale, *The Captive Press in the Third Reich*, pp. 1, 143.
10. Ibid., p. 4.
11. Ibid., p. 3.
12. Now the Polish cities of Cztuchów and Walcz.
13. John Sieg, *Einer von Millionen Spricht*, p. 8.
14. A decade later Halfeld was known as a Nazi writer, and published screeds of anti-Semitic prose.
15. Sieg, *Einer von Millionen Spricht*, p. 20.
16. Ibid., insert following p. 64.
17. *Protokoll des Genossen Hermann Grosse*, September 29, 1967, GDW archive.
18. "Nebel" means "fog."
19. Heinrich Scheel, introduction to Sieg, *Einer von Millionen Spricht*, p. 9.
20. In January 1924, the month of Lenin's death, Stalin asked to meet privately with German Communist representatives in Moscow, ferreting out information about the German party structure and the best means to control it. Alan Bullock, *Hitler and Stalin*, quoting Ruth Fischer, p. 194.
21. Ibid., p. 206.
22. Ibid., p. 426.

Chapter 4: **THE MASSES AND THE MEDIA**

1. Greta Kuckhoff, *Vom Rosenkranz zur Rote Kapelle*, p. 105.
2. Ibid.
3. Leuppi's "Untitled," 1933.

4. Kuckhoff, *Vom Rosenkrantz zur Rote Kapelle*, p. 105.
5. Ibid., p. 114.
6. The Social Democrats had moved their government temporarily to the provincial city of Weimar after World War I, seeking to avoid Berlin's civil unrest.
7. Mildred Fish to mother, October 29, 1931, GDW archive.
8. Mildred Fish to mother, December 29, 1928, GDW archive.
9. Mildred Fish to mother, February 1, 1930, GDW archive.
10. Mildred Fish to mother, October 18, 1930, GDW archive.
11. Alexandra Richie, *Faust's Metropolis*, p. 349. The trajectory of Berlin's political satire was reflected in the career of composer Friedrich Holländer. In 1926 he could afford to mock the political system by having a comic feminist proclaim: "Throw all the men out of the Reichstag . . . they're blinded by their vanity. . . . They're flushing the whole country down the toilet." In 1931, riding on the success of his songs for Marlene Dietrich, Holländer opened a nightclub called the Tingeltangel. By this time much of the repertory was devoted to attacking the Nazis. One ditty about Hitler included the refrain: "Liar! Liar! Liar! Liar!" Holländer fled the country in 1933. See http://www.cbs.com/specials/rise_of_evil/cast/hollander.shtml.
12. Peter Fritzche, *Germans into Nazis*, p. 150.
13. Ibid., p. 133.
14. Ibid., p. 189.
15. Detlef Mühlberger, *The Social Bases of Nazism, 1919–1933* (2003), p. 46. See also Fritzche, *Germans into Nazis*, p. 188.
16. Fritzche, *Germans into Nazis*, p. 157.
17. Russel Lemmons, *Goebbels and Der Angriff*, p. 36.
18. William Shirer, *The Rise and Fall of the Third Reich*, pp. 180–182.
19. This can be clearly observed in two pre-1933 Nazi campaign posters. A 1932 election poster shows a large cross with a swastika at the center, publicizing the Nazi "martyrs" who have fallen in street battles. Another pre-1933 poster shows an angelic figure resembling St. George poised beside a Nazi, thrusting a sword into a dragon labeled with the abbreviations of the Communist and the Social Democratic parties. See http://www.calvin.edu/academic/cas/gpa/posters1.htm.
20. The manuscript had languished for eight years before it was finally released in 1929—by Eher Verlag, the Nazi publishing house.
21. Lemmons, *Goebbels and Der Angriff*, p. 37.
22. The term, borrowed from electrical engineering, referred to the process of wiring a generator to make a connected motor run at the same speed.
23. Jan-Christopher Horak, "Prometheus Film Collective."
24. Goebbels Diary, October 10, 1939. Quoted in Michael H. Kater, "Jazz in the Third Reich," *American Historical Review* 94, no. 1, February 1989, p. 31.

Chapter 5: THINGS FALL APART

1. Quoted in Shareen Brysac, *Resisting Hitler*, p. 110.
2. Jonathan Wright, *Gustav Stresemann: Weimar's Greatest Statesman*, p. 211.
3. Regina Griebel, Marlies Coburger, and Heinrich Scheel, *Erfasst?*, p. 72.
4. Brysac, *Resisting Hitler*, p. 107.
5. Ibid., pp. 107–119.
6. Ibid., p. 110. See also Wolfgang Schivelbusch, *The Culture of Defeat*, p. 307. The

new director, Friedrich Schönemann, called Walt Whitman, a favorite poet of Mildred's, one of the northern "loser intellectuals" because he mourned the human cost of the Civil War.

7. Brysac, *Resisting Hitler*, pp. 110–111.
8. Ibid., p. 117; Griebel, Coburger, and Scheel, *Erfasst?*, p. 60.
9. Named after an early practitioner, Grigori Potemkin, a courtier of Catherine the Great.
10. Brysac, *Resisting Hitler*, p. 117.
11. Ibid., p. 123.
12. Martin Kitchen, *Cambridge Illustrated History of Germany*, p. 253.
13. Richard Evans, *The Coming of the Third Reich*, p. 317.
14. Roderick Stackelberg et al., *The Nazi Germany Sourcebook: An Anthology of Texts*, pp. 130–132.
15. The question of responsibility is still debated.
16. The Reichsbanner was a militant mass organization supported by the Social Democrats.
17. Quoted in Evans, *The Coming of the Third Reich*, pp. 330–331.
18. Ibid., p. 331.
19. William Shirer, *The Rise and Fall of the Third Reich*, p. 195.
20. Brysac, *Resisting Hitler*, p. 128.
21. Evans, *The Coming of the Third Reich*, p. 357.
22. Mildred Fish to mother, May 2, 1933, GDW archive.
23. Evans, *The Coming of the Third Reich*, p. 357.

Chapter 6: THE TAKEOVER

1. Max Reinhardt died in New York in 1943. Jessner died in Los Angeles in 1945. Piscator died in West Germany in 1966.
2. Ilse Brauer and Werner Kayser, *Günther Weisenborn*, p. 68. Weisenborn's coauthor, Dadaist Richard Hülsenbeck, fled to Prague the next day, and reinvented himself as "Charles Hubeck," a noted New York psychoanalyst.
3. Eric Johnson, *Nazi Terror: The Gestapo, Jews, and Ordinary Germans*, p. 162.
4. Ibid., p. 534.
5. Ibid., p. 162.
6. Lion Feuchtwanger, *The Oppermanns*, p. 279.
7. Shareen Brysac, *Resisting Hitler*, p. 128.
8. February 26, [1928?] GDW archive.
9. Brysac, *Resisting Hitler*, p. 111.
10. Mildred Fish to mother, August 7, 1934, GDW archive.
11. Brysac, *Resisting Hitler*, p. 126. Massing later emigrated to the United States and taught at Columbia and Rutgers, before returning to Germany after the war.
12. Greta Kuckhoff, *Vom Rosenkranz zur Rote Kapelle*, p. 117.
13. Ibid., p. 120.
14. Mannheim fled to Britain, where he became a leading scholar at the London School of Economics.
15. Kuckhoff, *Vom Rosenkranz zur Rote Kapelle*, pp. 120–121.
16. Regina Griebel, Marlies Coburger, and Heinrich Scheel, *Erfasst?*, p. 72.
17. Mordecai Paldiel, *The Path of the Righteous: Gentile Rescuers of Jews During the Holocaust*, pp. 170–173. In 1967 the Yad Vashem Holocaust Martyrs' and Heroes'

Remembrance Authority recognized Wegner (like Oskar Schindler) as "Righteous Among the Nations." See also www.yadvashem.org/righteous/index_righteous .html.

18. The most detailed account of Sieg's experience in Berlin was published by his friend Heinrich Scheel after the war (by an East German publishing house).

19. *The Guardian,* March 16, 1933.

20. Reinhard Rürup, *Topography of Terror,* p. 93; John Sieg, *Einer von Millionen Spricht,* p. 10. Haubach, who was repeatedly arrested and sent to a concentration camp for anti-Nazi activities, was hung at Plötzensee in January 1945.

21. Interview with Hermann Grosse, GDW archive, p. 3.

22. Sieg, John, *Einer von Millionen Spricht,* p. 10. Karl Ernst was murdered by his fellow Nazis in 1934, during "The Night of the Long Knives."

23. Goebbels's quotes and material on radio from David Welch, *The Third Reich: Politics and Propaganda,* pp. 38–39.

24. As reported in the *Völkischer Beobachter,* May 12, 1933. This quote and the following material about book burning are taken from http://dizzy.library .arizona.edu/images/burnedbooks/goebbels.htm.

25. Robert Gellately, *Backing Hitler,* p. 21.

26. Ibid., pp. 58–59.

27. See United States Holocaust Memorial Museum, http://www.ushmm.org/ wlc/article.php?lang=en&ModuleId=10005263, Oranienburg film footage.

28. Gellately, *Backing Hitler,* p. 59.

29. Albert Speer, *Spandau: The Secret Diaries,* p. 261.

30. Ibid., p. 103.

31. Ibid.

32. Curt Trepte and Jutta Wardetzky, *Hans Otto: Schauspieler und Revolutionär,* p. 131.

33. Quoted in ibid., p. 68.

34. Ibid., reproduced after p. 88.

35. Bergner pursued her career in London, Reinhardt in Hollywood and New York, with mixed results. They never recovered the success they enjoyed in Weimar Germany.

36. Klaus Mann, *Mephisto,* pp. 238ff. A 1981 film version of the novel won an Academy Award for best foreign film.

37. Trepte and Wardetzky, *Hans Otto,* p. 71.

38. Armin-Gerd Kuckhoff, *Hans Otto Gedenkbuch,* 1948, p. 46.

39. Kuckhoff, *Hans Otto Gedenkbuck,* pp. 85–86. See also Rürup, *Topography of Terror,* p. 50.

40. Haffner is referring to Adalbert Matkowsky (1857–1909), a legendary German actor who performed in Hamburg and Berlin.

41. Sebastian Haffner, *Defying Hitler,* p. 195.

42. Kuckhoff, *Hans Otto Gedenkbuch,* p. 91.

Chapter 7: DENIAL AND COMPLIANCE

1. Peter Hoffmann, *The History of the German Resistance,* p. 251.

2. Shareen Brysac, *Resisting Hitler,* p. 131.

3. Richard J. Evans, *The Coming of the Third Reich,* p. 382. See also www.britannica .com.

4. Greta Kuckhoff, *Vom Rosenkranz zur Rote Kapelle,* p. 115.

5. Ibid., p. 125.
6. Ibid., pp. 124–125.
7. Vinogradov was the charming young diplomat who would soon embark on a turbulent affair with Martha Dodd, the U.S. ambassador's daughter.
8. Stephen Koch, *Double Lives*, p. 136. There is no suggestion of the identity of "Faigt."
9. These secret exercises were conducted in violation of the Versailles Treaty.
10. Author Stephen Koch reproduces the memo and speculates on its meaning in *Double Lives*, his book on Willi Münzenberg. But Koch's interpretation of this memo includes a number of errors (including the misspelling of Kuckhoff's and Niedermayer's names). He also links Vinogradov and Martha Dodd, though their courtship does not appear to have begun until the following year. Given the mixed political identifications of the individuals in Radek's memo, it seems that they represented a list of possible contacts rather than confirmed Soviet agents. Niedermayer died in a Soviet POW camp after the war, while Vinogradov and Radek were both executed in Stalin's purge, Vinogradov in 1938 and Radek in 1939.
11. As of 1933, Thälmann effectively disappeared. He was held in solitary confinement in a series of prisons and concentration camps for eleven years, until he was finally shot at Buchenwald in August 1944.
12. Pierre Ayçoberry, *The Social History of the Third Reich*, p. 39.
13. See Sergio Bologna, "Nazism and the Working Class," translated by Ed Emery. Paper presented at the Milan Camera del Lavoro, 3 June 1993.
14. John Sieg, *Einer von Millionen Spricht*, p. 10; and GDW, http://www.gdw-berlin.de/b17/b17-2-flug-e.php.
15. Sieg, *Einer von Millionen Spricht*, p. 11.
16. Evans, *The Coming of the Third Reich*, ill. following p. 222.
17. See www.calvin.edu/academic/cas/gpa.
18. See 1992 BBC documentary, *Goebbels: Master of Propaganda*, as cited in http://194.3.120.243/humanities/igcsehist/term3/persuasion/resources.htm.
19. *Kuhle Wampe* was also shown in New York, as was the 1939 Nazi propaganda film *Der Feldzug in Polen*, which elicited cheers from the audience. See Sabine Hake, *Popular Cinema in the Third Reich*.
20. "A Nazi Youth Film," *New York Times*, July 7, 1934.
21. George promptly hired his and Brecht's former collaborator, Günther Weisenborn, as lead dramaturge.
22. Ronald Taylor, *Berlin and Its Culture*, p. 267.

Chapter 8: GOING TO GROUND

1. Author interview with Genie Allenby, October 2007.
2. Shareen Brysac, *Resisting Hitler*, p. 125.
3. See U.S. Holocaust Memorial Museum, http://www.ushmm.org/bonhoeffer/b3.htm.
4. *Holocaust Encyclopedia*, U.S. Holocaust Memorial Museum, see http://www.ushmm.org/wlc/article.php?lang=en&ModuleId=10005206.
5. Brysac, *Resisting Hitler*, p. 152.
6. Ibid., p. 142.
7. Ibid., p. 147.

8. Nigel Hamilton, *Reckless Youth*, p. 108; and George Mason University website, http://hnn.us/articles/697.html. See Doris Kearns Goodwin, *The Fitzgeralds and the Kennedys*, p. 470. Young Kennedy fought in World War II and died during an air force mission against the Nazis in 1944.
9. Brysac, *Resisting Hitler*, p. 141.
10. Ibid.
11. Robert Tucker, *Stalin in Power*, p. 275.
12. Brysac, *Resisting Hitler*, p. 156.
13. Brysac, *Resisting Hitler*, p. 169.
14. http://www.traces.org/marthadodd.html#livingquarters.
15. Greta Kuckhoff, *Vom Rosenkranz zur Rote Kapelle*, pp. 189–190.
16. Brysac, *Resisting Hitler*, p. 177, quoting correspondence to Maxwell Perkins.
17. Ibid., p. 196.
18. Ibid.
19. Ibid., pp. 196–197.
20. Ibid., p. 231.
21. Ibid.

Chapter 9: **THE PRAGUE EXPRESS**

1. See John Sieg files, GDW archive. See also Ian Kershaw, *The Nazi Dictatorship*, p. 208.
2. Giles MacDonogh, *A Good German*, p. 72.
3. Shareen Brysac, *Resisting Hitler*, p. 199.
4. John Sieg files, GDW archive, pp. 33–34. John Sieg, *Einer von Millionen Spricht*, introduction.
5. SOPADE Berichte, November 1935, quoted in Detlev Peukert, *Inside Nazi Germany: Conformity, Opposition, and Racism in Everyday Life*, p. 64.
6. David Barclay and Eric Weitz, *Between Reform and Revolution*, p. 364.
7. See Tim Mason, "The Workers' Opposition in Nazi Germany," *History Workshop Journal*, citing London's Wiener Library collection, pp. 4–6.
8. John Sieg files, GDW archive, pp. 15–21.
9. John Sieg, *Einer von Millionen Spricht*, p. 11.
10. Ibid., photo inserts.
11. Stephan Hermlin, *Die Erste Reihe*, p. 186.
12. Regina Griebel, Marlies Coburger, and Heinrich Scheel, *Erfasst?*, pp. 154, 240.
13. Hans Coppi and Geertje Andresen, eds., *Dieser Tod Passt zu Mir*, p. 256.
14. Ibid., p. 243.

Chapter 10: **THE GENTLEMEN'S CLUB**

1. Greta Kuckhoff, *Vom Rosenkrantz zur Rote Kapelle*, p. 196.
2. Shareen Brysac, *Resisting Hitler*, p. 201.
3. Regina Griebel, Marlies Coburger, and Heinrich Scheel, *Erfasst?*, p. 60.
4. Brysac, *Resisting Hitler*, p. 197.
5. Trade unionists organized alternate games, held at Randalls Island in New York City.
6. Douglas Chandler, "Changing Berlin," *National Geographic*, February 1937, pp.

131–170. During World War II, Chandler broadcast Nazi propaganda under the name "Paul Revere." After the war he was sentenced to life imprisonment.

7. William Dodd Jr. and Martha Dodd, eds., *Ambassador Dodd's Diary*, p. 430.

8. Ibid., p. 400.

9. Ibid., p. 403.

10. Ibid., p. 414.

11. Dodd's daughter, Martha, deprived of her status, continued to consort with Soviets and play her lovers off one another. She published several successful books in the United States about her Berlin experience. She married a wealthy American leftist and fell afoul of Joseph McCarthy's House Un-American Activities Committee (HUAC) after World War II. The couple fled to Prague, where she died in 1990.

12. https://www.cia.gov/cia/publications/oss/art02.htm. See also H. Montgomery Hyde, *Room 3603*, p. 151.

13. In the late 1930s, Dwight Eisenhower, then an army lieutenant colonel, offered a withering opinion of military intelligence officers: "Socially acceptable gentlemen; few knew the essentials of intelligence work. Results were almost completely negative and the situation was not helped by the custom of making long service as a military attaché, rather than ability, the essential qualification for appointment as head of the Intelligence Division in the War Department." Joseph Persico, *Roosevelt's Secret War*, p. 11.

14. See http://cryptome.org/fdr-astor.htm; Jeffery M. Dorwart, "The Roosevelt-Astor Espionage Ring," *New York History, Quarterly Journal of New York State Historical Association* 62, no. 3, July 1981, pp. 307–322.

15. Richard Breitman, *Official Secrets*, p. 24.

16. Kuckhoff, *Vom Rosenkranz zur Rote Kapelle*, p. 182.

17. Ibid., pp. 194–195.

18. See Theodor Pfizer, "Hans Hartenstein, ein preussischer Schwabe," *Schwäbische Heimat*, no. 1, 1979. See also Kuckhoff, *Vom Rosenkranz zur Rote Kapelle*, p. 172.

19. Griebel, Coburger, and Scheel, *Erfasst?*, p. 202.

20. Kuckhoff, *Vom Rosenkranz zur Rote Kapelle*, pp. 176–177.

21. Ibid., p. 199.

Chapter 11: **A FARAWAY COUNTRY**

1. Robert H. Keyserlingk, *Austria in World War II: An Anglo-American Dilemma*, p. 43.

2. Robert Gellately, *Backing Hitler*, p. 46. For Coffey's background, see James Allan Matte, *Forensic Psychophysiology Using the Polygraph*, p. 29.

3. Agostino von Hassell and Sigrid MacRae, *Alliance of Enemies*, p. 22.

4. Quoted in Allen Dulles, *Germany's Underground*, p. 16.

5. Leopold Trepper, *The Great Game*, p. 23. Most of Trepper's friends settled in the autonomous Jewish "homeland" of Birobidzhan, which Stalin had established on the Manchurian border. It attracted Jewish Communists from around the world, including Florida and California. See "Stalin's Forgotten Zion," http://www.swarthmore.edu/Home/News/biro/html/panel01.html.

6. Robert Tucker, *Stalin in Power*, p. 506. One of Trepper's classmates was Yugoslavian Josip Broz, nicknamed "Tito." See Trepper, *The Great Game*, p. 38.

7. See Robert Conquest, *The Great Terror*, pp. 485–488.

8. Alexandra Richie, *Faust's Metropolis*, pp. 619–620.
9. Ruth Fischer, *Stalin and German Communism*, p. 44. Neumann was also known for ordering the assassination of two anti-Communist Berlin policemen in 1931.
10. Conquest, *The Great Terror*, p. 401.
11. Tucker, *Stalin in Power*, p. 507.
12. Bertolt Brecht, *Journals 1934–1955*, p. 20.
13. Regina Griebel, Marlies Coburger, and Heinrich Scheel, *Erfasst?*, p. 240.
14. Conquest, *The Great Terror*, p. 402.
15. Tucker, *Stalin in Power*, p. 510.
16. Stephen Walsh, *Stalingrad: The Infernal Cauldron*, p. 16.
17. Conquest, *The Great Terror*, pp. 344, 394.
18. Shareen Brysac, *Resisting Hitler*, p. 214.
19. Ibid., p. 215.
20. Stefan Roloff and Mario Vigl, *Die Rote Kapelle*.
21. Quoted in Brysac, *Resisting Hitler*, p. 227.
22. Donald Heath to Sumner Welles, October 21, 1940, FDR Library, see http://www.fdrlibrary.marist.edu/psf/box31/t296j05.html. Quoted in Roloff and Vigl, *Die Rote Kapelle*, pp. 123–124.
23. Quoted in Brysac, *Resisting Hitler*, p. 227.
24. Roloff and Vigl, *Die Rote Kapelle*, p. 124. Donald Heath Jr. grew up to be a U.S. intelligence officer and served as a witness to Arvid Harnack's efforts on behalf of the Americans.
25. Brysac, *Resisting Hitler*, p. 425.
26. See John Weitz, *Hitler's Banker*.
27. Brysac, *Resisting Hitler*, p. 425, quoting State Department cable traffic September 16, 1937, citing *Völkischer Beobachter*.
28. Richard Grunberger, *The 12-Year Reich: A Social History of Nazi Germany, 1933–1945*, pp. 401–402.
29. Grunberger, *The 12-Year Reich*, p. 402.
30. Peter Hoffmann, *The History of the German Resistance*, p. 252.
31. Terry Parssinen, *The Oster Conspiracy of 1938*. Also see Hoffmann, *The History of the German Resistance*, pp. 90–91, 255; and Brysac, *Resisting Hitler*, p. 299.
32. Parssinen, *The Oster Conspiracy of 1938*, p. 158.
33. Ibid., p. 186.
34. Brysac, *Resisting Hitler*, p. 249.
35. Author interview with Richard Hottelet, December 14, 2006.
36. Donald Heath Jr., cited in Brysac, *Resisting Hitler*, p. 270.
37. Brysac, *Resisting Hitler*, pp. 250–251; and Hoffmann, *The History of the German Resistance*, pp. 117–119.

Chapter 12: **THE DINNER PARTY**

1. Regina Griebel, Marlies Coburger, and Heinrich Scheel, *Erfasst?* says the date was in 1939, but Hans Coppi places it in fall 1940.
2. Griebel, Coburger, and Scheel, *Erfasst?*, p. 72.
3. Karl-Heinz J. Schoeps, *Literature and Film in the Third Reich*, p. 259.
4. Edwin Zeydel, "A Survey of German Literature During 1937" *Modern Language Journal* 22, no. 7, 1938, p. 516. Zeydel was restrained with his praise; he listed

Kuckhoff among Germany's minor writers, and called his novel "too much a case study to be a work of art."

5.   Tobis Film evolved from a parent company called Deutsche Tonfilm. In 1928, Deutsche Tonfilm merged into a conglomerate called Tonbild Syndicat, whose name was condensed to "Tobis." The company was designed to monopolize the technology of sound-film production in Germany. See Klaus Kreimeier, *The UFA Story*, p. 179.

6.   Ingeborg Malek-Kohler, *Im Windschatten des Dritten Reiches*, p. 144.

7.   Langbehn would be arrested, tortured, and executed for his involvement with the 20th of July plot by the end of the war.

8.   Tobis was fully integrated into UFA in 1942, but still had its own releases.

9.   Malek-Kohler, *Im Windschatten des Dritten Reiches*, p. 142.

10.   Ibid., pp. 148–149. Dorsch's 1936 film was *Die Frau ohne Bedeutung*, a German version of Oscar Wilde's *A Woman of No Importance*.

11.   Malek-Kohler, *Im Windschatten des Dritten Reiches*, pp. 157–158.

12.   Author interview with Robby Lantz. Gustaf Gründgens, another Göring favorite and object of Klaus Mann's scorn, also used his influence to help colleagues suffering under the Nazis; see Malek-Kohler, *Im Windschatten des Dritten Reiches*, p. 163. Thomas Mann's son Klaus, writing from exile in Paris, took a cynical view of Emmy Göring in his novel *Mephisto:* "It was said of her, admiringly, that she occasionally pleaded with her husband for Jews in high social positions—yet Jews were still being sent to concentration camps. Lotte was called the Good Angel of the prime minister; yet his cruelty had become no milder since she had gone to work on him."

13.   See David Clay Large, *And the World Closed Its Doors: The Story of One Family Abandoned to the Holocaust*, p. 111.

14.   Malek-Kohler, *Im Windschatten des Dritten Reiches*, pp. 182–183.

15.   Greta Kuckhoff, *Vom Rosenkranz zur Rote Kapelle*, p. 226; Griebel, Coburger, and Scheel, *Erfasst?*, p. 58; Shareen Brysac, *Resisting Hitler*, p. 235.

16.   Elsa Boysen, *Harro Schulze-Boysen*, p. 6.

17.   Ibid., pp. 8–9. See also Stefan Roloff and Mario Vigl, *Die Rote Kapelle*, p. 95.

18.   Heinz Höhne, *Codeword: Direktor*, pp. 158–159.

19.   The offices were on Eichhornstrasse, off Potsdamer Platz.

20.   Kuckhoff, *Vom Rosenkranz zur Rote Kapelle*, pp. 227–228; Brysac, *Resisting Hitler*, p. 127.

21.   Günther Weisenborn, "Reich Secret," in Eric Boehm, *We Survived*, p. 193.

22.   Kuckhoff, *Vom Rosenkranz zur Rote Kapelle*, p. 128.

23.   Hans Coppi and Geertje Andresen, eds., *Dieser Tod Passt zu Mir*, p. 162.

24.   Brysac, *Resisting Hitler*, p. 128.

25.   Coppi and Andresen, *Dieser Tod Passt zu Mir*, p. 226—literally, "*Man solle die alten Kamellen lassen.*"

26.   They included sculptor Kurt Schumacher and Walter Küchenmeister. See Griebel, Coburger, and Scheel, *Erfasst?*, p. 130.

27.   Malek-Kohler, *Im Windschatten des Dritten Reiches*, p. 160.

28.   Thomas Doherty, *Pre-Code Hollywood: Sex, Immorality, and Insurrection in American Cinema, 1930–1934*, pp. 94, 385.

29.   Brysac, *Resisting Hitler*, p. 233; Hans Coppi and Johannes Tuchel, *Libertas Schulze-Boysen und die Rote-Kapelle*, p. 10.

30. The American film industry appeared to take it in stride: "American attitude on the matter is that American companies cannot afford to lose the German market no matter what the inconvenience of personnel shifts," *Variety* reported. Doherty, *Pre-Code Hollywood*, p. 94.

31. Coppi and Tuchel, *Libertas Schulze-Boysen und die Rote Kapelle*, p. 13.

32. Coppi and Andresen, *Dieser Tod Passt zu Mir*, pp. 206, 212.

33. Ibid., p. 228.

34. Ibid., pp. 229–230.

35. Malek-Kohler, *Im Windschatten des Dritten Reiches*, p. 184.

36. Ibid., p. 159.

37. Ibid.

38. After the war Göring told his Nuremberg interviewers: "Hitler didn't like wood carvings but was an enthusiast of bronze or stone. I prefer wood. Hitler was a south German—an Austrian really—and I was more influenced by my northern German ancestry." Leon Goldensohn, *The Nuremberg Interviews*, p. 106.

39. Höhne, *Codeword: Direktor*, p. 167.

40. Weisenborn, *Memorial*, p. 183; Sigrid Bock and Manfred Hahn, *Erfahrung Nazideutschland*, p. 255.

41. Weisenborn's play *Die Neuberin*, written under the name "Christian Munk," was a major success. It was produced as a feature film starring Käthe Dorsch, the actress who wheedled Göring into winning permission for Jews to leave the country and for the Engelsings to marry.

42. Griebel, Coburger, and Scheel, *Erfasst?*, p. 168.

43. See Malek-Kohler, *Im Windschatten des Dritten Reiches*.

44. Coppi and Andresen, *Dieser Tod Passt zu Mir*, p. 256.

45. Ibid. See also Wulf Koepke, "Günther Weisenborn's Ballad of his Life," in Neil Donahue and Doris Kirchner, eds., *Flight of Fantasy*, p. 235. All of Germany was gripped by the metaphor of epidemiology. Another example was the 1938 classic *La Habanera*, directed by Douglas Sirk and starring Zarah Leander and Ferdinand Marian. The film depicts German scientists outperforming their American rivals from the Rockefeller Foundation in wiping out an epidemic in Puerto Rico.

46. Günther Weisenborn, *Memorial*, pp. 212–214. Quoted in Wulf Koepke, "Günther Weisenborn's Ballad of his Life," Neil Donahue and Doris Kirchner, eds., *Flight of Fantasy*, p. 246, fn. 13.

47. Coppi and Andresen, *Dieser Tod Passt zu Mir*, p. 244.

Chapter 13: **THE BIRTHDAY PARTY**

1. Hans Coppi and Geertje Andresen, eds., *Dieser Tod Passt zu Mir*, p. 237. See also Regina Griebel, Marlies Coburger, and Heinrich Scheel, *Erfasst?*, pp. 58–59. Dissel survived the war to become an important film actor in East Germany. Some of his best-known films (*Naked Among Wolves*, *The Gleiwitz Case*, *The Architects*) touched on themes of resistance and dissent.

2. Coppi and Andresen, *Dieser Tod Passt zu Mir*, p. 229.

3. Ibid., p. 252. See also Shareen Brysac, *Resisting Hitler*, p. 237.

4. Coppi and Andresen, *Dieser Tod Passt zu Mir*, pp. 252–253.

5. Brysac, *Resisting Hitler*, p. 238.

6.   Stefan Roloff and Mario Vigl, *Die Rote Kapelle*, p. 104.
7.   Hans Sussmann, "Errinerungen des KPD-Mitglieds Hans Sussmann," Deutsches Historisches Museum, www.dhm.de/lemo/forum/kollektives-gedaechtnis/043/index.html.
8.   Coppi and Andresen, *Dieser Tod Passt ʒu Mir*, pp. 240, 255.
9.   Roloff and Vigl, *Die Rote Kapelle*, p. 104.
10. Griebel, Coburger, and Scheel, *Erfasst?*, p. 130.
11. "We Are the Peat Bog Soldiers" was recorded by Norman Luboff, folk-singers Theodore Bikel and Tom Glazer, and Ernst Busch, among many others.
12. David Barclay and Eric Weitz, *Between Reform and Revolution*, p. 366.
13. Griebel, Coburger, and Scheel, *Erfasst?*, p. 100. Langhoff became a major figure in postwar German theater, and was called the "Communist Gustaf Gründgens." See Wolfgang, Schivelbusch, *In a Cold Crater*, chapter 3.
14. Coppi and Andresen, *Dieser Tod Passt ʒu Mir*, p. 270.
15. Günther Weisenborn, "Reich Secret," in Eric Boehm, *We Survived*, p. 195.
16. Coppi and Andresen, *Dieser Tod Passt ʒu Mir*, p. 270.
17. Although the promotion was welcome, it was not a sign of special favor. Harro took five years to reach the rank of lieutenant, which was not remarkable progress in a period of rapid military expansion.
18. Weisenborn, "Reich Secret," in Eric Boehm, *We Survived*, p. 192.
19. Coppi and Andresen, *Dieser Tod Passt ʒu Mir*, p. 275.
20. Roloff and Vigl, *Die Rote Kapelle*, p. 104.
21. Robert Tucker, *Stalin in Power*, p. 603.
22. Ibid., pp. 606–607, and Michael Burleigh, *The Third Reich*, p. 669.
23. Robert Conquest, *The Great Terror*, p. 402.
24. Ruth Fischer, *Stalin and German Communism*, pp. 446, 605.
25. "Poland: Misery, Pride and Fear Call the Tune for the Post-War State Called Poland," *Life*, August 29, 1938, pp. 46–56.
26. Coppi and Andresen, *Dieser Tod Passt ʒu Mir*, p. 277.
27. George Kennan, *Memoirs, 1925–1950*, p. 108.
28. Coppi and Andresen, *Dieser Tod Passt ʒu Mir*, pp. 278–280.
29. Hugo Buschmann, quoted in Coppi and Andresen, *Dieser Tod Passt ʒu Mir*, p. 280.

Chapter 14: **THE INNER FRONT**

1.   John Waller, *The Unseen War in Europe*, p. 17.
2.   William Shirer, *The Rise and Fall of the Third Reich*, p. 596.
3.   Richard Breitman, *Official Secrets*, p. 84.
4.   Peter Hoffmann, *The History of the German Resistance*, p. 265.
5.   Terry Parssinen, *The Oster Conspiracy of 1938*, p. 7.
6.   Hoffmann, *The History of the German Resistance*, p. 103.
7.   Shareen Brysac, *Resisting Hitler*, p. 228; and Giles MacDonogh, *A Good German*, p. 235. Author interviews with Genie Allenby and Rainer von Harnack.
8.   Brysac, *Resisting Hitler*, p. 258.
9.   Ibid., p. 259.
10. Ibid., p. 240.
11. Eric Boehm, *We Survived*, p. xviii.
12. Nicholaus Wachmann, *Hitler's Prisons*, p. 56. Over the fourteen years of the

Weimar government, 1,141 death sentences were passed, but only 184 people were executed, and many influential leaders argued for the abolishment of the death penalty. See also Brigitte Oleschinski, *Gedenkstätte Plötzensee*, p. 15.

13. Brysac, *Resisting Hitler*, p. 226.
14. Stefan Roloff and Mario Vigl, *Die Rote Kapelle*, p. 124.
15. Welles was the nephew and namesake of famed abolitionist Senator Charles Sumner.
16. Ensnared by innuendo about his personal life, Welles was forced out of the State Department a few years later.
17. Donald Heath to Sumner Welles, October 21, 1940, FDR Library (online), box 31.
18. Russell S. Garner, "My Brush with History," *American Heritage Magazine*, September/October 1990. As a young FBI agent Garner tailed Trott to the Washington Monument, Mount Vernon, and a pacifist convention, only to have Trott stop him on the street "with a knowing smile on his face" and ask him how to get to the German embassy. "Our investigation produced no evidence indicating that he had engaged in subversive activity while in Washington . . . for the very good reason that he was a dedicated anti-Nazi and an avowed enemy of Adolf Hitler, a fact that I learned only long after the war," he wrote.
19. See "Restless Conscience" by Hava Beller, PBS. See also Hoffmann, *The History of the German Resistance*, pp. 117–119. Trott wrote a memorandum on the German situation that the Roosevelt administration ignored. An exiled German newspaper editor tried to help him publish a version of it in *The Atlantic*, but that effort failed as well.
20. In 1944, Trott attempted to set up a meeting with the Soviet ambassador in Sweden through sociologist Gunnar Myrdal. See Walter A. Jackson, *Gunnar Myrdal and America's Conscience*, p. 184. See also Zechlin memoir, GDW archive; Brysac, *Resisting Hitler*, pp. 106, 319.
21. Hoffmann, *The History of the German Resistance*, p. 252.
22. George Kennan, *Memoirs*, p. 118. Kennan regretted his position in later years, and like Allen Dulles, wrote that the United States had lost an important opportunity to work with the German resistance. Kennan believed that the entire U.S. policy had been based on a set of false premises, emphasizing the need to put Germans "in their place" over the possibility of working with German antifascists to save lives and avert calamity.
23. Leopold Trepper, *The Great Game*, pp. 102–103.
24. Brysac, *Resisting Hitler*, p. 280; David Murphy, *What Stalin Knew*, p. 97.
25. Michael Burleigh, *The Third Reich*, p. 669.
26. Griebel, Coburger, and Scheel, *Erfasst?*, p. 61. See also Roloff and Vigl, *Die Rote Kapelle*, pp. 115–116.
27. Greta Kuckhoff, *Vom Rosenkranz zur Rote Kapelle*, pp. 236–237.
28. Ibid., p. 238.
29. Brysac, *Resisting Hitler*, p. 270.
30. Roloff and Vigl, *Die Rote Kapelle*, p. 121.
31. Kuckhoff, *Vom Rosenkranz zur Rote Kapelle*, p. 260.
32. *Glenarvon*'s director, Max Kimmich, often hired Adam to write dialogue. Kimmich's career had soared after he married Joseph Goebbels's youngest sister. See Kuckhoff, *Vom Rosenkranz zur Rote Kapelle*, p. 261.
33. Ibid.

Chapter 15: **"THE NEW ORDER"**

1. John Sieg papers, GDW archive, p. 31.
2. John Sieg, *Einer von Millionen Spricht*, preface.
3. Greta Kuckhoff, *Vom Rosenkranz zur Rote Kapelle*, p. 259.
4. Interview with Hermann Grosse, GDW archive, p. 7.
5. Kuckhoff, *Vom Rosenkranz zur Rote Kapelle*, p. 274.
6. See Stefan Roloff, and Mario Vigl, *Die Rote Kapelle*, p. 85.
7. Graudenz was praised in *Scribner*'s magazine, 1939.
8. See the Bauhaus-Archiv, http://www.bauhaus.de/english/bauhaus1919/kunst/kunst_mappe_gropius.htm.
9. Author interview with Karin Graudenz Reetz, November 2007.
10. Regina Griebel, Marlies Coburger, and Heinrich Scheel, *Erfasst?*, pp. 98–99, 106–107.
11. Author interview with Sophie Templar-Kuh, February 2007.
12. Terry Parssinen, *The Oster Conspiracy of 1938*, pp. 172–173.
13. Agostino von Hassell and Sigrid MacRae, *Alliance of Enemies*, p. 79.
14. John Waller, *The Unseen War in Europe*, p. 126. See also Joachim Fest, *Plotting Hitler's Death*, p. 141.
15. Interviewed in "Restless Conscience" (documentary) by Hava Kovav Beller.
16. Allen Dulles, *Germany's Underground*, pp. 60–61.
17. Parssinen, *The Oster Conspiracy of 1938*, p. 174.
18. See Anne O'Hare McCormick, "Four Capitals of Destiny" *New York Times Magazine*, April 23, 1939.
19. William Shirer, *Berlin Diary*, p. 336.
20. Ibid., p. 451.
21. Ibid., pp. 460–601.
22. Waller, *The Unseen War in Europe*, pp. 154–156.
23. Hans Coppi and Geertje Andresen, eds., *Dieser Tod Passt zu Mir*, p. 301; Ingeborg Malek-Kohler, *Im Windschatten des Dritten Reiches*.
24. Coppi and Andresen, *Dieser Tod Passt zu Mir*, pp. 304–305.
25. Ibid., p. 304.
26. Alexander Kirk to Marguerite LeHand, June 19, 1940, www.fdrlibrary.marist.edu/box31/a296g07.html.
27. As Doris Kearns Goodwin wrote, "The [United States] lacked an arms industry. Its productive capacity was invested in the output of cars, washing machines, and refrigerators, in all of which it was the world leader." *No Ordinary Time*, p. 23.
28. Philip Knightley, *The First Casualty*, p. 260.
29. Marie Vassiltchikov, *The Berlin Diaries*, p. 22.
30. Brigitte Oleschinski, *Gedenkstätte Plötzensee*, p. 22.
31. Friedrich Wilhelm University's Institute of Anatomy and Biology was located near the grounds of the Charité Hospital Medical School. See http://www.charite.de/ch/presse/chronik/chrengl2.html.

Chapter 16: **ALL POSSIBLE FOOLISH RUMORS**

1. Marie Vassiltchikov, *The Berlin Diaries*, entry for January 15, 1940.
2. See Tadeusz Piotrowski, *Poland's Holocaust*, pp. 23–24.

3. Agostino von Hassell and Sigrid MacRae, *Alliance of Enemies*, p. 77.

4. Joachim Fest, *Plotting Hitler's Death*, pp. 116–118.

5. Quoted in Giles MacDonogh, *A Good German*, p. 208.

6. Blaskowitz spent the rest of the war on the western front. He was arrested and detained as a minor war criminal at Nuremberg, but died under mysterious circumstances awaiting trial. Stieff was later promoted to major-general. He joined the July 20 military conspiracy against Hitler, and was tortured and executed in 1944. See Fest, *Plotting Hitler's Death*, and MacDonogh, *A Good German*. Other generals who protested the *Einsatzkommandos'* murders included Walter von Brautitsch, Wilhelm Ulex, and Wilhelm von Leeb. See von Hassell and MacRae, *Alliance of Enemies*, p. 77.

7. William Shirer, *Berlin Diary*, pp. 542–543.

8. *Deutsche Wochenschau*, October 16, 1940.

9. Stefan Roloff and Mario Vigl, *Die Rote Kapelle*, p. 125.

10. Ibid., p. 108, and Hans Coppi and Geertje Andresen, eds., *Dieser Tod Passt zu Mir*, p. 315.

11. Coppi and Andresen, *Dieser Tod Passt zu Mir*, p. 315.

12. See Ansgar Diller, ed., *Rundfunkpolitik im Dritten Reich*. Munich, DTV, 1980.

13. Hans Coppi, Jürgen Danyel, and Johannes Tuchel, eds., *Die Rote Kapelle in Widerstand gegen den Nationalsozialismus*, pp. 110–112; and Shareen Brysac, *Resisting Hitler*, pp. 262–268.

14. David Murphy, *What Stalin Knew*, p. 262.

15. Ibid., p. 208.

16. Coppi, Danyel, and Tuchel, *Die Rote Kapelle*, p. 112.

17. Murphy, *What Stalin Knew*, p. 102.

18. Coppi and Andresen, *Dieser Tod Passt zu Mir*, pp. 313–314.

19. Shareen Brysac, *Resisting Hitler*, p. 283.

20. Murphy, *What Stalin Knew*, p. 97.

21. Ibid.

22. Ibid., p. 257.

23. "Barbarossa" was named after the twelfth-century monarch Frederick I called "red beard," ruler of the Holy Roman Empire, who expanded his territory through conquest.

24. Murphy, *What Stalin Knew*, p. 97; and Brysac, *Resisting Hitler*, p. 272.

25. Coppi and Andresen, *Dieser Tod Passt zu Mir*, p. 320.

26. Ibid.

27. Ibid., p. 322.

Chapter 17: THE ROAD TO BARBAROSSA

1. The following quotes from Harnack's and Schulze-Boysen's reports are from David Murphy, *What Stalin Knew*, pp. 99–101.

2. Hans Coppi and Geertje Andresen, eds., *Dieser Tod Passt zu Mir*, p. 320.

3. Ibid., p. 324.

4. Hans Coppi, Jürgen Danyel, and Johannes Tuchel, *Die Rote Kapelle im Widerstand gegen den Nationalsozialismus*, p. 113. See also Agostino von Hassell and Sigrid MacRae, *Alliance of Enemies*.

5. Murphy, *What Stalin Knew*, pp. 167–169; see also p. 97.

6. Coppi, Danyel, and Tuchel, *Die Rote Kapelle*, p. 114.
7. Ibid.
8. Alan Bullock, *Hitler and Stalin*, p. 707.
9. March 12, 1941, Coppi, Danyel, and Tuchel, *Die Rote Kapelle*, p. 115.
10. Ibid., p. 119.
11. Ibid., pp. 122–123.
12. Bullock, *Hitler and Stalin*, p. 779.
13. Coppi and Andresen, *Dieser Tod Passt zu Mir*, p. 336.
14. Ibid., pp. 329–330.
15. Coppi, Danyel, and Tuchel, *Die Rote Kapelle*, p. 128.
16. Coppi and Andresen, *Dieser Tod Passt zu Mir*, p. 328.
17. Shareen Brysac, *Resisting Hitler*, p. 286.
18. Memorandum from Merle Cochran to Secretary Morgenthau, May 8, 1941.
19. Greta Kuckhoff, *Vom Rosenkranz zur Rote Kapelle*, p. 276.
20. Ibid., p. 279.
21. Brysac, *Resisting Hitler*, p. 285.
22. Kuckhoff, *Vom Rosenkranz zur Rote Kapelle*, p. 280.
23. Brysac, *Resisting Hitler*, p. 287.
24. Ibid., p. 286; Stefan Roloff and Mario Vigl, *Die Rote Kapelle*, p. 34.
25. Kuckhoff, *Vom Rosenkranz zur Rote Kapelle*, pp. 284–285. Carl von Ossietsky (1889–1938) was a pacifist journalist who was one of the earliest of the Nazis' public critics. He was awarded the Nobel Peace Prize as a concentration camp inmate, and died shortly after.
26. Murphy, *What Stalin Knew*, p. 100.
27. Ibid.
28. Coppi, Danyel, and Tuchel, *Die Rote Kapelle*, p. 133; Regina Griebel, Marlies Coburger, and Heinrich Scheel, *Erfasst?*, p. 131. Schumacher was in the Third Company of Battalion 662.
29. Griebel, Coburger, and Scheel, *Erfasst?*, pp. 84–85; Coppi and Andresen, *Dieser Tod Passt zu Mir*, p. 336.
30. Coppi and Andresen, *Dieser Tod Passt zu Mir*, p. 336.
31. Griebel, Coburger, and Scheel, *Erfasst?*, p. 166.
32. Brysac, *Resisting Hitler*, p. 245.
33. Ibid., p. 277.
34. Murphy, *What Stalin Knew*, p. 101.
35. Coppi, Danyel, and Tuchel, *Die Rote Kapelle*, p. 137.
36. Murphy, *What Stalin Knew*, p. 101.
37. Coppi and Andresen, *Dieser Tod Passt zu Mir*, p. 336; and Coppi, Danyel, and Tuchel, *Die Rote Kapelle*, p. 137.
38. Murphy, *What Stalin Knew*, p. xv.
39. Michael Burleigh, *The Third Reich*, pp. 485–487, 492.
40. Murphy, *What Stalin Knew*, p. 163.
41. Ibid.
42. Bullock, *Hitler and Stalin*, p. 792.
43. Burleigh, *The Third Reich*, p. 492.
44. Murphy, *What Stalin Knew*, p. 259.
45. Kuckhoff, *Vom Rosenkranz zur Rote Kapelle*, pp. 290–291.
46. Brysac, *Resisting Hitler*, p. 435. The three were Rose Schlösinger, Karl Behrens,

and Leo Skrzypczynski. The three individuals were from varied political back-grounds, and met and joined the group through Mildred Harnack's night-school classes.

47. Brysac, *Resisting Hitler*, p. 290.
48. Ibid.
49. Coppi, Danyel, and Tuchel, *Die Rote Kapelle*, p. 137. See also Brysac, *Resisting Hitler*, p. 290.
50. Griebel, Coburger, and Scheel, *Erfasst?*, pp. 84–85. Author interview with Hans Coppi, November 21, 2007, GDW archive.

Chapter 18: OTHER WORLDS

1. John H. Waller, *The Unseen War in Europe*, p. 198.
2. Joseph Persico, *Roosevelt's Secret War*, pp. 98–99.
3. Roessler headed the Deutsches Bühnen-Volksbundes, or German theater association, under the administration of the Prussian Ministry of Culture, then run by Adam Kuckhoff's friend Adolf Grimme. Roessler's publications quoted Kuckhoff extensively. See Gaetano Biccari, *"Zuflucht des Geistes?": Konservativ-revolutionäre, faschistische und nationalsozialistische*, p. 65.
4. Roessler survived the war but took the identities of his military contacts to the grave. Intelligence files reveal nothing more than code names and ranks in the Germany army and air force. At least one Swiss military historian, Hans Rudolf Kurz, explored the possibility that Harro Schulze-Boysen was one of Roessler's sources, pointing to Roessler's 1941 publication of *The War Scenario and the Conditions for the War's Conduct*, written under the pseudonym "R. A. Hermes." Kurz suggested that the book corresponded to Harro's areas of military expertise and echoed Harro's idiosyncratic theory of revolutionary antifascist activity. See R. A. Hermes, *Die Kriegesschauplatze und die Bedingungen der Kriegführung* (Lucerne: Vita-Nova-Verlag, 1941); Hans Rudolf Kurz, *Nachrichten Zentrum Schweiz: Die Schweiz im Nachrichtendienst des zweiten Weltkriegs*, pp. 39–40. Gilles Perrault, the French author of *The Red Orchestra*, discounted the idea of Harro as Hermes, as does German expert Hans Coppi.
5. Persico, *Roosevelt's Secret War*, p. 101.
6. Once the Soviet Union was conquered, Hitler planned to turn his attention back to the conquest of Great Britain. The Nazis drew up an "enemies list" of 2,300 Britons slated for arrest or execution under German occupation. Most were Jews. Others included Virginia Woolf, E. M. Forster, and Noël Coward. See *The Independent*, March 3, 2000.
7. The Nazis argued that they were not legally obliged to offer Soviet prisoners humane treatment, because the USSR had not ratified the 1929 Geneva Convention on Prisoners of War, or made a commitment to the 1907 Hague Convention on the Rules of War. See http://www.ushmm.org/wlc/article.php?lang=en&ModuleId=10007183.
8. Hitler's *Kommissarbefehl*, issued June 6, 1941, was canceled on May 6, 1942, on the grounds that it backfired by giving the Soviets a greater will to resist.
9. Some thirty thousand Wehrmacht soldiers were executed by the notorious military courts over the course of the war, for offenses that included helping Jews, criticizing the regime, and desertion. See "Germany Considers Rehabilitating Soldiers Executed for Treason," Spiegel Online, June 29, 2007.

10. See postwar indictment, http://www.einsatzgruppenarchives.com/trials/fsix
.html.
11. The arrest orders instructed the police to target "well-off Jews," and many Jewish prisoners were released in return for ransom payments.
12. Author interview with Hans Coppi, November 22, 2007, GDW. See also
http://www.ushmm.org/wlc/article.php?lang=en&ModuleId=10007183.
13. http://www.chgs.umn.edu/Visual_Artistic_Resources/Public_Holocaust
_Memorials/Sachsenhausen_Concentration_Ca/Introduction_Sachsenhausen
_/introduction_sachsenhausen_.html.   http://www.ushmm.org/wlc/article
.php?lang=en&ModuleId=10007183.
14. See George Rosenthal, "The Evolution of Tattooing in the Auschwitz Concentration Camp Complex," http://www.chgs.umn.edu/Educational_Resources/
Curriculum/Auschwitz_Tattooing/auschwitz_tattooing.html.
15. See http://www.ushmm.org/wlc/article.php?lang=en&ModuleId=10007183.
See also Mark Roseman, *The Wannsee Conference*, p. 42.
16. http://www.ushmm.org/wlc/article.php?lang=en&ModuleId=10007178.
17. Greta Kuckhoff, *Vom Rosenkranz zur Rote Kapelle*, p. 275.
18. Howard K. Smith, "Berlin: Autumn 1941," *Reporting World War II: Part I*, Library of America, 1995, p. 226.
19. Regina Griebel, Marlies Coburger, and Heinrich Scheel, *Erfasst?*, p. 120. Stefan
Roloff and Mario Vigl, *Die Rote Kapelle*, pp. 42–43.
20. Roloff and Vigl, *Die Rote Kapelle*, pp. 42–43.
21. Kuttner's mother was murdered at Auschwitz, but she and her brother survived
and emigrated to Queens. Affadavit, Annemarie Klimmeck nee Kuttner, October 16, 1963 (Roloff papers). Interviews with Roloff family. See also Roloff and
Vigl, *Die Rote Kapelle*, pp. 49ff.
22. Interview published in Norbert Molkenbur and Klaus Hörhold, *Oda Schottmüller:
Tänzerin, Bildhauerin Antifaschistin, Eine Dokumentation*, pp. 44–46.
23. See also Griebel, Coburger, and Scheel, *Erfasst?*, p. 90.
24. Tim van Beek, quoted in Roloff and Vigl, *Die Rote Kapelle*.
25. See John Michalczyk, *Resisters, Rescuers, and Refugees*, pp. 72–74.
26. Author interview with Katja Casella Meirowsky, Pankow, November 18, 2007.
27. Griebel, Coburger, and Scheel, *Erfasst?*, p. 193.
28. Only one copy of one issue, number fifteen, has survived. See http://www
.gdw-berlin.de/b17/b17-2-flug-e.php.
29. James Edward Young, *Texture of Memory*, p. 42.
30. The Zwangsarbeiter Memorial at Hermannstrasse, Neukölln.
31. Kuckhoff, *Vom Rosenkranz zur Rote Kapelle*, p. 259.
32. Ibid.
33. Leopold Trepper, *The Great Game*, p. 102.
34. Ibid., p. 140.
35. Ibid., p. 97.
36. Suzanne Spaak's husband collected the work of René Magritte, who painted an
exquisite portrait of her in 1936. Spaak was arrested by the Germans in connection with her work for Trepper and murdered in 1944, thirteen days before the
liberation of Paris.
37. Trepper, *The Great Game*, p. 134.
38. Ibid., pp. 99–100.
39. Ibid., p. 147.

40. Ibid., p. 139.
41. Roloff and Vigl, *Die Rote Kapelle*, p. 135.
42. Shareen Brysac, *Resisting Hitler*, pp. 306–307.
43. Kuckhoff, *Vom Rosenkranz zur Rote Kapelle*, p. 311.
44. Ibid., pp. 308–309.
45. This was the "Arier Group," which included journalist and KPD member Ilse Stöbe, who had been working for Soviet intelligence since 1929. Her group also had difficulty maintaining contact with Moscow after the invasion. See Griebel, Coburger, and Scheel, *Erfasst?*, p. 86.
46. Trepper, *The Great Game*, p. 132.
47. Brysac, *Resisting Hitler*, pp. 308–310.
48. Ibid., p. 312.
49. Richard Breitman, *Official Secrets*, p. 241.
50. Ibid., p. 104.
51. Ian Kershaw, *Hitler: 1936–1945: Nemesis*, p. 453.
52. Ibid., p. 442.
53. Ibid.
54. Waller, *The Unseen War in Europe*, p. 211.
55. Hans Coppi and Geertje Andresen, eds., *Dieser Tod Passt zu Mir*, p. 342.
56. Ibid., p. 343.
57. Ibid., p. 344.
58. George Kennan, *Memoirs*, pp. 136–137. George Kennan, serving as a kind of internment camp counselor, irritably noted that his colleagues spent their time complaining about their food allotments, which were based on German civilian rations.
59. Griebel, Coburger, and Scheel, *Erfasst?*, pp. 158, 160.
60. Kuckhoff, *Vom Rosenkranz zur Rote Kapelle*, p. 297.
61. Brysac, *Resisting Hitler*, p. 304.
62. Coppi and Andresen, *Dieser Tod Passt zu Mir*, p. 345.
63. Kuckhoff, *Vom Rosenkranz zur Rote Kapelle*, pp. 314–318. For passage on Ingeborg Engelsing visiting, see Ingeborg Malek-Kohler, *Im Windschatten des Dritten Reiches*, p. 215.

Chapter 19: "DISTRESS ABOUT GERMANY'S FUTURE"

1. See "UFA Kulturfilm," German Film Institute, Frankfurt, www.filmportal.de.
2. Hans Coppi and Johannes Tuchel, *Libertas Schulze-Boysen und die Rote Kapelle*, p. 14.
3. Ibid., pp. 14–16. See also Heinz Höhne, *Codeword: Direktor*, p. 178.
4. Ingeborg Malek-Kohler, *Im Windschatten des Dritten Reiches*, p. 211. Baarova did disappear, until she was rediscovered decades later by Fassbinder and cast in *The Bitter Tears of Petra von Kant*.
5. Ibid., p. 168.
6. Ibid., p. 143.
7. Ibid., p. 210.
8. Morgan died in 1938 and Grünbaum died in January 1941.
9. *Time* magazine, March 9, 1942.
10. See entry on Gottschalk and German film at http://www.umass.edu/defa/filmtour/sjmarriage.shtml.

11. Malek-Kohler, *Im Windschatten des Dritlen Reiches*, p. 163. They included Erich Ziegler, Paul Henckels, and Theo Lingen.
12. Ibid.
13. Ibid., p. 162.
14. Anthony Bevor, *The Mystery of Olga Chekhova*, p. 152.
15. Heinz Höhne, *Codeword: Direktor*, p. 171.
16. Greta Kuckhoff, *Vom Rosenkranz zur Rote Kapelle*, pp. 157–158.
17. Christopher Browning and Jürgen Matthaus, *The Origins of the Final Solution*, p. 410.
18. Mark Roseman, *The Wannsee Conference and the Final Solution*, p. 149.
19. Kuckhoff, *Vom Rosenkranz zur Rote Kapelle*, pp. 309–310.
20. Shareen Brysac, *Resisting Hitler*, p. 299.
21. Allen Dulles, *Germany's Underground*, p. 73. It is unknown how much the Schulze-Boysens and Canaris/Dohnanyi group knew of each others' parallel archival efforts. There were several figures, including Albrecht Haushofer, a professor of geopolitics, and Werner von Trott, who moved between the two circles. Canaris's diary was captured by the Gestapo and reportedly destroyed.
22. Brysac, *Resisting Hitler*, p. 437.
23. "Die Sorge um Deutschlands Zukunft geht durch das Volk!" pamphlet from the GDW archive, winter 1941–42.
24. Hans Coppi and Geertje Andressen, eds., *Dieser Tod Passt zu Mir*, p. 349.
25. Interview with Helmut Roloff, "The Red Orchestra" (documentary).
26. Stefan Roloff and Mario Vigl, *Die Rote Kapelle*, p. 70.
27. Coppi and Andresen, *Dieser Tod Passt zu Mir*, p. 350.

Chapter 20: **THE ANTIWELLE**

1. Interview with Sophie Sieg, John Sieg papers, GDW archive.
2. Interview with Max Grabowski, February 8, 1967. GDW archive.
3. Author interview with Hans Coppi, November 2007.
4. Greta Kuckhoff, *Vom Rosenkranz zur Rote Kapelle*, pp. 315–317.
5. Ibid., p. 307.
6. Richard Breitman, *Official Secrets*, p. 48.
7. Ibid., pp. 92, 98.
8. Ibid., p. 54.
9. Ibid., p. 48.
10. Ibid., p. 111.
11. Shareen Brysac, *Resisting Hitler*, p. 299.
12. See Beatrix Herlemann, *Auf verlornenem Posten: Kommunistischer Widerstand im Zweiten Weltkrieg: Die Knöchel Organisation*, p. 44, 64 and 104. See also *Der Friedenskämpfer, Sonderausgabe Juni 1942*, from the GDW archive.
13. Regina Griebel, Marlies Coburger, and Heinrich Scheel, *Erfasst?*, p. 103.
14. Kuckhoff, *Vom Rosenkranz zur Rote Kapelle*, p. 319.
15. Günther Weisenborn, "Reich Secret," in Eric Boehm, *We Survived*, p. 195.
16. Ibid. See also Griebel, Coburger, and Scheel, *Erfasst?*
17. Günther Weisenborn, "Reich Secret," in Eric Boehm, *We Survived*, p. 194.
18. See German Propaganda Archive, Randall Bytwerk, http://www.calvin.edu/academic/cas/gpa/paradise.htm.
19. Kuckhoff, *Vom Rosenkranz zur Rote Kapelle*, p. 318.

20. Griebel, Coburger, and Scheel, *Erfasst?; "Die Rote Kapelle,"* www.gdw-berlin.de.

21. "Die Rote Kapelle," www.gdw-berlin.de.

22. Author interview with Hans Coppi, November 2007.

23. Kuckhoff, *Vom Rosenkranz zur Rote Kapelle*, p. 321.

24. Griebel, Coburger, and Scheel, *Erfasst?*, p. 279.

25. Hans Coppi and Geertje Andresen, eds., *Dieser Tod Passt zu Mir*, p. 360.

26. Heinz Höhne, *Codeword: Direktor*, p. 209.

27. Coppi and Andresen, *Dieser Tod Passt zu Mir*, p. 361. See also Griebel, Coburger, and Scheel, *Erfasst?*, p. 176.

28. Convoy PQ17, which departed Iceland for Murmansk on June 27, 1942, lost two-thirds of its thirty-four merchant ships in a little over a week See the U.S. Merchant Marine site, www.usmm.org.

29. Heinrich Scheel, *Vor den Schranken des Reichskriegsgerichts.*

30. Harro also spoke with Werner von Trott, whose diplomat brother, Adam von Trott, was deeply involved in the conspiracy. Harro might have been better off meeting with Werner's brother Adam, who was promoting the idea of a broad united front. Werner von Trott, a Communist aristocrat, subscribed to the notion of "inner immigration," that is, remaining in Germany but withdrawing from society. He had a conflicted relationship with his activist brother Adam. See Giles MacDonogh, *A Good German.*

31. Egmond Zechlin, "Arvid und Mildred Harnack zum Gedächtnis," GDW archive.

32. MacDonogh, *A Good German*, p. 264.

33. Spoerl reported that they also worked with documentary producers Wolf and Edith Hardt. Wolf Hardt had been one of Leni Riefenstahl's cameramen for her documentary on the 1936 Olympic Games.

34. Brysac, *Resisting Hitler*, p. 448.

35. Alexander Spoerl, "Memoir of Libertas Schulze-Boysen," GDW archive.

36. Karl Hess, statement, John Sieg papers, GDW archive.

37. According to some accounts, they carried two radios.

38. Brysac, *Resisting Hitler*, p. 314.

39. Ibid.

Chapter 21: **CRIME AND PUNISHMENT**

1. Ingeborg Malek-Kohler, *Im Windschatten des Dritten Reiches*, p. 193.

2. The actress was Reva Holsey and the director was Oscar Ingenohl. See Heinz Höhne, *Codeword: Direktor*, p. 223.

3. Ibid.

4. See Alexander Spoerl, "Memoir of Libertas Schulze-Boysen," GDW archive; and Greta Kuckhoff, *Vom Rosenkranz zur Rote Kapelle*, pp. 321–325.

5. Malek-Kohler, *Im Windschatten des Dritten Reiches*, p. 195.

6. Poznanska had been recruited by Leopold Trepper on their kibbutz in Palestine over a decade earlier. The State of Israel awarded her a posthumous citation for fighting the Nazis. See Neri Livneh, "A Woman Called Zosha," *Ha'aretz*, April 25, 2003.

7. Shareen Brysac, *Resisting Hitler*, p. 315.

8. Ibid., p. 318.

9. Stefan Roloff and Mario Vigl, *Die Rote Kapelle*, p. 153.

10. Hans Coppi and Geertje Andresen, eds., *Dieser Tod Passt zu Mir*, p. 371.

11. Höhne, *Codeword: Direktor,* pp. 230–201.
12. Kuckhoff, *Vom Rosenkranz zur Rote Kapelle,* p. 326.
13. Roloff and Vigl, *Die Rote Kapelle,* p. 155.
14. Regina Griebel, Marlies Coburger, and Heinrich Scheel, *Erfasst?,* p. 131.
15. Günther Weisenborn, "Reich Secret," in Eric Boehm, *We Survived,* p. 192.
16. Höhne, *Codeword: Direktor,* p. 241.
17. Brysac, *Resisting Hitler,* p. 338.
18. "Bezirksleutung" memoirs, p. 43, John Sieg papers, GDW archive.
19. Höhne, *Codeword: Direktor,* p. 231.
20. Ibid., pp. 232–233.
21. Roloff and Vigl, *Die Rote Kapelle,* p. 195.
22. Höhne, *Codeword: Direktor,* p. 240. See also Peter Steinbach and J. Tuchel, eds., *Lexikon des Widerstandes.*
23. Brysac, *Resisting Hitler,* p. 342. See also Höhne, *Codeword: Direktor,* p. 240.
24. Spoerl, "Memoir of Libertas Schulze-Boysen," GDW archive.
25. Weisenborn, "Reich Secrets," in Boehm, *We Survived,* pp. 201–202.
26. Interview with Karin Graudenz Reetz, "The Red Orchestra" (documentary).
27. Kuckhoff, *Vom Rosenkranz zur Rote Kapelle,* pp. 348, 357ff.
28. Höhne, *Codeword: Direktor,* p. 245.
29. Interview with Johannes Haas-Heyes, "The Red Orchestra" (documentary).
30. Martin Gilbert, *The Second World War,* p. 332.
31. Höhne, *Codeword: Direktor,* p. 247.
32. Ibid., pp. 252–254.
33. Brysac, *Resisting Hitler,* p. 340.
34. Interview with Helmut Roloff, "The Red Orchestra" (documentary).
35. Höhne, *Codeword: Direktor,* pp. 263–265.
36. Interview with Johannes Tuchel "The Red Orchestra" (documentary).
37. Brysac, *Resisting Hitler,* pp. 351–352.
38. Höhne, *Codeword: Direktor,* p. 269.
39. Ibid.
40. Interview with Hartmut Schulze-Boysen, "The Red Orchestra" (documentary).
41. Egmont Zechlin, "Arvid und Mildred Harnack zum Gedächtnis," GDW archive.
42. Höhne, *Codeword: Direktor,* pp. 271–272.
43. *Ernst von Harnack: Jahre des Widerstands 1932–1945,* Gustav-Adolf von Harnack, ed., p. 158.
44. Ibid.
45. Höhne, *Codeword: Direktor,* p. 282.
46. Spoerl, "Memoir of Libertas Schulze-Boysen," GDW archive.
47. Richard Breitman, *Official Secrets,* p. 156.
48. Allen Dulles, *Germany's Underground,* p. 125.
49. R. W. Johnson, "Cads, a review of Persico, *Roosevelt's Secret War,*" *London Review of Books,* 4 April 2002.
50. Lucas Delattre, *A Spy at the Heart of the Third Reich.*
51. Coppi and Andresen, *Dieser Tod Passt zu Mir,* p. 361.
52. Höhne, *Codeword: Direktor,* p. 275.
53. Ibid., p. 276.
54. Kuckhoff, *Vom Rosenkranz zur Rote Kapelle,* pp. 364, 373ff.
55. Ibid., p. 373.
56. Ibid.

57. Ibid., p. 383.
58. Griebel, Coburger, and Scheel, *Erfasst?*; author interview with Hans Coppi, August 7, 2003.
59. David Murphy, *What Stalin Knew*, p. 90.
60. Material on Falk Harnack from correspondence with Rainer von Harnack, September 19, 2007. Katerina Kritsiki, *Der Anteil deutscher Antifaschisten am Widerstandskampf des griechischen Volkes im zweiten Weltkrieg;* letter from Dr. Günter Groll to Richarda Huch, May 31, 1947 (Harnack/Roloff papers). See also interview with Käthe Braun, *Neues Deutschland*, February 3, 1993, p. 3.
61. "Die Rote Kapelle," www.gdw-berlin.de.
62. Kuckhoff, *Vom Rosenkranz zur Rote Kapelle*, p. 386.
63. Griebel, Coburger, and Scheel, *Erfasst?*, p. 354.
64. "Power, Responsibility and Abuse in Medicine: Lessons from Germany," William E. Seidelman, in Rochelle L. Millen, (ed.), *The Holocaust: A New Guide for Educators*, p. 327. Brigitte Oleschinski, *Gedenkstätte Plötzensee*, pp. 28, 46–47. See also Doris Claudia Mandel, *Die Zähmung des Chaos*, p. 138. Stieve was never investigated for his actions, and was a much-honored medical researcher in East Germany until his death in 1952.
65. Brysac, *Resisting Hitler*, p. 394.
66. Kuckhoff, *Vom Rosenkranz zur Rote Kapelle*, pp. 391ff.

Chapter 22: **THE SURVIVORS**

1. Peter Hoffmann, *The History of the German Resistance*, p. 293.
2. Terry Parsinnen, *The Oster Conspiracy of 1938*, p. 179; Hava Kovav Beller, "The Restless Conscience" (documentary).
3. Hava Kovav Beller, "The Restless Conscience" (documentary).
4. Agostino von Hassell and Sigrid MacRae, *Alliance of Enemies*, p. 343.
5. Giles MacDonogh, *A Good German*, pp. 230–231.
6. Eric Boehm, *We Survived*, p. xviii.
7. See Hoffmann, *The History of the German Resistance*, pp. 510–523.
8. Poelchau also actively participated in resistance activities himself. He helped many of the prisoners, smuggling messages to their families. He also combed bomb sites for identity papers to give to Jews. See also Peter Schneider, "The Good Germans," *New York Times Magazine*, September 13, 2000; and Ian Kershaw, *Hitler: 1936–1945: Nemesis*, p. 693.
9. Greta Kuckhoff, *Vom Rosenkranz zur Rote Kapelle*, p. 418.
10. Author interview with Saskia von Brockdorff, Berlin, November 2007.
11. Robert Solomon Wistrich, *Who's Who in Nazi Germany*, p. 137.
12. Gunther Weisenborn, "Reich Secret," in Boehm, *We Survived*, p. 210.
13. Hans Coppi and Geertje Andresen, eds., *Dieser Tod Passt zu Mir*, pp. 373–374.
14. Schneider, "The Good Germans," *New York Times Magazine*.
15. Boehm, *We Survived*, p. xviii.
16. Ibid., p. xxi.
17. Shareen Brysac, *Resisting Hitler*, p. 384.
18. Four were acquitted, one died during the trial, and another was granted a mistrial on the basis of severe illness.
19. These trials served as the basis for the Broadway play and 1961 Oscar-winning film *Judgment at Nuremberg*, starring Spencer Tracy and Marlene Dietrich.

20. William Shirer, *The End of a Berlin Diary*, p. 223.

21. Ibid., p. 224.

22. Ibid., p. 357.

23. Ibid., p. 356.

24. Norman Goda, "Tracking the Red Orchestra: Allied Intelligence, Soviet Spies, Nazi Criminals," from Richard Breitman, et al., *U.S. Intelligence and the Nazis*, pp. 298–299.

25. See "Reversal of Fortune: Robert Kempner," http://www.ushmm.org/wlc/article.php?lang=en&ModuleId=10007164. In a twist of fate, Kempner, who had once been legal adviser to the Prussian police, led the prosecution of Hermann Göring, the man who had fired him for anti-Nazi activities in 1933. Göring took cyanide before he was scheduled to be hung in October 1946.

26. Regina Griebel, Marlies Coburger, and Heinrich Scheel, *Erfasst?*, p. 203.

27. Richard Cutler, *Counterspy*, p. 64.

28. These included Marie Terwiel, Cato Bontjes van Beek, Hilde Coppi, and Liane Berkowitz. The huge Radio Berlin facility, once Goebbels's Reichs Radio, where Günther Weisenborn had once worked, was now in Soviet hands. See Markus Wolf, *Man Without a Face*, p. 38.

29. Allen Dulles, *Germany's Underground*, p. 100.

30. Dulles's own record was mixed. He received some of the earliest notification of the Holocaust and expressed private distress over the fate of the Jews. But he advised against publicizing the news, to avoid provoking U.S. and British anti-Semitism. See introduction to new edition of *Germany's Underground*.

31. Greta Kuckhoff files, GDW archive.

32. Major Earl S. Browning, US Army Counter-Intelligence Corps memorandum, August 28, 1947, National Archives.

33. Major Earl Browning, CIC memorandum, May 20, 1948 National Archives.

34. Goda, "Tracking the Red Orchestra," in Breitman et al., *U.S. Intelligence and the Nazis*, p. 299.

35. Ibid.

36. Ibid., p. 301.

37. Ibid., p. 302.

38. Barbie remained in Bolivia from 1951 until 1983. He was finally extradited to France and died there in prison in 1991. See Ted Morgan, "The Barbie File," *New York Times Magazine*, May 10, 1987, and "Klaus Barbie, 77, Lyons Gestapo Chief," obituary, *New York Times*, September 26, 1991.

39. Memorandum reproduced in Breitman, et al., *U.S. Intelligence and the Nazis*, p. 305.

40. See Paul Brown, "Report on the IRR File on The Red Orchestra," http://www.archives.gov/iwg/research-papers/red-orchestra-irr-file.html.

41. Brysac, *Resisting Hitler*, pp. 385–386.

42. Goda, "Tracking the Red Orchestra" in Breitman et al., *U.S. Intelligence and the Nazis*, p. 302.

43. Manfred Roeder, *Die Rote Kapelle: Europäische Spionage*, pp. 13, 33–36.

44. Stefan Roloff and Mario Vigl, *Die Rote Kapelle*, p. 332.

45. See Giles Perrault, *The Red Orchestra*.

46. Goda, "Tracking the Red Orchestra," in Breitman et al., *U.S. Intelligence and the Nazis*, pp. 314–315. Nuremberg's justice was not necessary for Nazi jurist Roland Freisler, the "hanging judge" of the People's Court. Freisler had been the

scourge of the German resistance, condemning over two thousand prisoners to death, including the youth of the White Rose and scores of the 20th of July military conspirators. On February 1945, only three months before the end of the war, an Allied air raid struck Freisler's Berlin courthouse, and Freisler was crushed to death by debris. He was holding the file of one of the 20th of July conspirators, who escaped execution as a result.

47. Harold Marcuse, *Legacies of Dachau*, p. 98.
48. Michael Burleigh, *The Third Reich*, p. 805.
49. Edith Anderson, *Love in Exile*, p. 64.

Chapter 23: LIFE IN A COLD CLIMATE

1. Quoted in Ronald Taylor, *Berlin and Its Culture*, p. 288.
2. "Günther Weisenborn," in Viktoria Hertling, *Dictionary of Literary Biography* (2005–06).
3. Günther Weisenborn, *Memorial*, p. 267.
4. Staudte collaborated on a number of film projects with both Weisenborn and Falk Harnack over the following decades, in both East and West Germany.
5. Rosemarie Reichwein, quoted in *Courageous Hearts: Women and the Anti-Hitler Plot of 1944* by Dorothee von Meding, p. 97.
6. Ibid., pp. 94–95.
7. Ibid., p. 88.
8. Freya von Moltke, quoted in von Meding, *Courageous Hearts*, p. 69.
9. Allen Dulles, *Germany's Underground*, p. 22.
10. Author's interview with Rainer von Harnack, October 2007.
11. Greta Kuckhoff, *Adam Kuckhoff zum Gedenken*, p. 11.
12. See Edith Anderson, *Love in Exile*, p. 66, and Saskia von Brockdorff interview, November 2007.
13. Shareen Brysac, *Resisting Hitler*, p. 386.
14. These experiences were mixed. After the war began, political prisoners were usually treated less viciously than Jewish prisoners. In some cases political prisoners in concentration camps abused and exploited Jewish prisoners. In other cases, they protected, assisted, and collaborated with them.
15. Michael Burleigh, *The Third Reich*, p. 512. This horrific figure still did not approach the rate of Soviets who died in German detention. See Alon Rachamimov, *POWs and the Great War*, p. 107.
16. Markus Wolf, *Man Without a Face*, p. 40.
17. Dulles, *Germany's Underground*, p. 76.
18. Burleigh, *The Third Reich*, p. 803.
19. Wolf, *Man Without a Face*, p. 65.
20. The case of the American Communist in question, Noel Field, remains a mystery. See Anderson, *Love in Exile*, and *Time* magazine, November 19, 1954.
21. In 1956, a West German court had ruled against punishing the judge who had sentenced him to death, ruling that he had acted to uphold "the right of the state to maintain itself." See Alan Cowell, "After 50 Years, German Court Exonerates Anti-Hitler Pastor," *New York Times*, August 16, 1996.
22. For more on East Germany's treatment of the Holocaust, see Jeffrey Herf, *Divided Memory*.
23. Regina Griebel, Marlies Coburger, and Heinrich Scheel, *Erfasst?*, p. 71.

24. Greta Kuckhoff files, GDW archive.
25. Or "Notenbank." See http://www.politeia.uni-bonn.de/archiv/kuckhoff/kuckhoff_a13.html.
26. Author interview with Hans Coppi, November 2007.
27. See Wolf, *Man Without a Face*, pp. 61–62.
28. Peter Thomson and Glendyr Sacks, *Cambridge Companion to Brecht*, quoting the *Buckow Elegies* (ca 1953), p. 215. In 1954 one of Brecht's young protégés, Martin Pohl, was arrested on trumped-up charges of anarchism; he was abused and·sentenced to four years in prison. The playwright worked hard for his release and was outraged at Pohl's report of his treatment at the hands of the Stasi. Brecht died suddenly two years later. Shortly afterward, the acting head of the Stasi made a secret speech denouncing Brecht and his intent to lodge a complaint about the treatment of Pohl. Some East Germans even suspected that the Stasi had a hand in his death. See Peter von Becker, "Erich Mielke und des Dichters Herzschlag," *Tagesspiegel*, August 14, 2006.
29. *Washington Post*, July 20, 1958.
30. Open Society Archives, http://www.osa.ceu.hu/files/holdings/300/8/3/text/24-1-12.shtml.
31. Joanne Sayner, *Women Without a Past?: German Autobiographical Writings and Fascism*, p. 236.
32. See Wolf, *Man Without a Face*, pp. 56–57.
33. Heinz Höhne, *Codeword: Direktor*, p. 336.
34. Ibid., pp. 333–334.
35. Ibid., p. 329.
36. Ibid., p. 262.
37. Ibid., p. 263.
38. Wolf, *Man Without a Face*, p. 341.·
39. Ibid., p. 342.
40. Hans Coppi and Geertje Andresen, eds., *Dieser Tod Passt ʒu Mir*, pp. 13–17. Interview with Stefan Roloff, September 2008.
41. Greta Kuckhoff interviews with Biernat, Greta Kuckhoff files, GDW archive.
42. The East German film was released in 1971. Höhne's television series was broadcast in 1972.
43. Greta Kuckhoff files, GDW archive.
44. Wolf, *Man Without a Face*, p. 114.
45. "Bemerkungen zum Manuskript von Genossin," Greta Kuckhoff, December 1971, GDW archive.
46. Ibid., pp. 12, 14.
47. Ibid., p. 28.
48. "Bermerkungen zum Manuskript von Genossin," Greta Kuckhoff, December 1971, GDW archive.
49. Greta Kuckhoff, "Begegnung mit dem Siebten Kreuz Über Anna Seghers," p. 151, in Anna Seghers, *The Seventh Cross*, p. 427.

Epilogue: TO THOSE BORN AFTER

1. Regina Griebel, Marlies Coburger, and Heinrich Scheel, *Erfasst?*, p. 171.
2. Marcus Wolf, *Man Without a Face*, p. 208. See also http://www.wilsoncenter.org/index.cfm?topic_id=1409&fuseaction=topics.item&news_id=105150.

3. The 1955 amnesty applied to "Soviet citizens who assisted the foreign invaders in the Great Patriotic War of 1941–1945." See http://www.peoples.ru/military/scout/gurevich/.

4. "Günther Weisenborn," in Victoria Hertling, *Dictionary of Literary Biography*,

5. From "An die Nachgeborenen," in Bertolt Brecht *Werke: Gedichte 2. Vol. 12*, pp. 85–87.

Select Bibliography

BOOKS

Accoce, Pierre, and Pierre Quet. *A Man Called Lucy, 1939–45*. Coward-McCann, Inc., New York, 1966.

Anderson, Edith. *Love in Exile: An American Writer's Memoir of Life in Divided Berlin*. Steerforth Press, Hanover, N.H., 1999.

Andrew, Christopher, and Vasili Mitrokhin. *The Sword and the Shield: The Mitrokhin Archive and the Secret History of the KGB*. Basic Books, New York, 2000.

Ayçoberry, Pierre. *The Social History of the Third Reich*. The New Press, New York, 1999.

Barclay, David E., and Eric D. Weitz, eds. *Between Reform and Revolution: German Socialism and Communism from 1840 to 1990*. Berghahn Books, Oxford and New York, 1998.

Baum, Vicki. *Grand Hotel*. International Collectors Library, Garden City, 1957.

———. *Hotel Berlin '43*. Doubleday, Doran & Company, New York, 1944.

Berghahn, V. R. *Modern Germany: Society, Economy and Politics in the Twentieth Century*. Cambridge University Press, Cambridge, 1987.

Biccari, Gaetano. *"Zuflucht des Geistes"?: Konservativ-revolutionäre, fascistische und nationalsozialistische*. Gunter Narr Verlag, Tübingen, 2001.

Blumenthal, W. Michael. *The Invisible Wall: Germans and Jews, a Personal Exploration*. Counterpoint, Washington, 1998.

Bock, Sigrid, and Manfred Hahn. *Erfahrung Nazideutschland: Romane in Deutschland 1933–1945*. Aufbau Verlag, Berlin and Weimar, 1987.

Boehm, Eric H. *We Survived: Fourteen Histories of the Hidden and Hunted in Nazi Germany*. Westview Press, Boulder, Colo., 2003.

Boysen, Elsa. *Harro Schulze-Boysen: Das Bild eines Freiheitskämpfers*. Komet-Verlag, Dusseldorf, 1947.

Brauer, Ilse, and Werner Kayser. *Günther Weisenborn*. Hans Christians Verlag, Hamburg, 1971.

Brecht, Bertolt. *Journals, 1934–1955*. Routledge, New York, 1993.

———. *Werke: Gedichte 2. Vol. 12*, Aufbau Verlag, Berlin, 1988.

Breitman, Richard, Norman J. W. Goda, Timothy Naftali, and Robert Wolfe. *U.S. Intelligence and the Nazis*. Cambridge University Press, New York, 2005.

———. *Official Secrets: What the Nazis Planned, What the British and Americans Knew*. Hill and Wang, New York, 1998.

Breuer, William. *Top Secret Tales of World War II*. Wiley & Sons, New York, 2000.

Browning, Christopher R., and Jürgen Matthaus. *The Origins of the Final Solution: The Evolution of Nazi Jewish Policy, September 1939–March 1942*. University of Nebraska Press, Lincoln, Neb., 2007.

Brysac, Shareen Blair. *Resisting Hitler: Mildred Harnack and the Red Orchestra*. Oxford University Press, New York, 2000.

Bullock, Alan. *Hitler and Stalin: Parallel Lives*. Vintage Books, New York, 1993.

Burleigh, Michael. *The Third Reich: A New History*. Hill and Wang, New York, 2000.

Carr, E. H. *The Comintern and the Spanish Civil War*. Macmillan, London and Basingstoke, 1984.

Ceplair, Larry. *Under the Shadow of War: Fascism, Anti-Fascism, and Marxists, 1918–1939*. Columbia University Press, New York, 1987.

Conquest, Robert. *The Great Terror: A Reassessment*. Oxford University Press, New York, 1990.

Coppi, Hans. *Harro Schulze-Boysen—Wege in den Widerstand: Eine biographische Studie*. Verlag Dietmar Fölbach, Koblenz, Germany, 1995.

Coppi, Hans, and Geertje Andresen. *Dieser Tod passt zu mir: Harro Schulze-Boysen, Grenzgänger im Widerstand*. Aufbau-Verlag, Berlin, 1999.

Coppi, Hans, Jürgen Danyel, and Johannes Tuchel, eds. *Die Rote Kapelle im Widerstand gegen den Nationalsozialismus*. Gedenkstätte Deutscher Widerstand, Berlin, 1994.

Coppi, Hans, and Johannes Tuchel. *Libertas Schulze-Boysen und die Rote Kapelle*. Gedenkstätte Deutscher Widerstand, Berlin (undated).

Cutler, Richard W. *Counterspy: Memoirs of a Counter-Intelligence Officer in World War II and the Cold War*. Potomac Books, Dulles, Va., 2005.

Delattre, Lucas. *A Spy at the Heart of the Third Reich: The Extraordinary Story of Fritz Kolbe*. Atlantic Monthly Press, New York, 2005.

Dodd, Martha. *Sowing the Wind*. Harcourt, Brace & Co., New York, 1945.

———. *Through Embassy Eyes*. Harcourt, Brace & Co., New York, 1939.

Dodd, William E. Jr., and Martha Dodd, eds. *Ambassador Dodd's Diary*. Harcourt, Brace & Co., New York, 1941.

Doherty, Thomas. *Pre-Code Hollywood: Sex, Immorality, and Insurrection in American Cinema, 1930–1934*. Columbia University Press, New York, 1999.

Donahue, Neil, and Doris Kirchner, eds. *Flight of Fantasy: New Perspectives of Inner Immigration on German Literature, 1933–1945*. Berghahn Books, New York and Oxford, 2005.

Dulles, Allen. *Germany's Underground*. MacMillan, New York, 1947.

Eggenberger, David. *An Encyclopedia of Battles*. Dover Books, Mineola, N.Y., 1985.

Esslin, Martin. *Brecht: The Man and His Work*. Doubleday, New York, 1961.

Evangelischen Akademie Berlin (West) Im Evangelischen Bildungswerk. *In der Gestapo-Zentrale Prinz-Albrecht-Strasse 8: Berichte ehemaliger Häftlinge*. Evangelischen Akademie Berlin (West), 1989.

Evans, Richard J. *The Coming of the Third Reich*. The Penguin Press, New York, 2004.

Fest, Joachim C. *Plotting Hitler's Death*. Macmillan, New York, 1997.

Feuchtwanger, Lion. *The Oppermanns*. Carroll & Graf, New York, 2001.

Fischer, Ruth. *Stalin and German Communism*. Harvard University Press, Cambridge, Mass., 1948.

Fleming, Thomas. *The New Dealers' War: FDR and the War Within World War II*. Basic Books, New York, 2001.

Foner, Philip Sheldon. *The T.U.E.L. 1925–1928: A History of the Labor Movement in the United States*. International Publishers Co., Long Island City, N.Y., 1994.

Friedrich, Otto. *Before the Deluge: A Portrait of Berlin in the 1920s*. Harper & Row, New York, 1972.

Fritzche, Peter. *Germans into Nazis*. Harvard University Press, Cambridge, Mass., 1999.

Gellately, Robert. *Backing Hitler: Consent and Coercion in Nazi Germany*. Oxford University Press, New York, 2001.

Gilbert, Martin. *The Second World War*. Macmillan, London, 2004.

Goldensohn, Leon. *The Nuremberg Interviews*. Random House, New York, 2005.

Gollwitzer, Helmut, Käthe Kuhn, and Reinhold Schneider, eds. *Dying We Live: The Last Messages of Men and Women Who Resisted Hitler and Were Martyred*. Pantheon, New York, 1956.

Goodwin, Doris Kearns. *The Fitzgeralds and the Kennedys: An American Saga*. Macmillan, New York, 1991.

————. *No Ordinary Time*. Simon & Schuster, New York, 1995.

Griebel, Regina, Marlies Coburger, and Heinrich Scheel. *Erfasst? Das Gestapo-Album zur Roten Kapelle*. Audioscop, Halle, 1992.

Grunberger, Richard. *The 12-Year Reich: A Social History of Nazi Germany, 1933–1945*. Da Capo Press, Cambridge, Mass., 1995.

Gründgens, Gustaf. *Briefe, Aufsätze, Reden*. Deutscher Taschenbuch Verlag, Munich, 1970.

Haffner, Sebastian. *Defying Hitler*. Picador, New York, 2003.

Hake, Sabine. *Popular Cinema in the Third Reich*. University of Texas Press, Austin, 2002.

Hale, Oron J. *The Captive Press in the Third Reich*. Princeton University Press, Princeton, N.J., 1964.

Hamilton, Nigel. *Reckless Youth*. Random House, New York, 1992.

Harnack, Gustav-Adolf von, ed. *Ernst von Harnack: Jahre des Widerstands 1932–1945*. Verlag Günther Neske, Pfullingen, 1989.

Hassell, Agostino von, and Sigrid MacRae. *Alliance of Enemies: The Untold Story of the Secret American and German Collaboration to End World War II*. St. Martin's Press, New York, 2006.

Henderson, Nevile. *Failure of a Mission, Berlin 1937–1939*. G. P. Putnam's Sons, New York, 1940.

Herf, Jeffrey. *Divided Memory: The Nazi Past in the Two Germanys*. Harvard University Press, Cambridge, Mass., 1997.

Herlemann, Beatrix. *Auf verlorenem Posten: Kommunistischer Widerstand im Zweiten Weltkrieg*. Verlag Neue Gesellschaft, Bonn, 1986.

Hermlin, Stephan. *Die Erste Reihe*. Verlag Neues Leben, Berlin, 1985.

Hoffmann, Peter. *The History of the German Resistance 1933–1945*. The MIT Press, Cambridge, Mass., 1977.

Höhne, Heinz. *Codeword: Direktor: The Story of the Red Orchestra*. Coward, McCann & Geoghegan, New York, 1971.

Hyde, H. Montgomery. *Room 3603*. The Lyons Press, Guilford, Conn., 2001.

Innes, C. D. *Erwin Piscator's Political Theatre: The Development of Modern German Drama*. Cambridge University Press, New York, 1972.

Isherwood, Christopher. *Goodbye to Berlin*. Penguin Books, London, 1974.

Jackson, Walter A. *Gunnar Myrdal and America's Conscience*. University of North Carolina Press, Chapel Hill, 1990.

Jacobi, Jutta. *Zarah Leander: Das Leben einer Diva*. Hoffman und Campe, Hamburg, 2006.

Johnson, Eric. *Nazi Terror: The Gestapo, Jews, and Ordinary Germans*. Basic Books, New York, 1999.

Kennan, George. *Memoirs: 1925–1950*. Pantheon, New York, 1967.

Kershaw, Ian. *Hitler: 1936–1945: Nemesis*. Norton, New York, 2001.

————. *The Nazi Dictatorship: Problems and Perspectives of Interpretation.* Arnold, London, 2000.

Keyserlingk, Robert H. *Austria in World War II: An Anglo-American Dilemma.* McGill-Queen's Press, Montreal, 1990.

Kitchen, Martin. *Cambridge Illustrated History of Germany.* Cambridge University Press, New York, 2000.

Klemperer, Klemens von. *German Resistance Against Hitler: The Search for Allies Abroad.* Oxford University Press, New York, 1994.

Knightley, Philip. *The First Casualty: The War Correspondent as Hero and Myth-Maker from the Crimea to Iraq.* Johns Hopkins University Press, Baltimore, Md. 2004.

Koch, Stephen. *Double Lives.* Enigma Books, New York, 1994.

Koehler, John O. *Stasi: The Untold Story of the East German Secret Police.* Westview Press, Boulder, Colo., 1999.

Koestler, Arthur. *The Invisible Writing.* Macmillan, New York, 1954.

Kreimeier, Klaus. *The UFA Story.* Hill & Wang, New York, 1996.

Kritsiki, Katerina. *Der Anteil deutscher Antifaschisten am Widestandskampf des griechischen Volkes im zweiten Weltkrieg,* dissertation. Universität Rostock, 1971.

Kuckhoff, Adam. *Der Deutsche von Bayencourt.* Rowohlt, Berlin, 1937.

————. *Fröhlich Bestehn: Prosa, Lyrik, Dramatik.* Aachen, 1985.

———— (with Peter Tarin). *Strogany und die Vermissten.* Universitas Verlag, Berlin, 1941.

Kuckhoff, Armin-Gerd. *Hans Otto Gedenkbuch.* Verlag BrunoHenschel und Sohn, Berlin, 1948.

Kuckhoff, Greta, ed. *Adam Kuckhoff zum Gedenken: Novellen, Gedichte, Briefe.* Berlin, 1946.

————. *Vom Rosenkranz zur Roten Kapelle—Ein Lebensbericht.* Verlag Neues Leben, Berlin, 1974.

Kurz, Hans Rudolf. *Nachrichten Zentrum Schweiz: Die Schweiz im Nachrichtendienst des zweiten Weltkriegs.* Verlag Huber, Frauenfeld und Stuttgart, 1972.

Large, David Clay. *Berlin.* Basic Books, New York, 2000.

————. *And the World Closed Its Doors: The Story of One Family Abandoned to the Holocaust.* Basic Books, New York, 2003.

Lemmons, Russel. *Goebbels and Der Angriff.* University of Kentucky Press, Lexington, 1994.

MacDonogh, Giles. *A Good German: A Biography of Adam von Trott zu Solz.* Overlook Press, Woodstock, N.Y., 1992.

MacMillan, Margaret. *Paris 1919.* Random House, New York, 2003.

Malek-Kohler, Ingeborg. *Im Windschatten des Dritten Reiches.* Verlag Herder, Freiburg, 1986.

Malraux, Andre. *Days of Wrath.* Random House, New York, 1936.

Mandel, Doris Claudia. *Die Zähmung des Chaos.* Gegenbergsche, Halle, Germany, 1999.

Mann, Klaus. *Mephisto.* Penguin, New York, 1983.

Marcuse, Harold. *Legacies of Dachau: The Uses and Abuses of a Concentration Camp, 1933–2001.* Cambridge University Press, New York, 2001.

Matte, James Allan. *Forensic Psychophysiology Using the Polygraph: Scientific Truth Verification—Lie Detection.* J. A. M. Publications, Williamsville, N.Y., 1998.

McDonough, Frank. *Opposition and Resistance in Nazi Germany.* Cambridge University Press, New York, 2001.

Meding, Dorothee von. *Courageous Hearts: Women and the Anti-Hitler Plot of 1944.* Berghahn Books, Oxford and New York, 1997.

Michalczyk, John J. *Resisters, Rescuers, and Refugees: Historical and Ethical Issues.* Rowman & Littlefield, Lanham, Md. 1997.

Millen, Rochelle L., ed. *The Holocaust: A New Guide for Educators.* NYU Press, New York, 1996.

Molkenbur, Norbert, and Klaus Hörhold. *Oda Schottmüller: Tänzerin, Bildhauerin, Antifaschistin.* Henschelverlag, Berlin, 1983.

Möller, Horst, Volker Dahm, and Hartmut Mehringer, eds. *Die tödliche Utopie: Bilder, Texte, Dokumente, Daten zum Dritten Reich.* Instituts für Zeitgeschichte, Munich and Berlin, 1999.

Mühlberger, Detlef, ed. *The Social Bases of Nazism, 1919–1933.* Cambridge University Press, Cambridge and New York, 2003.

Murphy, David E. *What Stalin Knew: The Enigma of Barbarossa.* Yale University Press, New Haven, Conn., 2005.

Noakes, J., and G. Pridham. *Nazism 1919–1945, Vol. 2: State, Economy and Society 1933–1939,* and *Vol. 3: Foreign Policy, War and Racial Extermination.* University of Exeter Press, Exeter, England, 1995.

Oleschinski, Brigitte. *Gedenkstätte Plötzensee.* Gedenkstätte Deutscher Widerstand, Berlin (year unknown).

Paldiel, Mordecai. *The Path of the Righteous: Gentile Rescuers of Jews During the Holocaust.* KTAV Publishing House, Jersey City, N.J., 1992.

Parssinen, Terry. *The Oster Conspiracy of 1938: The Unknown Story of the Military Plot to Kill Hitler and Avert World War II.* HarperCollins, New York, 2003.

Payne, Stanley G. *The Spanish Civil War, the Soviet Union, and Communism.* Yale University Press, New Haven and London, 2004.

Perrault, Gilles. *The Red Orchestra.* Simon & Schuster (Pocket Books), New York, 1970.

Persico, Joseph. *Piercing the Reich: The Penetration of Nazi Germany by American Secret Agents during World War II.* Viking, New York, 1979.

———. *Roosevelt's Secret War.* Random House, New York, 2001.

Peukert, Detlev. *Die KPD im Widerstand: Verfolgung und Untergrundarbeit an Rhein und Ruhr 1933 bis 1945.* Peter Hammer Verlag GmbH, Wuppertal, 1980.

———. *Inside Nazi Germany: Conformity, Opposition, and Racism in Everyday Life.* Yale University Press, New Haven, Conn., 1989.

Piotrowski, Tadeusz. *Poland's Holocaust.* MacFarland & Co., London, 1997.

Poelchau, Harald. *Die letzten Stunden: Erinnerungen eines Gefängnispfarrers.* Verlag Volk und Welt, Berlin, 1987.

Rachamimov, Alon. *POWs and the Great War: Captivity on the Eastern Front (Legacy of the Great War)* Berg Publishers, Oxford, England, 2002.

Remarque, Erich Maria. *Spark of Life.* Dell, New York, 1964.

Richie, Alexandra. *Faust's Metropolis: A History of Berlin.* Carroll & Graf, New York, 1998.

Roeder, Manfred. *Die Rote Kapelle: Europäische Spionage.* Siep-Verlag, Hamburg, 1952.

Roessler, Rudolf, ed. *Das Nationaltheater.* Bühnen-Volksbund, Berlin, 1929–1933.

——— ed. *Thespis* (1929–1933). Bühnen-Volksbund, Berlin, 1929–1933.

Roloff, Stefan, and Mario Vigl. *Die Rote Kapelle.* Ullstein, Berlin, 2002.

Roseman, Mark. *The Wannsee Conference and the Final Solution.* Metropolitan Books, New York, 2002.

Roth, Karl Heinz, and Angelika Ebbinghaus, eds. *Rote Kapellen—Kreisauer Kreise—Schwarze Kapellen: Neue Sichtweisen auf den Widerstand gegen die NS-Diktatur 1938–1945.* VSA Verlag, Hamburg, 2004.

Rürup, Reinhard, ed. *Topography of Terror: Gestapo, SS and Reichssicherheitshauptamt on the "Prinz-Albrecht-Terrain."* Verlag Willmuth Arenhövel, Berlin, 1997.

Sayner, Joanne. *Women Without a Past?: German Autobiographical Writings and Fascism,* Rodopi, Amsterdam and New York, 2007.

Scheel, Heinrich. *Vor den Schranken des Reichskriegsgerichts: Mein Weg in den Widerstand,* edition q, Berlin, 1993.

Schivelbusch, Wolfgang. *The Culture of Defeat: On National Trauma, Mourning, and Recovery.* Metropolitan Books, New York, 2003.

———. *In a Cold Crater: Cultural and Intellectual Life in Berlin, 1945–1948.* University of California Press, Berkeley and Los Angeles, 1998.

Schlabrendorff, Fabian von. *The Secret War Against Hitler.* Westview, Boulder, Colo., 1994.

Schoeps, Karl-Heinz J. *Literature and Film in the Third Reich.* Camden House, Rochester, N.Y., 2004.

Schweitzer, Eva. *Amerika und der Holocaust: Die Verschwiegene Geschichte.* Knaur Taschenbuch Verlag, Munich, 2004.

Seghers, Anna. *The Seventh Cross.* David R. Godine, Boston, 2004.

Shirer, William L. *Berlin Diary: The Journal of a Foreign Correspondent, 1934–1941.* Knopf, New York, 1941.

———. *The End of a Berlin Diary.* Knopf, New York, 1947.

———. *The Rise and Fall of the Third Reich.* Simon & Schuster, New York, 1960.

Sieg, John. *Einer von Millionen Spricht: Skizzen, Erzählungen, Reportagen, Flugschriften.* Dietz Verlag, Berlin, 1989.

Sozialdemokratischen Partei Deuttschlands (Sopade). *Deutschland-Berichte.* Verlag Petra Nettelbeck, Frankfurt-am-Main, 2001.

Speer, Albert. *Spandau: The Secret Diaries.* Macmillan, New York, 1976.

Stackelberg, Roderick et al. *The Nazi Germany Sourcebook: An Anthology of Texts.* Routledge, New York, 2002.

Steinbach, Peter, and J. Tuchel, eds. *Lexikon des Widerstandes, 1933–1945.* Verlag C. H. Beck, Munich, 1998.

Taylor, Ronald. *Berlin and Its Culture.* Yale University Press, New Haven, Conn., 1997.

Thomasett, Michael C. *German Opposition to Hitler: The Resistance, the Underground, and Assassination Plots, 1939–1945.* McFarland & Co., Jefferson, N.C., 1997.

Trepper, Leopold. *The Great Game.* McGraw Hill, New York, 1977.

Trepte, Curt, and Jutta Wardetzky. *Hans Otto: Schauspieler und Revolutionär.* Henschelverlag, Berlin, 1970.

Tucker, Robert C. *Stalin in Power: The Revolution from Above, 1928–1941.* W. W. Norton & Company, New York, 1990.

Vassiltchikov, Marie. *The Berlin Diaries.* Vintage, New York, 1988.

Wachmann, Nicholaus. *Hitler's Prisons: Legal Terror in Nazi Germany.* Yale University Press, New Haven, Conn., 2004.

Waller, John H. *The Unseen War in Europe: Espionage and Conspiracy in the Second World War.* Random House, New York, 1996.

Walsh, Stephen. *Stalingrad: The Infernal Cauldron.* St. Martin's Press, New York, 2000.

Watt, Donald Cameron. *How War Came: The Immediate Origins of the Second World War 1938–1939.* Pantheon, New York, 1989.

Weisenborn, Günther. *Die Illegalen.* Berlin, 1948.

———. *Memorial.* Aufbau-Verlag, Berlin, 1948.

Weiss, Peter. *The Aesthetics of Resistance.* Duke University Press, Durham and London, 2005.

Weitz, John. *Hitler's Banker.* Little, Brown, Boston, 1997.

Welch, David. *The Third Reich: Politics and Propaganda*. Routledge, New York, 2002.

Welles, Sumner. *The Time for Decision*. World Publishing Company, Cleveland and New York, 1945.

Willett, George. *A Few Days in Russia*. George F. O'Connell Printing Company, New York, 1936.

Willett, John. *Art and Politics in the Weimar Period*. Pantheon, New York, 1978.

Wistrich, Robert Solomon. *Who's Who in Nazi Germany*. Routledge, New York, 2001.

Wolf, Markus. *Man Without a Face*. Crown Publishers, New York, 1997.

Wright, Jonathan. *Gustav Stresemann: Weimar's Greatest Statesman*. Oxford University Press, New York, 2002.

Young, James Edward. *Texture of Memory: Holocaust Memorials and Their Meaning*. Yale University Press, New Haven, Conn., 1993.

ARTICLES

Baxandall, Lee, trans. Introduction to *The Mother*, by Bertolt Brecht. Grove Press, New York, 1989.

Becker, Peter von. "Erick Mielke und des Dichters Herzschlag." *Tagesspiegel*. August 14, 2006.

Bologna, Sergio. "Nazism and the Working Class." Paper presented at the Milan Camera del Lavoro, June 3, 1993.

Brown, Paul. "Report on the IRR file on The Red Orchestra." http://www.archives.gov/iwg/research-papers/red-orchestra-irr-file.html.

Chandler, Douglas. "Changing Berlin." *National Geographic*. February 1937.

Cowell, Alan. "After 50 Years, German Court Exonerates Anti-Hitler Pastor." *New York Times*, August 16, 1996.

Craig, Gordon A. "Berlin, the Hauptstadt." *Foreign Affairs*. July/August 1998.

Dorwart, Jeffery M. "The Roosevelt-Astor Espionage Ring." *New York History, Quarterly Journal of New York State Historical Association*, 62, no. 3. July 1981.

Garner, Russell S. "My Brush with History." *American Heritage Magazine*. September/October 1990.

Goda, Norman J. W. "Tracking the Orchestra: Allied Intelligence, Soviet Spies, Nazi Criminals." In *U.S. Intelligence and the Nazis* (Breitman et al). Cambridge University Press, New York, 2005.

Goetze, Dieter. "Ein Idealist der Linken: Adam Kuckhoff." www.luise-berlin.de, 1997.

Hahn, Manfred. "Ein Linker im Widerstand: Günther Weisenborn: 'Die Furie,' " *Erfahrung Nazideutschland: Romane in Deutschland 1933–1945*. Aufbau Verlag, Berlin and Weimar, 1987.

Hertling, Victoria. "Günther Weisenborn." *Dictionary of Literary Biography*. Thomson-Gale, Farmington Hills, Mich., 2005.

Hoffmann, Peter. introduction to new edition of Allen Dulles's *Germany's Underground*. Da Capo Press, New York, 2000.

Horak, Jan-Christopher. "Prometheus Film Collective." *Jump Cut*, no. 26. December 1981.

Johnson, R. W. "Cads, a review of Persico, *Roosevelt's Secret War*." *London Review of Books*. April 4, 2002.

Kater, Michael H. "Jazz in the Third Reich." *American Historical Review*, vol. 94, no. 1. February 1989.

Koch, Stephen. "Lying for Truth: Münzenberg and the Comintern." *The New Criterion*. November 1993.

Life staff. "Poland: Misery, Pride and Fear Call the Tune for the Post-War State Called Poland." *Life* magazine, August 29, 1938.

Livneh, Neri. "A Woman Called Zosha." *Ha'aretz*. April 25, 2003.

Mason, Tim. "The Workers' Opposition in Nazi Germany." *History Workshop Journal*, no. 11. Spring 1981.

McCormick, Anne O'Hare. "Four Capitals of Destiny." *New York Times Magazine*. April 23, 1939.

Meech, Tony. "Brecht's Early Plays." *Cambridge Companion to Brecht*, ed. Peter Thomson and Glendyr Sacks. Cambridge University Press, 1994.

Morgan, Ted. "The Barbie File." *New York Times Magazine*. May 10, 1987.

Pfizer, Theodor. "Hans Hartenstein, ein preussischer Schwabe." *Schwäbische Heimat*, no. 1, 1979.

Schneider, Peter. "The Good Germans." *New York Times Magazine*. February 13, 2000.

Smith, Howard K. "Berlin: Autumn 1941." *Reporting World War II: Part I*, Library of America, New York, 1995.

Zeydel, Edwin. "A Survey of German Literature During 1937." *Modern Language Journal*, 22, no. 7. 1938.

ARCHIVAL MATERIALS

Donald Heath correspondence. www.fdrlibrary.marist.edu/psf/box31/t296j05.html

Materials on German resistance activities from the archives of the Gedenkstätte Deutscher Widerstand, including:

"Arvid und Mildred Harnack zum Gedächtnis," Prof. Dr. Egmont Zechlin. May 1945.

"Bemerkungen zum Manuskript von Genossin," Greta Kuckhoff. December 1971.

Interview with Max Grabowki. August 2, 1967.

Interview with Hermann Grosse. September 29, 1967.

Interview with Kurt Heims. August 31, 1967.

Interview with Willy Schumacher. November 1, 1967.

Correspondence of Arvid and Mildred Harnack.

Correspondence of Greta Kuckhoff.

Greta Kuckhoff interviews with Karl Heinz Biernat.

Memoirs of the "Bezirksleutung."

Memoir of Libertas Schulze-Boysen, by Alexander Spoerl.

FAMILY PAPERS

Ernst von Harnack (Rainer von Harnack).

Helmut Roloff (Stefan Roloff).

U.S. Army's Investigative Records Repository (IRR), The National Archives.

WEBSITES

THE BAUHAUS PAINTING PROJECT UTILIZING JOHN GRAUDENZ'S PHOTO

www.bauhaus.de/english/bauhaus1919/kunst/kunst_mappe_gropius.htm

ON NAZI PROPAGANDA (RUSSEL LEMMONS)

www.calvin.edu/academic/cas/gpa

ON U.S. INTELLIGENCE
   www.cia.gov/cia/publications/oss/art02.htm
INTERVIEWS WITH MEMBERS OF THE GERMAN RESISTANCE
   www.dhm.de/lemo/forum/kollektives-gedächtnis/043/index.html
ON GOEBBELS'S 1933 BOOK-BURNING
   www.dizzy.library.arizona.edu/images/burnedbooks/goebbels.htm
ON POSTWAR TRIALS OF EINSATZGRUPPEN
   www.einsatzgruppenarchives.com/trials.fsix.html
ON GERMAN CINEMA
   www.filmportal.de
GEDENKSTÄTTE DEUTSCHER WIDERSTAND WEBSITE
   www.gdw-berlin.de
ON EAST GERMAN PURGES (SCHIRDEWAN ET AL.): OPEN SOCIETY ARCHIVES
   (RADIO FREE EUROPE ARCHIVES)
   http://www.osa.ceu.hu/files/holdings/300/8/3/text/24-1-b12.shtml.
ON ALLIED CONVOYS TO SOVIET UNION
   www.usmm.org
ON THE HOLOCAUST AND ABUSES OF SOVIET POWS
   www.ushmm.org
ON HOLOCAUST AND RIGHTEOUS GENTILES
   www.yadvashem.org

DOCUMENTARIES

"Bonhoeffer." 2006, by Martin Doblmeier.
"Jeder Tod war mir ein tiefer Schmerz." Harald Poelchau, Gefängnispfarrer 1933–1945.
   2001, by Irmgard von zur Mühlen.
"The Red Orchestra." 2002, by Stefan Roloff.
"The Restless Conscience." 1991, by Hava Kovav Beller.
"Widerstand: Kampf gegen Hitler." 1995, by Michael Kloft.

Photo Credits

*All photographs courtesy of
the author except as noted below*

...

INSERT PAGE 1 — Gedenkstätte Deutscher Widerstand, Berlin

INSERT PAGE 2 — Gedenkstätte Deutscher Widerstand, Berlin

INSERT PAGE 3 — *middle:* bpk Berlin, Carl Weinrother, 2008

INSERT PAGE 4 — *bottom:* Donald Heath, Jr.

INSERT PAGE 5 — *middle and bottom:* Gedenkstätte Deutscher Widerstand, Berlin

INSERT PAGE 6 — *top and middle:* Gedenkstätte Deutscher Widerstand, Berlin

INSERT PAGE 7 — *top and bottom:* Gedenkstätte Deutscher Widerstand, Berlin

INSERT PAGE 8 — *top and bottom:* Gedenkstätte Deutscher Widerstand, Berlin

INSERT PAGE 9 — Gedenkstätte Deutscher Widerstand, Berlin

INSERT PAGE 10 — *middle:* Gedenkstätte Deutscher Widerstand, Berlin

INSERT PAGE 11 — *middle:* Stefan Roloff

bottom: Karin Reetz

INSERT PAGE 12 — *top:* Tim Bontjes van Beek

middle: Katja Meirowsky

INSERT PAGE 13 — *top and bottom:* Gedenkstätte Deutscher Widerstand, Berlin

middle: National Archives

INSERT PAGES 14 AND 15 — *mug shots:* Gedenkstätte Deutscher Widerstand, Berlin

INSERT PAGE 16 — *top and middle:* Gedenkstätte Deutscher Widerstand, Berlin

bottom: Gerald Wesolowski

ABOUT THE AUTHOR

ANNE NELSON is an acclaimed journalist, playwright, and lecturer. She has been the recipient of numerous awards and grants, including a 2005–2006 Guggenheim Fellowship and the 1989 Livingston Award for international reporting. Her books and articles have been published widely and her play *The Guys*, one of the first plays to address the September 11 attacks, has been published and staged throughout the world. She has written and reported on humanitarian and human rights issues around the globe, with an emphasis on the role of the media. As a war correspondent in El Salvador and Guatemala from 1980 to 1983, she published reports and photography in the *Los Angeles Times*, the *New York Times*, and many other publications. She is a member of the Council on Foreign Relations, a graduate of Yale University, and teaches at Columbia University.

DATE DUE

JE 0 8 '09		
APR 0 7 2010		
	SUBJECT TO	
	RECALL	